THE EROTIC AS RHETORICAL POWER

INTERSECTIONAL RHETORICS
Karma R. Chávez, Series Editor

# THE EROTIC AS RHETORICAL POWER

## ARCHIVES OF ROMANTIC FRIENDSHIP BETWEEN WOMEN TEACHERS

Pamela VanHaitsma

THE OHIO STATE UNIVERSITY PRESS
COLUMBUS

Copyright © 2024 by The Ohio State University.
All rights reserved.

Library of Congress Cataloging-in-Publication Data
Names: VanHaitsma, Pamela, author.
Title: The erotic as rhetorical power : archives of romantic friendship between women teachers / Pamela VanHaitsma.
Other titles: Intersectional rhetorics.
Description: Columbus : The Ohio State University Press, [2024] | Series: Intersectional rhetorics | Includes bibliographical references and index. | Summary: "A queer feminist history of rhetoric that forwards a new theory of the erotic that recovers the civic contributions of nineteenth-century women teachers in same-sex romantic friendships where these friendships have been ignored or simplified and dismissed as normative instances of sexual repression and social constraint"—Provided by publisher.
Identifiers: LCCN 2024021261 | ISBN 9780814215609 (hardback) | ISBN 0814215602 (hardback) | ISBN 9780814283714 (ebook) | ISBN 0814283713 (ebook)
Subjects: LCSH: Lesbian teachers. | Women educators. | Lesbian couples. | Feminist theory. | Queer theory. | Feminism and rhetoric.
Classification: LCC HQ75.5 .V36 2024 | DDC 306.76/630883711—dc23/eng/20240805
LC record available at https://lccn.loc.gov/2024021261

Other identifiers: ISBN 9780814259245 (paperback) | ISBN 0814259243 (paperback)

Cover design by Alexa Love
Text design by Juliet Williams
Type set in Adobe Minion Pro

# CONTENTS

| | |
|---|---|
| Acknowledgments | vii |
| List of Archives, Collections, and Databases | xi |
| Cast of Characters | xiii |
| Prologue | xv |

| | | |
|---|---|---|
| INTRODUCTION | The Erotic as Rhetorical Power in the Long Nineteenth Century | 1 |
| | Introduction to Interludes:<br>Imagined Pasts beyond the Archives | 38 |
| CHAPTER 1 | A Radical Erotic of Antislavery Affection: Abolitionist Lecturing and Freedmen's Teaching, 1848–1893 | 45 |
| | Interlude 1:<br>A School Girl Again | 87 |
| CHAPTER 2 | A Conservative Erotic of Emulating Beauty: Commonplace Rhetorics and Belletristic Instruction, 1868–1900 | 92 |
| | Interlude 2:<br>My Husband | 128 |
| CHAPTER 3 | A Progressive Erotic of Sapphic Egalitarianism: Communication and Leadership among Equals, 1897–1922 | 133 |
| | Conclusion to Interludes:<br>Future Archives | 172 |
| CONCLUSION | Erotics of Rhetorical Power | 176 |

| | |
|---|---|
| Bibliography | 185 |
| Index | 211 |

## ACKNOWLEDGMENTS

I began this project with archival research about Irene Leache and Annie Wood when I, too, lived and worked on the occupied Lumbee and Chesapeake territories that are now known as Norfolk, Virginia, and have been home to the Leache-Wood Seminary as well as Old Dominion University.[1] At ODU, I thank former department chair Dana Heller and graduate research assistant Sarah Spangler for their support of this project. I am grateful for an Office of Research Summer Research Fellowship that supported my earliest archival research on Sallie Holley, Caroline Putnam, and Gertrude Buck in University of Michigan collections. Also, for their support and assistance while at ODU, I thank Jo Ann Mervis Hofheimer from the Irene Leache Memorial, along with Erik H. Neil, Jeannine Harkleroad, Joshua Weinstein, and especially Allison Termine from the Chrysler Museum's Jean Outland Chrysler Library. Finally, I thank Mary Lamb Shelden as well as Garfield Parker and Harold Blackwell from Holley Graded School.

I completed my archival research and wrote this book while living and working on occupied Susquehannock territory that is now home to State

---

1. "Whose land are you on, dear reader?" asks Driskill. "What are the specific names of the Native nation(s) who have historical claim to the territory on which you currently read this book? What are their histories before European invasion? What are their historical and present acts of resistance to colonial occupation?" See Driskill, *Asegi Stories*, 23; and Native Land Digital. See also Simpson, "Symposium."

College, Pennsylvania, and Penn State University's University Park campus.[2] At Penn State, I have been fortunate to have ample research funding and writing support. I thank heads Denise Solomon and Kirt Wilson, along with all of my colleagues in the Department of Communication Arts and Sciences, for their labor to cultivate and maintain a departmental climate that is both intellectually rigorous and materially supportive of faculty research. I thank former graduate students Haley Schneider, Marguerite Nguyen Lehman, Robin Duffee, and Jeff Nagel for their indispensable research assistance. Their research was supported by the Department as well as a Research in Democracy Support Grant from the McCourtney Institute for Democracy. I thank Clarence Lang in the College of Liberal Arts and Ted Toadvine in the Rock Ethics Institute for the course releases provided by a Sherwin Early Career Professorship. Finally, I thank colleagues Mary Stuckey, Debra Hawhee, Michele Kennerly, and Cheryl Glenn for their expert feedback on my book proposal, grant proposals, and other related writing.

My research has relied on the expertise and assistance of countless archivists. In addition to those already named above, I thank Caitlin Rizzo for inspiring collaborations around the concept of archival imaginaries. At Vassar College, my research was partly supported by a Charlotte I. Hall Archives and Special Collections Library Research Grant, and I thank archivist Dean Rogers. At the Connecticut Historical Society, I thank Andrea Rapacz and Tasha Caswell; at the Schlesinger Library, Jennifer Fauxsmith; at the Massachusetts Historical Society, Hannah Elder; and at the Handley Regional Library, Rebecca Ebert and Kylie Feiring. I continue to be indebted to the early work of Farah Jasmine Griffin to make transcribed, edited versions of Addie Brown and Rebecca Primus's correspondence widely available. Finally, while there are too many names to include them all here, I thank the archival staff from every institution listed on the pages to follow. They worked to make digitized materials available even through the period of COVID-19 when their doors were closed and I could not travel.

I wrote portions of the manuscript during virtual and in-person writing dates with Elizabeth Groeneveld and Joshua Trey Barnett. My now–associate professor buddy Steph Ceraso helped me stay on track with my writing and revision plans. I am grateful to Ames Hawkins for collaboration on the Rhetoric Society of America Summer Institute workshop, "Queer(ing) Archival Imaginaries," which sparked my desire and courage to embrace imaginative erotohistoriography in my own writing. Beyond these friends and colleagues, I want to thank several others whose writing has inspired me. Whether you are

---

2. Native Land Digital. Also see "Acknowledgement"; and Lee and Ahtone, "Land-Grab."

a close friend, distant colleague, or complete stranger, you have enacted your scholarly work on the page in ways that I aspire to learn from: Alexis Pauline Gumbs, Saidiya Hartman, Jo Hsu, Hil Malatino, Jacqueline Jones Royster, Julietta Singh, and Stacey Waite. Earlier drafts of portions of chapters 1 and 2, along with methodological reflections on my archival research, have benefited from editorial guidance, technical support, and reviewer feedback from anonymous reviewers as well as Jessica Enoch and David Gold; Arthur Walzer; Karrin Vasby Anderson, Courtney Rivard, Heather Froehlich, and Tara LaLonde; and Tom Nakayama and Charles E. Morris.

Tara Cyphers and Karma Chávez from The Ohio State University Press's Intersectional Rhetorics series have been an editorial dream team to work with on this project. I thank them for their expert guidance and selection of such helpful reviewers. All three reviewers provided crucial, encouraging, critical feedback. I am especially grateful to Aimee Carrillo Rowe, who read my manuscript not once but twice, pushing me to make the project stronger in ways that are particularly important to me. While any failures of this project remain my own, the book is absolutely better because of Tara, Karma, Aimee, and the other reviewers' expertise.

Any royalties from this book project will be divided between my family and redistribution to the Audre Lorde Project, which "is a Lesbian, Gay, Bisexual, Two Spirit, Trans and Gender Non-Conforming People of Color center for community organizing, focusing on the New York City area," where Lorde was from.[3] "Through mobilization, education and capacity-building," the Audre Lorde Project "work[s] for community wellness and progressive social and economic justice."

My own intimate and domestic life changed radically between the time when I began archival research for this book and when I finished revising it. My time and energy for research and writing depended absolutely on my spouse, Jess, who showers me with love and, just as crucially, shares in household and parenting responsibilities. My work on this project depends, equally so, on the labor of those who helped us care for the incredible bundle of joy and burst of energy who has joined our family. I am especially grateful to Yamiya, Maggie, Ms. Tammy, Ms. Amber S. and Ms. Amber R., Ms. Rachel and Ms. Gretchen, and everyone else at Easterseals Child Development Center in State College. I also thank all of the LGBTQ+ and reproductive justice activists, scientists, and everyday people who have fought to make families like ours possible. Most of all, I thank Francis, who teaches me more about love and wonder with every day.

---

3. Audre Lorde Project, "About."

# ARCHIVES, COLLECTIONS, AND DATABASES

| | |
|---|---|
| AAA | Archives of American Art, Smithsonian Institution, New York, NY |
| AAS | Abigail Kelley Foster papers, 1836–91, American Antiquarian Society, Worcester, MA |
| AF/HL | Alcott family papers, 1830–88, Houghton Library, Harvard University, Cambridge, MA |
| AHN | America's Historical Newspapers, 1690–1922 |
| APS | American Periodical Series, 1740–1900 |
| BHL | Fred Newton Scott papers, Bentley Historical Library, University of Michigan, Ann Arbor, MI |
| CP/CLMT | Caroline F. Putnam papers, William L. Clements Library, University of Michigan, Ann Arbor, MI |
| CRNL | Emily Howland papers, #2681, Division of Rare and Manuscript Collections, Carl A. Kroch Library, Cornell University, Ithaca, NY |
| CWM | Virginia Taylor McCormick papers, MSS 65 M13, Special Collections Research Center, Swem Library, College of William and Mary, Williamsburg, VA |

| | |
|---|---|
| FD/LOC | Frederick Douglass papers, 1841–1967, Manuscript Division, Library of Congress, Washington, DC |
| FHSC | Emily Howland family papers, RG5/066, Friends Historical Library, Swarthmore College, Swarthmore, PA |
| HF/CLMT | Harriet deGarmo Fuller papers, William L. Clements Library, University of Michigan, Ann Arbor, MI |
| HT | Hathi Trust Digital Library |
| JOCL | Irene Leache papers, Jean Outland Chrysler Library, Chrysler Museum of Art, Norfolk, VA |
| LOC | Library of Congress, Washington, DC |
| MHS | Samuel May papers, Massachusetts Historical Society, Boston, MA |
| NCN | Nineteenth-Century US Newspapers (Gale) |
| NPL | Sargeant Memorial Collection, Norfolk Public Library, Norfolk, VA |
| PF/CHS | Primus family papers, 1853–1924, MS 44012, Connecticut Historical Society, Hartford, CT |
| RH/CHS | Rudd and Holley family papers, 1788–2006, MS 100906, Connecticut Historical Society, Hartford, CT |
| RL/CLMT | Rochester Ladies' Anti-Slavery Society papers, William L. Clements Library, University of Michigan, Ann Arbor, MI |
| SLRI | Rebecca Primus papers, 1854–72, A/P9537, Schlesinger Library, Radcliffe Institute, Harvard University, Cambridge, MA |
| UVA | Louise Collier Willcox papers, MSS 11390, Albert and Shirley Small Special Collections Library, University of Virginia, Charlottesville, VA |
| VCL | Laura Johnson Wylie papers, Archives and Special Collections Library, Vassar College, Poughkeepsie, NY |
| WF/HL | Wendell Phillips papers, 1555–1882, MS Am 1953, Houghton Library, Harvard University, Cambridge, MA |
| WFHS | Elizabeth Engle Collection, Stewart Bell Jr. Archives, Handley Regional Library, Winchester-Frederick County Historical Society, Winchester, VA |
| WG/CLMT | Weld-Grimké family papers, William L. Clements Library, University of Michigan, Ann Arbor, MI |

# CAST OF CHARACTERS

Sallie Holley (1818–93)[1]
　　Abolitionist lecturer. Met Putnam at Oberlin College and taught formerly enslaved African Americans together at the Holley School.

Caroline Putnam (1826–1917)
　　Colporteur on abolitionist lecture circuit. Met Holley at Oberlin, taught together at Holley School.

Rebecca Primus (1836–1932)
　　Freedman's teacher at the Primus Institute. Met Brown in Hartford.

Irene Kirke Leache (1839–1900)
　　Published author. Taught at Valley Female Seminary, a boarding school for white girls in the South, where she met then-student Wood. Taught together at another boarding school, the Leache-Wood Seminary.

Addie Brown (1841–70)
　　Domestic laborer, Sunday school teacher. Met Primus in Hartford. Supported her teaching at the Primus Institute.

---

　　1. I draw the title "Cast of Characters" and partly model my list after Hartman, *Wayward Lives,* xvii.

Annie Cogswell Wood (1850–1940)
    Published author. Met Leache at Valley Female Seminary, taught together at Leache-Wood Seminary.

Laura Johnson Wylie (1855–1932)
    Published literary scholar and suffrage activist. Hired and taught with Buck at Vassar.

Gertrude Buck (1871–1922)
    Published rhetorical theorist. Met Wylie when hired to teach at Vassar College.

# PROLOGUE

*The Erotic as Rhetorical Power: Archives of Romantic Friendship between Women Teachers* theorizes the erotic as rhetorical power through exploration of how it not only animated same-sex intimate friendships between women teachers but also helped make it possible for the most privileged of these women to sustain decades-long careers as teachers of rhetoric and rhetors in their own right. At its core, the book is an archival investigation of the women's romantic relationships, teaching careers, and rhetorical practices during the long nineteenth century. Yet my curiosity about the rhetorical possibilities of same-sex relationships originated long before the idea of this book or the archival research that grounds it. That curiosity emerged from my own academic career as a rhetorician as well as my own intimate relationships as a queer femme.

When I was a PhD candidate completing the dissertation research that would later inform my first book, I learned about the romantic relationship and correspondence of two freeborn African American women, Rebecca Primus and Addie Brown.[1] Primus and Brown sustained a cross-class romantic friendship through letter writing for nearly a decade (1859–68). Whereas my book focused on how rhetors like Primus and Brown learned and developed

---

1. VanHaitsma, "Queering the Language"; and VanHaitsma, *Queering Romantic Engagement.*

queer epistolary practices, I also noticed how the women's romantic relationship seemed to support Brown's self-education and Primus's freedmen's teaching. I later wrote about how the women's romantic friendship helped make possible their education for racial uplift, at least for a period of time, although their relationship was cut short because of an economic need to marry.[2]

As I conducted early archival research on Primus and Brown, I also noticed what my own queer relationship seemed to make possible. In my thirties, I had recently moved in with my partner and, countering all U-Haul stereotypes, this was my first time living with anyone I dated. While the desires that motivated this move had nothing to do with my work, I soon found that many aspects of sharing a domestic life made research, writing, and teaching much easier and more enjoyable: affording a two-bedroom apartment with multiple places to sit and write, instead of the tiny efficiency where I had lived previously; organizing my dissertation writing and teaching in relation to her/their eight-to-five work schedule; sharing the pet care and household responsibilities; and, just as importantly, finding a new degree of contentment and pleasure in my life that I brought to my work every morning as I sat down to write. In short, our relationship helped support my rhetorical labors. Realizing this, I started to wonder about the relationships of my peers, colleagues, and mentors in other domestic arrangements.

I began to pay more attention to the articles circulated on social media by feminist friends about the gendered distribution of domestic and emotional reproductive labor. I read over and over again that, in presumably cisgender heterosexual couples, twenty-first-century women still do a disproportionate amount of the household and caretaking work, even when they work full-time outside of the home (and yes, most studies continue to focus largely on couples defined by a cisgender binary).[3] I read also that, in same-sex couples, unpaid reproductive labor generally is shared in a more egalitarian manner.[4] These research findings mirrored what I had observed in the lives of cisgender women teachers, writers, and academics with partners who were cisgender men—especially with human children in the picture, and even if both of the adult partners self-identified as feminists. Sitting with these observations, I became increasingly curious about how same-sex and other queer

---

2. VanHaitsma, "Romantic Correspondence."

3. See, for example, Altintas and Sullivan, "Fifty Years"; Bianchi et al., "Housework"; Donner, "Household Work"; Rodsky, *Fair Play*; Hochschild and Machung, *Second Shift*; Orbuch and Eyster, "Division"; Rao, "Even Breadwinning Wives"; and Sullivan, "Gendered Division."

4. For a recent summary of the research, along with new research on transgender and nonbinary couples, see Tornello, "Division." See also Bauer, "Gender Roles"; Brewster, "Lesbian Women"; Kelly and Hauck, "Doing Housework"; Kurdek, "Allocation"; van der Vleuten, Jaspers, and van der Lippe, "Same-Sex Couples"; Pfeffer, "'Women's Work'?"; and Sutphin, "Division."

relationships, each understood in their own cultural and historical contexts, might be possible to sustain and, in turn, might help make possible the careers of women rhetoricians.

Just as my questions about the rhetorical possibilities of such relationships originated long before the idea of this book, my interests in these possibilities exceed the archives available for research. Primus and Brown are a case in point. What available archives most fully document are the romantic friendships, teaching careers, and rhetorical practices that middle- and upper-class white women were able to maintain over the course of multiple decades. But what if the material conditions of Primus's and Brown's lives as African American women—especially Brown's as a domestic laborer—had been different? What if they both could have accessed formal education? What if they could have lived as a married couple and worked together as teachers for the rest of their lives? Continued attention to the example of Primus and Brown, as a point of comparison, makes clear the relative privilege of the settler white women teachers centered in the archives and this book. At the same time, such attention throws into relief the material conditions of settler archives themselves. Who are the other BIPOC women who did tenaciously and creatively carve out lives together as romantic friends, teachers of rhetoric, and rhetors during the nineteenth century? What if their rhetorical labors go unacknowledged partly because they were not preserved in archives? Or what if they were preserved, and I have failed thus far to find those archival materials? These what-ifs encircle this book's archival study, taking shape as imaginative interludes between the main chapters. Each interlude enacts, imaginatively and beyond the available archives, another past for Primus and Brown—with the goal of another future for us all.

I first drafted this prologue during the summer of 2020, in a present marked by the COVID-19 pandemic with its widespread losses and its differential impacts, and by the time I found myself rewriting, the pandemic had persisted long past when most of us expected. Again my social media feeds were filled with stories about the inequitable distribution of care labor. Women continued to bear disproportionately the responsibilities to care for children who were home from day care and school.[5] Articles about this problem continued to focus almost entirely on presumed cisgender women within opposite-sex domestic arrangements. And still, too few people who read the phrase "distribution of care labor" will think first of all the service workers—working in grocery stores and warehouses, delivering packages, and cleaning

---

5. See, for example, Feintzeig, "Women"; T. Gross, "Pandemic"; and Savage, "How COVID-19."

health care sites—who helped make it possible for the relatively privileged among us to keep going, however grief-stricken, worried, screen-weary, and exhausted we may have been a lot of the time.[6]

I also wrote this prologue in a present marked by white supremacist violence, both persistent and shape-shifting. George Floyd. Jacob Blake. Breonna Taylor. Ahmaud Arbery. These losses—their murders—garnered wider recognition within mainstream public conversations, including among white people. But whatever degree of recognition arose and persisted in any meaningful sense was born of tremendous struggle. The activist gains of the Black Lives Matter movement and their reach into dominant discourse during the summer of 2020 must be traced, at the very least, to the vision of Alicia Garza, Patrisse Cullors, and Ayọ Tometi. Their ongoing organizing to affirm Black life and resist anti-Black racism is, in Garza's words, "rooted in the labor and love of queer Black women."[7] Also within LGBTQ+ communities in the United States, the summer of 2020 saw further reckoning with the history of Pride, as Black Lives Matter activists pushed large LGBTQ+ rights organizations to alter Pride events in recognition of its historical roots in BIPOC-led activism against police harassment and violence.[8] These activists and others writing about their labor have emphasized the central role of Black and brown transgender women, drag performers, and lesbian women including Marsha P. Johnson, Sylvia Rivera, Miss Major Griffin-Gracy, and Stormé DeLarverie in the Stonewall Riot and subsequent activism against police brutality.[9] In each case, what we have witnessed is born of significant rhetorical labors made over time by LGBTQ+ women and gender-nonconforming people of color—and subject to predictably racist, homophobic, and transphobic forms of backlash.

All of this is to say: the questions driving this book's research about women's rhetorical labors in the past are also questions about our work and relationships in the present. What forms of relation enable our work as rhetors participating in activism? And our work as teachers of rhetoric? What material conditions help make those relations possible? And, just as vitally, what erotics energize us, allowing us to keep loving and keep working in spite of all that makes doing so difficult?

---

6. For another important perspective on care labor, see Malatino, *Trans Care*.

7. Garza, "Herstory." Also see Black Lives Matter, "Herstory"; and Petermon and Spencer, "Black Queer Womanhood."

8. Allaire, "How Pride"; Fitzsimons, "Pride"; Giuliani-Hoffman, "LGBTQ Communities"; and Hylton, "Black Lives." Importantly, these actions in the US are preceded by organizing around Toronto Pride in 2016. See, for example, K. Davis, "Transnational Blackness"; Costa, "Pride"; and Greey, "Queer Inclusion."

9. Bergin, "Remembering"; Borge, "Queer Black History"; and Corrigan, "Queering."

All of this is also to say: the questions driving this book's research are born of my earliest archival research about African American women who were *not* able to maintain a domestic partnership over time, and, equally so, of my own career and relationship as a queer white woman. I share this bit of backstory within a tradition of feminist scholarship that acknowledges the limits and possibilities associated with researcher positionality, as well as the complex but potentially productive relationships between women's so-called private and public work.[10] It is these very relationships, in both their inspiring and their troubling forms, that this book examines at length.

---

10. On the limitations of positionality statements that emphasize an individual author, see Carrillo Rowe, *Power Lines*, 14–15.

INTRODUCTION

# The Erotic as Rhetorical Power in the Long Nineteenth Century

This book advances a theory of the erotic as a rhetorical power that holds variable political possibility, fueling rhetorical practices and pedagogies with the potential to both transform and instantiate existing hierarchies of difference. Within this theory, I understand the erotic as an interanimation of desires—simultaneously intimate, intellectual, pedagogical, and political—that, in being passionately shared, becomes imbued with the creative power to forge connections as well as foment change. This creative power takes on a specifically rhetorical valence as intimate connections blur the boundaries between so-called private and public life, energizing rhetorical activities that include public speaking, published writing, and the teaching of rhetoric oriented to social change. Importantly, although the pursuit of such change is more often idealized as creating connections across difference in order to facilitate positive transformation, in actuality the erotic may fuel rhetorical practices that move in directions radical, progressive, or conservative.

My theory of the erotic as rhetorical power emerges from historiographic and imaginative engagements with the archives of romantic friendship. Working with materials from over twenty manuscript and digital collections, I have investigated the rhetorical activities of (presumably cisgender) women who sustained same-sex romantic friendships and teaching careers for decades, separated from each other only by death. From what I have found, perhaps unsurprisingly, the women who were able to sustain such relationships and careers were white; they were born into families privileged by the "violent inheritances" of settler colonialism and slavery in occupied territories now known as the United States.[1] In this sense, the women's romantic friendships and career opportunities stand in contrast to those of the African American couple already introduced in my prologue, Rebecca Primus (1836–1932) and Addie Brown (1841–70). I imagine another past for Primus and Brown, one less constrained by anti-Black racism, within the imaginative interludes woven between the book's body chapters. In the chapters themselves, my historiography centers three couples who were more privileged and whose lives, relationships, and rhetorical activities are relatively well documented in archives.

First are "lifelong companions" Sallie Holley (1818–93) and Caroline Putnam (1826–1917).[2] During their forty-five years as a couple, these white women from the North traveled together on the antislavery lecture circuit and then moved to the South to teach at a freedmen's school. Another couple, Irene Kirke Leache (1839–1900) and Annie Cogswell Wood (1850–1940), shared an "opulent friendship" for more than three decades.[3] Both conservative women who published their writing, Leache and Wood taught at a boarding school for white girls in the South. Also published authors, Gertrude Buck (1871–1922) and Laura Johnson Wylie (1855–1932) were active as a rhetorical theorist and suffrage activist. Teaching and administering the rhetoric program at Vassar College, they shared a "close personal and professional relationship" for almost twenty-five years.[4] My historiographic focus on the extensively archived activities of these three couples allows for investigation of the erotic as rhetorical power across the latter portion of the "long nineteenth century," from the years of abolitionist activism leading up to the Civil War and then into the Progressive Era reform movements.[5] These couples also reflect the complexities of the erotic as rhetorical power, because it fueled the women's teaching at diverse educational sites as well as their speaking and writing to competing political ends.

In the remainder of this introductory chapter, I flesh out my theory of the erotic as rhetorical power through engagement with a range of thinkers from ancient times to the present. I then more fully situate my investigation

---

1. Cram, *Violent Inheritance*, xv.
2. Buchanan, *Regendering*, 147; Clifford, *Those Good Gertrudes*, 164; Shelden, "'Such a Great Light,'" 69; and Pease and Pease, "Sallie," 205.
3. Wood, *Story*, 12, NPL.
4. Bordelon, *Feminist Legacy*, 24.
5. On the idea of the "long nineteenth century," see Hobsbawm, *Age of Revolution*; Hobsbawm, *Age of Capital*; and Hobsbawm, *Age of Empire*. Hobsbawm focuses on Europe, but the term has been used with reference to the US as well. Although I am not interested in delineating historical periods, I use the term to acknowledge that my case studies, like the practices of romantic friendship itself, extend just past the nineteenth century and into the early twentieth century.

of the erotic as rhetorical power in the long nineteenth century. Specifically, I introduce the place of the erotic within women's romantic friendships and show how the teaching profession was particularly conducive to enabling such relationships between privileged women. I also underscore how, even as the erotic of these romantic friendships fueled the women's rhetorical activities toward sometimes transformational ends, settler colonialism and slavery were the conditions of possibility for both that erotic and its archives. Within this context, the erotic as rhetorical power energized rhetorical activities that alternately challenged and reinforced problematic power dynamics. My goal in what follows, then, is not to recover the erotic between women in romantic friendships as universally positive or inherently radical or progressive. Rather, I argue for the significance of the erotic as a rhetorical power that, while directed to conflicting social and political aims, is central to rhetorical theory and history as well as feminist and LGBTQ+ historiography.

## The Erotic as Rhetorical Power

My conception of the erotic as rhetorical power brings together and extends diverse perspectives from ancient Greek rhetoric to nineteenth-century progressivism, from Audre Lorde's Black lesbian feminist theory of the 1970s and 1980s to present-day feminist, queer, and queer of color studies. From among these various theories of the erotic, I take as my central touchstone Lorde's groundbreaking and oft-cited 1984 essay, "Uses of the Erotic: The Erotic as Power."[6] This most direct articulation of Lorde's theory of the erotic was first delivered as a conference talk in 1978 and later published and recirculated in multiple forums.[7] Yet as biographer Alexis De Veaux illustrates, the power of the erotic suffused Lorde's life across all of her writing, relationships, and activism.[8] This section fleshes out my theory of the erotic as a specifically rhetorical power through extended engagement with Lorde's body of work,

---

6. While I follow other scholars in engaging with Lorde's conception of the erotic as theory, it is important to note that her own understanding of the relationship between theory and poetry—between the "ideas" that "were what the white fathers told us were precious" and the "feelings" that are "hidden sources of . . . power from where true knowledge and, therefore, lasting action comes"—are complex. Lorde, "Poetry Is Not a Luxury," 37. See also Bereano, "Introduction," 7–8; and Lorde, "Poetry Makes," 185–86.

7. On the details surrounding Lorde's delivery, see De Veaux, *Warrior Poet*, 220–21; Gill, "In the Realm," 183; Olson, "Intersecting Audiences," 125–46; Olson, "Traumatic Styles," 271–72; and Carrillo Rowe, "Erotic Pedagogies," 1035.

8. De Veaux, *Warrior Poet*. In addition to De Veaux's biography, another is forthcoming. See Gumbs, *Survival*. For additional examples of Lorde's writing about the erotic, see "My Words," 164; Lorde and Star, "Sadomasochism," 52–53; and Lorde and Parker, *Sister Love*, 90–91.

its more recent interdisciplinary uptakes, and resonances with ideas about the erotic from earlier historical periods.

The erotic is grounded, first and foremost, in shared intimacy.[9] As Lorde theorizes, the power of the erotic "comes from sharing deeply any pursuit with another person . . . whether physical, emotional, psychic, or intellectual."[10] The erotic consists of "those . . . expressions of what is deepest and strongest and richest within each of us, being shared: the passions of love, in its deepest meanings."[11] Of note within this conception of intimacy is the emphasis on sharing love, passion, and deep feeling. Genuine sharing requires mutual consent. Only under that condition can the erotic foster an "intimate connection" that is "a shared connection" between people.[12] Once shared, such connection gathers strength through "how deeply one feels."[13] The power of the erotic emerging from this shared intimacy, as Godfried Asante notes, "takes love as its point of convergence."[14] What marks a connection as erotic, then, is not the presence of sexual desire but the depth of shared feeling, passion, and love.

But the relationship between sex and the erotic often gets confused in at least two ways. In the first, the erotic becomes "a mere euphemism for sex acts."[15] In Lorde's conception, by contrast, the erotic is not synonymous with or reducible to the sexual.[16] Along similar lines, bell hooks and Ela Przybylo urge that "we must move beyond thinking of these forces solely in terms of the sexual" to recognize "erotic energies not tethered to sex."[17] Whereas some mistakenly reduce the erotic to the sexual, others overly distance the erotic from sexuality, which is a second way the erotic is misunderstood. The problem, Joan Morgan explains, is how some "have chosen to map a binary and heteronormative read onto Lorde's erotic that implies that the erotic can only be

---

9. Whereas this study considers the intimate connections between romantic friends who were teachers, the erotic also functions as a source of power within collective relations of alliance- and coalition-building. See Asante, "Decolonizing," 113; and Carrillo Rowe, *Power Lines*.

10. Lorde, "Uses of the Erotic," 56.

11. Lorde, "Uses of the Erotic," 56.

12. Baker, "Revisiting," 472, 474.

13. Baker, "Revisiting," 471. As Musser writes, this connection is forged through "bonds between women" that become "avenues for nurturing and collaboration." Musser, "Re-Membering," 348.

14. Asante, "Decolonizing," 115.

15. Gill, "In the Realm," 178.

16. Lorde laments that women "are taught to separate the erotic demand from most vital areas of our lives other than sex." See Lorde, "Uses of the Erotic," 55.

17. hooks, "Eros," 60; and Przybylo, *Asexual Erotics*, 1. As Allen also urges, the erotic "is not only about the power of one's own sexual energy but also, more profoundly, the erotic includes and goes well beyond associations with sensuality, sex, and sexuality." Allen, *Venceremos*, 96.

achieved by a transcendence of mere sex."[18] This distancing from sex may be a response, at least partly, to Lorde's view that the erotic is "antithetical to the pornographic."[19] While her stance on pornography is complex and beyond my scope, I share with Lorde, as well as Morgan and many others, the insistence that the erotic may include, even as it is not limited to, diverse forms of sexual desire and practice. In this sense, I follow Omise'eke Natasha Tinsley, who articulates the erotic as "a sharing of deep, possibly but not necessarily sexual feeling."[20] Tinsley's understanding of the relationship between the erotic and the sexual is particularly important to have in mind when considering the erotics of romantic friendships between nineteenth-century white women, because, as I discuss further in the next section, those relationships were (and are) often desexualized through racist and cisheterosexist interpretations. These nineteenth-century relationships are best understood as marked, in the words of Martha Vicinus, by "many varieties of erotic love, ranging from the openly sexual, to the delicately sensual, to the disembodied ideal."[21]

With shared intimacy as its foundation, the erotic is defined most forcefully by its creative power: its capacity to not only forge intimacy between people but also become a source of energy extending beyond those relations. This "source," "force," "resource," and "lifeforce," as Lorde variously refers to the erotic, may become "a considered source of power" in women's lives.[22] She thus endows the erotic with "a creative power."[23] That creative power takes shape beyond interpersonal or sexual intimacy, as Roderick A. Ferguson, Qwo-Li Driskill, and Eric Darnell Pritchard all point out. "Activating and illuminating all parts of life," the erotic "becomes a lens through which we scrutinize all aspects of our existence," and "this kernel of energy animates the entire enterprise of our interventions, and indeed, of our lives as whole."[24]

18. Or, Morgan continues, "by eschewing sex that isn't regulated to the realms of romantic love or the spiritual." Morgan, "Why We Get Off," 39. One example Morgan cites is Collins, *Black Sexual Politics*.

19. Cruz, *Color*, 35. In Lorde's own words, "pornography is a direct denial of the power of the erotic, for it represents the suppression of true feeling. Pornography emphasizes sensation without feeling." "Uses of the Erotic," 54. Lorde's commentary about the pornographic, along with her perspectives on S/M, have been taken up and appropriated in various ways during the so-called lesbian sex wars of the 1980s and ongoing conversations about the complexities of Black women's sexuality and the erotic. In addition to Cruz, see Chude-Sokei et al., "Race"; Lorde and Star, "Sadomasochism"; Miller-Young, *Taste*; and Nash, *Black Body*.

20. Tinsley, *Thiefing*, 20. See also Gill, "In the Realm," 178; and Olson, "Intersecting Audiences," 128.

21. Vicinus, *Intimate Friends*, xx.

22. Lorde, "Uses of the Erotic," 53–55, 57, 53.

23. Baker, "Revisiting," 470.

24. Ferguson, "Of Sensual Matters," 298; Lorde, "Uses of the Erotic," 57, qtd. in Driskill, "Stolen," 52; and Pritchard, *Fashioning Lives*, 202. For further theorization of what Driskill terms the "Sovereign Erotic," see *Asegi Stories*, 36; and Driskill, "Call Me Brother."

Where these "parts of life" include public life, the creative power of the erotic is rhetorical in that it blurs lines between intimate and civic domains. The erotic's distinctly rhetorical power is rooted in a refusal to be contained within the so-called private realm. The refusal to reduce "the transformative charge that exists among people" to a power within interpersonal relationships and domestic spaces amounts to, in the words of Aimee Carrillo Rowe, "an erotics of pubic intimacy."[25] More often, the charge of shared intimacy is only "acknowledged in the private sphere, between lovers," where "we are sanctioned to feel the desire to strive toward another, to take a risk, to step into the unknown."[26] What distinguishes the erotic as rhetorical power is that this "rush of energy that flows between people" is rearticulated "as a public and political act of social change."[27] In this formulation, the desires that constitute the erotic are expansively understood, so as to include a broad spectrum of what Sharon Patricia Holland calls "the personal and political dimensions of desire."[28] For nineteenth-century teachers in same-sex romantic friendships, these desires animated the seemingly domesticated couple form of the romantic friendship and, simultaneously, drove the women's public intimacy in the form of social and political activities.

This view of the erotic as a power with both intimate and civic potentiality is by no means limited to the historical, cultural, and political contexts of Lorde's Black lesbian feminist theory and women of color feminisms.[29] Nineteenth-century thinkers also contemplated the specifically same-sex erotics through which intimate relationships could animate public contributions. British philosopher Edward Carpenter (1894) drew on Greek conceptions of *eros* to theorize "homogenic love"—*homos* for "same" and *genos* for "sex"— which he claimed could make possible progressive social change.[30] Writing about this same-sex *eros*, Carpenter reflected, "I think myself that the best philanthropic work—just because it is the most personal, the most loving, and the least merely formal and self-righteous—has a strong fibre of the Uranian heart running through it."[31] Carpenter acknowledged homogenic love

---

25. Carrillo Rowe, "Erotic Pedagogies," 1032, 1040. On the erotic's potential to fuel both so-called private and public life, also see Allen, *Venceremos*, 97; and Gill, "In the Realm," 178.
26. Carrillo Rowe, "Erotic Pedagogies," 1040.
27. Carrillo Rowe, "Erotic Pedagogies," 1040, 1053.
28. Holland, *Erotic Life*, 9.
29. Whereas I focus here on the long nineteenth century, also of relevance is the question of how Lorde's conception departs from that of Plato as well as Freud and de Beauvoir. See Holland, *Erotic Life*, 46–51, 59; Przybylo, *Asexual Erotics*, 3, 20–23; and Willey, *Undoing*, 94.
30. Carpenter, *Homogenic Love*, 4.
31. During the nineteenth century, the term *Uranian* was used to describe a "third sex"— meaning homosexuality, particularly among men—and should not be confused with present-day uses of the term *intersex*.

among both men and women and, as Julia M. Allen shows, his ideas reached and were taken up by white women in what is now the US.[32] Central to this erotic in women's lives was coming "together in a common purpose—and ultimately a partnership," often through shared participation in homosocial and homoerotic spaces, such that their "expansive, activist love . . . enabled some to foster same-sex relationships."[33] At least some nineteenth-century people thus recognized the simultaneously erotic and rhetorical potential of their same-sex relationships.

For women teachers, this power of the erotic emerged through a shared passion for intellectual and educational desires. Lorde recognizes this form of passion in characterizing the erotic as "the nurturer . . . of all our deepest knowledge," as "fuel for intellectual production."[34] Also emphasizing the importance of knowledge within Lorde's theory of the erotic as a "source of power and information," Cait McKinney points out how "Lorde's use of the term 'information' is not generally remarked on in turns to her theory of the erotic. Information implies that the erotic is in part a communication practice: the erotic transmits actionable knowledge between a scene and a woman who has opened herself to this kind of knowledge."[35] For each of the women in this study, the "scene" she "opened herself to" in meeting her romantic friend was explicitly educational, with the erotic of their relationship constituted by a shared passion for women's "intellectual production" and "actionable knowledge." Decades before becoming freedmen's teachers, Holley and Putnam met in the coeducational setting of Oberlin College, which is generally credited with being the first college in the country to admit women. Leache and Wood met and later taught within the homosocial settings of boarding schools for white girls in the South. Buck and Wylie also developed their relationship and careers together in homosocial educational settings, in their case the women's

---

32. Allen, *Passionate Commitments*.

33. Allen, *Passionate Commitments*, 65; and Cima, *Performing*, 123. These partnerships stood in contrast to most opposite-sex marriages, which involved a "withdrawal from public life" for the woman, "a turning away from speaking to focus on an intimate relationship." See Hanly, "'Then Alone,'" 287.

While I extend Lorde's theory of the erotic in ways that continue to center presumably cisgender women, this conception of the erotic as rhetorical power is productive for archival research on other marginalized rhetors as well. As Carrillo Rowe reflects, "this female power also may be announced as queer power, marginal power because the work of (re)claiming erotic power involves transfiguring the distortions placed on the bodies of the disenfranchised." Carrillo Rowe, "Erotic Pedagogies," 1035. This expansion of the erotic beyond cisgender women is discussed further in Baker, "Revisiting"; Gill, "In the Realm," 185, 187; E. P. Johnson, "Revelatory Distillation," 312; and Musser, "Re-Membering," 349, 351.

34. Lorde, "Uses of the Erotic," 56. Also qtd. in Ferguson, "Of Sensual Matters," 298. On the erotic and Black women's self-knowledge, see Baker, "Revisiting," 471, 473.

35. McKinney, *Information*, 21.

college at the turn of the century. A passion for educational pursuit brought the couples together, developed into an admiration of each other's minds, and energized a shared intellectual stimulation that constituted the erotic of their relationships.

The erotic animated by shared passions for intellectual and educational life functioned as a rhetorical power that fueled the women's pedagogical activities as teachers. Lorde observes this potential of the erotic to energize work, so that it, too, becomes "a longed-for bed . . . from which I rise up empowered."[36] As Lester C. Olson discusses, she "reclaim[s] work, not primarily for profit but rather as a deeply satisfying experience," as "another meaning of the erotic."[37] Theorizing the work of teaching in particular, hooks writes of "the place of eros or the erotic in our classrooms," Carrillo Rowe of the "the classroom" as a space for the "public rearticulation of the erotic," and William P. Banks of the "great passion" animating the teaching of writing.[38]

For rhetoricians especially, these linkages between the erotic and pedagogy have precedents in Western rhetorical history. As not only Carpenter but also Lorde notes, "the very word *erotic* comes from the Greek word *eros*."[39] References to *eros* likely call to mind the pedagogical relationship between Plato's Socrates and Phaedrus, because the homoeroticism of such relations are acknowledged across histories of classical rhetoric. As Patricia Bizzell and Bruce Herzberg explain, "intense homoerotic relationships often developed between mentor and pupil, which apparently were considered appropriate aids to emulation."[40] "In the most socially approved version of such a relationship," they continue, "the younger partner accepted a passive sexual role out of gratitude for the older partner's kindnesses to him, which often included . . . instruction, and out of admiration for his accomplishments." Offering this account in a widely used textbook, Bizzell and Herzberg capture a broadly shared understanding of eroticized pedagogical exchanges between ancient Greco-Roman men.[41] However, rhetorical scholars have yet to explore the par-

---

36. Lorde, "Uses of the Erotic," 55.

37. Olson, "Traumatic Styles," 269. Within communication and rhetorical studies, Lorde's larger body of work has been examined extensively by Olson. In addition to the essays already cited, see "Anger"; "Liabilities"; "On the Margins"; and "Personal."

38. hooks, "Eros," 60; Carrillo Rowe, "Erotic Pedagogies," 1043; and Banks, "Written," 27–28. For additional discussion of the erotic and present-day pedagogy, see Carbine, "Erotic Education"; McNinch, "Queering Seduction"; Rasheed, "Sexualized Spaces"; Siejk, "Awakening"; and Young, "'Uses of the Erotic.'"

39. Lorde, "Uses of the Erotic," 55.

40. Bizzell and Herzberg, *Rhetorical Tradition*, 26.

41. See, for example, Gunderson, *Declamation*; Hawhee, *Bodily Arts*, 105–8; and Kennerly, *Editorial Bodies*, 204–6.

allel yet discrete dynamics that evolved in other cultural contexts and historical periods, particularly for women.[42]

For the women couples in this study, their teaching of rhetoric together was fueled by the interanimation of their shared desires for each other and intellectual pursuit, with other desires for the various forms of social change that motivated their teaching. The erotic of Brown and Primus's romantic friendship energized their participation, as learner and teacher, in African American self-education for racial uplift and justice. Holley and Putnam's relationship was animated by an erotic of radical antislavery affection, with their desires for abolition shaping their teaching of rhetoric in service of racial justice alongside the African American community at the Holley School. Leache and Wood developed an "opulent friendship" through a passion for the conservative emulation of "beauty," which informed their teaching at the Leache-Wood Seminary of belletristic rhetoric modeled after beautiful writing. Buck and Wylie's relationship was fueled by a "homogenic" and "sapphic" erotic of progressive egalitarianism that shaped their administration of the rhetoric program at Vassar, where rhetoric was taught as an idealized form of cooperative communication between equals. The erotic as rhetorical power thus shaped the women's teaching according to different cultural, political, and pedagogical values within each couple.

For the white women with relatively privileged access to public forums, the erotic also functioned as a source of rhetorical power by fueling their own rhetorical practices as public speakers and published writers who shared desires for social and political transformation. Lorde theorizes this capacity of the erotic to "give us the energy to pursue genuine change within the world."[43] Along similar lines, Lore/tta LeMaster and Pritchard build on Lorde's work to conceptualize "desire in critical terms that labor toward transformational worldmaking," such that the erotic becomes "an affective power within both individual and collective struggles against oppression."[44] For Holley and Putnam, the radical erotic of their relationship energized their rhetorical activities as speakers on the abolitionist lecture circuit and activists fighting for voting rights alongside African American men. The conservative erotic of Leache and Wood's romantic friendship became a source of rhetorical power within their work to advance educational opportunities for white girls in the South.

---

42. On literary representations of the same-sex erotics of women's education in the late nineteenth and early twentieth centuries, see Kent, *Making*, 19, 157–61, 169, 178–83.

43. Lorde, "Uses of the Erotic," 59. Also on this point, see Ferguson, "Of Sensual Matters," 298.

44. LeMaster, "Felt Sex," 106; and Pritchard, *Fashioning*, 202.

Finally, for Buck and Wylie, the progressive erotic of their relationship fueled their efforts on behalf of higher education and suffrage for white women. For all of these women, the erotic amounted to a rhetorical power in that it not only constituted their intimate relationships but also motivated and informed their access to participation in civic life.

From Carpenter to Lorde and into the present, this creative power of the erotic is usually idealized as transformative in a politically radical or progressive sense. However, as my mentions of the conservative erotic of Leache and Wood's relationship may already foreshadow, my historiography confronts such idealized views of the erotic, because, especially with respect to questions of difference, the erotic may fuel rhetorical labors that both challenge and instantiate existing power structures. I thus want to probe at the onset the relationship between the erotic and difference. As Holland points out, Lorde is often read as suggesting "the view that the erotic 'functions' as a means to undo difference, rather than facilitate its entrenchment."[45] I believe this (mis)reading emerges in response to two important and often quoted passages from "Uses of the Erotic." In the first, Lorde emphasizes how the erotic may empower women to "do that which is . . . self-affirming in the face of a racist, patriarchal, and anti-erotic society."[46] But her emphasis needs to be understood with respect to her own context, purpose, and positionality, concerned as she was with the erotic's power to be "self-affirming" especially by, for, and among Black women and other women of color. As Amber Jamilla Musser observes, Lorde's erotic is "a response to very particular experiences of racism, patriarchy, and capitalism."[47] In the second key passage, speaking directly to questions of difference, Lorde writes that erotic sharing "forms a bridge between the sharers which *can be* the basis for understanding much of what is not shared between them, and lessens the threat of their difference."[48] Important in this line is her word choice of "can be" rather than "is" or "will be." While she recognizes the possibility for erotic sharing to serve as a "bridge" that "lessens the threat" of difference, she in no way claims that the erotic inevitably or necessarily has this effect in all cases.

Quite the contrary. Here Lorde's essay on the erotic needs to be read alongside her broader body of work on difference and power, which is animated at virtually every turn with an insistence on recognizing both the differences between women (as well as across the Black diaspora) and the

---

45. Holland, *Erotic Life*, 59.
46. Lorde, "Uses of the Erotic," 59.
47. Musser, "Re-Membering," 353. See also Byrd, "Introduction," 18.
48. Lorde, "Uses of the Erotic," 56, emphasis added.

multiple possible responses to such difference.[49] On the one hand, she does indeed celebrate the capacity for difference to serve a "creative function . . . in our lives" as "that raw and powerful connection from which our personal power is forged"—"a creative and necessary force for change."[50]

On the other hand, even as Lorde approached difference in this way, she recognized that most people—and especially those who are relatively privileged in a given situation—more frequently respond to difference in ways that reject rather than embrace its capacity to empower creativity and change. In an essay focused on differences between women, she writes that "members" of "a profit economy . . . have *all* been programmed to respond to human differences between us with fear and loathing and to handle that difference in one of three ways."[51] People "ignore it, and if that is not possible, copy it if we think it is dominant, or destroy it if we think it is subordinate." Unfortunately, she laments, "we have no patterns for relating our human differences as equals. As a result, those differences have been misnamed and misused in the service of separation and confusion." Insofar as Lorde advocates for the erotic's capacity to energize the embrace of difference as a source of creative power, then, she does so precisely because most people are so ill-equipped for responding to difference productively. Even though feminist and queer scholarly engagements with Lorde have tended toward "the erotic's *disarticulation* from racist practice," explain Holland and Lyndon K. Gill, "the erotic has been and can be used to reinscribe and entrench differences."[52] Along these lines, I conceive of the erotic as a rhetorical power that holds the potential to be enacted in ways

---

49. Pritchard, "'As Proud,'" 159. For additional examples of Lorde's speaking and writing on difference, beyond what is already discussed in this introductory chapter, see Lorde, "Burst," 88, 94, 96, 98, 102, 112, 120; Lorde, "Commencement," 216, 218; Lorde, "Difference," 201–6; Lorde, "Foreword," 170, 171, 176; Lorde and Star, "Sadomasochism," 53; Lorde, "There Is," 219; Lorde, "Transformation," 40, 43; Lorde, "What Is," 223; and Lorde, *Zami*, 81–82, 149, 204–5.

50. Lorde, "Master's Tools," 111–12; and Lorde, "Learning," 135. In a speech on behalf of the National Coalition of Black Lesbians and Gays, for example, Lorde addressed Black Civil Rights Movement organizers and activists. "We know we do not have to become copies of each other," she said, "in order to be able to work together. We know that when we join hands across the table of our difference, our diversity gives us great power." Lorde thus urged her audience to "join hands across" differences of sexuality, taking "great power" from the "diversity" of Black communities. "When we can arm ourselves with the strength and vision for all of our diverse communities," she concluded, "then we will in truth all be free at last." See Lorde, "Address," 212. I learned of this speech from Pritchard, "'As Proud,'" 165. Pritchard not only analyzes the speech but also explains the activism involved in getting Lorde to the podium on that occasion. Lorde further characterizes difference as a potential source of creative power across her larger body of work. See, for example, Lorde, "My Words," 162; Lorde, "Turning," 78; and Lorde, "When Will," 209.

51. Lorde, "Age, Race, Class," 115. Emphasis is in the original here and throughout, except where otherwise indicated. Lorde also speaks about three possible responses to difference in "Difference and Survival," 201–2.

52. Holland, *Erotic Life*, 12; and Gill, "In the Realm," 188.

that both challenge and perpetuate hierarchies of difference as structured with societies that are racist, settler colonial, patriarchal, heterosexist, transphobic, capitalist, and so on.

With privileged women like those centered in my archival study, even as they worked to effect other forms of social change, they were especially prone to enacting the erotic in ways that reinscribed difference through investments in white femininity. As Lorde notes, the power of the erotic "is not easily shared by women who continue to operate under an exclusively europeanamerican male tradition."[53] It is too easy "for white women," she writes, "to believe the dangerous fantasy that if you are good enough, pretty enough, sweet enough, quiet enough, teach the children to behave, hate the right people, and marry the right men, then you will be allowed to co-exist with patriarchy in relative peace."[54] Obviously the lifelong same-sex couples in my study did not "marry the right men." But as I will explore further in a later section of this introductory chapter, they still fell for other aspects of nineteenth-century fantasies of white femininity, such that the erotic fueling their rhetorical labors did so in ways that reinscribed as much as it transformed existing power structures of settler colonialism and slavery.

Part of what the women passionately shared within their intimate relationships was an investment in white femininity. The erotic of the relationships amounted to what Carrillo Rowe theorizes as a "power-evasive intimacy," one "contingent upon segregated belongings" and conducive to the "power-evasive communication styles" common among white women.[55] The kind of relational "experiences that arise within segregated alliances allow" many "white women to experience power and marginality as an exclusively gender-based phenomenon."[56] During the long nineteenth century, and against the cultural backdrop of US miscegenation laws, the primary form of relational belonging between the women in this study was one of sameness.[57] Through their shared experiences and investments in white femininity, the erotic of their romantic friendships empowered social change, but not change accountable to transracial alliances among people or even women specifically. Rather, the women's passionately shared sameness, along with their evasive approach to difference, created "limit points" even as the erotic functioned as a rhetorical power within their teaching, speaking, and writing.[58]

---

53. Lorde, "Uses of the Erotic," 59.
54. Lorde, "Age, Race, Class," 119.
55. Carrillo Rowe, *Power Lines*, 73. See also *Power Lines*, 80, 145; and Frankenberg, *White Women*, 43–55, 142–57.
56. Carrillo Rowe, *Power Lines*, 131.
57. Frankenberg, *White Women*, 72.
58. Carrillo Rowe, *Power Lines*, 18.

Thus the erotic's progressive and radical potential with respect to difference is just that: a potential.[59] The rhetorical power of the erotic holds the potential to challenge as well as entrench existing power dynamics. For women teachers in romantic friendships, the rhetorical power of the erotic was indeed transformational. But this power was grounded in settler colonialism and slavery, and the transformation worked to ends variously radical, progressive, and conservative. Moreover, among all the women, no matter how progressive or radical their ideals, they pedagogically and rhetorically reproduced troubling dynamics of systemic racism and its intersections with other forms of oppression.

As I move forward with this view of the erotic's complex and politically variable relationship to difference, I want to underscore two clarifications regarding how my own theory simultaneously builds upon and extends the work of others. First, in extending the work of Lorde and other scholars engaged throughout this section, I am building a specifically *rhetorical* theory of the erotic. By this I mean a theory of the erotic not only as a creative power for change but as one that blurs the boundaries between so-called private and public domains, fueling rhetorical practices that include public speaking, published writing, and the teaching of rhetoric oriented to social and political change.

Second, my theory of the erotic as rhetorical power emphasizes political variability with respect to divergent historical contexts and hierarchies of differences between women. As such, I am in no way suggesting that the erotic enacted by settler white women in the long nineteenth century is the same as the erotic conceptualized by Lorde as energizing the feminist pursuit of social change in the 1970s and 1980s.[60] Although feminist, queer, and queer of color uptakes of Lorde's writing frequently idealize the erotic for its potential to transcend difference, the white women in my study certainly did not embrace this potential, much less ally themselves with the Black and Indigenous women living and working in geographic proximity to them. Instead, and in every instance, whether the erotic of their relationships energized politically radical, conservative, or progressive visions, these white women materially relied on and rhetorically perpetuated their unearned privileges with harmful effects that undermined their rhetorical contributions.

---

59. For further discussion of the erotic and potentiality, see E. P. Johnson, "Revelatory Distillation," 312–13; and LeMaster, "Felt Sex," 106–8.

60. Lorde, "Uses of the Erotic," 59. For additional feminist and LGBTQ+ perspectives on the erotic beyond those already discussed, see brown, *Emergent Strategy*, 33; Driskill, "Call Me Brother"; Garber, *Vice Versa*; Ghisyawan, "Social Erotics"; Gomez and Munt, "Femme"; Kemp, "Writing"; Montgomery and Bergman, *Joyful Militancy*, 61; Musser, "On the Erotic"; Rifkin, *Erotics*; Smith, "Toward"; Stallings, *Funk*; and J. Taylor, "Enduring Friendship."

Why advocate for theorizing and investigating the erotic as rhetorical power, if it partially reinforced the very systems of settler colonialism and racism that enabled the women I study to have sustained their romantic relationships and careers as teachers of rhetoric? When even the most politically radical of these women still enacted the erotic in ways that rhetorically reproduced those systems so as to perpetuate hierarchies of differences? These questions have arisen for me through the process of research, writing, and especially revision. When I first started this project, I realized the problematic dimensions of the rhetorical practices and pedagogies advanced by the women. But I initially saw these problems as separate from the erotic itself, which, like many other feminist and queer scholars, I understood in an almost entirely positive valence.

Through the revision process, however, I have learned from the insights of readers who pushed me to more fully contextualize the erotic as a rhetorical power among these privileged white women as people who upheld settler colonialism and anti-Black racism. This process has shifted my theory of the erotic as rhetorical power, complicating my own and others' surface-level interpretations of Lorde's ideas. Such interpretations are tied to a widespread idealization of the erotic as inherently transformational in a necessarily progressive way. Still, my shift in thinking has not minimized the significance of the erotic as a specifically rhetorical power. Rather, a conception of the erotic as a politically variable form of power underscores its importance to rhetorical study. This more nuanced view of the erotic takes us further into the complicated, messy terrain that is rhetoric and power. From this place, scholars may recognize more fully how the erotic life of intimate relations is inextricable from the public life of rhetoric and politics. We need a theory of the erotic as rhetorical power in order to account for LGBTQ+ rhetoric and historiography—and to understand the mutually constitutive rhetorical dynamics of intimate and public life writ large.

## Romantic Friendships between Women

Before I discuss further the contexts of settler colonialism and slavery across the long nineteenth century, I first need to situate the erotic as rhetorical power in relation to historically specific notions of romantic friendship. Women's romantic friendships took various forms during the period and, depending on the setting and participants, have been known also as intimate friendships, smashes and crushes, and Wellesley and Boston marriages. The nature of the relationships is debated among historians of sexuality.

In the 1970s, early histories of romantic friendship characterized it as passionate but probably not sexual. These historical accounts suggested that, although some nineteenth-century women's diaries and letters described friendships using emotionally charged, sentimentalized language, this language was common to the period and did not amount to evidence of sexual practices. Early studies of romantic friendship also emphasized how it was socially acceptable prior to sexological discourse and its invention of sexual identity categories.[61] Certainly women's same-sex relationships should be situated within their historical contexts. Current LGBTQ+ historiography is rightly framed by recognition of the historical specificity of identity categories such as *lesbian, gay, bisexual, trans, queer,* and *two-spirit,* not to mention *straight* and *cisgender.* Since at least the mid-1990s, however, scholarship focused on women's romantic friendships has complicated the earlier studies. With increased access to a wider range of archival materials, historians have pointed to a more nuanced understanding of a range of romantic friendships that were (or were not) sexual or socially accepted to varying degrees.[62] Their research makes clear that, while all relationships should be contextualized historically, it is important to allow for the diversity of women's romantic friendships across the long nineteenth century—as well as the complexity of over forty years of ongoing study and debate about them.[63]

Unfortunately, outside of interdisciplinary LGBTQ+ studies and historiography, there is a tendency to pass over this complex understanding of romantic friendship. Where evidence of romantic friendship shows up in the archives, scholars often write off those relationships in relatively simple terms that repeat only the earliest historiographic claims about them. Specifically, some scholars are quick to point out that the relationships were common, socially accepted, and nonsexual—that they should not be claimed, by implication, as part of LGBTQ+ history. Scholarship about the white women in my study is no exception. Early research on Putnam and Holley references Carol Smith-Rosenberg's foundational and still widely cited 1975 essay on intimate

---

61. The oft-cited early studies include Faderman, *Surpassing*; and Smith-Rosenberg, "Female World." For discussion and complication of the idea that sexual identity was invented in the late nineteenth century, see Foucault, *History*; Sedgwick, *Epistemology*; and Somerville, *Queering*.

62. See, for example, Cleves, *Charity*; Diggs, "Romantic Friends"; Hansen, "'No Kisses'"; Vicinus, *Intimate Friends*; Faderman, *To Believe*; Smith-Rosenberg, "Discourses"; Halberstam, *Female Masculinity*; and Love, *Feeling Backward*.

63. Other important works that attend to the complexities of nineteenth-century sexuality with respect to gender identity, trans practices, and intersex embodiment include Cleves, "Beyond the Binaries"; Malatino, *Queer Embodiment*; Manion, *Female Husbands*; Mesch, *Before Trans*; Meyer, "Signifying Invert"; Sloop, "Lucy"; and Snorton, *Black*.

friendship in order to suggest that "probably [Putnam and Holley's] physical intimacy skirted the erotic; there are no hints in their letters that they actually made love."[64] In similar terms, the most extensive study of Wood and Leache's relationship repeats claims that "affectionate friendships between women" were socially accepted and "held no sexual connotation."[65] Wood and Leache were "celibate lovers" and "thoroughly Victorian women," according to this study, who "had neither the concept of, nor the terms for, a lesbian relationship."[66] Within feminist rhetorical studies, where Buck and Wylie have been studied already, scholars explain the romantic dimensions of Buck and Wylie's relationship by also repeating claims made in the early work of Smith-Rosenberg as well as Lillian Faderman, the other most frequently referenced historian of romantic friendship.[67]

These accounts of romantic friendship reflect a larger pattern across feminist rhetorical studies in particular. The fact that some nineteenth-century women rhetors shared their lives in same-sex couples and women-identified communities is by no means denied. These women and their relationships are acknowledged within feminist histories of rhetoric. However, these acknowledgments are made only in passing. Or, where more than a single sentence is granted to the women's same-sex relationships, the discussion rarely moves beyond the insights of Smith-Rosenberg and Faderman's earliest research on romantic friendship—although this research has since been complicated, including by Smith-Rosenberg and Faderman themselves.[68] Especially in reading the rich body of feminist research on Buck and Wylie and recognizing the continued weight of patriarchal histories within the discipline of rhetoric, I find it understandable that feminist scholars have focused first on underscoring Buck's rhetorical contributions, even though doing so has meant relegating the romantic dimensions of her relationship with Wylie to passing reference. Still, there remains much to learn about the specifically romantic dimensions as well as the rhetorical significance of their and other women's same-sex romantic friendships.

The centrality of gender as well as sexuality to virtually every realm of rhetorical theory, history, and practice is now well demonstrated within LGBTQ+ rhetorical studies.[69] An impressive number of scholars—such as Jonathan Alexander, Jean Bessette, Karma R. Chávez, E Cram, Qwo-Li Driskill, Thomas

---

64. Herbig, "Friends," 165.
65. Hofheimer, *Annie*, 43.
66. Hofheimer, *Annie*, 45.
67. Bordelon, *Feminist Legacy*, 24; and Campbell, *Toward*, xvi–xvii, xxii.
68. Faderman, *To Believe*; Smith-Rosenberg, "Discourses."
69. For an overview of LGBTQ+ rhetorical studies, see Cox and Faris, "Annotated Bibliography."

R. Dunn, Ames Hawkins, V. Jo Hsu, E. Patrick Johnson, Charles E. Morris III, Lester C. Olson, Eric Darnell Pritchard, Erin J. Rand, K. J. Rawson, Jacqueline Rhodes, and J. Logan Smilges—have undertaken archival and oral history research to examine discourse related to diverse forms of LGBTQ+ relationships and activism.[70] However, historiography in LGBTQ+ rhetorical studies has rarely focused on the era of romantic friendship.[71]

I see two probable reasons for this lack of scholarly attention. The first concerns historical period and publicity, in that the widespread practice of romantic friendships as such preceded the development of Western sexological discourse just before and after the turn of the century. Sexology played a role in not only the invention of sexuality as a category of identity but also the pathologizing of lesbianism and, perhaps most importantly with respect to the study of rhetoric, the mass dissemination of ideas about so-called deviant sexuality within the public. Romantic friendships also preceded, quite obviously, the homophile and post-Stonewall public activism that organized around gender and sexual identities. Within LGBTQ+ studies of specifically public discourse, then, rhetorical practices from the era of romantic friendship may seem outside the domain of rhetorical study. A second reason romantic friendships have been underexamined within LGBTQ+ rhetorical studies is the tendency to focus on that which is "queer," as in nonnormative.[72] With some privileged women's romantic friendships accepted under certain circumstances during the nineteenth century—and often assumed to be universally accepted—this form of relationship may seem decidedly unqueer. Insofar as LGBTQ+ rhetorical studies focuses on the nonnormative, the rhetorics of romantic friendship remain far afield from the study of "self-conscious and critical engagement with normative discourses of sexuality in the public sphere."[73]

In my view, romantic friendships are interesting precisely because of their complex status with respect to publicity, rhetoric, and sexuality. Generally these relationships were accepted only to the extent that a public performance

---

70. See, for example, Alexander and Rhodes, "Queer Rhetoric"; Bessette, *Retroactivism*; Chávez, *Borders*; Cram, *Violent Inheritance*; Driskill, *Asegi Stories*; Dunn, *Queerly Remembered*; Hawkins, *Love(d) Letters*; Hsu, *Constellating*; E. P. Johnson, *Black. Queer.*; E. P. Johnson, *Sweet Tea*; Morris, "Kentucky Homo"; Olson, "Traumatic Styles"; Pritchard, *Fashioning*; E. J. Rand, *Reclaiming*; Rawson, "Rhetorical Power"; and Smilges, *Queer Silence*.

71. Morris's work on public memory and Abraham Lincoln is an important exception, though obviously focused on men's friendship. For these and other rhetorical studies of relationships during the period, see L. Harris, *State*; Morris, "Hard Evidence"; Morris, "My Old Kentucky Homo"; Morris, "Sexuality"; Morris, "Sunder the Children"; and Sloop, "Lucy." For a rhetorical study of women's same-sex friendships in the early twentieth-century context, see Allen, *Passionate Commitments*.

72. Bessette, "Queer Rhetoric," 149–52. See also Wiegman and Wilson, "Introduction."

73. Alexander and Rhodes, "Queer Rhetoric." Also see Rhodes and Alexander, *Routledge Handbook*.

of passion was accompanied by a domestication (and apparent absence) of sexual potential. Somewhat paradoxically, the popular understanding of romantic friendship as celibate actually made possible women's same-sex erotic and sexual relations, because it functioned as what Marylynne Diggs calls a "cover."[74] Diggs finds evidence in nineteenth-century women's diaries that they "were aware of the popular notion of nonsexual romantic friendships and engaged in sexual relationships under that cover."[75] She explains further that "such relations were tolerated only to the extent they were *mis*understood as 'romantic friendship.'"[76] Along similar lines, to the extent that intimate relationships between the women in this study were understood and accepted as romantic friendships, the popular idea of romantic friendship could have functioned as a "cover" for erotic or sexual possibilities that were not made public. Indeed, it is only within a culture of compulsory heterosexuality—both in the women's own time and in present-day historiography—that the lack of overt statements about sexual practice or identity are interpreted as proof of heterosexuality or celibacy.[77] It is cisheterosexism that demands a public speech act, a coming out, that is convinced everyone was and is straight (and cisgender) until proven otherwise.[78] Driskill makes this point with respect to the "colonial, heterosexist, and gender-binary thinking that would assume" a historical figure, in this case the Lady of Cofitachequi, "is someone who would now be considered heterosexual and gender normative."[79] Reflecting on descriptions of a dance by Waxhaw women, ze states, "there is no evidence that the women were people we would now call Two-Spirit. There is

---

74. Diggs, "Romantic Friends," 319.

75. Diggs, "Romantic Friends," 319, 328. Diggs discusses, for example, the diaries of English gentlewoman Anne Lister (1791–1840), "which describe her sexual relationships with other women and her doubts that the famed 'Ladies of Llangollen' had a purely 'platonic' relationship." Also on the Ladies of Llangollen and Anne Lister, see Castle, *Apparitional Lesbian*; and Whitbread, *I Know*.

76. Here Diggs quotes sexologists who "explained the relatively scant medical attention to lesbianism by arguing that 'inverted sexual intercourse among women is less noticeable, and by outsiders is considered mere friendship.'" See Kraft-Ebing, *Psychopathia Sexualis*, 396–97.

77. Rich, "Compulsory Heterosexuality."

78. To put it another way, the heterosexist assumption that romantic friendship, as a form of relationship, was nonsexual relies on interpreting it, to repurpose Ahmed's words, "in [a] way that straightens that form." "Straightening devices" function to "keep things in line" so that any queer effects get "corrected." Along these lines, the potential queerness in the archives of romantic friendships—the evidence that women, in enacting intimacy, passion, and domesticity with and toward one another, strayed from the normative path of marriage, home, and children—has been reread via the "straightening device" of heteronormativity, such that the queer effects of their same-sex relationships were "corrected." The very form of the romantic friendship has been straightened. See Ahmed, "Orientations," 561–62; and VanHaitsma, "Stories."

79. Driskill, *Asegi Stories*, 56.

no evidence they were not."[80] For the settler white women in my study, there is no evidence they engaged in sexual acts that we would now associate with LGBTQ+ identities and practices. There is no evidence they did not.

To be clear, I am not implying these women's relationships needed to be sexual for their same-sex erotics to be worthy of sustained attention within feminist and LGBTQ+ historiography. Such a move would be bound up in "compulsory sexuality," as in "the ways in which sexuality is presumed to be natural and normal to the detriment of various forms of asexual and nonsexual lives, relationships, and identities."[81] By contrast, as Przybylo explains, "the asexual, or ace, community" conceptualizes asexuality—whether as identity, practice, or resonance—in order to "suggest that sexual attraction is not an innate aspect of intimate or interpersonal life, thus challenging compulsory sexuality or the belief that sex and sexuality are core components of being human."[82] Along these lines, it is possible that the erotic energizing the romantic friendships of the women in my study was, in at least some instances, asexual.[83] There is a difference, though, between the act of claiming asexuality and the imposition of what Eunjung Kim terms "desexualization."[84] Within compulsory sexuality, sex and sexuality are expected and encouraged as normative among some people, whereas others are discouraged from reproductive and/or pleasurable sex.[85] During the long nineteenth century, economically privileged settler white women in romantic friendships were among the groups desexualized.[86] Their gender, class, race, and nation were all tied to idealized notions of nonsexual femininity and central to this desexualization.[87] To understand desexualized women as "asexual" would involve "misusing the

---

80. Driskill, *Asegi Stories*, 85. Also see 45, 48, 98.

81. Przybylo, *Asexual Erotics*, 1. This concept from asexuality studies builds upon the foundational lesbian feminist theorization of "compulsory heterosexuality" by Rich, "Compulsory Heterosexuality." See also Emens, "Compulsory Sexuality"; and Gupta, "Compulsory Sexuality."

82. Przybylo, *Asexual Erotics*, 4. See also Przybylo and Cooper, "Asexual Resonances."

83. Kahan, *Celibacies*; and Rothblum and Brehony, *Boston Marriages*.

84. Kim, "Asexuality."

85. Przybylo, *Asexual Erotics*, 15. See also Gupta, "Compulsory Sexuality," 141.

86. Przybylo's work focuses on the twentieth century but acknowledges a longer history of asexual resonances that includes, in the nineteenth century, intimate friendships and Boston marriages. See Przybylo, *Asexual Erotics*, 65, 76.

87. Owen's account of historical linkages between asexuality and race shows how an idealized desexualization of white women was linked to the simultaneous hypersexualization and desexualization of Black women, which was used to justify practices of enslavement and sexual abuse as well as structures of misogynoir. For white women, desexualization occurred through "a racial and sexual trope" of "asexuality-as-ideal." See Owen, "On the Racialization," 122–23. On the desexualization of Black women through the figure of the mammy, also see Collins, *Black Feminist*; Owen, "Still, Nothing"; and Wallace-Sanders, *Mammy*.

term 'asexuality' in the process."[88] Nor do I want to perpetuate lines of discussion that implicitly reinforce a normative conception of sex itself by counting only some physical acts—usually those consisting of or resembling heterosexual genital intercourse—as sex. Thus, while I affirm the asexual potential of the same-sex erotic energizing these women's romantic friendship, I reiterate that there is no reason to assume, one way or another, whether the relationships were sexual, nonsexual, or asexual.

One might wonder, then, why I use the term *romantic friendship* at all, if it usually conjures a straightened vision of nineteenth-century women's relationships as necessarily nonsexual—or why I attend to romantic friendship as such when so much of queer historiography has moved on from this "backward" relational form, whether in its dismissed or its idealized iterations.[89] I embrace the term because I seek to reinvigorate scholarship on romantic friendship, on relationships too easily left behind within feminist rhetorical histories that are heteronormative as well as queer rhetorical histories that emphasize the nonnormative.[90] In doing so, I treat romantic friendship as a form of intimate same-sex relationship between women that was marked by varying degrees of passionate expression, erotic intensity, and domestic entanglement. This view neither presumes these relationships were asexual nor understands them as inherently sexual in keeping with compulsory sexuality (or a normative view of what "counts" as sex).[91] While the "cover" of romantic friendship allowed privileged women to develop erotic and sexual relationships of various kinds, my focus as a rhetorician is not on what the women did sexually but on how the erotic of their relationships became a source of rhetorical power. Yet, even as I focus on the erotic, I also recognize the more practical ways that the teaching profession in particular enabled women's intimate relations and rhetorical activities.

---

88. Przybylo, *Asexual Erotics*, 15.
89. Love, *Feeling*, 25, 76.
90. Bessette, "Queer Rhetoric"; Love, *Feeling*; and Marcus, "State's Oversight."
91. As Manion suggests, writing about eighteenth- and nineteenth-century "female husbands," "maybe it is time that we embrace—rather than continue to fight—the ephemeral nature of sex, especially the way that illicit, non-normative, non-procreative sex eludes the archive's reach, refusing any notion of certainty or permanence." Manion explains further, "Historians often get bogged down in these details, assuming that nothing other than conventional heterosexual intercourse involving a penis and vagina could constitute sex—or be as pleasurable. We must not indulge this distraction." Manion, *Female Husbands*, 10, 22. Also see Coviello, *Tomorrow's Parties*.

## Women in the Teaching Profession

In a practical sense, straying from the heteronormative path most available to cisgender women during the long nineteenth century could open up time for a greater focus on public careers, social activism, and rhetorical practice. I do not mean to deny the incredible familial, cultural, and economic pressures to follow that path. Nor do I ignore the uneven distribution of that pressure among women variously located at the intersections of gender and sexuality with race, ethnicity, class, educational access, disability, family makeup, and so on. Understanding the historical and rhetorical contributions of women in same-sex romantic friendships requires, however, a simultaneous recognition of how that form of relational and domestic intimacy could enable privileged women's public activities. In the words of Faderman, same-sex relational "arrangements freed . . . women to pursue education, professions, and civil and social rights for themselves and others far more effectively than they could have if they had lived in traditional heterosexual arrangements."[92] Women were "freed," that is, from the gendered expectations of opposite-sex relationships, in which cisgender women (including those who needed to work outside the home) were disproportionately responsible for the reproductive labor of giving birth and raising children, performing or managing domestic labor, and carrying out the emotional labor of familial relationships.[93] As Trisha Franzen observes, women's same-sex "partnerships most often complemented and aided their professional activities, in contrast to the energy-draining conflicts recorded when their married counterparts tried to combine marriage and career."[94] In short, women in same-sex romantic friendships were released from at least some forms of reproductive labor and were more likely to share others equitably, which left energy for the rhetorical labors of other professional, educational, and political pursuits.

Whereas Faderman and Franzen survey the range of professional activities to which women in same-sex intimate friendships contributed, I focus on the profession most associated with women during the period: teaching. "To Americans," notes Geraldine J. Clifford, "the female schoolteacher is so commonly experienced and taken for granted that one can hardly accept that

---

92. Faderman, *To Believe*, 1–2.

93. I do not mean to suggest, of course, that people in same-sex romantic friendships had less housework than opposite-sex married couples. Rather, it is that domestic responsibilities were more likely to be shared between two women in a same-sex couple instead of falling to the one woman in an opposite-sex marriage.

94. Franzen, *Spinsters*, 119.

she was not always a *she*."⁹⁵ This "feminization of teaching"—the gendering of teaching as labor carried out by women—occurred over the course of the century.⁹⁶ As education at all levels started to become more accessible to a wider range of learners, teaching transformed from a relatively high-status occupation primarily open to privileged white men, to one of the few professional careers deemed fitting for women. As Jacqueline Jones Royster explains, "teaching was a type of work that was sanctioned as being appropriate for women."⁹⁷ Especially following the Civil War, more African American and white women were able to participate in the profession of teaching. The sanctioning of teaching as "the profession of a woman" occurred in part, according to Jessica Enoch, through arguments about women's "'natural' capacity to nurture and guide" within the context of "a national shift in educational priorities from classical learning . . . to moral education, social etiquette, and basic literacy."⁹⁸ As teaching became more similar to the reproductive labor women already carried out in the home, the profession opened up to at least some women, although African American women were paid less and usually restricted to teaching at segregated schools.⁹⁹ In this context, teaching was one of the few professional careers for formally educated women, not to mention one of the domains in which some could pursue advanced education.

This limited cultural openness to women's teaching careers was married to constraints surrounding the terms of such a career. Mainly, women were expected to teach only until marriage, and then leave the reproductive work of guiding the young minds of their students to instead carry out the reproductive work of supporting their husbands and raising biological children. These cultural expectations were codified in nineteenth-century "marriage bar" laws, which required women to leave their teaching careers if they married or became pregnant.¹⁰⁰ Clifford cautions against simplistic accounts of marriage bars, underscoring how their presence and enforcement were uneven

---

95. Clifford, *Those Good Gertrudes*, 4. On historic women teachers, see also Hoffman, "'Inquiring.'"

96. Clifford, *Those Good Gertrudes*, 19. Also see Enoch, "Woman's Place."

97. Royster, *Traces*, 178.

98. Enoch, "Woman's Place," 1.

99. While I have not encountered evidence of same-sex romantic relationships between Indigenous women teachers, there is room for further research in this area. Sources that focus on Chickasaw, Cherokee, and Sioux women's education and teaching during the long nineteenth-century include Cobb, *Listening*; Enoch, *Refiguring*; Mihesuah, *Cultivating*; and Moulder, "Cherokee Practice." Driskill speculates further on the possibilities of "same-sex intimacy and love" between Cherokee students at missionary schools. "The missionaries' insistence," ze writes, "on separating Cherokee students along a binary gender system opens up ruptures for radical imaginings of same-sex love and bonding." Driskill, *Asegi Stories*, 123.

100. Clifford, *Those Good Gertrudes*; and Oram, *Women Teachers*, 185–219.

by region.[101] Marriage bars were less common, for instance, in the South.[102] Still, even in Virginia, where Holley, Putnam, Leache, and Wood taught, one survey found that marriage bars remained in place into the early twentieth century in 33 percent of urban school districts.[103] Where sexist marriage bar policies and practices existed, same-sex friendships could function as practical supports for women's teaching careers. By remaining unmarried, instead forming romantic friendships with each other, at least some women were able to continue their professional careers as teachers over the course of decades rather than being forced to retire.

Marriage bars functioned in conjunction with the cultural figure of the spinster. Early spinsters were understood in terms of both lack and excess, as "lacking a partner" yet marked by "the 'excess and extraness' of erotic energy unchanneled into heterosexual partnering."[104] Within the context of Victorian colonialism, this spinster figure was "repackaged as a national commodity for use in nation building."[105] In the nineteenth-century US, spinster schoolteachers were viewed as central to settler-colonial nation-building—until, that is, they came to be associated with lesbianism.[106] For a period, though, unmarried white women could live together as "spinster" teachers and be recognized as contributing to the civic life of the nation through their careers in education. As Franzen writes of the "independent womanhood" practiced by both spinsters and lesbians, "if there is one cause, a common thread, among this diverse group it is the waged and political work which was shared between the two."[107] For unmarried women whose work involved teaching, it was often their careers in education that brought them together.

The women in this study fit this category, and they taught rhetoric at three of the educational sites most open to women over the course of the long nineteenth century. The first site, following the Civil War, was the freedmen's school. I discussed already the example of Primus, an African American freedmen's teacher whom I have written about elsewhere and whose life and relationships continue to capture my imagination in the interludes

---

101. Clifford, *Those Good Gertrudes*, 128–34.
102. Clifford, *Those Good Gertrudes*, 130.
103. Clifford, *Those Good Gertrudes*, 131.
104. Kent, *Making*; and Przybylo, *Asexual Erotics*, 129.
105. Przybylo, *Asexual Erotics*, 129. For further discussion of this point, see Kranidis, *Victorian Spinster*.
106. On teaching and nation-building, see Clifford, *Those Good Gertrudes*; and Enoch, *Refiguring*. On the emergence of an association between spinsters with lesbianism, see Cavanagh, *Sexing*, 7; and Przybylo, *Asexual Erotics*, 129.
107. Franzen, *Spinsters*, 119. For further discussion of the spinster figure, see Ensor, "Spinster Ecology"; Kahan, *Celibacies*; and Love, "Gyn/Apology."

threaded between chapters.[108] Her freedmen's teaching at the Primus Institute was supported by the erotic of her cross-class romantic friendship with another freeborn African American woman, Brown, although Brown worked as a domestic and the women were unable to live together over time.[109] In contrast, as privileged white women, Putnam and Holley were able to live and work together as freedmen's teachers for decades.[110] After meeting at Oberlin and then spending their early years together on the antislavery lecture circuit, Putnam and Holley taught at a freedmen's school alongside formerly enslaved African Americans. Holley and Putnam taught there together until Holley's passing in 1893, with Putnam continuing to do so until her own death in 1917. Putnam and Holley were far from alone as women who taught at freedmen's schools following the War. Many nineteenth-century women did so, including both white and Black women, as well as women from the North and South.[111] Freedmen's schools offered literacy instruction that served as a vital ground for nineteenth-century African American rhetorical education.[112] At the Holley School, Putnam and Holley notably taught rhetoric in ways that explicitly served the goal of racial justice rather than mere assimilation.[113]

The most extensively documented romantic friendships are those that developed in the homosocial educational settings of boarding schools and colleges catering to privileged white girls and young women. So-called mashes, smashes, crushes, and raves—often cultivated between a younger and older student, and at times between a student and teacher—were common

---

108. VanHaitsma, "Archival Framework"; and VanHaitsma, "Gossip."

109. VanHaitsma, "Romantic Correspondence."

110. Another example is Mary Grew (1813–96) and Margaret Jones Burleigh (1817–92), who are frequently mentioned alongside Putnam and Holley as fellow abolitionists in a romantic friendship with each other. See Chadwick, *Life*, 99; Cima, *Performing*, 123; and Faderman, *To Believe*, 20–22. Burleigh taught with Grew at Mary Grew's School for Young Women in Philadelphia, where abolitionist and freedmen's teacher Emily Howland studied. Grew also taught at a school for Black children opened by the Philadelphia Female Anti Slavery Society. When Burleigh married abolitionist Cyrus Burleigh in 1855, he passed away just one month later, at which point she moved in with Grew, who never married, and the women were "housemates" until Burleigh's death in 1892. As Grew wrote in an 1892 letter following Burleigh's passing, "the nature of the relation which existed" between the women "seems to have been a closer union than that of most marriages. We know that there have been other such between two men, & also between two women And why should there not be." See I. Brown, *Mary*, 15; Dixon, "Grew" 1–2; and correspondence from Grew to Howland, April 27, 1892, CRNL, quoted in Faderman, *To Believe*, 20–21.

Still another possible example is the relationship between Laura Towne and Ellen Murray, freedmen's teachers who started the Penn School in South Carolina, which later became a normal school. See Butchart, *Schooling*, 90; and Towne and Holland, *Letters*.

111. Butchart, *Schooling*, xi.

112. Logan, *Liberating*.

113. VanHaitsma, "African-American."

at these residential institutions.[114] In this category, a second educational site open to teaching by white women was the boarding school for white girls and young women.[115] In 1871, Leache and Wood helped found a boarding school, the Leache-Wood Seminary. They administered the school together and taught there for twenty years, until their shared retirement in 1891. Leache and Wood had met at another boarding school, where Leache was a teacher and Wood her student, though Wood was already nineteen years old when they met. Private boarding schools, seminaries, and academies generally served privileged young women, increasing their access to intellectual opportunities while also "inculcating in them the social and domestic skills they would need as republican mothers."[116] Especially in the domestic setting of the boarding school, where students and teachers lived together, women were seen as the ideal guides to such learning. Rhetoric was among the subjects women taught, though more attention usually went to grammar, literature, and composition. So, too, at the Leache-Wood Seminary, where rhetorical education took a belletristic form that, while common to the period, played a part in improved access to specifically academic training for young white women in the South.

The women's college was a third educational site that opened to white women teachers, especially late in the century.[117] In 1897, Buck and Wylie met

---

114. Inness, "Mashes"; Sahli, "Smashing"; and Vicinus, "Distance."

115. Just as Wood had been Leache's student in the South, teacher Maria Louisa Spear (1804–81) maintained a decades-long relationship with her former student from the Hillsborough Female Academy, Mary Ruffin Smith (1814–85). Spear never married and, in 1867, moved in with Smith at a Price's Creek plantation. There Spear opened another school on the property, for white students, and the women lived together until Spear's death in 1881. See Hoffert, "Earnest Efforts."

116. Hoffert, "Earnest Efforts," 815.

117. Two final examples resemble Buck and Wylie's relationship as faculty members teaching together at Vassar in the late nineteenth and early twentieth centuries. First is Bryn Mawr president M. Carey Thomas (1857–1935), whose "diaries of 1877 and 1878 indicate that she fell in love with Mamie [Gwinn] and Mary [Garrett] simultaneously." Later Carey would hire Gwinn to teach in Bryn Mawr's English department, and "the two women lived together as a couple in the Deanery until 1904," at which point Gwinn married another professor. With Mary Garrett, Thomas's "mutual attraction . . . never ceased. As letters indicate, it grew more intense through the years, apparently becoming physical after . . . 1890." A wealthy donor, Garrett's financial support apparently played a role in Thomas securing the presidency at Bryn Mawr. See Faderman, *To Believe*, 201–4; and Thomas, *Making*.

Second is the relationship between Mount Holyoke president Mary Woolley (1863–1947) and English department head Jeannette Marks (1875–1964). The women met when Woolley was Marks's professor at Wellesley. Marks graduated in 1900, at which point she and Woolley would "import a Wellesley marriage to Mount Holyoke." From 1901 to 1937, Woolley lived with Marks as a "life partner" and "devoted companion." See Faderman, *To Believe*, 223, 225; and Faderman, "Foreword," xi–xv.

at one of the Seven Sisters, Vassar, after Wylie had hired Buck to teach and administer the English department's program in rhetoric and composition. Particularly on the English side of interdisciplinary rhetorical studies, Buck is the best-known teacher in my study, because she was the first person to earn a PhD in rhetoric, from the University of Michigan, and she published widely as a scholar. Wylie's PhD was from Yale. The two women ran the department and taught together at Vassar for almost twenty-five years, until Buck passed away in 1922, and Wylie retired shortly after. Like boarding schools, residential women's colleges were central to increased educational opportunities for privileged young women. The elite Seven Sisters in particular also offered important employment opportunities for a first generation of women PhDs, though they were paid less than men. As at boarding schools, women faculty were seen as models for the students' gendered social and intellectual development. Yet, as a "true college," Vassar "boldly offered the full liberal arts curriculum to women."[118] That curriculum included training in rhetoric that, under Buck and Wylie's shared leadership, prepared privileged young women for participation in public discourse while emphasizing an egalitarian form of cooperative communication.

At freedmen's schools, boarding schools, and women's colleges, women teachers shared the passions of same-sex romantic friendship. To be sure, these intimate relationships supported their teaching, especially against the backdrop of marriage bar laws and cultural expectations about women abandoning the profession of teaching once married. In practical terms, these legally unmarried women found space within their lives together for the professional work of teaching. In the words of Franzen, "a woman without conventional domestic responsibilities had more time and energy to devote to causes—and if she lived with another woman who shared her interests and inclinations (or who would take care of their shared home while she pursued social housekeeping), the time and energy available for such work were expanded."[119] These causes were many and included the work of expanding access to educational opportunities on behalf of African Americans as well as white girls and women. Yet romantic friendships were not the only enabling conditions for privileged women's work as teachers and rhetors. Their rhetorical activities across the long nineteenth century were also made possible by settler colonialism and slavery.

---

118. Horowitz, *Alma Mater*, 28.
119. Franzen, *Spinsters*, 100.

## Settler Colonialism and Slavery

The erotic as rhetorical power in these women's romantic friendships was itself enabled by the settler colonialism and anti-Black racism of "stolen land and stolen labor."[120] In the words of Naomi Greyser, settler colonialism and slavery were the material "grounds" and "conditions of possibility" for the erotic as rhetorical power.[121] For all of the women in this study, the lands on which they were born—and where they practiced and taught rhetoric—were stolen from Indigenous peoples through forced removals, coerced "treaties," and attempted genocide. The buildings where the women learned and taught were erected and maintained by enslaved and exploited labor. The logics of settler colonialism and slavery—the extraction and exhaustion of Indigenous lands and people as well as the African diaspora in order to energize and empower white settlers—constitute what E Cram theorizes as a "violent inheritance" for the women in this study.[122] Crucially, these same logics that enabled the erotic as rhetorical power for some privileged white women functioned to constrain the educational, relational, and professional opportunities available to women such as Brown, Primus, and many others who remain unaccounted for in settler-colonial archives.

At the intersections of race, nation, and class, all of the white women in this study inherited their place on stolen lands along with access to generational wealth and the educational and professional opportunities it afforded. Beginning with Holley, she was born in the occupied Haudenosaunee and Seneca territories known as Canandaigua, New York.[123] Her father, Myron Holley, was a college graduate, a lawyer-turned-elected-official, and an abolitionist who founded the Liberty Party.[124] He "took an active interest in her education" at home.[125] She was also formally educated as a day student at a nearby boarding school and later Oberlin.[126] Less is known about Putnam's family and education. But she was born on occupied territory that is now Massachusetts, her father was a physician who passed away during her childhood, and she later moved to New York after her mother remarried.[127] Although records of Putnam's early education do not exist, "she immediately qualified

---

120. Hsu, *Constellating*, 113.
121. Greyser, *Sympathetic Grounds*, 31.
122. Cram, *Violent Inheritance*, 4–5.
123. Native Land Digital.
124. Pease and Pease, "Sallie," 205–6; and Herbig, "Friends," 16.
125. Herbig, "Friends," 25.
126. Pease and Pease, "Sallie," 205; and Herbig, "Friends," 17, 24.
127. Herbig, "Friends," 58.

as a second year student" upon her arrival at Oberlin, so it is safe to presume that "she had received solid preparatory-level education at some point before then."[128] Oberlin, where the couple met, was founded on occupied Erie and Kaskaskia territories by a minister and missionary with expressly settler-colonialist goals of westward expansion.[129] It is on these stolen grounds that Holley and Putnam developed the erotic of antislavery affection that animated their romantic friendship and rhetorical activities.

Leache and Wood were born on occupied Manahoac, Massawomeck, and Shawandasse Tula territories known as Virginia.[130] Leache's grandfather owned a plantation, so her family's generational wealth was made possible by their direct participation in the systemic enslavement of Africans, African Americans, and Indigenous people in the South.[131] Her "parents were conscientious about the education of their children," and Leache "was self-educated" through her father's library and "under the supervision of an intellectual mother" until she first left home as a governess and tutor.[132] This work included Leache's own involvement in slavery, living on another plantation, where she tutored white children and "taught Bible to the young slaves."[133] Wood's father "came from a large and prominent family of property and position," her mother from "an illustrious New England family, prominent from Colonial times."[134] Wood's maternal grandfather graduated from Harvard, which was built and maintained through slave labor, and her father purchased a home from his parents, with the family's generational wealth also being an inheritance of settler colonialism and slavery.[135] Wood's formal education included attendance at private schools in the North and the Valley Female Seminary in Winchester, Virginia.[136] The school, also located on occupied Manahoac, Massawomeck, and Shawandasse Tula territories, is where Wood met Leache, then her teacher. Here, on the grounds of settler colonialism and with the inheritances of slavery, they developed the erotic of emulating "beauty" that would make possible their own teaching and practices of rhetoric.

Buck was born in Kalamazoo, Michigan, on occupied Peoria and Bodwéwadmi territories. Her father, an attorney and judge, "may have spurred Buck's interest in education, rhetoric, and social reform," and her mother was

128. Herbig, "Friends," 61.
129. Native Land Digital; and Oberlin College and Conservatory, "Oberlin."
130. Hofheimer, *Annie*, 9, 35; and Native Land Digital.
131. Hofheimer, *Annie*, 35.
132. Hofheimer, *Annie*, 35–36. For further discussion of Leache's self-education, see Engle, "Valley Seed," 2, WFHS.
133. Hofheimer, *Annie*, 36.
134. Hofheimer, *Annie*, 18–19.
135. Hofheimer, *Annie*, 17, 19; and Hartocollis, "Major Findings."
136. Engle, "Valley Seed," 2, WFHS; and Hofheimer, *Annie*, 33.

"a descendent of Gov. William Bradford," an early English colonialist.[137] Buck earned her bachelor's, master's, and doctorate at the University of Michigan, which was funded by the sale of land taken from the Ojibwe, Odawa, and Bodwéwadmi nations.[138] Wylie was born on occupied Susquehannock territory known as Milton, Pennsylvania.[139] Although "from a less privileged background than Buck," Wylie's father was a seminary-educated minister.[140] Wylie's school attendance was "irregular," but she was educated partly by her father, graduated Vassar as the valedictorian of her class, and earned her doctorate at Yale.[141] As at Harvard, portions of Yale's campus were constructed by enslaved people of the African diaspora, and many early leaders of the college were slaveholders.[142] Wylie met Buck at Vassar, located in what is now Poughkeepsie, New York, on occupied Mohican, Munsee Lenape, and Schaghticoke territories.[143] On these grounds, Wylie and Buck developed and sustained the erotic of sapphic egalitarianism that energized their rhetorical activities. Settler colonialism and systemic racism thus afforded all three couples access to formal education and then teaching careers, not to mention greater financial freedom than most nineteenth-century women experienced.

Moreover, racist assumptions about white women's sexuality played a part in their romantic friendships being able to function as what Diggs calls a "cover."[144] Again, Diggs argues that at least some women were able to develop erotic and sexual relationships precisely because of the cover provided by popular understandings of romantic friendships as nonsexual.[145] It is important to keep in mind, though, that this understanding was grounded in cultural assumptions about middle- and upper-class white women's so-called sexual "purity" and relative lack of interest in sex for the sake of pleasure. In part, these were sexist and heterosexist assumptions about women as nonsexual until their desires were activated by a man. But these were also assumptions made primarily about economically privileged white women. Many white women advanced or went along with these ideas, presenting "their morality and controlled passions in stern opposition to the 'uncontrolled' and 'immoral' behavior of other classes and races."[146] Their "purity" was contrasted with distorted and damaging views of poor white women, eastern and south-

---

137. Bordelon, *Feminist Legacy*, 17; and *Britannica*, "William Bradford."
138. Tobin, "Wait."
139. Native Land Digital.
140. Bordelon, *Feminist Legacy*, 74.
141. Bordelon, *Feminist Legacy*, 74.
142. Dennehy and Gonzalez, "Yale."
143. Native Land Digital. See also Hertz, "Hidden."
144. Diggs, "Romantic Friends," 319.
145. Diggs, "Romantic Friends," 319, 328.
146. Franzen, *Spinsters*, 171.

ern European immigrant women, Indigenous women, and African American women.¹⁴⁷ For the women in this study, heterosexist dismissals of their erotic lives together are linked to colonialist, racist, and classist thinking about the supposed sexual purity of white women of means.

Yet it is not merely that these women were born into material conditions of possibility that were not of their own choosing. In each case, the women themselves rhetorically reproduced the troubling power dynamics of settler colonialism and slavery. Most troublesome but perhaps least surprising is how they reproduced the unearned privileges of white femininity, though in different ways and to different degrees. Subsequent chapters discuss how Holley's and Putnam's rhetorical practices and pedagogies reproduced white saviorism, racial paternalism, and regional prejudices against Black worship practices in the South; how Leache's and Wood's maintained an anti-reform stance that defended pro-Confederate beliefs and eugenics discourse about the superiority of upper-class white people; and how Wylie's and Buck's perpetuated racist, Eurocentric ideas about education and civilization that were wrapped up in imperialism and colonialism. Even as these women labored for the advancement of some rights and reforms, they were complicit in the undermining of—and sometimes even outright resistance to—other forms of racial justice and progressive social change. They are not heroines of feminist or LGBTQ+ history to be celebrated uncritically, in other words, but people who enacted the erotic as rhetorical power in ways both helpful and harmful.

Just as the individual women should not be idealized, nor should the erotic of their same-sex romantic friendships. While it may be tempting to associate same-sex relationships between women with an inherent or inevitable equality, there are power dynamics to recognize within each relationship itself. Most concerning, as the next chapter discusses, is the fact that Holley's behavior in her relationship with Putnam involved the power imbalance and pattern of control now associated with intimate abuse.¹⁴⁸ Additionally, as already noted, Wood was Leache's former student. While there is no evidence that Leache abused the power of this former student/teacher dynamic, it is clear from primary sources that Wood continued to look up to, admire, and emulate Leache for the remainder of her life. Along similar lines, Wylie hired Buck at Vassar and technically remained her supervisor, even as the women's

---

147. Franzen, *Spinsters*, 170. For discussion of the racist hypersexualization of African American women during and following chattel slavery, see Collins, *Black Feminist*, 71–73, 77–78; and Pritchard, *Fashioning*, 42. On the sexualization of Indigenous women in what is now the US, see Driskill, *Asegi Stories*, 78–81. On the history of imperialism and the hypersexualization of African and Indigenous women, see McClintock, *Imperial Leather*.

148. Kaschak, *Intimate Betrayal*.

relationship was animated by an erotic of sapphic egalitarianism that took shape partly through their shared administrative work. Although these six women were similarly positioned by nation, race, class, gender, education, and profession, then, there were differences of power between the individual women in each couple.

The erotic as rhetorical power holds the potential to allow women to acknowledge rather than deny these differences. Again, as Lorde claims, the erotic "can be the basis for understanding much which is not shared between them, and lessens the threat of their difference."[149] But the white couples in my study did not embrace fully this capacity of the erotic, instead grasping at the privileges of white femininity when doing so seemed to serve the cultivation of their intimate relations, rhetorical practices, and professional careers. In this sense, their exercise of the erotic as rhetorical power affirms Holland's insistence that "we can't have our erotic life—a desiring life—without involving ourselves in the messy terrain of racist practice."[150] Holland thus counters most uptakes of Lorde by "positioning difference at the center of the erotic."[151] Joining Holland, I underscore that the same erotic that made possible the rhetorical pedagogies and practices of the romantic friends in this study also energized their rhetorical and pedagogical reproductions of difference in ways that reinforced settler colonialism and slavery.

It was these conditions of possibility that simultaneously limited the rhetorical and relational opportunities of working-class and BIPOC women in romantic friendships. Consider again the example of Primus and Brown, whose extant romantic correspondence was cut short at exactly the point when Brown, who worked as a domestic, determined that she needed to marry a man for economic reasons. In her letters to the middle-class Primus, Brown tried to explain her economic justifications and convince Primus to see the situation differently. Although the erotic of their relationship animated Brown's support for Primus's work as a freedmen's teacher for formerly enslaved African Americans, it was that work that took Primus to the South. Still, Brown insisted in her letters that if the women could be together physically even part of the time, Brown would not marry. Although these African American women in a cross-class relationship were an early inspiration for the research questions that drive this project, and I return to them in my imaginative interludes, Brown and Primus were not able to persist in their relationship like the white women in this study. How many other BIPOC women also

---

149. Lorde, "Uses of the Erotic," 56. On Lorde's conception of difference, also see Pritchard, "'As Proud,'" 159.
150. Holland, *Erotic Life*, 46.
151. Musser, "Re-Membering," 353.

shared interanimating desires for each other, education, and social change but were not able to continue their romantic friendships or teaching careers because of the ways that systemic racism, settler colonialism, and capitalism constrained their lives? How many BIPOC women's intimate relationships and rhetorical activities go unacknowledged for these reasons? These are not rhetorical questions. I pose them because I sincerely hope the questions will invite future research that can be expected to clarify and complicate the findings of my own archival study and its theory of the erotic as rhetorical power.

## Erotohistoriography in Settler-Colonial Archives

A challenge confronting such research is the availability of archival materials. The settler colonialism and racism that enabled and constrained women's rhetorical and relational options across differences of nation, race, and class are also the conditions of possibility for archives themselves—not to mention my own historiographic engagements with archives. As previously noted, my study of the erotic as rhetorical power is grounded in archival research conducted in over twenty different manuscript and digital collections. (A full list of these collections precedes the book's prologue.) While I pride myself on carrying out such extensive archival research, it is important to recognize how archives and the knowledge-making they (dis)allow are implicated in settler colonialism and racism.

Perhaps most obviously, there is the problem of what archives are available. Marked by the intersections of cisheterosexism, settler colonialism, racism, and capitalism, the availability of LGBTQ+ and BIPOC archives is constrained by histories of enslavement, attempted genocide, literacy bans, forced removals and migrations, generational poverty, employment discrimination, gentrification, and housing crises. These histories and their ongoing effects produce material conditions of housing precarity, which often prohibit the preservation of materials across generations (not to mention the acquisition of those built spatial resources required to establish and maintain brick-and-mortar archives).[152] Also relevant is the appraisal of documents according to collections policies that have long reflected dominant cultural values.[153] Indeed, within this broader archival context, Primus is truly remarkable as an African American woman whose same-sex romantic friendship is

---

152. Chávez, *Borders*, 13; Holmes, "What's the Tea," 59–60; Lee, *Producing*, 81; and Van-Haitsma, "Archival Framework," 32–34.

153. For an introduction to appraisal as understood within archival studies, see Caswell, "Archive."

documented through romantic letters that she was able to save and others were willing to preserve. The same-sex relationships and rhetorical practices of most BIPOC women, especially across the long nineteenth century, have not been documented and preserved. By contrast, for the white women in this study, their unearned privileges played a part in not only the relational, educational, and professional opportunities available to them but also the likelihood that print records of their lives would be preserved in archives and special collections. They were able to create, save, leave behind, and have collected extensive records of their relationships and work together, including correspondence, scrapbooks, public speeches, published articles and books, and school records.[154]

However, it is not only that the available LGBTQ+ and BIPOC archives are limited—a fact that can too easily be used as an excuse for historiography that remains unimaginatively complicit in ongoing structures of epistemological violence.[155] Rather, archives themselves are colonial "technologies of rule," and historiography that allows itself to be ruled by their easy availability is itself implicated.[156] As Melissa Adams-Campbell, Ashley Glassburn Falzetti, and Courtney Rivard explain, "the birth of the modern concept of the archive emerged alongside the Western European nation-state, together with its quest for empire and colonial domination. The growth in population in eighteenth-century Europe and the need to document and report on colonial populations and holdings required the creation of an institution to store and maintain these records—the archive."[157] In specifically settler-colonial contexts, such as the occupied territories that now make up the US, "technologies of rule" take on "unique features" linked to "the continued erasure of indigenous communities within settler-colonial nation-states."[158] These features include the building of archives on stolen Indigenous lands, the development of archives through practices of extraction and captivity that extend to records and artifacts, and

---

154. That is not to say, however, that these women's archives are not marked by the elisions and absences routinely grappled with by feminist and LGBTQ+ historiographers. See Duberman, Vicinus, and Chauncey, *Hidden*; and Kumbier, *Ephemeral Material*.

155. The very framing of archives in terms of "loss" within histories of sexuality may be rooted in Western colonial logics. On "radical abundance," as opposed to loss, see Arondekar, "In the Absence," 110; and Arondekar, *Abundance*.

156. Stoler, "Colonial Archives," 87.

157. Adams-Campbell, Falzetti, and Rivard, "Introduction," 109.

158. Stoler, "Colonial Archives," 87; and Adams-Campbell, Falzetti, and Rivard, "Introduction," 110. On the distinctions and relations between colonialism and settler colonialism, see also Veracini, "Introducing," 2.

their descriptive framing according to settler cisheteropatriarchal conceptions of gender and sexuality.[159]

Recognizing these archival complicities, LGBTQ+ historiography often turns from "the archive" to what Diana Taylor theorizes as "the repertoire."[160] Like the archive, the repertoire is a mediated "system of transfer" for cultural memory, but the repertoire "enacts embodied memory" through "acts usually thought of as ephemeral, nonreproducible knowledge."[161] Within LGBTQ+ historiography, these acts include practices of storying, double weaving, oral history, ephemera, regeneration, and gossip.[162] Importantly, for Taylor and myself, the archive and repertoire are not a binary ("true versus false, mediated versus unmediated, primordial versus modern"), nor is their relation "by definition antagonistic or oppositional."[163] Rather, the problem is that within Western logocentrism, the archived written word is valorized over the repertoire.[164] I introduce the repertoire to this critical account of archives to emphasize that, although my study is archival, I do not subscribe to the settler-colonial view that archives provide greater access to knowledge or memory than does the repertoire. I refuse, in other words, the scholarly arrogance that my archival research offers a more valuable account of the erotic as rhetorical power than might other methods focused on cultural memory through LGBTQ+ practices like those listed above.

To counter the risk of inadvertently perpetuating such a view, I want to emphasize the extent to which this project, even as it is grounded in extensive archival research, is as much a work of historiography as any other rhetorical analysis of the archive or repertoire. I practice an intentionally feminist and queer historiography, by which I mean a selective rewriting of both histories of rhetoric and histories of these women for the explicit purposes of centering the role of the erotic. As Nancy F. Partner observes, "the silent shared conspiracy of . . . historians . . . is to talk about the past as though it were really 'there,'" when in truth, "history is the definitive human audacity imposed on formless time and meaningless event with the human meaning

---

159. Cushman et al., "Decolonizing Projects," 2, 10, 13; Driskill, *Asegi Stories*, 18–19; Lee, *Producing*, 8, 76; and Powell, "Dreaming," 117. On archival description as a rhetorical practice of power, see Rawson, "Rhetorical Power."

160. D. Taylor, *Archive*.

161. D. Taylor, *Archive*, xvii, 20.

162. Cram, *Violent Inheritance*; Driskill, *Asegi Stories*; Holmes, "What's the Tea"; Hsu, *Constellating*; Kumbier, *Ephemeral Material*; Lee, *Producing*; Muñoz, "Ephemera"; and VanHaitsma, "Gossip."

163. D. Taylor, *Archive*, 22, 36.

164. D. Taylor, *Archive*, 6, 24, 34.

maker: language."¹⁶⁵ This imposition through "the artistry of historical writing . . . consists of selection and pattern."¹⁶⁶ Specifically, the "shared conspiracy" is manifested through "an adroit selection and display of facts and quoted evidence" that are "woven together with nicely modulated comment by the author" in order to "make a firm pattern or generalization seem to 'emerge' from the materials with only modestly unobtrusive couching from the historian."¹⁶⁷ Of course, among feminist and queer historiographers as well as rhetoricians, many scholars have elected to emphasize the role of the author or historiographer in these purposeful rhetorical practices of selection, arrangement, framing, and style.¹⁶⁸

My own historiographic engagements with archives are no exception, as I purposefully select from the available records and arrange my "quoted evidence" in order to tell a story about the erotic as rhetorical power for women teachers in romantic friendships during the long nineteenth century. This is not to say that my historiography is fiction. As Partner emphasizes, the "genre distinction to be made between fiction and history" relies "on the highly specialized, rigorously evolved methods for discerning, selecting, and interpreting the materials from which a narrative claiming nonfictional status may be constructed."¹⁶⁹ However, "these are distinctions of degree, not kind, and they underlie claims to acceptable knowledge, not certainty."¹⁷⁰ Indeed, I do move further into the realm of fiction in the imaginative interludes that interrupt this book's dominant historiography. As I discuss further in the first of these interludes, they enact Black feminist methodologies of "critical imagination" and "critical fabulation" as theorized by Royster and Saidiya Hartman in order to invent alternative pasts for Primus and Brown.¹⁷¹

Throughout my archival, historiographic, and imaginative practices, the erotic itself also plays a role. Elizabeth Freeman's theorization of erotohistoriography comes to mind. I do not enact her method fully; I do not, that is, linger over descriptions of my embodied, affective pleasures (and pains) in desiring the women's stories, seeking out their archives, and crafting this historiography. I own, however, that the erotic animates my historiographic desires, research, and writing. Freeman, in characterizing her erotohistoriographic

165. Partner, "Making Up," 97.
166. Partner, "Making Up," 102.
167. Partner, "Making Up," 97, 102.
168. See, for example, Biesecker, "Of Historicity"; Glenn and Enoch, "Drama"; and Morris, "Archival Queer."
169. Partner, "Making Up," 112.
170. Partner, "Making Up," 112.
171. Royster, *Traces*, 83; and Hartman, "Venus," 11.

method as "a counterhistory of history itself," writes that "erotohistoriography admits that contact with historical materials can be precipitated by particular bodily dispositions, and that these connections may elicit bodily responses, even pleasurable ones, that are themselves a form of understanding."[172] In the words of Julietta Singh, there is an "erotic relay at work" in "the historian's erotic desire for her archived object."[173] Following Freeman and Singh, I want to reiterate that it was the queer dispositions and pleasures of my own same-sex intimate life, as well as my early encounters with Primus and Brown's romantic and erotic correspondence, that precipitated the early research questions giving rise to this archival research and historiographic account. I admit that I desire these materials, stories, and histories in ways that are not distant but close to my embodied experiences of pleasure within romantic relationships, rhetorical activities, and queer feminist historiography.

There is a risk with erotohistoriography—as with uptakes of Lorde's theory of the erotic—that it will be idealized as necessarily oriented to feminist, queer, and other progressively or radically transformative ends. But erotohistoriography can also be driven by and productive of harmful desires and practices. "Freeman is aware of the potential romanticism and racism that can result from an *ars erotica* of history," explains Tyler Bradway," and "Freeman's own erotohistoriography . . . refus[es] to sacrifice the violence of racist history for a redemptive intimacy with, or a reparative erasure of, the traumatic past."[174] Freeman considers such racism—what Holland theorizes as "the erotic life of racism"—in relation to "erotohistoriography's limit-case—sadomasochistic role-play . . . between black people and white people," including "the use of props and costuming that suggest specific social forms of power such as police officer or prison guard, and/or historically specific time periods such as Nazi Germany or the Spanish Inquisition."[175] Like Freeman's erotohistoriography, my own risks erasing or ignoring the racist and settler-colonial dimensions of the erotic as a rhetorical power. It risks embracing, in the words of Musser, a "particular fantasy about present reinterpretations of the past to claim queerness without racial baggage."[176]

I am driven by my desires for and fantasies of a past (as well as a present and future) in which more women were able to share their lives and work, with the erotic of their same-sex romantic relationships fueling their rhetorical activities and, importantly, their capacity to enact transformative social

---

172. Freeman, *Time*, 95–96.
173. Singh, *No Archive*, 82. See also Lee, "Be/Longing," 36–37; and Olivares, "Thoughts."
174. Bradway, "How to Do," 4.
175. Freeman, *Time*, 137.
176. Musser, "Queering," 69.

change. But the pleasures experienced wherever I find evidence of such desires realized must not slip into denial about the "baggage" of racism and settler colonialism that made possible both the erotic as rhetorical power in some women's lives and the erotohistoriography in my own archival research. Such denial is confronted, in part, through the imaginative interludes that interrupt the dominant historiographic arc of this book.

# INTRODUCTION TO INTERLUDES

## Imagined Pasts beyond the Archives

My questions about the erotic as rhetorical power in romantic friendships between women teachers were originally sparked by the relationship between Rebecca Primus and Addie Brown, which supported their pursuit of self-education for racial uplift and justice.[1] In my subsequent research, however, I have found substantial archival records of sustained relationships between women teachers only among white women with economically privileged access to formal education. Unsurprisingly, these women's national, racial, economic, and educational privileges played a central role in how the erotic animated their intimate and professional partnerships, as well as what records of their rhetorical labors have been preserved and made available for research in settler-colonial archives.[2] Rather than merely acknowledge such privilege, however, I want to push back against it by imagining alternate lives and archives that might have been possible for Brown and Primus had they, too, benefited from access to a wider range of educational, professional, and relational opportunities. I imagine these possibilities within interludes that are threaded between and around the archival studies of Sallie Holley and Caroline Putnam, Irene Leache and Annie Wood, and Gertrude Buck and Laura Wylie. The interludes are freed from the bounds of existing archives—and

---

1. VanHaitsma, "Romantic Correspondence."
2. Cram, *Violent Inheritance*.

even actual history—in order to imagine Primus and Brown as also able to live and work together as romantic friends and teachers.

Still, the imaginative interludes are grounded, at least initially, in the details of Primus's and Brown's actually existing lives and archives. Trained as a schoolteacher, Rebecca Primus (1836–1932) was born into a middle-class family that was prominent in the African American community of Hartford, Connecticut, which exists on Tunxis, Wangunk, Sicaog (Saukiog), and Poquonock territories.[3] While less is known about the family of Addie Brown (1841–70), she spent her early years in Philadelphia and worked primarily as a domestic in multiple locations across New York and Connecticut.[4] The women met in Hartford, where Brown may have boarded with the Primus family. Brown and Primus were often separated by their work: Brown left Hartford to find employment as a domestic, and Primus moved following the Civil War to help establish a freedmen's school in Royal Oak, Maryland, on the occupied land of Susquehannock, Choptank, and Ozinie nations.[5] Primus worked with the Hartford Freedmen's Aid Society and the Baltimore Association for the Moral and Educational Advancement of the Colored People in order to start the school for formerly enslaved children and adults. Across the physical distances separating them, Primus and Brown maintained a cross-class romantic friendship through letters for nearly a decade (1859–68). As existing scholarship makes clear, the women's correspondence describes relations that were not merely romantic but explicitly erotic and sexual.[6]

In my ongoing archival research about their erotic and rhetorical practices, I have now consulted two collections of the women's letters. The first and more widely studied collection is the Primus family papers. Acquired by the Connecticut Historical Society in 1934, the Primus family papers consist of two boxes: one box containing Primus's letters to her parents and sister along with her brother's and other miscellaneous family letters, and the other box well over a hundred of Brown's romantic letters to Primus. Unfortunately, as is often the case, only Brown's half of the romantic exchange with Primus is available. The extant romantic letters cease in 1868, after Brown married Joseph Tines. Primus went on to marry Charles Thomas but saved her letters from Brown for over sixty years, until her own death in 1932.[7] A second archival collection, the Rebecca Primus papers, became available through its

---

3. Griffin, *Beloved Sisters*, 10; Beeching, *Hopes*, 19, 38; and Native Land Digital.
4. Griffin, *Beloved Sisters*, 10–12; and Beeching, *Hopes*, 138.
5. Native Land Digital.
6. Griffin, *Beloved Sisters*; Hansen, "'No Kisses'"; and VanHaitsma, *Queering Romantic Engagement*.
7. Griffin, *Beloved Sisters*, 284; and Beeching, *Hopes*, 189.

acquisition in 2017 by the Arthur and Elizabeth Schlesinger Library on the History of Women in America.[8] This collection, now digitized, consists of two folders containing just over forty letters, most of them written to Primus. The collection documents more of Primus's later life and thus includes some letters from Thomas, but none from Brown.[9]

Departing from what these archives suggest about Primus and Brown's romantic friendship, I imagine a different past for them—a past in which the women were able to live and work together as teachers throughout their lives. In doing so, I draw on methodologies for imaginative engagements with archival materials by and about Black women. Specifically, I use methodologies of "critical imagination" and "critical fabulation" as theorized by Jacqueline Jones Royster and Saidiya Hartman.[10] Royster developed critical imagination as a methodology for scholars seeking to develop histories of Black women's rhetoric and literacy practices even where primary archival materials are limited.[11] The methodology involves "making connections and seeing possibility" based on what "traces" of evidence are available; it consists of "finding whatever pieces of the complex puzzle . . . that still exist and then . . . hypothesizing from the evidence, however skeletal it might seem, about what else seems likely to be true."[12] Hartman theorizes critical fabulation in compatible terms.[13] Writing about fleeting traces of Black women in the archive of slavery, Hartman characterizes critical fabulation as a methodology "to imagine what might have happened or might have been said or might have been done."[14] Critical fabulation proceeds through "advancing a

---

8. Correspondence to Primus, 1854–72, SLRI.

9. Correspondence to Primus, 1854–72, SLRI; and VanHaitsma, "Archival Framework," 34–36.

10. Royster, *Traces*, 83; and Hartman, "Venus," 11. My imaginative interludes are methodologically framed by Royster's critical imagination and Hartman's critical fabulation, which are theorized specifically for understanding and engaging with the archives of Black women's lives and rhetoric. Yet another possible approach may be through feminist and queer Afrofuturism. In rhetoric and communication, for example, see Brooks, "Cruelty"; Dickerson, "'Don't Get Weary'"; Hall, "Slippin' In"; and Pirker and Rahn, "Afrofuturist Trajectories."

Also relevant are imaginative approaches offered by Anne J. Gilliland and Michelle Caswell in archival studies. Gilliland and Caswell theorize "imagined records" that are of an "aspirational nature (i.e., because an individual or community wants it to exist, or wills it into an imagined existence)," as well as "archival imaginaries," which "may work in situations where the archive and its hoped-for contents are absent or forever unattainable." Gilliland and Caswell, "Records," 56, 61.

11. Royster, *Traces*, 83. Royster expands on this earlier concept of critical imagination with Kirsch in *Feminist Rhetorical Practices*, 71.

12. Royster, *Traces*, 80, 83, 81.

13. Hartman, "Venus," 11.

14. Hartman, "Venus," 11.

series of speculative arguments and exploiting the capacities of the subjunctive (a grammatical mood that expresses doubts, wishes, and possibilities), in fashioning a narrative."[15]

On the one hand, the narratives I fashion about Primus and Brown enact critical imagination and critical fabulation as I actively embrace the methodological possibilities of imagination, all while using extant archives as my starting point. Hartman points out, for instance, that even as she works to "exceed or negotiate the constitutive limits of the archive," her critical fabulation "is based upon archival research."[16] Like Hartman's critical fabulation, my imaginative interludes are grounded in archival research. When I imagine an alternative past in which Brown had the opportunity to continue her education as Primus's student, this possibility is something that Brown's letters show she herself fantasized about. When I imagine Brown being able to live and work with Primus as a married couple, instead of working as a domestic or marrying a man for economic reasons, this, too, is a wish that Brown expressed in her own writing. In these respects, the alternative pasts that I imagine for Brown and Primus are based on my sustained research in the two archival collections now available. Stylistically speaking, I make transparent these ties to primary records by following Hartman's practice of using italics.[17] My imaginative interludes specifically italicize any words, phrases, and sentences that are drawn directly from the archival records or secondary sources.

On the other hand, I depart from Royster's and Hartman's methodologies of critical imagination and critical fabulation in that, at least in this rendering, I let my imagination run wild a bit. I do not limit my imagination only to what could or might have been. Instead, I begin with what the archives suggest to be true, in order to imagine what should have been possible. By that I mean what might have been possible under different "conditions of possibility" in a more just past—a past not located on the "grounds" of slavery and settler colonialism—a past not so entirely circumscribed by the systemic racism, capitalism, and "racialized heteronormativity" that restricted the professional, intimate, and rhetorical options available to freeborn African American women.[18] To be clear, it is not simply that the pasts I imagine were not archived. It

---

15. Hartman, "Venus," 11.

16. Hartman, "Venus," 11. Royster especially emphasizes the need for epistemological care when advancing narratives that exceed available archives. She urges, "the necessity is to acknowledge the limits of knowledge and to be particularly careful about 'claims' to truth, by clarifying the contexts and conditions of our interpretations and by making sure that we do not overreach the bounds of either reason or possibility." Royster, *Traces*, 84.

17. Hartman, *Wayward Lives*, xiv.

18. Greyser, *Sympathetic Grounds*, 31. I understand the concept of racialized heteronormativity following Pritchard, *Fashioning*, 26. Also on this concept, see Ferguson, *Aberrations*, 17.

is that they did not occur. When I imagine what could have been, then, it is what could have been in a different world. In this way, I do indeed "overreach the bounds" of both "reason" and "possibility."[19]

In so doing, I am inspired, too, by Hartman's more recent approach in another narrative engagement with archival records of Black women's lives, in this case with a focus on the period from 1890 to 1935.[20] Here Hartman slips into imagining alternative pasts based on, but in excess of, the available archives. She presents this work as "an archive of the exorbitant, a dream book for existing otherwise."[21] When contemplating a series of images, for example, Hartman writes, "in such pictures, it is easy to imagine the potential history of a black girl that might proceed along other tracks. Discern the glimmer of possibility, feel the ache of what might be. It is this picture I have tried to hold on to."[22] My goal for the imaginative interludes to follow is "to imagine the potential history" of Brown and Primus "that might proceed along other tracks"—to "discern the glimmer of possibility"—to acknowledge and invite readers to "feel the ache" of what was not, yet should have been, possible for these African American women. This is the ache, I want to insist, of an erotohistoriography in which the erotic functioned as a source of rhetorical power for white women teachers, but so many other women labored rhetorically and pedagogically while separated from the women they desired.

It is risky, of course, to respond to this ache by imagining alternative pasts. First, there is a scholarly risk of admonishment by those who are skeptical of any and all imaginative engagements with history—much less forms of imagination that are deliberately untethered from the world as it actually was. Fear of such charges will not stop me. Instead, I write for readers who have the capacity to simultaneously hold yet distinguish between the imaginative interludes, careful archival research, and historiographic narratives on offer.

Second, and more important to my mind, are the ethical and political risks that my intentions in imagining alternative pasts for Brown and Primus will be, in the words of Hartman, "overshadowed by the inevitable failure of any attempt to represent" them.[23] My own inevitable failure is marked especially by my position as a twenty-first-century white woman who is imagining alternative pasts for nineteenth-century Black women. I will return to and reflect further on these failures in my concluding interlude, even as it refuses to

---

19. Royster, *Traces*, 84.
20. Hartman, *Wayward Lives*, xv.
21. Hartman, *Wayward Lives*, xv.
22. Hartman, *Wayward Lives*, 30.
23. Hartman continues, "I think this is a productive tension and one unavoidable in narrating the lives of the subaltern, the dispossessed, and the enslaved." Hartman, "Venus," 12.

"provide closure."²⁴ What I want to recognize at the onset is that, while I carefully attend to what Brown's archived letters suggest regarding how *she* likely wanted different possibilities for her life with Primus, there is still an incredible imposition in *me* imagining an alternate past for the women based on the desires driving my erotohistoriography. In a sense, this imaginative imposition "replicates," according to Hartman, "the very order of violence that it writes against by placing yet another demand upon the [women], by requiring that [their] li[ves] be made useful or instructive, by finding in [them] a lesson for our future or a hope for history."²⁵ Moreover, my imaginative imposition, as that of a specifically white scholar engaging in archival research for a book focused mainly on white women, risks that what I replicate is yet another archival violence of whiteness.²⁶

I move forward aware of these risks, sure to fail in at least some respects, yet insistent on carving out space for women like Brown and Primus in this erotohistoriography. My decision is to underscore (rather than merely note and then move on quickly) how the violence of settler colonialism and anti-Black racism made possible the forms of the erotic that functioned as sources of rhetorical power for women like Holley, Putnam, Leache, Wood, Buck, and Wylie. It is to remind readers, at each turn and between every chapter, how this same violence delimited the erotic and rhetorical possibilities available to Brown, Primus, and many other BIPOC women whose records remained unarchived. It is to not only recognize that violence but also write back against it. It is, again in the words of Hartman, "a history written with and against the archive," "a critical reading of the archive that mimes the figurative dimensions of history" in order "both to tell an impossible story and to amplify the impossibility of its telling."²⁷

Ultimately, the imaginative interludes interrupt the erotohistoriography developed through my studies of Holley and Putnam, Leache and Wood, and Buck and Wylie. These interludes, while woven into the story with attention to thematic connections and chronological order, intervene in the dominant historiographic narrative to insist that we—both my readers and myself—keep in mind four points. First, the form of the erotic as rhetorical power made possible by the romantic friendships between white women was not available equally to all women, as illustrated through the example of Brown and Primus.

---

24. Hartman, "Venus," 12.
25. Hartman, "Venus," 14.
26. On whiteness and archives, see Dunbar, "Introducing"; Espinal, Sutherland, and Roh, "Holistic Approach"; Powell, "Dreaming"; Ramirez, "Being"; and Williams and Drake, "Power."
27. Hartman, "Venus," 12, 11. Malea Powell also theorizes and enacts a form of "writing back to the archive" and its imperial and settler-colonial project. Powell, "Dreaming," 118.

Second, women who were not able to sustain their same-sex romantic friendships or professional careers for the remainder of their lives still creatively crafted erotic relations that enriched their rhetorical contributions. Third, in spite of what women like Brown and Primus accomplished, settler-colonial archives of their romantic relationships, rhetorical practices, and rhetorical pedagogies are limited. Fourth and finally, we ourselves do not need to limit our investigations of feminist and LGBTQ+ rhetorical history, or our imaginations and desires for its possibilities, to the archival records of what actually occurred. Indeed, it is imperative that we do not, if we are to fully understand the erotic as a source of rhetorical power that is, in the words of Audre Lorde, "creative energy empowered, the knowledge and use of which we are now reclaiming in our language, our history . . . our love, our work, our lives."[28] The erotohistoriography of my imaginative interludes reclaims the "knowledge and use" of the erotic as a rhetorical power that, even where grounded in settler colonialism and slavery, simultaneously imagines love, work, and lives in erotic excess of archives.

---

28. Lorde, "Uses of the Erotic," 55.

CHAPTER 1

# A Radical Erotic of Antislavery Affection

## Abolitionist Lecturing and Freedmen's Teaching, 1848–1893

> But one can hardly think of Mary Grew at all without thinking of her friends Sarah Pugh and Margaret Burleigh, especially the latter, devoted to her with that affection *passing the love of men* which many of the anti-slavery women manifested toward each other; in the affection of Caroline Putnam for Sallie Holley finding one of its loveliest illustrations.
>
> —John White Chadwick, *A Life for Liberty: Anti-Slavery and Other Letters of Sallie Holley*, 1899

Sarah (Sallie) Holley (1818–93) and Caroline F. Putnam (1826–1917) met in 1848 while they were students at the settler institution of Oberlin.[1] After graduating in 1851, Holley began speaking as an agent for the American Anti-Slavery Society. Rather than return to Oberlin to complete her own studies, Putnam joined Holley on an early speaking tour that traveled with Abigail Kelley Foster, Parker Pillsbury, and Sojourner Truth. Delivering hundreds if not thousands of antislavery lectures over the course of her career, Holley faced "the ordeal of becoming a *Woman Lecturer* on the everywhere odious, despised & rejected Garrisonian Anti-Slavery platform," which meant that she was "banned & barred from all respectable churches & society, as Infidel."[2] While Holley lectured publicly before "promiscuous audiences," Putnam went door to door distributing tracts, selling subscriptions, and participating in the "conversational rhetorics" deemed more acceptable for nineteenth-century

---

1. As previously introduced, Oberlin was founded on occupied Erie and Kaskaskia territories by a white minister and missionary who had settler-colonialist goals of westward expansion. See Native Land Digital; and Oberlin College and Conservatory, "Oberlin."

2. Correspondence from Putnam to May, January 22, 1887, MHS. Also quoted in Baylor, "Holley School for Freedmen," 53.

women.³ Putnam and Holley shifted from this abolitionist work to freedmen's teaching following the Civil War. In 1868, Putnam moved South to teach alongside the African American community in a freedmen's school. In time, Holley joined Putnam at what was by then named the Holley School. Holley passed away in 1893, and Putnam remained at the Holley School until her own death in 1917. For forty-five years, Putnam and Holley's relationship was animated by shared desires for racial justice, pursued through their work together first as abolitionists and later as freedmen's teachers.

Nineteenth-century biographer John White Chadwick's (1899) observation in my epigraph—that Putnam and Holley's relationship was one of the "loveliest illustrations" of the "affection *passing the love of men* which many of the anti-slavery women manifested toward each other"—is recognized in scholarship on the women's abolitionist rhetoric and freedmen's teaching.⁴ As Putnam and Holley's twentieth-century biographer, Katherine Lydigsen Herbig (1977), characterizes the relationship, they "had been close friends, then something more, perhaps ardent lovers, who wrote love letters to one another."⁵ According to Lillian Faderman, Putnam and Holley's work together allowed them to enjoy "each other's company rather than settling down with a husband."⁶ "Instead of having a conventional marriage," Faderman explains, they "created a virtual marriage, managing also to forge careers as reformers." In concert with Faderman, I understand Putnam and Holley's friendship as an alternative to marriage. This alternative was available to them as nineteenth-century abolitionists and freedmen's teachers, and their shared passion for racial justice defined the erotic of their friendship. Building on the feminist and queer theories of the erotic already introduced, I argue that the erotic of Putnam and Holley's romantic friendship functioned as a radical source of rhetorical power. In this version of the erotic as rhetorical power, Putnam and Holley's erotic desires for each other interanimated with passionately shared intellectual, pedagogical, and political desires that were all marked by an antislavery affection. This erotic of antislavery affection not only brought to life the women's intimate relationship but also fueled their public pursuit of racial justice through abolitionist rhetoric and freedmen's teaching.

The erotic as rhetorical power in Putnam and Holley's romantic friendship is distinctive in that, instead of catering to settler white girls and women, like Annie Wood, Irene Leache, Gertrude Buck, and Laura Wylie did, Putnam and Holley acted on their shared desires for racial justice by teaching rhetoric at

---

3. Donawerth, *Conversational Rhetoric*; and Zaeske, "'Promiscuous Audience.'"
4. Chadwick, *Life*, 99.
5. Herbig, "Friends," 354.
6. Faderman, *To Believe*, 101.

a freedmen's school within the African American community. In the wake of laws against reading instruction among enslaved people, freedmen's schools in the post–Civil War South necessarily taught basic forms of literacy. Yet as Jessica Enoch, Shirley Wilson Logan, and Jacqueline Jones Royster make clear, this literacy instruction was a crucial component of African American rhetorical education in the period.[7] With support in some instances from the Freedmen's Bureau and the American Missionary Association, freedmen's schools were made possible by the drive for education among newly free people. The simple fact that Putnam and Holley taught at a freedmen's school was by no means unique. Many nineteenth-century women—white and Black, Northern and Southern—did so.[8] However, Putnam and Holley taught rhetoric in service of racial justice, whereas the dominant freedmen's institutions encouraged pedagogical approaches oriented to social stability rather than political change.[9] Moreover, with the Holley School functioning as a private school supported by local African Americans as well as abolitionist networks in the North, Putnam was able to sustain her teaching for racial justice for almost fifty years—long after institutional support was withdrawn from most freedmen's schools in the South.

Also notable with respect to Putnam and Holley is the wide range of settler-colonial archives that document their lives together. By contrast, my research on the other couples in this study relies in each case on a few manuscript collections that hold most extant materials documenting the women's romantic friendships and rhetorical labors. Yet Holley's public activity as an abolitionist orator has resulted in databases of digitized nineteenth-century periodicals that contain countless references to her lecturing.[10] In addition,

---

7. Enoch, *Refiguring*; Logan, *Liberating*; and Royster, *Traces*. Additional scholarship on freedmen's teachers and schools includes Butchart, *Schooling*; Cimbala, *Under the Guardianship*; Faulkner, *Women's Radical Reconstruction*; J. Jones, *Soldiers*; R. C. Morris, *Reading*; and Williams, *Self-Taught*.

8. As Butchart argues, historical accounts of freedmen's teachers have been "distorted" by the presumption they were "white, single women from New England." Butchart, *Schooling*, xi. This distortion is particularly troubling in overlooking the role of African American women in freedmen's schooling. In fact, many Black women went South as freedmen's teachers. Royster, *Traces*, 178. Among these teachers were Emma V. Brown, Hallie Quinn Brown, Jane Deveaux, Charlotte Forten [Grimké], Blanche V. Harris, Edmonia Highgate, Ellen Garrison Jackson, Louisa Jacobs, Susie King, Mary S. Peake, Rebecca Primus, Sara G. Stanley, and Fannie Barrier Williams. See Enoch, "Woman's Place"; Griffin, *Beloved Sisters*; Royster, *Traces*; and VanHaitsma, "African-American."

9. Enoch, "Woman's Place"; and VanHaitsma, "African-American."

10. Materials are available, for example, through America's Historical Newspapers, 1690–1922; American Periodical Series, 1740–1900; and Nineteenth-Century US Newspapers (Gale). Elsewhere I detail digital methods for working with these databases. VanHaitsma, "Between Archival Absence."

both Holley and Putnam were avid letter writers, corresponding with each other when separated as well as with many others in their well-established abolitionist networks. Edited versions of some of these letters are published.[11] Other letters are preserved in manuscript collections. Specifically, I conducted archival research in the Caroline F. Putnam papers at the University of Michigan's William L. Clements Library. The Putnam papers consist of 111 items, most of them letters, which were sent between 1868 and 1877. The papers include some correspondence from Putnam to Emily Howland, another Northern white woman and fellow abolitionist-turned-freedmen's-teacher, who encouraged and supported Putnam in starting the Holley School.[12] Most of the letters from Putnam are addressed to Holley, sent before she joined Putnam at the school and during periods of travel. Yet in the Clements Library alone, writing by and about Putnam and Holley also appears in at least three additional collections: the Rochester Ladies' Anti-Slavery Society papers; the Harriet deGarmo Fuller papers, which include materials from the Michigan Anti-Slavery Society; and the Weld-Grimké family papers.[13] Furthermore, I have consulted digitized archival materials from multiple other collections that hold Holley's scrapbooks, other letters between the two women, and both women's correspondence with supporters, including the Alcott family, Frederick Douglass, Emily Howland, Abigail Kelley Foster, Samuel May, Wendell Phillips, and Theodore Dwight Weld. This chapter thus benefits from considerable documentation of Putnam and Holley's romantic relationship and rhetorical labors.

Grounded in this archival research, I investigate how the erotic of Putnam and Holley's intimate relationship functioned as a source of rhetorical power that made possible their activities as rhetors and teachers. My analysis, here as well as in subsequent chapters, is organized into four sections. First, I characterize in each case the development of a specific erotic in the couple's relationship, underscoring the variously radical, conservative, and progressive forms this erotic took. In the second and third sections of each chapter, I analyze the role of the erotic in fueling the women's rhetorical practices as public speakers and published writers, and then in informing their rhetorical pedagogies as teachers. Fourth and finally, I emphasize the problematic power dynamics reproduced because of how those rhetorical practices and pedagogies were

---

11. Chadwick, *Life*.

12. Howland taught in another freedmen's school in the same region of rural Virginia. It was Howland who had informed Putnam and Holley of the need for a teacher at Lottsburgh. See Baylor, "Emancipation," 79–92; and Chambers-Schiller, *Liberty*, 153.

13. See RL/CLMT; HF/CLMT; and WG/CLMT.

"used to reinscribe and entrench differences."[14] In so doing, I counter idealized conceptions of the erotic as rhetorical power within women's same-sex relationships, especially as enacted among white women on the "grounds" of slavery and settler colonialism.[15]

In the case of Putnam and Holley, I begin by describing their first meeting while at Oberlin and the subsequent development of their romantic friendship. I show how the relationship was animated by a radical erotic of same-sex, antislavery affection, even as the women's rhetorical activities were marked by a "white savior complex" and a division of labor between public and private roles. Turning to the ways this complicated erotic enabled their rhetorical practices, I discuss how Putnam supported Holley's career on the antislavery lecture circuit. While Holley addressed "promiscuous audiences" from the podium, Putnam went door-to-door, speaking one-on-one within more domestic spaces, with assumptions about white women's sexual "purity" allowing the women's travel together to allay potential accusations of promiscuity.[16] The women's shared passions, white saviorism, and division of labor also shaped their pedagogical work as freedmen's teachers. Each contributing to the cause in different ways, they worked together alongside African Americans to teach rhetoric in service of racial justice at the Holley School. Putnam consistently maintained the school and household over the course of decades, even as Holley frequently traveled away, and Putnam used indirect forms of persuasion to encourage Holley's participation in the more traditionally feminized work of teaching. Holley, in turn, used her extensive networks as a former antislavery lecturer to garner public support for the rhetorical education for racial justice at the Holley School. Yet both Putnam and Holley, as white women, took undue credit for what was accomplished by African Americans at the school.

Moreover, although Putnam's and Holley's teaching in the South was animated by an erotic of antislavery affection, even this more radical form of the erotic as rhetorical power was grounded in and made possible by the conditions of settler colonialism and slavery.[17] As with the other white women in this study, Putnam and Holley's erotic of rhetorical power was enabled, materially speaking, through these conditions. More importantly, they themselves reproduced problematic dimensions of white femininity through their rhetorical practices and pedagogies. Specifically, Holley and Putnam carried with them a regionalized form of anti-Black racism directed against Southern

---

14. Gill, "In the Realm," 188. See also Holland, *Erotic Life,* 59.
15. Greyser, *Sympathetic Grounds,* 31.
16. Buchanan, *Regendering Delivery,* 147.
17. Greyser, *Sympathetic Grounds,* 31.

African American worship practices. This racism was characterized by the "fear and loathing" of difference that Audre Lorde theorizes as undermining the power of the erotic.[18] Moreover, while Holley's and Putnam's rhetorical labors otherwise sought to redress dominant power structures, the division of labor within their own romantic friendship evolved so as to ultimately reproduce troubling power imbalances between the women. I thus argue that even as the radical erotic of antislavery affection functioned as a power fueling their rhetorical practices and pedagogies for racial justice, they simultaneously reproduced the violent power dynamics of both systemic racism and intimate abuse.

## Radical Erotic of Antislavery Affection

To lay the groundwork for my analysis of how Putnam and Holley's "affection passing the love of men" fueled their rhetorical practices and pedagogies, this section characterizes their initial meeting, the development of their relationship, and the defining features of its radical erotic of antislavery affection.[19] Fortunately there are extant letters between Putnam and Holley. Here I examine these letters and other primary materials alongside biographical work by Chadwick (1899) and Herbig (1977) as well as more recent historical scholarship. These sources show how Putnam's and Holley's passion for abolitionist rhetoric—their "sharing deeply" of the antislavery "pursuit"—animated their romantic friendship from the start.[20] Over time this friendship developed into a marriage alternative, which made their antislavery work possible in part through a typically gendered division of labor.

It was abolitionist rhetoric that brought Putnam and Holley together at Oberlin. Having interviewed Putnam about this initial meeting after Holley's death, Chadwick (1899) reported that Putnam "was drawn to Sallie Holley at Oberlin, she tells me, by anti-slavery kinship."[21] Putnam had been introduced to abolitionist rhetoric when, as a girl, she attended the "last public address" of Myron Holley, Sallie's father. "The recollection by Putnam of Holley's father helped cement the friendship of the two young women," explains Mary Lamb Shelden, "when they first met at Oberlin."[22] This coming together through abolitionist rhetoric was solidified further when "the women attended a

---

18. Lorde, "Age, Race, Class," 115.
19. Chadwick, *Life*, 99.
20. Lorde, "Uses of the Erotic," 56.
21. Chadwick, *Life*, 51.
22. Shelden, "'Such a Great Light,'" 70.

rousing antislavery speech by Abby Kelley Foster."[23] Specifying the form of antislavery rhetoric to which the women would commit their own labors following Holley's graduation, Putnam recounted to Chadwick that she and Holley "found themselves 'the only ultra radicals there,'" as in, "the only Garrisonian abolitionists."[24] As students, Putnam and Holley thus identified with each other, in a Burkean sense, through a shared investment in radical Garrisonian antislavery rhetoric.[25]

Putnam and Holley's early meeting at Oberlin was marked by a relationship dynamic common among young white women at nineteenth-century colleges, often referred to as a "smash" or "crush," in which a slightly younger student looked up to, admired, and was mentored by an older student. These were "dominant-subordinate relationships," as identified in Helen Lefkowitz Horowitz's study of women's colleges, often linking "an erotic element to a power relationship."[26] When Putnam and Holley met, "Holley immediately aroused Putnam's admiration" because she was "sophisticated and independent-minded."[27] In the words of Lindal Buchanan, "Holley's antislavery zeal dazzled Putnam."[28] According to Herbig, "Holley served as Putnam's intellectual mentor and spiritual advisor during their years at Oberlin."[29] This same-sex intellectual mentoring has ties, as already introduced, with the homoerotic pedagogies of emulation in ancient Greece.[30] Predictably, there is no evidence suggesting that Putnam and Holley, as nineteenth-century women, engaged in the specific sexual practices common to men in the ancient context. But an "admiration" for Holley's antislavery rhetoric did motivate the development of Putnam's relationship with her.

That Holley "served as a model for Putnam" is apparent in lines of admiration from an 1852 letter.[31] Having left Oberlin to join Holley on the abolitionist lecture circuit the year before, Putnam wrote to her, "I never have in all my life, felt more fully the extent of my obligations to you, how large is my indebtedness to the Truth you had received before me—and of which you became the Interpreter to me. . . . It is indeed a great thing to render so valuable a service to any soul, by which it may attain a higher worth, and is

---

23. Chadwick, *Life*, 52.
24. Chadwick, *Life*, 52.
25. K. Burke, *Rhetoric*, 20–21.
26. Horowitz, *Alma Mater*, 166.
27. Chambers-Schiller, *Liberty*, 150.
28. Buchanan, *Regendering*, 147.
29. Herbig, "Friends," 92.
30. Bizzell and Herzberg, *Rhetorical Tradition*, 26.
31. Chambers-Schiller, *Liberty*, 152.

enabled to enter upon a life of superior excellence."³² While Putnam did not become a public lecturer herself, she clearly admired Holley, seeing her as a rhetorical model to learn from. Putnam's affection for Holley only encouraged such emulation. "What sparked Putnam's imagination and inspired her effort," writes Herbig, "was the desire to be worthy of Holley's love and the hope that they could work together."³³ Nor was the affection one-sided. Interspersed within Holley's lecture notes on rhetoric taken while at Oberlin, she added (1848), "Miss Putnam is with me today, she reminds me of what Solomon says 'the lips of knowledge are like a precious jewel.'"³⁴ This dynamic of affection and admiration served as a motivating "force" in the development of the women's friendship.³⁵

Extant letters between Putnam and Holley suggest that, at some point, the relationship became more passionate, taking shape in keeping with cultural norms and epistolary conventions for romantic love. Herbig's interpretation, again, was that the initial friendship developed into "something more, perhaps ardent lovers."³⁶ During their lecture tour together in 1851 and 1852, "their relationship apparently deepened from friendship into love."³⁷ This view of the women's romantic friendship is warranted by passages of their letters written in a manner consistent with conventions for the romantic letter genre, including affectionate terms of address, pet names, and expressions of emotional and physical longing.³⁸ One example is an 1861 letter that Holley wrote to Putnam when they were apart from each other. "Oh, my heart yearns toward you this morning," Holley wrote, "and the heaviest disappointment of my life would fall if *you* should die. Again and again I thank you for all your love to me. I wish I were more deserving of it. Please God I may be some day. How I should love to put my arms around your neck and kiss you!"³⁹ Putnam's

---

32. Correspondence from Putnam to Holley, October 1, 1852, CRNL, quoted in Chambers-Schiller, *Liberty*, 150, 249 n. 85.
33. Herbig, "Friends," 150.
34. Holley, commonplace book, [1847]–52, RH/CHS. In addition to Holley's notes taken while at Oberlin, her commonplace books and scrapbooks consist of clippings about her own abolitionist lectures, her family members, and, to a lesser extent, the Holley School. The albums also contain clippings of poems, articles, lectures and speeches, and letters concerned with questions of abolitionism, women's rights and responsibilities, and religion.
35. Lorde, "Uses of the Erotic," 54.
36. Herbig, "Friends," 354.
37. Herbig, "Friends," 92.
38. VanHaitsma, *Queering Romantic Engagement*.
39. Correspondence from Holley to Putnam, November 18, 1861, quoted in Chadwick, *Life*, 186–87. For other discussion of the romantic passages in Putnam and Holley's letters, see Chambers-Schiller, *Liberty*, 153; Herbig, "Friends," 93, 102; Faderman, *To Believe*, 101–2; Speicher, and *Religious World*, 52.

letters to Holley include similar expressions of affection and longing. Putnam "cheered [Holley] on during these separations," writes Faderman, "addressing her as 'Dear Loving Heart' and 'My Best Angel' and assuring her that she too longed for 'the old delight of working, sleeping, and talking by your side.'"[40]

The shared desires of Putnam and Holley's relationship were by no means limited to conventional (albeit same-sex) romantic letters. Instead, their romantic friendship became a long-term alternative to marriage, which they seem to have chosen not only out of love for each other but in order to share the work of lecturing and teaching for racial justice. The long-term nature of their forty-five-year "virtual marriage" is recognized across the secondary scholarship, with Putnam referred to again and again as Holley's "lifelong companion."[41] Importantly, there is reason to believe that Putnam and Holley actively chose this alternative to marriage. They had considered their other options: the women rejected suitors who were men, and they briefly "tried out the lives" of spinsters who lived with and took care of extended family.[42] Ultimately, they chose same-sex romantic friendship over opposite-sex marriage or spinsterhood. This choice opened up space for Putnam and Holley "to forge careers as reformers at a time when there was almost no such thing as a career for women."[43]

Following the War, when Holley was no longer employed as an antislavery lecturer, she and Putnam refashioned their romantic friendship to allow for continued reform work, but in combination with domestic life rather than travel. Lee Virginia Chambers-Schiller observes that this arrangement was especially appealing to Putnam. In a letter to Howland, the more established freedman's teacher, Putnam (1858) wrote, "you join school and housekeeping," which "is a kind and style of life that always captivated my imagination—Far more than the ordinary mode of domesticity—the family proper."[44] In the words of Chambers-Schiller, Putnam "longed for an integrated life and sought a way to combine work and home which neither marriage nor itinerant lecturing provided."[45] Holley did not join Putnam in freedmen's teaching immediately, and would continue to travel on and off throughout their years together, with Putnam writing letters to convince Holley to join and stay with

---

40. Faderman, *To Believe*, 102.
41. Faderman, *To Believe*, 101; Buchanan, *Regendering*, 147; Clifford, *Those Good Gertrudes*, 164; Shelden, "'Such a Great Light,'" 69; and Pease and Pease, "Sallie," 205.
42. Chambers-Schiller, *Liberty*, 47; and Herbig, "Friends," 56, 219.
43. Faderman, *To Believe*, 101.
44. Correspondence from Putnam to Howland, March 29, 1858, CRNL, cited in Chambers-Schiller, *Liberty*, 153, 250 n. 96.
45. Chambers-Schiller, *Liberty*, 153.

her in rural Virginia. But helping to establish and teach at the Holley School allowed Putnam to create and maintain this "integrated life," a life devoted to both antislavery affection and the woman she loved.

While the emphasis in my subsequent analysis is on the specifically rhetorical dimensions of the erotic of Putnam and Holley's romantic friendship, I want to recognize before proceeding an alternative interpretation of the relationship itself. In keeping with the complexities of scholarly debates about romantic friendship, it could be argued that Putnam and Holley's letters represent their friendship as romantic but in no way erotic (much less sexual). Writing in the early days of scholarship on romantic friendship, for instance, Herbig hypothesizes, "probably their physical intimacy skirted the erotic; there are no hints in their letters that they actually made love."[46] Herbig seems to have equated "the erotic" with the sexual in ways that, following Lorde, I do not.[47] Yet Herbig proceeds to quote multiple letters showing that Putnam and Holley "did appreciate one another's physical attributes and presence," including through embracing, kissing, holding hands, and sleeping together. After discussing this documentation of the women's physical relationship, Herbig references Carol Smith-Rosenberg's foundational and widely cited essay on romantic friendships in order to claim such affection between women "was open and common."[48] Indeed, physically affectionate romantic friendships were common during the period. As Geraldine J. Clifford notes, Putnam and Holley "were shunned by their Virginia neighbors not for being lifelong companions but for teaching ex-slaves."[49] What was nonnormative about this relationship, in other words, was not its romantic dimensions but its orientation to racial justice. In this sense, Herbig's historical contextualization of the relationship within the nineteenth century is important to keep in mind.

However, we should not be so quick to dismiss the erotic and sexual possibilities of Putnam and Holley's romantic friendship. Herbig's assertion about the likelihood that their "physical intimacy skirted the erotic"—and especially her basing of this claim on an observation that "there are no hints in their letters that they actually made love"—anticipates similar claims in Faderman's early work. There Faderman considers it "unlikely" that romantic friendships were sexual during the presexological nineteenth century and, as Marylynne Diggs notes, draws this conclusion based on "the dearth of explicit references to sex between women in correspondence or diaries, ignoring the similar lack

---

46. Herbig, "Friends," 165.
47. Lorde, "Uses of the Erotic," 54.
48. Herbig, "Friends," 165; and Smith-Rosenberg, "Female World."
49. Clifford, *Those Good Gertrudes*, 164.

of such discussions of heterosexual sex."⁵⁰ Like Diggs, I urge that a couple's lack of epistolary discussions about having "actually made love"—as much with same-sex couples as opposite-sex couples—is by no means an indication of whether and how they expressed affection or acted on desires through sexual practices.⁵¹ Again, I am not suggesting that Putnam and Holley's relationship was necessarily sexual. Instead, I am interested in how the erotic dimensions of Putnam and Holley's romantic friendship enabled their activities as rhetors and teachers of rhetoric. I ask how their shared desires for each other and racial justice functioned as a radical source of rhetorical power fueling their work through antislavery lecturing and freedmen's teaching.

As I turn next to these rhetorical activities, I want to emphasize two themes from the development of Putnam and Holley's relationship. First, as already introduced, their rhetorical labors were facilitated by the antislavery erotic that animated their romantic friendship from the start. While political commitments and civic life generally are not viewed through the lens of the erotic within normative strands of rhetorical studies, such an approach is more common within feminist and queer theory and throughout the history of social movements focused on reproductive rights, nonnormative kinship, and sexual freedom.⁵² The erotic functioned powerfully for Putnam and Holley in that their simultaneous desires for each other and for racial justice were interanimating, serving as the foundation for their relationship and work. In Lorde's words, the erotic as rhetorical power within their intimate relationship gave them "the energy to pursue genuine change."⁵³ By sharing their intimate lives and focusing so much of their energy on public life, Putnam and Holley certainly subverted the patriarchal expectations of their time. Yet, whereas many other white women did so in order to pursue rights on behalf of other white girls and women, Putnam and Holley focused on racial justice for African Americans, seeing the work of antislavery lecturing as part of a larger project of antiracism.⁵⁴

Holley opposed the disbanding of the American Anti-Slavery Society following the abolition of slavery, for example, because the work of resisting "complexional hatred" in multiple forms was far from complete.⁵⁵ Seeing anti-

---

50. Diggs, "Romantic Friends," 337 n. 2. See also Faderman, *To Believe*, 18–19, 250–51, 414.
51. Herbig, "Friends," 165.
52. On the limitations of normative histories of rhetoric, see Chávez, "Beyond Inclusion."
53. Lorde, "Uses of the Erotic," 59.
54. Speicher, *Religious World*, 103, 122, 144.
55. Faulkner, *Women's*, 38. The phrase "complexional hatred" was used by Holley in writing an 1859 speech about school segregation, which was delivered by "Miss Parker," a young African American woman, in Holley's absence. S. Holley, "Address," 91, NCN. For further discussion of this speech with respect to questions of delivery and race, see VanHaitsma, "Between Archival Absence," 39–40.

slavery work as incomplete, Holley even resisted the initial formation of the freedmen's aid movement. Holley and Putnam "were among the only agents who continued to raise funds to support the American Anti-Slavery Society and its newspaper, the *National Anti-Slavery Standard*, after 1865."[56] In Holley's words (1868), "the American Anti-Slavery Society is the only Society in all this broad land, amid thirty millions of people—that demands unfalteringly, a guaranteed equal liberty, equal justice, for the black race!"[57] As Holley and Putnam continued to enact their commitment to racial justice through post-War freedmen's teaching, they also participated in activism to support voting rights for African American men, departing from other well-known white women suffragists by prioritizing these men's right to vote.[58] Even as the white women in this study most committed to a vision of racial justice, however, Holley and Putnam reproduced racism through their harmful representations of Southern Black worship practices. To both productive and problematic ends, what fueled Putnam's and Holley's activism across the board was the radical erotic of antislavery affection that defined their lives and work together.

Second, while Putnam and Holley's relationship was animated by a shared commitment to working for racial justice, they simultaneously divided their roles in ways common to opposite-sex relationships. In short, Holley took a public role while Putnam supported her through more behind-the-scenes rhetorical activities. Holley delivered antislavery lectures at public podiums before "promiscuous audiences," a rhetorical activity historically reserved mainly for privileged white men in the West.[59] As Holley's traveling companion on the abolitionist lecture circuit, Putnam participated in "conversational rhetoric," in which women were more likely to exert their influence through relatively interpersonal and small group interactions.[60] Putnam's participation included "organizing tours, scheduling lectures, hiring halls, arranging transportation and lodging, and selling antislavery literature and subscriptions."[61] Through the former especially, Putnam "proselytized on a smaller level" within the

---

56. Faulkner, *Women's*, 36.
57. "Letter from Miss Sallie Holley, March 7, 1868," *National Anti-Slavery Standard*. Also quoted in Faulkner, *Women's*, 38.
58. Correspondence from Putnam to Holley, [November 9–16, 1868] and December 1, 1869, CP/CLMT. On racism among white women within the suffrage movement, as well as public memory about the movement, see Ginzberg, *Elizabeth*; Goodier, "Doublespeak"; Hsu, "Voting"; M. S. Jones, *Vanguard*; McDaneld, "White Suffragist"; Palczewski, "1919"; Sneider, "Impact"; and Tetrault, *Myth*.
59. Zaeske, "'Promiscuous Audience.'"
60. Donawerth, *Conversational Rhetoric*. See also Zaeske, "'Promiscuous Audience,'" 200.
61. Buchanan, *Regendering*, 147. Also see Chambers-Schiller, *Liberty*, 151.

domestic spaces of the "homes" that she visited "on behalf of the cause."[62] As Herbig puts it, Putnam "became for Holley what her society expect from a dutiful wife."[63] Even within the context of a same-sex relationship, this gendering of their roles was complicit with patriarchal values. As "the supportive partner," Putnam "play[ed] a conventionally feminine and, therefore, largely unappreciated role, one that often goes unnoticed."[64] Over time, Putnam and Holley's gendered division of rhetorical labor seems to have contributed to troubling power dynamics within the relationship, especially during their later years as freedmen's teachers. At least at the onset, however, and especially given the patriarchal context in which they lived and worked, Putnam and Holley's division of labor on behalf of a shared cause, fueled as it was by a radical erotic of antislavery affection, enabled both women's rhetorical practices.

## Antislavery Lecturing and Conversational Rhetorics

This erotic functioned as what Lorde characterizes "as a considered source of power" enabling both Holley's and Putnam's rhetorical activity on the abolitionist lecture circuit.[65] Following the women's first antislavery tour together, Holley would go on to deliver hundreds and likely thousands of lectures as an agent of the American Anti-Slavery Society.[66] She spoke before "promiscuous audiences," as in those containing people of more than one gender, mainly in

---

62. Speicher, *Religious World*, 52. See also Jeffrey, *Great Silent Army*, 203.
63. Herbig, "Friends," 385.
64. Buchanan, *Regendering*, 147.
65. Lorde, "Uses of the Erotic," 53. Other studies of women's abolitionist and antislavery rhetoric include Bacon, *Humblest*; Bacon, "'Do You'"; Browne, *Angelina*; Carlacio, "'Ye Knew'"; Fiesta, "Homeplaces"; L. J. Harris, "Motherhood"; Henry, "Angelina Grimké's Rhetoric"; Hoffman, "Teaching"; Hoganson, "Garrisonian Abolitionists"; Huxman, "Mary"; Japp, "Esther"; Logan, *We Are Coming*; Mandziuk and Fitch, "Rhetorical Construction"; Rycenga, "Greater Awakening"; Yee, *Black Women*; and Zaeske, "Signatures."

While my focus is on the antislavery abolitionism of the nineteenth century, it is important to note present-day iterations of abolitionism in the movement to abolish the prison system as an extension of slavery. See, for example, Davis and Rodriguez, "Challenge"; Hsu, "(Trans) Forming"; Reed, *Love*; Spade, *Normal Life*; and Stanley, Smith, and McDonald, *Captive Genders*.

66. I discuss the complexities and challenges involved in attempting to count the number of speeches that Holley delivered in VanHaitsma, "Between Archival Absence," 39–40. In her letters and a commonplace book, Holley herself sometimes reported on the number of lectures she had given during a period of time. In a letter to Abby K. Foster, for example, Holley wrote, "I have only given six lectures since I came back to this state—I wanted rest." Correspondence from Holley to Foster, [1851?], AAS. An 1852 commonplace book entry listed "the Places in which I have lectured," noting the number of lectures delivered in each town. Holley, commonplace book, [1847]–52, RH/CHS. For other references to the number of lectures Holley delivered, see Chadwick, *Life*, 87; Faulkner, *Women's Radical Reconstruction*, 37; and Herbig, "Friends," 194.

small-town schools, town halls, and churches.[67] In so doing, Holley followed in the footsteps of Maria W. Stewart, the first US "American-born woman, black or white," on record as having "mounted a lecture platform and raised a political argument before a 'promiscuous' audience."[68] Although Holley's public speaking career has been underexamined within rhetorical studies for reasons I discuss elsewhere, her significance as an orator is recognized within Lillian O'Connor's early study of women's public address, *Pioneer Women Orators: Rhetoric in the Ante-Bellum Reform Movement* (1954).[69] Putnam's supportive role on the antislavery lecture circuit is also acknowledged within Buchanan's study of the "offstage elements" that made public delivery possible for some women in the period.

Certainly Putnam's and Holley's rhetorical activities, as with those of the other women in this study, were possible in practical terms because their romantic friendship with each other, as opposed to an opposite-sex marriage, freed up the women's time from childbearing, child-rearing, and some forms of domestic labor. Yet what the wide-ranging archives of Putnam and Holley's abolitionist work make especially clear is the role of Putnam's support within the women's romantic friendship. The documentation of Putnam's participation on the antislavery lecture circuit takes two main forms. The first is correspondence Putnam and Holley wrote to each other and fellow abolitionists. The second consists of nineteenth-century periodicals, now available through digital databases, which report and offer commentary on Holley's lectures. These sources show how the antislavery affection animating Putnam and Holley's relationship, enacted as it was through a division of labor, involved Putnam supporting and making possible Holley's more public rhetoric.

For both women, the radical antislavery erotic that brought them together motivated their decision to continue traveling together and speaking on the abolitionist circuit following that first tour in 1851. As Lorde defines the erotic, it consists of "what is deepest and strongest and richest within each of us, being shared: the passions of love, in its deepest meanings."[70] These passionately shared desires may function as a source of "power" and "strength," demanding of life a pursuit of "satisfaction" that "does not have to be called *marriage*."[71] Where the erotic empowers the pursuit of satisfaction beyond marriage, its power may include "the energy to pursue genuine change in

---

67. Zaeske, "'Promiscuous Audience.'"
68. Stewart and Richardson, *Maria W. Stewart*, xiii. See also Bacon, *Humblest*, 50, 166; Byrd, "Introduction," 6; and Logan, *With Pen*, 1–16.
69. O'Connor, *Pioneer Women*, 96–97; and VanHaitsma, "Between Archival Absence."
70. Lorde, "Uses of the Erotic," 56.
71. Lorde, "Uses of the Erotic," 57.

the world." For Putnam and Holley, as this section illustrates, their shared desires for abolition provided a source of power and strength that fueled their commitments to travel and speak on the antislavery lecture circuit.

Understanding the full significance of this rhetorical power, especially as it was acted on over the course of a decade, requires recognition of the nineteenth-century attitudes about women's public speaking that confronted Holley. *The Liberator* (1858) reported on the critical reception Holley encountered, noting "much bitter pro-slavery prejudice . . . both in regard to abolition, and the right and propriety of woman speaking in public."[72] Reflecting the cultural resistance to abolitionist lecturers more broadly, it was frequently reported that Holley's planned addresses had been sabotaged and ultimately canceled after local ministers failed to notify the public or barred her from their meeting spaces. The prejudice facing women in particular was rehearsed by other periodicals. *Frederick Douglass' Paper* (1852) reprinted an article that praised Holley's speaking but perpetuated "prejudices against the public speaking of women."[73] The article maintained that "although there was nothing in her bearing that was not perfectly becoming," the authors "could not but feel a regret . . . to see her occupying the position of a public lecturer." "Whatever may be her talents for debate or . . . discourse," they "opine that she will soon find that she has mistaken her vocation," as she is "so eminently fitted for the acknowledged sphere of woman." As I. B. Holley Jr. observes, Holley faced "hecklers in the audience who disapproved of women daring to speak in public."[74] Such disapproval of women's public speaking was typical for the period. For any abolitionist lecturer to persist in her work in the face of these cultural attitudes required a deep and passionate commitment to the antislavery cause.

In Holley's case, that commitment was buoyed by the antislavery erotic of her relationship with Putnam. While Putnam and Holley's shared political desires sustained their work on the abolitionist lecture circuit, so too did their desires to be with each other. As Faderman explains, "there is no question that Holley and Putnam were sincerely committed to their work."[75] At the same time, "that work also provided them with an exciting, legitimate means of grasping the personal freedom that was otherwise denied women in their day. It allowed them to travel in each other's company rather than settling down with a husband, and it provided an escape from the drudgery

---

72. Claflin, "Miss Holley," 111, APS.
73. "Sallie Holley," NCN.
74. Holley, "Schooling," 479. I. B. Holley explained his relation to Sallie Holley, whose father, Myron Holley, was I. B. Holley's "great, great uncle" (478).
75. Faderman, *To Believe*, 101.

and confines of mere domesticity." For Holley and Putnam, the passionately shared desires of their romantic friendship and abolitionist work were simultaneous and interanimating. These desires constituted an erotic of antislavery affection that fueled the relationship itself as well as their rhetorical practices on the lecture circuit.

Whereas this antislavery erotic motivated Putnam and Holley, their sustained participation as abolitionist rhetors was also made possible, at least in part, by the gendered and racialized discourses of "purity" that generally presumed romantic friendships between middle- and upper-class white women were nonsexual. In advance of a mainstream reach for sexological discourse, these presumptions provided a "cover" for diverse relationships that were variously romantic, erotic, or sexual.[76] The cover of romantic friendship paradoxically benefited all of the women in this study, but it enabled Putnam and Holley's abolitionist rhetoric in a specific way. Namely, a same-sex romantic friendship assumed to be nonsexual could function to allay the accusations of sexual immorality that were often leveraged to discredit women who traveled alone and spoke in public. Susan Zaeske details the emergence of charges about "promiscuous audiences," which were leveled at women praying publicly during the 1820s and then, beginning in the 1830s, at women abolitionists lecturing before mixed-gender audiences. These women were charged with immodesty and impropriety for their public speaking, and the charges were "increasingly linked with the morality and sexuality of women."[77] In other words, a woman abolitionist "was not only criticized for speaking to a 'promiscuous audience,' but her 'modesty,' or sexual purity, was questioned in the same breath."[78] This linking of women's public speaking with sexual impurity is grounded in a longer history of Western rhetoric in which, because it was believed that "woman by nature was irrational and could persuade only through seduction," a woman's "suasory powers" were "associated . . . with sexuality rather than with rational argument."[79]

Holley, by speaking publicly as an abolitionist within both this patriarchal rhetorical tradition and her current historical moment, risked being accused of sexual immorality. For this reason, Buchanan explains, women lecturers "had to consider traveling arrangements carefully" and often "sought traveling companions."[80] During Holley's antislavery lecture tours, Putnam's

---

76. Diggs, "Romantic Friends," 319. See also Castle, *Apparitional Lesbian*, 93–96.
77. Zaeske, "'Promiscuous Audience,'" 193.
78. Zaeske, "'Promiscuous Audience,'" 195.
79. Zaeske, "'Promiscuous Audience,'" 197. Also see Ballif, *Seduction*; and Bizzell, "Chastity Warrants."
80. Buchanan, *Regendering*, 146–47.

"presence on the road" could actually function to "diffuse[ ] suspicions of the speaker's sexual promiscuity and thus contributed indirectly to the success of the lectures."[81] In this sense, assumptions about nineteenth-century women's romantic friendships could act in yet another way as a "cover," activating assumptions that the relationship was nonsexual, rather than provoking accusations of promiscuity.[82] For public speakers in particular, the cover of a romantic friendship like Holley's with Putnam could function as what Patricia Bizzell terms a "chastity warrant," a means "to naturalize the woman public speaker for American audiences, not only defending her chastity but also giving her an appropriately feminine social mission."[83]

Importantly, to the extent that assumptions of sexual chastity do seem to have been activated, this process depended on Holley and Putnam's white femininity. During the long nineteenth century, as already introduced, economically privileged white women in romantic friendships were among the social groups desexualized. The colonialist, racist, and classist expectation within the dominant culture was that middle- and upper-class white women were sexually "pure": that they had little interest in sex for the sake of pleasure unless desire was activated by a man with whom they were to form a family and have children. Privileged women often perpetuated these damaging notions of difference by framing "their morality and controlled passions in stern opposition to the 'uncontrolled' and 'immoral' behavior of other classes and races."[84] In the US, this supposed "purity" of white settler women was contrasted with the harmful stereotypes used to justify sexual harassment and violence against other women, especially Indigenous and African American women.[85] Holley and Putnam's travel alone together provided a "cover" and "chastity warrant" that diffused rather than aroused potential accusations of sexual promiscuity, because they were in a position to enact a desexualized white femininity within the context of heterosexism and settler racism.

Putnam's role in allaying potential accusations of sexual immorality was particularly crucial given that Holley's arguments, like those of most abolitionists, were grounded in settler-colonial Christianity. Indeed, the charge that women public speakers were sexually suspect and immoral was often

---

81. Buchanan, *Regendering*, 147.
82. Diggs, "Romantic Friends," 319.
83. Bizzell, "Chastity Warrants," 388.
84. Franzen, *Spinsters*, 171.
85. Franzen, *Spinsters*, 170. Men of color have also been subject to racist stereotypes and hypersexualization in order to justify violence against them. See Bacon, *Humblest*, 45; Collins, *Black Feminist*, 71–73, 77–78; Driskill, *Asegi Stories*, 78–81; Frankenberg, *White Women*, 75–76; and Pritchard, *Fashioning*, 42.

advanced against women abolitionists in specifically religious terms.[86] So this charge needed to be diffused in order for Holley's religiously patterned moral claims and ethical appeals to be persuasive. A representative example of this pattern can be found in Holley's own words in a letter to *The Liberator* along with an account by a correspondent to the paper. Reporting on two lectures Holley gave in Wellsville, New York, the correspondent (1857) characterized "the first discourse" as showing "the debasing influence of slavery, and that the toleration of it is . . . subversive of true religion." The second was "designed to show the wide distinction between true religion, and the idle formality which is apt to assume its name." In this second speech, Holley emphasized "the glory of virtue" and, in contrast, "the active and eternal antagonism between real Christianity on the one hand, and all oppression and injustice on the other."[87] Holley, in her published letter (1858), characterized herself as an "apostle of the Gospel of Liberty."[88] She articulated the same distinction made by the correspondent, between the true practice of Christianity, which demands antislavery sympathy and action, and the mere practice of religious formalities like church attendance, baptism, and communion.[89]

These kinds of religious appeals, common among antislavery women, were reflected in abolitionist Abby Kelley's proclamation (1842), "abolitionism is Christianity applied to slavery."[90] But while Holley's religious appeals were common, their persuasiveness obviously required that her ethos not be tarnished by the charges of sexual immorality involving men that often targeted women who spoke before promiscuous audiences. In the cultural context and rhetorical situations that Holley navigated, Putnam's support as a same-sex traveling companion worked in concert with desexualized notions of white femininity such that her presence could reduce the likelihood of such charges undermining Holley's moral ethos.

Along with providing potential cover for accusations of sexual immorality, the women's romantic friendship occasioned Putnam's provision of direct and practical support for Holley's speaking career. While Holley delivered public lectures before promiscuous audiences, Putnam, in the words of Anna M. Speicher, "proselytized on a smaller level, visiting homes as a colporteur (a distributor of tracts) on behalf of the cause."[91] As Herbig notes, this work

---

86. Bacon, *Humblest*, 36–38, 140–41, 148; and Bizzell, "Chastity Warrants," 386, 388.
87. "Lectures of Miss Holley," 206, APS.
88. Holley, "Letter from Sallie Holley," AHN.
89. On various nineteenth-century conceptions of sympathy as proffered by abolitionists, see Cima, *Performing*.
90. Speicher, *Religious World*, 89.
91. Speicher, *Religious World*, 52.

involved "arguing the abolition case with individuals."⁹² I understand this proselytizing with individuals in relation to what Jane Donawerth calls "conversational rhetoric" in her study of "theories of women's rhetoric based on conversation, not on public speaking."⁹³ Donawerth underscores the need to view conversation in rhetorical terms if we are to account for the contributions of many women.

At least some nineteenth-century correspondents did recognize Putnam's labor in commentary on Holley's speeches. A piece in *The Liberator* (1858) referred to Putnam as "another devoted lady in the cause of genuine abolition," describing "the excellence and value of [Holley's] excellent friend and associate, Miss Putnam, who is worthily engaged in untiring efforts in circulating tracts, and in obtaining donations for the cause, and subscribers for the Liberator and Standard."⁹⁴ Here, too, Putnam's ability to assist Holley depended on the women's white femininity. In the nineteenth century, the designation "lady" was not only gendered but raced and classed, suggesting a privileged woman who was understood as fulfilling cultural standards for sexual chastity and purity. It was as a specifically white, middle-class woman that Putnam could safely move through public spaces in order to approach and enter the homes of white families and have this movement still be interpreted as the action of a "lady."

Beyond simply recognizing Putnam's conversational rhetoric when visiting homes as a colporteur, I want to emphasize that, as this behind-the-scenes rhetorical activity enabled Holley's public speaking, Putnam's support was marked by a typically gendered division of labor. As a correspondent wrote to *The Liberator* (1856), "Miss Putnam has a mission to visit families, as clearly as Miss Holley to address public assemblies."⁹⁵ Discussing what this division of labor made possible, Herbig writes, "Holley succeeded in her public career partly because of this support she received from Caroline Putnam."⁹⁶ Again, Herbig characterizes the role Putnam played in Holley's speaking career as that of "a dutiful wife." In order to join Holley on the lecture circuit, Putnam left her own studies at Oberlin early, although Holley had declined to do the same when she was first invited to begin lecturing.⁹⁷ Once the women were

---

92. Herbig, "Friends," 385–86.
93. Donawerth, *Conversational Rhetoric*, 2. Zaeske also discusses the idea that women could more appropriately exert their influence within domestic as opposed to public spaces. "'Promiscuous Audience,'" 200.
94. Claflin, "Miss Holley," 111. See also Stevens, "Sallie," 206, NCN.
95. J. R. Johnson, "Sallie," 22, NCN. Also cited in Speicher, *Religious World*, 52.
96. Herbig, "Friends," 385.
97. Speicher, *Religious World*, 45.

on tour together, Putnam "deferred her own needs so that Holley could continue the lecturing she loved."[98] Putnam "invested herself in Holley's more visible accomplishments," Herbig continues, "in the way homebound partners sometimes live vicariously through their spouses."[99] Over time, this deferral of Putnam's needs in service of Holley's career led to conflicts about the power dynamics of their relationship. At least during their early years on the antislavery lecture circuit, however, the division of labor served Holley's career.

Nor was this a role that just any traveling companion could have played. Putnam's contribution was that of a devoted partner rather than a mere colleague. In fact, abolitionist leaders James Miller McKim and Samuel May Jr. corresponded in 1860 about whether Holley could travel with and advise another young woman speaker, Anna Dickinson. According to Herbig, May wrote to McKim that "he judged Putnam to be the better traveling companion" for the other young woman, "but he did not expect she could be persuaded to leave Holley."[100] May was right, and Putnam did not leave Holley's side. Holley spoke publicly to promiscuous audiences, while Putnam traveled with her, able as a white woman to assist behind the scenes and allay public accusations of sexual immorality.

With Putnam's support, Holley could counter at least some cultural prejudices against "lady" abolitionists. A correspondent to *The Liberator* (1859) asserted that, following an address by Holley, "there was a great amount of prejudice against female speaking that found a grave that day, which will not be soon resuscitated."[101] Also reflecting the persistent yet shifting prejudices toward women as antislavery lecturers, one correspondent (1853) claimed that Holley was "decidedly the best lady orator we have heard," and another (1858) asserted more broadly that she was "one of the most effective and successful lecturers now in the field."[102] On the one hand, that at least some sources praised Holley as a lecturer, rather than underscoring her gender as a "lady" lecturer, is suggestive of her rhetorical effectiveness with audiences. On the other hand, that other commentators continued to emphasize her status as a "lady" was tied, again, to settler racism and presumptions of white femininity's sexual purity. As Jacqueline Bacon argues, white women abolitionists "could use the assumption that they were 'True Women' to their advantage" through appeals to audience assumptions about white femininity.[103] In con-

---

98. Herbig, "Friends," 385.
99. Herbig, "Friends," 386.
100. Herbig, "Friends," 209.
101. "Lectures of Miss Holley," 206; and Libby, "Sallie," 138. NCN.
102. "Anti-Slavery Lecture," *Liberator*, 72, NCN; and C.B., "Sallie," 206, AHN.
103. Bacon, *Humblest*, 42–43.

trast, African American women abolitionists faced greater risks and vulnerabilities to charges of promiscuity because of racist stereotypes of Black women as "driven by sexual desire and thus judged inherently inferior to 'pure' and 'modest' white women."[104] That Holley apparently was judged to be a sexually pure "lady" in spite of her abolitionist lecturing before promiscuous audiences can be attributed to not only her speaking abilities and romantic friendship with Putnam but also racialized notions of difference that simultaneously worked against African American women speakers.

Certainly Holley did not, as an individual, change attitudes toward abolitionist white women speaking in public. But with Putnam's support for her career, Holley was able to contribute to a slow but broad change in the gendered reception of women orators who addressed promiscuous audiences on the antislavery lecture circuit. Within the context of systemic anti-Black racism and its racialized stereotypes about women's sexuality, the radical erotic of antislavery affection that constituted Holley and Putnam's romantic friendship served as a form of rhetorical power that made possible the women's distinct yet complementary contributions to abolitionist rhetoric.

## Rhetorical Education for Racial Justice

Turning from Putnam's and Holley's rhetorical practices to their pedagogical work as teachers, this section considers how the same radical erotic of antislavery affection that animated the development of their relationship and participation on the antislavery lecture circuit also functioned as a "source of power" for their teaching of rhetoric.[105] The women taught alongside members of the African American community at the Holley School, which was located on occupied Sekakawon territory in Lottsburgh, Virginia.[106] In contrast with the white institutions discussed in later chapters, the Holley School was a freedmen's school that operated privately without ongoing support or oversight, even from the Freedmen's Bureau or American Missionary Association. As such, the school left relatively few records of the sort usually associated with larger educational institutions. In soliciting support for the Holley School, though, Putnam and Holley wrote many letters that described its pedagogical

---

104. Bacon, *Humblest,* 43. See also Bizzell, "Chastity Warrants," 389; Collins, *Black Feminist,* 71–73, 77–78; and Pritchard, *Fashioning,* 42.
105. Lorde, "Uses of the Erotic," 53.
106. Native Land Digital. Following Shelden, I use the spelling of Lottsburgh "generally used in the time that Holley and Putnam lived in Northumberland County, Virginia. Today the town's name is spelled 'Lottsburg.'" See Shelden, "'Such a Great Light," 138 n. 2.

goals and activities. These epistolary records show how the women's radical antislavery erotic, along with a "white savior complex," shaped their freedmen's teaching.[107] Their shared desires motivated their teaching of rhetoric and drove their curricular goals and activities in service of racial justice. Also from their work together on the antislavery lecture circuit, the women carried forward a traditionally gendered division of labor. Yet, whereas Putnam had followed Holley to a life on the lecture circuit, it was Holley who followed Putnam to the freedmen's school. In fact, Putnam had to persuade Holley to settle down there and join in the feminized work of teaching. Putnam persuaded Holley by appealing to the erotic of antislavery affection that infused their romantic friendship and giving Holley, a white woman, credit for the African American community's own accomplishments via the school. Holley in turn supported the school through more public-facing activities.

At the Holley School, Putnam and Holley collaborated with the local African American community to deliver rhetorical education in service of racial justice. This pedagogical goal was pursued through a curriculum enacted during a combination of daytime and evening sessions with children and adults, as well as Sunday school classes and community-wide political events.[108] Importantly, Putnam and Holley not only taught formerly enslaved African Americans but actively enacted a rhetorical pedagogy that continued the radical antislavery erotic of their romantic friendship and prior work on the abolitionist lecture circuit. As Frederick Douglass noted when he visited the Holley School in 1872, they were "doing up the unfinished work of the anti-slavery movement" by "devoting their time, strength, and talents to the education . . . of the class for whose emancipation they labored so long and effectively at the North."[109] This teaching of rhetoric in service of racial justice contrasted with the pedagogy that dominant freedmen's institutions encouraged. That pedagogy, according to Enoch, "did not encourage students to engage in a kind of active participation that effected social change; instead freedmen's institutions advocated that their teachers stress social stability through a pedagogy based in student obedience, acceptance, and passivity."[110] Freedmen's teachers were

---

107. Zakaria, *Against White Feminism*, 16. See also Murphy and Harris, "White Innocence."

108. I discuss this curriculum in greater detail in VanHaitsma, "African American," 296–301. See also Baylor, "Second Decade."

109. F.D., "Lotsburgh [sic], Virginia," LOC. Also quoted in Baylor, "Holley School and Zion Church," 11.

110. Enoch, *Refiguring*, 42. For additional discussion of how Putnam's and Holley's pedagogies differed from the dominant approach to freedmen's education, see Freeman, "Politics," 338–39.

encouraged, that is, to "teach black students to accept yet another form of subordinated status after the Civil War."[111]

In contrast, Putnam, Holley, and their white and Black assistant teachers at the Holley School instead collaborated with students and community members with the goal of securing rights of citizenship.[112] As Putnam wrote to Holley when preparing for a new school year to begin (1869), "the schoolhouse is being cleaned this morning for school to begin to-morrow—I mean to teach better than ever so these people shall know their rights & how to get them."[113] In this letter, both Putnam's commitment to civic education in service of racial justice and her own white savior complex are clear. As Rafia Zakaria explains, the white savior complex found within present-day white feminism has roots in the colonialism and settler colonialism of the long nineteenth century. Originating in the colonial mission of "spreading . . . civilized ways," a woman's enactment of this complex typically involves seeking to "show the crucial role that she, a white woman, is playing in the lives of" people of color, "positioning herself as their rescuer, the conduit through which emancipation must flow."[114] In Putnam's case, she positioned herself, a white woman, as the "rescuer" through which local African Americans would come to "know their rights & how to get them."[115] At the same time, she demonstrated a stronger pedagogical orientation to such rights of citizenship than most freedmen's teachers of the period. In this sense, even as Putnam worked to engage difference as "a creative and necessary force for change," she simultaneously "facilitate[d] its entrenchment" with respect to hierarchies of colonialism, racism, and white femininity.[116]

As part of the Holley School's civic orientation, at least two features of its rhetorical education are important to emphasize. These features illustrate how Putnam and Holley's radical erotic of antislavery affection—their complex and simultaneously shared desires for each other, as white women, as well as for the "pursuit" of racial justice—shaped their freedmen's teaching.[117] First,

---

111. Enoch, *Refiguring*, 25.

112. Other Northern white women would work as assistant teachers at the Holley School over time. For the names of these women, see Booth, "Study," 39–40. While the teachers were initially white women from the North, African American women who were former students would later teach at the Holley School. Among them were educators Susie Blackwell, Eliza Conner, and Cora Smith. See Booth, "Study," 40; and Herbig, "Friends," 372.

113. Correspondence from Putnam to Holley, August 16, 1869, CP/CLMT.

114. Zakaria, *Against White Feminism*, 103, 16.

115. Zakaria, *Against White Feminism*, 16; correspondence from Putnam to Holley, August 16, 1869, CP/CLMT.

116. Lorde, "Learning," 135; and Holland, *Erotic Life*, 59.

117. Lorde, "Uses of the Erotic," 56.

the women taught basic forms of literacy in combination with abolitionist rhetoric. Literacy instruction was politically significant in the post-War context, because it had been illegal to teach enslaved people to read.[118] As Royster explains, "African Americans understood the implications of literacy and learning in political, economic, and social progress. They could see clearly—from the extent to which they were denied access to it—that education could make a difference for individuals and for whole communities."[119] These political implications motivated Lottsburgh community members as they secured initial, one-time funding from the Freedmen's Bureau in order to erect the first building for their school and then sought out a teacher.[120] When community members welcomed Putnam in November of 1868, Glasgow Blackwell, "one of the community's leading men," spoke before those assembled.[121] Blackwell framed the school's exigency by contrasting Putnam with slaveholders, those "grand villains" who enforced prohibitions against literacy instruction with violence.[122] "They told me they would break off my fingers close to my hand if they catched me with a book in it," Blackwell said, "but now our children will have this good chance to learn to write."

---

118. Of course there were people who resisted by teaching and learning in spite of such laws. For further discussion of the political implications of literacy for African Americans during and following slavery, see Butchart, *Schooling*; and Cornelius, *"When I Can."*

119. Royster, *Traces*, 123. Moreover, as Royster makes clear, nineteenth-century freedmen's schools functioned within a broader tradition of African American rhetorical education through both self-education and formal instruction. For select examples of formal and extracurricular instruction from other periods, see Epps-Robertson, *Resisting*; Heath, "Finding"; Moss, "'Phenomenal Women'"; Pritchard, "'Like Signposts'"; Richardson, "'To Protect'"; and Royster and Williams, "History."

120. Baylor, "Holley School for Freedmen," 54. Other motivations were also at work, as community members first planned for the building to serve as a church. I discuss conflicts surrounding use of the building in this chapter's conclusion.

121. Herbig, "Friends," 243.

122. Blackwell's words are from Putnam's account in a letter to Holley that was published in the *National Anti-Slavery Standard*. See Herbig, "Friends," 243; and Shelden, "'Such a Great Light,'" 68–69. While histories of the Holley School necessarily rely on those primary materials available, it is important to keep in mind the politics of historiography and, in this case, whose records were preserved. We must remember that this is Putnam's representation of Blackwell's speech, and she crafted this account with her own purposes and audience in mind.

As Shelden notes in reference to another example—Holley's transcription of the words of the formerly enslaved woman Winnie Beale—"skepticism" is also warranted with respect to representations of Black speech: "Holley, a sympathetic listener who . . . had . . . lived among the former slaves and been immersed in their culture . . . had probably developed a good ear for the black speech of Virginia's Northern Neck. Even so, she had grown up in a white culture that transcribed and marked black speech in exaggerated and sometimes bizarre flourishes of spelling and punctuation." See Shelden, "'Broad, Generous.'"

While Holley School students learned to write, they simultaneously studied writing and speaking by and about figures who advanced abolitionist agendas before the War, argued for racial justice during Reconstruction, and celebrated the achievements of African Americans. Putnam and Holley devoted entire classes, for example, to John Brown, Wendell Phillips, and Charles Sumner.[123] The orator most often mentioned in Putnam's letters was Frederick Douglass, whom she and Holley knew through the American Anti-Slavery Society.[124] Students read Douglass and had the opportunity to hear him speak when he visited the school.[125] Insofar as Putnam and Holley meaningfully collaborated with the African American community to help make possible this rhetorical education, the erotic of the white women's romantic friendship did manage to engage difference in order "to pursue genuine change" to at least some extent.[126]

Second, and alongside the regular study of abolitionist rhetoric at the Holley School, Putnam's and Holley's pedagogy supported students and community members in developing their own speaking abilities and taking political action. Consider again the example of Blackwell, who delivered a speech upon Putnam's arrival in Lottsburgh. In May of 1869, Putnam, assistant teacher Miss Crosby, and community members including Blackwell and Alexander Day walked four miles to the county seat in Heathsville.[127] When stopping to rest, Putnam and Crosby read the *National Anti-Slavery Standard* aloud, just as they often did at the Holley School. Once in Heathsville, Blackwell and Day delivered speeches on behalf of Ephraim Nash, the candidate they supported for election to the state legislature. Writing to Holley about the trip, Putnam exclaimed, "Glasgow told last night what a stain of shame was on Virginia for selling her own sons & daughters—*you taught these black orators!*" Although Putnam praised Holley's teaching, now positioning Holley as the "white savior" and "conduit" through which the men's oratorical accomplishments became possible, Blackwell and Day of course deserved the primary credit for their public speaking abilities.[128] In Blackwell's case especially, he was probably chosen to speak on the occasion of Putnam's arrival precisely

---

123. Shelden, "'Such a Great Light,'" 92. Putnam and Holley also taught the speaking and writing of Lydia Maria Child, Thomas Wentworth Higginson, Oliver Wendell Holmes, Abraham Lincoln, Samuel May, Robert Gould Shaw, Gerrit Smith, Thaddeus Stevens, and John Greenleaf Whittier. On the period of Reconstruction, see Wilson, *Reconstruction*.

124. Shelden, "'Such a Great Light,'" 67.

125. Correspondence from Putnam to Holley, January 14, 1869, and July–August 1871, CP/CLMT. See also Shelden, "'Such a Great Light,'" 108.

126. Lorde, "Uses of the Erotic," 59.

127. Baylor, "Holley School for Freedmen," 56.

128. Zakaria, *Against White Feminism*, 16.

because he was a skilled orator already, long before any pedagogical intervention by the white women. Still, Putnam's exclamation to Holley makes clear how they aspired for their teaching to serve Black orators speaking on behalf of the African American community.

Moreover, Putnam and Holley did not teach rhetoric only to step back and observe how the community participated politically. Much to the chagrin of the local white people who resisted change, Putnam and Holley actively participated in politics alongside students, especially in terms of voting rights.[129] In an 1868 letter, writing to Holley about instances of election intimidation, Putnam declared, "I believe the influence of our boldness especially *yours* at the polls here, will never be forgotten or lost."[130] That Putnam wrote such letters to Holley underscores how both women desired to exert influence on issues of racial justice by teaching Black orators and arguing alongside them for full rights of citizenship. Again, though, Putnam positioned herself and Holley as the white saviors with crucial "influence" and "boldness."

This praise of Holley's "influence" and "boldness" also must be understood within the context of the women's romantic friendship, their erotic of antislavery affection as a source of rhetorical power, and Putnam's early efforts to persuade Holley to move to Lottsburgh and fully join together in the work of the Holley School. After the school's 1868 founding, Holley visited twice, staying for about five months each time, but it was not until 1870 that she moved there.[131] That Putnam desired for Holley to live and work with her as a freedmen's teacher is apparent in how she crafted her earliest descriptions of students when writing to Holley. In an 1868 letter, Putnam described a group of students, and then stated directly, "you will love dearly to be here & teach them."[132] This gesture was followed immediately by what was not Putnam's first statement about the need for teachers in rural Virginia: "I wonder hundreds of women don't come—Life is far more interesting here away from the towns than it can be (for us, at least) as in Richmond where all societies & teachers seek to establish themselves—E. is as happy as a queen. . . . She has wonderful genius & love for the people & work." After further description of how satisfying Emily Howland found her work, Putnam imagined Holley there, lamenting, "I am only sorry you can't see it all! As it goes on!" Although unsuccessful

---

129. One community member, using racist language, allegedly complained that the women "meddled with politics too much" and "had too much to do with the darkies votes!" Correspondence from Putnam to Holley, December 1, 1869, CP/CLMT.
130. Correspondence from Putnam to Holley, [November 9–16, 1868], CP/CLMT.
131. Baylor, "Holley School for Freedmen," 55.
132. Correspondence from Putnam to Holley, November 17, [1868], CP/CLMT.

in this particular attempt to persuade Holley to move South, Putnam was beginning to use a rhetorical strategy that would later prove effective.

Putnam's key strategy was to vocalize her desires for Holley to be there not only through conventional expressions of romantic longing but also through descriptions of Holley School students and in connection to the women's radical erotic of antislavery affection. These vocalizations were tied to Putnam and Holley's shared investments in a larger project of racial justice yet enacted a white savior complex. This complex showed up as Putnam, in trying to persuade Holley to join her in freedmen's teaching, gave undue credit to Holley, a white woman who was still largely absent, for "playing" a "crucial role" in what the African American students and community members were accomplishing already at their own school.[133] In another 1868 letter, for example, Putnam again followed a description of students with the exclamation, "O—how you would love to be with them & feel their gentle friendly natures."[134] Putnam exclaimed further, "they will adore you when you come—They have already named the school for you—in their meeting last Thursday night *Pyramus Nutt* the carpenter put it to vote—saying he was well pleased at it—& so they all are." Naming the freedmen's school after Holley was an obvious form of flattery that unfairly credited the role of the white woman (and we need to question the extent to which this alleged vote was urged by Nutt or Putnam herself). What I also want to emphasize is how Putnam's flattery was accompanied by the aspirational statement that students "will adore you when you come."[135] Putnam amplified this adoration, using her letter writing about the students to express her own desires for Holley to return.

In this sense, Putnam even romanticized and eroticized the women's white savior complex as abolitionists and now freedmen's teachers. This approach did not amount to persuasion in the form of logical argument, of course. Rather, Putnam's seductive rhetoric worked more indirectly. This rhetoric functioned against the backdrop of both the antislavery erotic of the women's romantic friendship and the racism with which they remained complicit, suggestively vocalizing their own feelings and desires through African American students and community members.[136] This is not to say that Putnam was never direct about her desires for Holley. In a letter from early in 1870, Putnam began, "I wish you were here!" and then continued on with praise of Holley's work on

---

133. Zakaria, *Against White Feminism*, 16.
134. Correspondence from Putnam to Holley, November 21, [1868], CP/CLMT.
135. For another example, also see correspondence from Putnam to Holley, October 22, 1869, CP/CLMT.
136. On seductive rhetorical strategies, see Ballif, *Seduction*; Erickson and Thomson, "Seduction"; Kelley, "Rhetoric"; and Werner, "Seductive Rhetoric."

behalf of the school: "no wonder you are all tired out, working so hard for this school & me! Your generous overflowing results ought to overwhelm us all with gratitude!"[137] Again, as Putnam conveys her own desires for Holley, she does so in ways that inflate Holley's role. Here the women rhetorically perform the erotic of specifically white femininity through not only white saviorism but also an individualization of power. In Aimee Carrillo Rowe's terms, the women emphasize Holley's "individualized" actions according to the "individualized logic" of whiteness rather than the collective actions of "transracial alliances" that in fact made possible rhetorical education at the Holley School.[138]

While I understand Putnam's expressions of praise and gratitude for Holley's contributions as an instance of white savior complex and form of seductive rhetoric, Holley did genuinely support Putnam's pedagogical efforts, just as Putnam had supported Holley's speaking career. Here too, though, the women's romantic friendship and rhetorical participation were marked by a traditionally gendered division of labor. Whereas Putnam carried out most of the more feminized work at the Holley School, maintaining their home and teaching from day to day, Holley engaged in public-facing activities to garner support for the school. For instance, Holley assisted Putnam in the early recruiting of assistant teachers, reporting in an 1876 letter, "already I have succeeded in persuading two Northern ladies to journey to Lottsburgh expressly to assist in teaching our School."[139] Alongside this teacher recruitment, most of Holley's documented support took the form of cultivating epistolary networks among largely white abolitionists in order to secure donations to financially support the Holley School.[140]

Holley's letter-writing campaigns were crucial due to a lack of funding from those sources that usually provided financial support for freedmen's schools. Although the Black community of Lottsburgh was successful in securing one-time funds from the Freedmen's Bureau in order to finish the first building for the school, the Bureau did not hire Putnam and Holley nor provide ongoing support for educational expenses. To compensate, Holley sought out donated goods that the women bartered with local community members in exchange for food and labor. As Holley wrote in a letter to one donor (1877), "your contributions of various literature" were bartered "for small supplies of eggs—butter fruit and milk."[141] "Seeing we have no salary or income," Holley

---

137. Correspondence from Putnam to Holley, January 3, 1870, CP/CLMT.
138. Carrillo Rowe, *Power Lines*, 29, 32.
139. Shelden, "'Such a Great Light,'" 111.
140. On the importance of letter writing to Putnam and Holley's rhetorical labors, and to the abolitionist movement more broadly, see Freeman, "Politics."
141. Shelden, "'Such a Great Light,'" 107.

explained, bartering was "a convenience not to be despised."[142] Securing private donations was a pressing and ongoing need, because, even after freedmen's organizations had largely withdrawn from the South, and as segregated public schools for African American students became more common, the Holley School remained private due to Putnam and Holley's commitment—likely solidified during their time as Oberlin students—to coeducation and desegregated schooling.[143] Responding to this need, Holley garnered financial support for the school through letter writing that targeted connections established through the women's prior involvement in abolitionist circles. In a letter characteristic of her networking, Holley (1879) wrote to Theodore Dwight Weld, "I go back to Virginia and my school at Lottsburgh next Monday—Miss Putnam and I remember most gratefully the kind gifts you sent our school—we thank you always in our hearts."[144] Received from donors across their abolitionist networks, similar gifts to the Holley School took a number of forms, including goods to barter as well as books and other pedagogical materials.[145]

Holley sought the donations at Putnam's request, and these requests intermingled with passages more generically conventional for romantic letters. Consider an 1868 letter in which Putnam requested Holley's help with book donations. After concluding her letter of request, Putnam wrote alongside the page, "with that I ought ever to keep warm for you."[146] It appears Holley made good on the sort of requests that kept Putnam warm for her, because another letter from within the month concluded, "you are as true as God, & generous in your affection & deed towards me as possible for a human being! & will have *your* great reward—Would that I was worthy the millionth part of it all!"[147] A year later, Putnam's letters continued to compliment Holley's generosity, one letter opening with, "you never do less than your generous promise and always do more," and going on to discuss "the *third* box" that had arrived.[148] Finally, in an undated letter she exclaimed, "it is a wonder to

---

142. Putnam did earn a "modest stipend as . . . postmistress." Shelden, "'Deep,'" 98. For discussion of ongoing challenges to Putnam's position as postmistress, see Baylor, "Holley School at Lottsburg," 60.

143. Shelden, "'Such a Great Light,'" 92.

144. Correspondence from Holley to Weld, November 12, 1879, WG/CLMT.

145. Holley secured the donation of barrels that included not only books but clothes, dry goods, and other items. The women gave these items to students as pedagogical rewards or, more often, used them to barter with their African American and white neighbors. One of Holley's widely documented epistolary networks for requesting these barrels was with author Louisa May Alcott, her mother "Abba" May Alcott, and their friends from a sewing circle in Concord, Massachusetts. See correspondence, AF/HL; Shelden, "'Such a Great Light'"; and Shelden, "'Deep.'"

146. Correspondence from Putnam to Holley, October 22, 1868, CP/CLMT.

147. Correspondence from Putnam to Holley, [October 23–30, 1868], CP/CLMT.

148. Correspondence from Putnam to Holley, August 29, 1869, CP/CLMT.

us how many things you send down—Thornton Parker said to Col. Hunter 'The Lord only knows where they come from!' But *I know* how hard *you* have worked!" While Holley's epistolary networks relied on the generosity of many in order to maintain material support for the Holley School, the center of this network was the warmth and affection of Putnam and Holley's romantic friendship.

The donations sought by Holley supported the Holley School's rhetorical education for racial justice, which continued long after Holley's passing and until Putnam's own death in 1917, for almost half a century. This commitment to racial justice, born of the radical antislavery affection fueling Putnam and Holley's romantic friendship, is noteworthy in contrast with the orientation of most white women's work at freedmen's schools of the time—not to mention the rhetorical training offered by Wood, Leache, Buck, and Wylie at educational sites catering to white girls and women. Of course, Putnam's delivery of rhetorical education—just as much as Holley's delivery of antislavery lectures—was made possible by what Buchanan termed "offstage elements."[149] Among these offstage elements were the women's collaborations with a range of stakeholders. Most obviously, they collaborated with the local African American community in Lottsburgh, although the women's own representations of this shared labor were marked by a white savior complex that flattered the women with the notion they played an outsized role in the community's own efforts on behalf of themselves. Also offstage to this collaboration at the Holley School, yet more available for study through extant archives, was Holley's support within the context of the women's romantic friendship.

In keeping with the division of labor that marked their relationship from the start, Putnam carried out the majority of the more feminized work of teaching. Appealing to the erotic of antislavery affection that fueled their relationship, Putnam persuaded Holley to join her at the school. Holley in turn supported Putnam's pedagogical work by developing and maintaining epistolary networks to garner donations for the school. As Putnam's own letters emphasize, she certainly could not have continued her work with Lottsburgh's African American community without the additional support provided through her romantic friendship with Holley. Although marked by a division of labor, the radical erotic of antislavery affection that energized their abolitionist rhetorical practices also served as a form of rhetorical power that sustained their support of racial justice through teaching rhetoric at the Holley School.

---

149. Buchanan, *Regendering*, 3.

## Reproducing Racialized Religious Prejudice and Intimate Abuse

Thus far this chapter has shown how Putnam and Holley's radical erotic of antislavery affection functioned as a source of rhetorical power that made possible their labors on behalf of racial justice. However, it is important to attend further to the problematic dimensions of the women's work and relationship. Even as the couple in this study whose rhetorical practices were more radically oriented, Holley and Putnam pedagogically reproduced abuses of power. Although their freedmen's teaching promoted racial justice, Putnam and Holley were like most white women from the North in that their teaching in the South reproduced regionalism, classism, and anti-Black racism. In addition, though the erotic of antislavery affection between Putnam and Holley was oriented toward challenging at least some dominant power structures, the division of labor that initially enabled their rhetorical labors developed into a troubling power dynamic and even intimate abuse.

As historians have established already, when Northern teachers moved to the South to teach and support the educational efforts of formerly enslaved communities, these settler teachers brought regional, class, and racial biases with them. They worked toward "uplifting the race" through education, but often "would look down on" students even while doing the "utmost to instruct" them in what Northern middle-class teachers considered appropriate behavior.[150] Among white teachers, these regional and class-based biases intersected with anti-Black racism. As this section will detail, Putnam and Holley were no exception, in spite of their commitments to racial justice. In the words of Stacey M. Robertson, "Sallie Holley devoted twenty years in the postwar period to teaching ex-slaves."[151] But even as Holley "offered evidence of advancement and intelligence among her students, she also maintained a tone of superiority."[152] Nor was Holley alone; a tone of superiority appeared in some of Putnam's letters too.[153] In Lorde's terms, the women's erotic fell short in using difference as a source of rhetorical power, in that their rhetorical labors entrenched existing hierarchies of racism, classism, and regionalism.

Putnam and Holley's rhetorical reproduction of systemic racism is most evident in their attitudes toward Black worship practices in the South. As Speicher observes, "Holley had ample opportunity to observe black worship

---

150. Beeching, "Primus," 164.
151. Robertson, "Remembering," 69.
152. Robertson, "Remembering," 69. See also Breitborde, "Learning," 38; and Herbig, "Friends," 353.
153. Speicher, *Religious World*, 104, 107.

and found it reprehensible."[154] For example, an 1878 letter is blatantly racist in its settler-colonial description of worship practices. Holley wrote, "the religion of these coloured people is very demoralising [sic]. It has no connection with moral principle. They have just had a 'three days' meeting' in the old stolen schoolhouse, and made night hideous with their horrible singing and prayers, and dancing in a wild, savage way."[155] Another letter from 1884 evidences little change in perspective over the years. Here Holley characterized a worship meeting as "hideous with terrible noises," asserting that "all this kind of religion seems to me *worthless*."[156] This racist perspective on Southern Black worship practices is tied as well as to settler-colonial logics of the "savage," representing African American worshipers as "limited by an innate primitivism and . . . in urgent need of white assistance," while positioning themselves as "civilizing" white saviors.[157] How did this racist, settler-colonial perspective impact students at the Holley School? As is too often the case, extant archives of the period offer little documentation created by African American students and community members. But it is easy to imagine that the freedmen's curriculum, however oriented to racial justice, was itself paradoxically "demoralising"—that it encouraged formerly enslaved African Americans to learn rhetoric in service of accessing rights of citizenship, while simultaneously disparaging those culturally rooted forms of worship that had helped sustain the community in the face of brutal enslavement and racism long before Putnam or Holley arrived.

The white women's racist biases toward Southern Black Christianity no doubt played into a debate about uses of the schoolhouse building for political purposes. Contrary to what the women's white savior complex may have led them to believe, they were not alone at the center of the Holley School. Rather, its sustained success depended absolutely on considerable labor by and support from the local Black community: African Americans built the initial schoolhouse, secured the one-time funds from the Freedmen's Aid Bureau, sought out their first teacher, attended and sent their children to the school in spite of discouragement and threats by former slaveholders, bartered goods and labor that allowed Putnam and Holley to survive in the area, and managed

---

154. Speicher, *Religious World*, 104.

155. Correspondence from Holley to Miller, December 30, 1878, quoted in Chadwick, *Life*, 229; and Speicher, *Religious World*, 104. Holley's judgment and biting tone were by no means limited to Black worship practices. In the lines directly preceding these, she wrote, "It is pitiful to see these poor whites with their blank, lean faces. Too silly or proud to attend, or to allow their children to attend our *coloured* school! And to grow up without knowing the alphabet!"

156. Correspondence from Holley to Tyler, August 15, 1884, quoted in Chadwick, *Life*, 238; and Speicher, *Religious World*, 104.

157. Zakaria, *Against White Feminism*, 25, 103.

to navigate these white Northern women's racism in order to work alongside them in any number of ways for decades.[158] Yet when the community erected that first building, the original plan was for it to serve as a church. Community members later changed their plans, determining the building would house both a school and a church, in part as a response to requirements by the Freedmen's Aid Bureau. While extant records and prior historical accounts suggest that most in the African American community supported the school, questions did arise surrounding Putnam and Holley's overt engagement with politics in a space that also served religious purposes.

After visiting the Holley School in 1872, for instance, Douglass reported to the *New National Era* that he "went to [Lottsburgh] to speak upon the political questions of the day, and especially to commend the candidates of the Republican party."[159] But he "found the colored people of Lottsburgh . . . divided, not in respect to Greeley and Grant, but upon the question whether I should speak upon political questions in the schoolhouse—that said house being used for religious worship on Sunday! Oh, how cunning are the devices of slavery!" Both Douglass and Putnam speculated about the larger political forces at work when local religious figures discouraged political discussions. In Douglass's view, "no longer able to enslave the negro by Scripture, that spirit now endeavors to prevent his enlightenment, and this by religion and superstition, teaching him that a pile of rude boards are too holy a place in which to teach political duties!" Douglass attributed this teaching to "a wily white minister . . . Dr. Smith, who has been at pains of preaching a special sermon on the subject," as well as an unnamed "colored preacher . . . who is allowing himself to be used by designing men against the interests of his people."[160] Douglass characterized such preaching as "religious Ku-Kluxism."

---

158. As Butchart explains, "the education of the freed people was, first and foremost, an education by African Americans. . . . The freed people welcomed the help of northern white teachers and northern aid organizations, though they resented the paternalism and arrogance of the white efforts. In the end, however, the black community gave much more toward their own educational emancipation than did the far wealthier and far more numerous people that surrounded them." See Butchart, *Schooling*, 3.

159. F.D., "Lotsburgh [sic], Virginia," 2, LOC. Also quoted in Baylor, "Holley School and Zion Church," 11.

160. Douglass pointed out that, "for the present," he would "spare the colored preacher of [Lottsburgh]" by not mentioning his name, "but he will do well to desist at once from his warfare." See F.D., "Lotsburgh [sic], Virginia," LOC. By Holley's account, writing to Wendell Phillips, the unnamed man was a "treacherous colored Baptist preacher" who "has been long the tool of the white rebels trying to rob our colored people of the schoolhouse—and make it a Baptist church—to prevent our school and Republican principles from being successfully carried on in it." Holley's reference to "our colored people" is a form of white paternalism common among white freedman's teachers. Correspondence from Holley to Phillips, March 14, 1874, WF/HL.

Disagreement about political instruction and speaking in the schoolhouse continued into the following year. African American federal employee R. D. Beckley visited Lottsburgh for political purposes, but he refused to speak at the schoolhouse.[161] After Putnam published a letter criticizing Beckley, he responded in the *New National Era and Citizen* (1873).[162] Beckley asserted that Putnam's "communications" were of a "malicious and scurrilous character," calling her a "female rhetorical charlatan." Responding to Putnam's claim that he said he would "whip" his wife if she attended a "political meeting," Beckley wrote that, "unfortunately for Miss Holley, she has no one to 'love, cherish, and protect' her . . . and, so long as her behaviour remains unreformed, it is a question of grave doubt whether she will ever succeed in obtaining one." While Beckley's heterosexism is blatant here, he also rightly questioned Putnam's and Holley's practices of soliciting donations for the school and exchanging some of the goods for African American labor. Finally, Beckley charged that Holley had "made Caroline F. Putnam write up that long letter of flagrant misrepresentations."[163] He concluded by warning both women, "I would advise you to keep quiet, or the people of [Lottsburgh], whom you have misrepresented, will tell some things on you that will make my honored friend, Frederick Douglas, blush with shame when he hears them."[164] Did the "things" that Beckley threatened to "tell . . . on" Putnam and Holley have to do primarily with the racial politics of the building site, donated goods, and African American labor at the school? Did they have anything to do with the nature of the white women's romantic friendship? Or perhaps both? Regardless, Putnam did not keep quiet. Of course, these disagreements about the political, religious, and educational uses of the first schoolhouse building could not have been helped by the women's overtly racist attitudes toward Southern Black workshop practices.[165] Ultimately, the need for physical space from which to continue Putnam's and Holley's educational and political work was addressed through the women's relationship and economic privilege. By 1875, Holley had purchased settler-occupied land for the couple's house together, and that same

---

161. Baylor, "Holley School and Zion Church," 16.

162. Beckley, "Letter," 1, LOC. Also quoted in Baylor, "Holley School and Zion Church," 17. According to Holley, in an 1874 letter to Wendell Phillips, "a miserable colored man R. D. Beckley made a shameful speech against Civil Rights here last October—and Miss P. reported him in Douglass' paper at Washington. He was stung to madness and made a scandalous reply." Putnam also wrote to Phillips about Beckley that year. See Correspondence from Holley to Phillips, March 14, 1874, and June 28, 1874, WF/HL.

163. Beckley, "Letter," 1, LOC. Also quoted in Baylor, "Holley School and Zion Church," 18.

164. Beckley, "Letter," 1, LOC.

165. For further discussion of the complexities of these conflicts, see Baylor, "Holley School and Zion Church"; and Baylor, "Holley School at Lottsburg."

land also became home to a new schoolhouse building, owned privately and thus less subject to pressures from religious or political officials.[166]

In addition to Putnam and Holley's rhetorical practices marked by racist, settler-colonial religious prejudice, another set of problematic power dynamics concerned their own romantic friendship. From the start, their erotic of antislavery affection involved Putnam admiring Holley and allowing her considerable influence.[167] But over the course of the relationship, this admiration and the women's division of rhetorical labor became imbued with an imbalance of power. Although many people still associate abusive power dynamics with opposite-sex relationships, intimate abuse of course may occur in any relationship, including same-sex romantic relationships between cisgender women.[168] Holley abused her power through controlling directives, harsh communication, and verbal abuse.

An 1867 letter from Holley to Putnam is representative of these controlling behaviors. Sent before their work at the Holley School had begun, Holley shared that she "felt *greatly hurt* that [Putnam] should send any extracts from [Holley's] letters to Mr. Powell, *without first sending them to [Holley]*."[169] But instead of delving into an emotionally vulnerable discussion of her hurt feelings, Holley followed this statement with a threat to withdraw her epistolary attentions if Putnam did not do as instructed. Holley threatened, "if you do not promise not to do it again, I must only write you very short and meagre letters." "*You* cannot take such a responsibility," Holley asserted, "*I* am the responsible one—you know it is always so." The letter devolves into a virtual "dos and don'ts" list of whom Putnam "may" or may not contact and in what form. Holley's commands in this single letter include all of the following: "don't do it & *don't write* or say anything about me"; "I wish you would go & make Mrs. Foster a visit—don't write to her"; "you can decide about going to [Emily Howland] *after* The Festival"; "don't you send anything to the Standard without first sending to me"; "don't write me such gossip—But write me for The Cause & my lectures"; and finally, in the last line of the letter, "do it at once." Other letters from Holley directed sarcasm and criticism at Putnam.[170] As Chambers-Schiller notes, Holley had a "style of extending love and

---

166. Baylor, "Holley School and Zion Church," 19.
167. Faulkner, *Women's Radical Reconstruction*, 37. Also see Herbig, "Friends," 385.
168. Select sources on same-sex intimate abuse among women include Duggan, *Sapphic Slashers*; Lobel, *Naming*; Lundy and Leventhal, *Same-Sex Domestic Violence*; and Ristock, *No More Secrets*. These sources are included within a fuller list of scholarship and other writing about same-sex and queer domestic violence offered by Machado, *In the Dream House*, 245–47.
169. Correspondence from Holley to Putnam, November 9, 1867, FHSC. Also cited in Baylor, "Holley School at Lottsburg," 70.
170. Chambers-Schiller, *Liberty*, 152.

approval then withdrawing both in a storm of verbal abuse"; she "had a sharp tongue and was perfectly capable of using it to prod Putnam in the name of the cause."[171]

Holley's tendency to engage in "verbal abuse" took an especially unfortunate turn during the women's later years. "Over the course of their lives together," Herbig explains, "an inadvertent symmetry evolved."[172] Holley's career as an abolitionist lecturer was "the high point of her life but a period of considerable sacrifice for Putnam." By contrast, during their time at the Holley School, "Putnam found fulfillment in direct involvement, teaching, and serving the poor, but Holley resigned herself to the school as martyrdom."[173] With the power dynamic of their relationship subject to a related shift, "the emotional balance between them eventually went askew."[174] It seems that, as Holley's public notoriety and related influence among white abolitionists began to wane, she reasserted even greater control over Putnam and her pedagogical work alongside African Americans. Among the women's friends, concerns rightly emerged that Holley was overly controlling and verbally and emotionally abusive.[175]

Concerns were documented especially in response to two conflicts. One was a conflict that emerged as many freedmen's schools became racially segregated public schools. Both Putnam and Holley opposed this shift, insisting that the Holley School remain private in order to resist mandated segregation (though, in practice, few white families and students actually chose to be involved in the school). But in a characteristically controlling move, Holley went so far as to prohibit visits by any of Putnam's friends who went along with the shifting of freedmen's schools into the public school system.[176] Isolation of a partner from friends is a maneuver of power and control that typifies abusive relationships and, as evidenced in the 1867 letter above, Holley had long attempted to control Putnam's interactions with others.[177] But isolating Putnam from potential visitors carried particular weight once the women were geographically and culturally isolated in rural Virginia, where very few of the local white people approved of their educational and political efforts.[178]

---

171. Chambers-Schiller, *Liberty*, 152.
172. Herbig, "Friends," 386.
173. Herbig, "Friends," 386.
174. Herbig, "Friends," 386.
175. Chambers-Schiller, *Liberty*, 152.
176. Chambers-Schiller, *Liberty*, 154. Nor was this the only time that Holley isolated Putnam by rejecting others who had been friends and supporters of the school. Also see Herbig, "Friends," 357–58.
177. National Domestic Violence Hotline, "Power."
178. Herbig, "Friends," 350; and Shelden, "'Such a Great Light,'" 71, 110, 117.

Holley's abusive isolation was recorded in the letters of Howland.[179] With her own freedmen's teaching also impacted by the conflict over segregating schools, Howland (1873) reported having asked another friend about visiting Putnam, and "he advised me not to, he knew Miss Putnam would like to see me if Miss Holley were gone, but I thought even in that case my visit might make trouble."[180] Seeming to recognize the abusiveness of isolation marked by fear, albeit with a tinge of what we now understand as victim-blaming, Howland wrote, "poor woman, what a voluntary bondage [Putnam] lives in not to dare to have a friend come to her home to see her."[181] Howland lamented further, "what a life of struggle Miss Putnam has, I think clinging to Miss Holley has thwarted what should have been her life."[182] Tellingly, it was "shortly after Holley's death" that Putnam "renewed" her "lively friendship with Emily Howland."[183] This dynamic of control, marked by the "bondage" of isolation and the fear of causing "trouble," is textbook relationship abuse.[184]

A second series of conflicts involved Holley's reputation following a newspaper story about the Holley School. Friends in the women's abolitionist networks criticized the story, because, consistent with the division of labor and power dynamics of the relationship, the story's account of the school focused on Holley without recognizing Putnam's more sustained role in collaborating with Lottsburgh's African American community.[185] Putnam commented on this conflict in a letter to Samuel May from early 1893, just a couple weeks

---

179. Chambers-Schiller, *Liberty*, 153.

180. Correspondence from Emily Howland to Hannah [Letchworth Howland], November 13, 1873, FHSC, quoted in Herbig, "Friends," 358.

181. Correspondence from Emily Howland to Hannah [Letchworth Howland], November 13, 1873, FHSC, quoted in Herbig, "Friends," 358.

182. Correspondence from Emily Howland to Hannah [Letchworth Howland], November 13, 1873, FHSC, quoted in Chambers-Schiller, *Liberty*, 154; and Herbig, "Friends," 358.

183. Herbig, "Friends," 378.

184. That said, identifying intimate abuse within the history of same-sex relationships between women is marked by incredible challenges of "archival silence." As Machado explains in her memoir about an abusive relationship, "I have spent years struggling to find examples of my own experience in history's queer women. I tore through book after book about the queer women of the past, pen poised over paper, wondering what would happen if they had let the world know they were unmade by someone with just as little power as they. Did Susan B. Anthony's womanizing extend to psychological torment? What did Elizabeth Bishop really say to Lota de Macedo Soares when she'd been drinking heavily? Did their voices crawl with jealousy? Did they hurl inkwells and figurines? Did any of them gingerly touch their bruises and know that explaining would be too complicated? Did any of them wonder if what had happened to them had any name at all?" See Machado, *In the Dream House*, 138, 227.

185. Although Putnam insisted the article did not bother her, and she attempted to reconcile the issue among their friends and with Holley, "Holley never felt that her friend had sufficiently cleared the air with the New England abolitionists whose regard she so valued." Chambers-Shiller, *Liberty*, 155.

after Holley passed away.[186] Apparently May had expressed concerns about the conflict, because Putnam wrote, "I have tried to answer your kind inquiries as frankly & fully as I know how."[187] Putnam's attempt to "answer" May's "inquiries" documented how Holley blamed Putnam for the consequences to Holley's reputation following the story. Putnam explained that when Holley's reputation came into question, "Miss Holley believed I had complained & talked in a self-pitying way—or looked as like an aggrieved person as to . . . her treatment of me." On these grounds, Holley charged Putnam with "base ingratitude." "To the last," according to Putnam, "Holley accused me of being the means of taking away her justly fair & beautiful New England reputation—so dear to her heart." Sympathizing with Holley, Putnam continued that Holley "suffered cruelly" following her loss of reputation, "& I have too." Further reflecting the isolation that had developed in their relationship, Putnam wrote that she "gave up the Marstons & Mrs. Joy's friendship, & others who undertook to pity me, as an abused person."[188] Again, the situation that Putnam described typifies intimate abuse: Holley blamed Putnam for her own loss of reputation, making accusations to justify that blame; friends recognized the situation as abusive to Putnam; and Holley's control was increased as Putnam was then separated from her concerned friends.[189]

Putnam's letter to May reports still other abusive behaviors of control, blame, and self-blame. Holley surveilled the contents of Putnam's letters. "She saw my letter lying ready for the mail," Putnam relayed to May, "& said 'I hope you haven't written any thing about me!'—I said 'you can read it'—but she didn't, & hadn't wished to hear your letter to me—since the last exchange of letters between you—not that she blamed you, but me." Nor was Holley's pattern of blaming Putnam limited to the conflict around Holley's reputation. In this same letter to May, Putnam recalled that Holley had said, "I would have had a beautiful school, if I could have had my way, but I couldn't with you." As if the reports of Holley's abusive behavior are not difficult enough to read, the very next line of Putnam's letter to May is "all of which is no doubt more than true—Alas."[190]

---

186. Correspondence from Putnam to May, January 27, 1893, MHS, cited in Herbig, "Friends," 365.

187. Correspondence from Putnam to May, January 27, 1893, MHS, cited in Herbig, "Friends," 365.

188. Correspondence from Putnam to May, January 27, 1893. MHS, cited in Herbig, "Friends," 365.

189. National Domestic Violence Hotline, "Power."

190. Correspondence from Putnam to May, January 27, 1893, MHS, cited in Herbig, "Friends," 365. In another set of letters, Putnam defended Holley's "coolness" toward Douglass, while insisting on the importance of Holley's "consecrated labors for the slave." Correspondence from Putnam to Douglass, April 19, 1888, FD/LOC.

Alas. Even in this letter where Putnam provided the most direct account of Holley's abuse, "candidly explaining the strains their relationship had suffered during the past ten years," Putnam engaged in self-blame and defended Holley—all of which is wholly consistent with the dynamics of an abusive relationship.[191] Ultimately, as Baylor points out, Putnam "had not seen herself through the eyes of those she called 'detractors,' and had refused the friendships of those who sought to pity her as an abused individual."[192] Defending Holley to the end, Putnam emphasized, "I owed Miss Holley the chief good, and happiness of my life."[193]

## Conclusion

While archival documentation of intimate abuse in same-sex romantic friendships is usually limited, Putnam's and Holley's complicity with the troubling power dynamics of white women's freedmen's teaching was unfortunately typical. With the erotic of their relationship made possible on the grounds of slavery and settler colonialism, Putnam and Holley reproduced anti-Black racism through their teaching of rhetoric in ways that pursued racial justice even as they enacted a colonizing white savior complex and demeaned African American religious practices in the South through the settler-colonial rhetoric of the "savage." These white women thus "misnamed and misused" difference "in the service of separation."[194] Still, what perhaps most stands out when Putnam and Holley are contrasted with the other white women in this study is how, in spite of their complicity, Putnam and Holley imperfectly but consistently pursued at least some forms of racial justice by seeking out ways to act on the radical erotic of antislavery affection that first brought them together in a romantic friendship.

For Putnam and Holley, the erotic functioned as a source of power, a passionate sharing of desires not only for each other and education but also for racial justice. Fueled by this erotic as a form of rhetorical power, they worked toward racial justice first through their rhetorical practices on the antislavery lecture circuit. Reflecting the typically gendered division of labor that characterized their relationship, Putnam supported Holley's career as an agent for the American Anti-Slavery Society.[195] Putnam went door-to-door,

---

191. Herbig, "Friends," 365.
192. Baylor, "Holley School at Lottsburg," 70.
193. Correspondence from Putnam to May, January 27, 1893, MHS. Also quoted in Chambers-Schiller, *Liberty*, 154.
194. Lorde, "Age, Race, Class," 115.
195. Faderman, *To Believe*, 101.

garnering support for the antislavery cause through conversational rhetoric within domestic spaces, while Holley spoke from the abolitionist podium before promiscuous audiences. Following the War, the women acted on their passionately shared desires for racial justice as teachers of rhetoric at the Holley School. Each contributing to the shared cause in distinct ways, they taught rhetoric in service of racial justice alongside formerly enslaved African Americans. Whereas Putnam did more of the feminized day-to-day work of maintaining the school and household over the course of decades, Holley used her extensive networks as a former antislavery lecturer to garner public support for the freedmen's school. Amid conflict about the educational, religious, and political purposes of the Holley School's first building, Holley also purchased the settler-occupied land on which it would come to stand.

When Holley passed away in 1893, she left the property to Putnam but "placed control over the school with a board of trustees."[196] While continuing to administer and teach at the school, Putnam soon dove into a new project to memorialize Holley's life and abolitionist rhetoric. With help from abolitionist friends and former assistant teachers, Putnam worked for six years to develop "a volume of Holley's letters, edited and pieced together with background information."[197] In the final year of the project, Unitarian minister John White Chadwick stepped in as editor, and *A Life for Liberty: Anti-Slavery and Other Letters of Sallie Holley* was published in 1899. In 1903, Putnam began to "ease gently into semi-retirement."[198] From then until 1917, Putnam continued to teach, but "various white teachers . . . ran the Holley School."[199] During this period, a former student, Cora Smith, became "a regular teaching assistant under" those white teachers.[200] Smith played a central role in the continuation of the Holley School. While herself teaching, Smith "assumed much of the responsibility for the day-to-day operation of the school and grounds."[201] Smith and her family were also the ones who cared for Putnam when her eyesight started to fail and she developed rheumatism.[202] It is consistent with the white saviorism of settler racism as well as Holley's own abusive pattern of behavior that both Putnam and the historical record have given so much

---

196. Herbig, "Friends," 366.
197. Herbig, "Friends," 368.
198. Herbig, "Friends," 373.
199. Herbig, "Friends," 372.
200. Herbig, "Friends," 372.
201. Herbig, "Friends," 373.
202. Herbig describes a "feud" that developed between Smith and some of Putnam's Northern white friends. To my mind, their suspicious accusations against Smith seem racist. See Herbig, "Friends," 379.

credit to Holley and so little to Smith (as well as Susie Blackwell, Eliza Conner, and other unnamed Black women teachers at the Holley School).[203]

Putnam remained at the school until she passed away in 1917, and her ashes were "buried in Lottsburg's segregated black cemetery, across the road from the Holley School."[204] At that point, "the school property passed from Putnam's estate to a black board of trustees and Holley Graded School became an all-Black public school."[205] This board of trustees consisted of Robert J. Diggs, Eugene Nelson, William D. Rich, Ernest Eskridge, L. C. Newman, Edward Diggs, Cora Smith, Maxwell Williams, Ella A. Knapp, Dr. Frank W. Lewis, and T. C. Walker.[206] In addition to the new name, Holley Graded School, a new building was constructed with funds raised by the Black community.[207] While the school took different forms in response to historical shifts, it continued as an elementary school for Black students until it closed in 1959.

Into the late twentieth and early twenty-first centuries, community members and Holley School alumni have continued to preserve the school's site and memorialize its importance to the African American community. After the school closed, neighbor Ruth Blackwell cared for the property until a new board of trustees formed in the 1980s and "began making plans to restore the school for use as a museum and community center."[208] In 1989 and 1990, the group secured recognition of the school through Virginia's Department of Historic Resources and then the National Register of Historic Places (NRHP).[209] In its NRHP application, the Holley Graded School is memorialized as "a source of great pride to the black community of Lottsburg," as the place "where most of Lottsburg's older generation of blacks received their educations," which "provided hope, support and social cohesion during an era of institutionalized racial discrimination."[210] Today the school serves as a museum, under the direction of Garfield Parker, a community meeting place, and an art gallery on the Northern Neck Artisan Trail.[211] The school is

---

203. Booth, "Study," 40; and Herbig, "Friends," 372.
204. Herbig, "Friends," 382.
205. Shelden, "'Such a Great Light,'" 84. See also Herbig, "Friends," 382.
206. O'Dell, "Holley," section 8, page 2.
207. O'Dell, "Holley," section 8, page 4.
208. Aiken, "Holley."
209. Virginia Department of Historic Resources, "066-0112"; and O'Dell, "Holley," section 1, page 1.
210. O'Dell, "Holley," section 8, page 6.
211. Aiken, "Holley." I had the opportunity to learn about the community's relatively recent preservation efforts during an August 2016 visit to the school's historic site and museum, which was made possible by Mary Lamb Shelden. I appreciate Garfield Parker, as well as Harold Blackwell, for taking time to share their important work.

also memorialized through the *Holley Graded School Historic Site* and *Holley School Histories* websites.[212] Created in collaboration with Mary Lamb Shelden, the former makes available audio recordings of excerpts from oral history interviews with former students and their families.[213]

In memorial efforts by present-day Lottsburg's Black community, the relationship between Putnam and Holley is recognized as central to the Holley School's founding.[214] The NRHP application characterizes Putnam as Holley's "friend and lifelong companion," and the historic marker at the site describes Holley as Putnam's "lifelong friend."[215] Still, in what recent popular coverage exists, the women are remembered simply as "college friends."[216] Although all of these descriptors are consistent with extant archives, what goes under-recognized is the importance of the specifically romantic and erotic dimensions of Putnam and Holley's friendship. It was the radical erotic of their antislavery affection—their passionately shared desires for each other, for education, and for racial justice—that served as a source of rhetorical power in their abolitionist rhetoric and freedmen's teaching.

---

212. Holley Graded School, "Home"; and "Holley School Histories."
213. "Oral Histories." See also Shelden, "'Such a Great Light,'" 84–87.
214. Though I have used the nineteenth-century spelling throughout, "Lottsburg" is the current spelling.
215. O'Dell, "Holley," section 8, page 1. I viewed the historic marker during my August 2016 visit with Shelden.
216. Aiken, "Holley."

# INTERLUDE 1

# A School Girl Again

> I have been thinking of you and wondering what you are about well I will imagine with you pupils all around you and also giving them good instructions I guess by this time they all very fond of you I sometime wish that I was a school girl again for this one reason so that I could be under you charge then I could be with the *object of my affections daily* and hourly. . . . Rebecca I want to see you very much I think of you daily & dream of you nightly.
>
> —Addie Brown, in a letter to Rebecca Primus, January 10, 1862

In 1862 Addie Brown worked for the Jacksons, a Black family in the settler-occupied territories of New York, while Rebecca Primus remained in her hometown of Hartford, Connecticut, where her teaching career had begun.[1] In a letter to Primus, Brown wrote that she *will imagine* Primus *with . . . pupils all around you.*[2] Brown imagined that Primus offered the students *good instructions* and they were *all very fond* of her.[3] Brown imagined further, and more evocatively, *I sometime wish that I was a school girl again . . . so that I could be under you charge—could be with the object of my affections daily and hourly.* Joining Brown in this *wish,* I imagine the earlier access to educational opportunities that might have helped make it possible for Brown to join Primus in a shared career as teachers, much like Sallie Holley and Caroline Putnam, with

---

1. Griffin, *Beloved Sisters,* 27. As previously introduced, Hartford was settled on the occupied land of Tunxis, Wangunk, Sicaog (Saukiog), and Poquonock territories. See Native Land Digital.

2. Correspondence from Brown to Primus, January 10, 1862, PF/CHS. In the Primus family papers held at the Connecticut Historical Society, box 1 includes Brown's letters to Primus, and box 2 Primus's letters to family. Letters are organized and cited by their date. Where transcribing the letters myself, I have maintained original spelling, capitalization, and punctuation.

3. In another 1861 letter, before Primus relocated to Maryland, Brown fantasized about watching her teach in "your private school." Brown wrote, "I often wish that I could take a birds eye view at you especially when you are playing some of my favorites." Griffin, *Beloved Sisters,* 51.

the erotic of their romantic friendship functioning as a rhetorical power that animated the women's self-education for racial uplift and justice.

It is 1859. Brown is in Hartford. She and Primus meet in the family's home, which *often served as a boardinghouse and employment agency for other African Americans, particularly young black women.*[4] Initially, the Primus family predictably supports Brown in securing yet another position working as a domestic.[5] But whenever Brown isn't cleaning, cooking, and caring for other families and Primus isn't teaching, the young women spend every spare minute together.

The women read voraciously, pouring over genres that range from novels to antislavery papers; from slave narratives to poetry; from speeches to books on politics and history.[6] They read Grace Aguilar's *Women's Friendship*, Frederick Douglass's *Narrative of the Life of Frederick Douglass*, and Harriet Beecher Stowe's *Uncle Tom's Cabin*. Late into the night, Brown and Primus discuss these books along with Frances Ellen Watkins Harper's poetry and speeches by Henry Ward Beecher and Henry Highland Garnet.[7]

Primus's parents, Holdridge and Mehitable Esther (Jacobs) Primus, can't help but notice. They see how Brown shares with Primus not only a special intimacy but also a passion for intellectual life and desire for self-education for racial uplift.[8] At dinner one night, Brown brings up a conversation with *a Lady* about Stowe's novel.[9]

"You *would be very much please with* this *Lady*," Brown says to the family, looking at Primus across the table. "The lady's *language is superb.*"

Recounting her own efforts to develop such language through the self-education of reading and letter writing, Brown adds, "*I often think when people has a chance to have a Education, why will they throw it away?*" She shakes her head.

"*They have lost golden opportunities.*" Everyone agrees.

---

4. Griffin, *Beloved Sisters*, 18.

5. Beeching, *Hopes*, 140–41; and Griffin, *Beloved Sisters*, 44.

6. Beeching, *Hopes*, 151; and Griffin, *Beloved Sisters*, 55, 79.

7. Correspondence from Brown to Primus, January 30, 1862; February 23, 1862; May 29, 1866; June 20, 1866; October 16, 1866, PF/CHS. Also quoted in Griffin, *Beloved Sisters*, 59, 60–61, 126, 131–32, 140. Correspondence from Rebecca Primus to family, November 1, 1868, PF/CHS. Also quoted in Griffin, *Beloved Sisters*, 249.

8. In addition to the sources cited already, other scholarship on nineteenth-century African American rhetorical education includes Bacon and McClish, "Reinventing"; Gold, *Rhetoric*; Jarratt, "Classics"; Logan, "Literacy"; Logan, "'To Get'"; McClish, "'To Furnish'"; McHenry, "'Dreaded Eloquence'"; and Wilson, "Racial Politics."

9. Correspondence from Brown to Primus, June 20, 1866, PF/CHS. Also quoted in Griffin, *Beloved Sisters*, 131–32.

Primus's parents recount this dinner table conversation later that night, in their own bed. The couple realizes that Brown's future will be better served by the *golden opportunities* of formal education. They make a decision to financially support Brown as a member of the extended family so that she may reduce her hours working as a domestic and begin attending the local school where Primus teaches. Although Brown is past the typical school age, she is welcomed into Primus's class.

Now *a school girl again,* Brown is *with the object of* her *affections daily and hourly,* not merely in the women's spare hours outside of paid work. Like all the students, Brown is *very fond of* Primus. But Brown's affection runs deeper. She takes pleasure in being *under* Primus's *charge* during the schooldays, fantasizing throughout the days about their nights together.

Primus stands at the blackboard, offering her *good instructions*.[10] Brown presses her left hand to her *bosom,* feeling a note from Primus tucked into her dress. Fondling a corner of the note, Brown recalls with pleasure the first time she unbuttoned her *night dress* so that Primus *could . . . get to* her *bosom*.[11]

It is about a week prior. Slipping out of Primus's bedroom, Brown leaves Primus a note placed to the left of her still-rumpled pillow:

> *Dearest Sister*
> *they tell me seek and ye shall*
> *find is that true no*
> *more this time*
> *your Darling little*
> *Sister Addie*
> or bad egg.[12]

In one sense, the note is nothing new. Both women enjoy playing flirtatious *seek and . . . find* games, trading notes with playful and often coded allusions to their erotic desires. In this case, though, after waiting longer than usual for Primus's reply—a full three days—Brown wants to provoke, with reference to the *bad egg* she keeps hinting about offering Primus while they cuddle in bed at night.

Much to Brown's surprise, Primus appears only minutes after Brown leaves behind the *bad egg* note. Primus stands in the entryway to Brown's sleeping

---

10. Correspondence from Brown to Primus, November 17, 1867, PF/CHS. Also quoted in Griffin, *Beloved Sisters,* 228.
11. On "bosom sex," see Hansen, "'No Kisses.'"
12. Undated note from Brown to Primus, PF/CHS. For further discussion of this note, see VanHaitsma, "Gossip."

area, which they usually avoid because of the other boarders. Primus slides into Brown's bed, hovers above her, and whispers into her ear.

"It is still *true, my little darling,* my *bad egg.* I am ready."

*Under* Primus, Brown starts to undo her buttons. She moves slowly, watching Primus's eyes, hoping that she has not misread the woman's expression of desire. Brown opens the *night dress,* so that Primus can get to her *bosom.* And she does. Primus *caresses* and *kisses* Brown's *bosom,* still whispering about *bad eggs.*[13] Brown stifles her moans.

Chalk scrapes across the blackboard and Brown is snapped back to the present. The note in her dress feels like it is radiating heat. She looks down at her *bosom,* sees a faint outline of the note, reorients herself to what Primus is saying at the blackboard.

In moments like this, all of Brown's desires intermix. She wants Primus's hands and mouth back on her *bosom.* She wants Primus in her bed. In Brown's mind, *the language and conventions of romantic love* that she uses to relive her nighttime pleasures with Primus carry over and into her thoughts about *a desire for a different kind of life, one in which she could enjoy the privileges that class mobility, literacy, and status make possible.*[14] Brown yearns for Primus, she yearns for education, she yearns for greater opportunities as an African American woman. Her desires for intimacy with Primus become so entangled with her desires for educational opportunity that they are nearly indistinguishable from each other.

So, too, with Brown's and Primus's desires for racial justice. Like most African American women, Brown and Primus are *fully aware of the material conditions of their lives and equally aware of the public discourses swirling around them.*[15] Whether at the family dinner table or alone in bed together at night, the women's conversations about their ideas and desires for change almost always circle back to the problem of systemic racism and collective efforts to counter it.[16]

One *Wednesday evening* Brown and Primus attend a *lecture at Talcott street Church* together on *the subject* of *Colored Mans Capacity.*[17] Returning home afterwards, the women offer to Primus's parents and siblings their shared assessment that the lecturer *spoke very well* about *Garnett, Douglass and other distinguish men.*[18]

---

13. Hansen, "'No Kisses,'" 187.
14. Grasso, "Edited Letter Collections," 259.
15. Royster, *Traces,* 110.
16. Griffin, *Beloved Sisters,* 5.
17. Correspondence from Brown to Primus, February 24, 1867; March 3, 1867, PF/CHS.
18. Correspondence from Brown to Primus, March 3, 1867, PF/CHS.

Brown lays awake that night, listening for the quiet that suggests everyone else is asleep, and then heads to Primus's room. Slipping into her bed, Brown opens her *night dress* right away this time, offering her *bosom* to Primus. But Brown can't stop thinking about the speaker's lecture.

"He said, *the day would come when states would allow every man vote.*"[19]

"I know," Primus replies, sliding Brown's *night dress* off her shoulders.

"When that *day would come,* he said *he was he was going back to Tennessee and take two blackest men one on each arm and go up to the ballot box.*"[20]

Primus buries her face in Brown's *bosom,* and both women stop talking.

Later that night, after Brown returns to her own bed, Primus imagines still another future day. She fantasizes about a day when the women can not only attend public lectures together but also speak more openly *of exchanging caresses, kisses, and hugs.* She imagines *sharing a bed* throughout the night, with no need to sneak back and forth while the rest of the house sleeps.[21]

Even so—with African Americans still unable to vote, with the fullness of their intimate relationship hidden in their own home, and with the arrival of the Civil War—Brown and Primus enjoy five glorious years together in Hartford. They live in the Primus family home as unmarried "single" women who share their passionate desires for each other, for intellectual life, and for racial uplift and justice. They sneak into each other's beds most nights and sneak out before the others are awake. Brown completes her studies, is trained as a teacher herself, and then begins as *a teacher in the Sunday school.*[22]

But everything changes in 1865. After the War comes to a close, Primus leaves *Hartford to teach the freedmen of Maryland.*[23] As one of two black teachers sponsored by the Hartford Freedmen's Aid Society, Primus establishes and teaches at what will become the Primus Institute. Brown supports Primus's move fully, as an opportunity to work toward their shared passions for self-education for racial uplift and justice—toward *the moral and educational improvement of the col'd. people,* through *teaching the Freedmen at the South.*[24]

Still, the women miss each other terribly.

---

19. Correspondence from Brown to Primus, March 3, 1867, PF/CHS.
20. Correspondence from Brown to Primus, November 17, 1867; March 3, 1867, PF/CHS.
21. Hansen, "'No Kisses,'" 187.
22. Griffin, *Beloved Sisters,* 56.
23. Griffin, *Beloved Sisters,* 77.
24. Correspondence from Primus to family, February 16, 1867, PF/CHS. Also quoted in Griffin, *Beloved Sisters,* 169. Correspondence from Brown to Primus, August 5, 1867, PF/CHS. Quoted in Griffin, *Beloved Sisters,* 215.

CHAPTER 2

# A Conservative Erotic of Emulating Beauty

## Commonplace Rhetorics and Belletristic Instruction, 1868–1900

> The subject of this memoir . . . was a beautiful personality because of her power to draw beauty out of the commonplace, and to make others do it; because she shook, roused, and waked up those who slept, demanding of them their best.
> —Anna Cogswell Wood, *The Story of a Friendship: A Memoir*, 1901

Irene Kirke Leache (1839–1900) and Anna (Annie) Cogswell Wood (1850–1940) met at the Valley Female Seminary, a boarding school for white girls in the South.[1] Wood was a student and Leache became her teacher. Wood reflected on their first meeting in *The Story of a Friendship: A Memoir* (1901), one of two books that she wrote about her life with Leache. It was "a September day, of the year 1868," Wood wrote, "that my eye first lighted on that rare woman whose influence was thenceforward to dominate my life."[2] "Thus our acquaintance began," Wood continued, "she as a teacher, I as pupil: but such is the catholicity of true friendship that it masters all other ties."[3] What began as a student-teacher relationship soon became a professional tie. In 1871, the women established another boarding school, the Leache-Wood Seminary. For twenty years, Leache and Wood lived at and administered the school, where they taught a belletristic form of rhetoric emphasizing the appreciation and emulation of "beautiful" writing. After retiring from formal teaching, they traveled abroad to Italy and throughout Europe and the Middle East, until Leache passed away in 1900. Also after retirement, both women became published writers. While compiling unpublished commonplace albums, Leache

---

1. As previously introduced, the Valley Female Seminary was located on occupied Manahoac, Massawomeck, and Shawandasse Tula territories. See Native Land Digital.
2. Wood, *Story*, 3, NPL.
3. Wood, *Story*, 4, NPL.

and Wood published a total of eight books. They were together, sharing their intimate lives and their work as teachers and writers, for over three decades.

The professional relationship that supported Leache's and Wood's rhetorical practices and pedagogies was also a romantic friendship. As Jane Turner Censer observes, Leache and Wood were among those women for whom "the friendships they formed with other teachers were a fulfilling alterative to or substitute for marriage," an alternative that "provided both love and intellectual stimulation."[4] I share with Censer the view that Leache and Wood's long-term friendship, their domestic and professional arrangement, was an alternative to marriage. This option was available to them, as with the other white women in my study, because of the privileged access to generational wealth, educational opportunities, and teaching careers that made it materially possible for them to live together and support themselves. In Wood's own words, her relationship with Leache was an "opulent friendship,"[5] which I understand as a form of romantic friendship characterized by a shared desire for the opulent "beauty" of white femininity specifically and white, Western culture more broadly. I argue that the erotic of this opulent friendship functioned as a distinctly conservative form of rhetorical power. In this conservative form, Leache and Wood's erotic desires for each other interanimated with passionately shared intellectual, pedagogical, and political desires that were marked by the emulation of traditional—as in settler, white, Western—beauty. Tied to notions of white superiority, this erotic of emulating beauty energized not only the women's intimate relationship but also their public development of commonplace rhetorics and teaching of belletristic rhetoric for privileged white girls in the South.

Considering how the women's opulent friendship enabled their teaching of rhetoric at the Leache-Wood Seminary, this chapter shifts attention from the freedmen's school to the boarding school, which was another of the educational sites open to some nineteenth-century women teachers. As previously introduced, these schools usually served white girls of economic means. In the North and the South, schools like the Leache-Wood Seminary increased access to intellectual opportunities for these young women while simultaneously "inculcating in them the social and domestic skills they would need as republican mothers."[6] In the domestic settings of boarding schools like the Leache-Wood Seminary, a few relational and pedagogical features are noteworthy. One is that women teachers were seen as the ideal guides to gendered instruction that included domestic skills, with teachers and even older

---

4. Censer, *Reconstruction*, 175.
5. Wood, *Story*, 12, NPL.
6. Hoffert, "Earnest Efforts," 815.

students often acting as models to emulate. Another is that, with academic subjects like rhetoric, instruction was predictably gendered, in that there was greater emphasis on belletristic rhetoric and beautiful writing than on political discourse and public speaking. Finally, as in other homosocial educational settings, same-sex romantic relationships between students, as well as older students and teachers, were common and largely accepted.[7] Wood was nineteen when Leache became her teacher.[8] Importantly, given the potential for abuse within this power dynamic, and in contrast with the case of Sallie Holley and Caroline Putnam, primary materials do not suggest an abusive relationship between Leache and Wood. Archival materials do show that Wood continued to see Leache as a model to learn from and emulate long after the early years of their student-teacher relationship.

In addition to turning to boarding schools, this chapter extends my scope with respect to geographic region and conservative politics. Whereas Holley and Putnam moved to Virginia for the purposes of their teaching careers, Leache and Wood were from the South. As David Gold and Catherine Hobbs urge, feminist histories of rhetoric still do not account fully for "the diversity of women's educational experiences . . . particularly in the South."[9] This relative lack of feminist scholarly attention results partly from "persistent public misperceptions of the South, which has long been portrayed as other to the enlightened North, nonrepresentative of the American experience and thus easily dismissed."[10]

Setting aside those stereotypes about the South that have been implicated in the under-examination of Southern women's rhetoric, it needs to be acknowledged that Leache and Wood were politically conservative women who upheld the white-supremacist stance of the nineteenth-century Confederacy. As Kimberly Harrison shows, there is also room within feminist rhetorical studies to consider more fully women rhetors whose politics were (and are) at odds with our own. While Holley and Putnam worked to teach in service of racial justice, however imperfectly, Leache and Wood were "privileged Southern women . . . whose politics were in support of maintaining slavery and their antebellum Southern culture."[11] Furthermore, as I discuss in a later section of this chapter, Leache and Wood continued to support Confederate

---

7. On student-student and student-teacher relationships at boarding schools, see Farnham, *Education*; Hoffert, "Earnest Efforts"; and Vicinus, "Distance." For discussion of similar relationships in other homosocial settings, including women's colleges, see Franzen, *Spinsters*; Horowitz, *Alma Mater*; Inness, "Mashes"; Jabour, *Scarlett's Sisters*; and Sahli, "Smashing."
8. Tunstall, "Story," 1, JOCL.
9. Gold and Hobbs, *Educating*, 2.
10. Gold and Hobbs, *Educating*, 4–5.
11. Harrison, *Civil War*, 6.

ideology even following the Civil War, with Leache refusing discussion of the War at the Leache-Wood Seminary. Far from trying to advance racial justice, the women supported settler-colonial hierarchies of race, ethnicity, and gender. Even as Leache and Wood worked to expand educational opportunities for privileged white girls in post–Civil War Norfolk, they urged that these young women should act according to the obligations of their "sex" and "race." Especially following Leache's death, Wood expressed overt opposition to the women's movement of the 1920s. In these respects, the conservative erotic that fueled Leache and Wood's partnership obviously went in an entirely different political direction than that envisioned by Audre Lorde.[12]

My study of the conservative erotic of Leache and Wood's opulent friendship is grounded in research conducted in settler-colonial archives.[13] The main collection of records from Leache, Wood, and the Leache-Wood Seminary is preserved in the Irene Leache Memorial Collection at the Chrysler Museum of Art's Jean Outland Chrysler Library. The archive is located, as was the boarding school itself, on occupied Lumbee and Chesapeake territories that were settled as Norfolk, Virginia.[14] Wood founded the Irene Leache Memorial in 1901 in order to honor Leache after her passing. Wood wanted to preserve memory of Leache's educational and cultural contributions as well as continue to advance the women's shared "passions."[15] Working with alumnae from the Leache-Wood Seminary, Wood and the Irene Leache Memorial loaned and later donated a private art collection of Leache's, which contributed to the eventual development of the Chrysler Museum and explains the location of the Irene Leache Memorial Collection. More central to the focus of my research, the Memorial group also donated the women's papers. This collection includes Leache's and Wood's publications, school catalogs and other records from the Leache-Wood Seminary, over twenty of the women's unpublished commonplace albums, and records from the Memorial group itself. Another Norfolk archive, the Sargeant Memorial Collection at the Norfolk Public Library, contains a more limited selection of the women's publications and additional records from the school. Other collections with select papers include the Stewart Bell Jr. Archives of the Handley Regional Library and the Albert and Shirley Small Special Collections Library at the University of Virginia.

Based on archival research in these collections, I investigate how Leache and Wood's intimate relationship empowered and inflected their conservative

---

12. Lorde, "Uses of the Erotic," 59.
13. See also VanHaitsma, "'Opulent Friendships.'"
14. Native Land Digital.
15. Lorde, "Uses of the Erotic," 56.

rhetorical practices and pedagogies. I begin by discussing the women's initial pedagogical encounters in order to set out the terms of their opulent friendship and its investments in white, Western aesthetics and rhetorical traditions. I consider how admiration of Leache's beauty, in a Platonic sense, inspired Wood to emulate her teacher as a rhetorical model for writing. Next I detail how this conservative erotic of emulating white, Western forms of beauty continued to shape Wood's development of rhetorical practices long after the women's student-teacher relationship had developed into a romantic friendship between fellow teachers. Associated with the rhetorical tradition of commonplace books, Wood's invention practices responded to Leache's rhetorical "power," described by Wood in this chapter's epigraph, "to draw beauty out of the commonplace."[16] Emulating Leache's rhetorical practices, Wood enacted what I term *commonplace rhetorics* within actual commonplace albums as well as published writing. Leache's and Wood's commonplace rhetorics also informed their work together as teachers and school administrators. With the conservative erotic of their opulent friendship fueling rhetorical emulation and pedagogy, they functioned as models of white femininity for the students at their school, much like Leache had for Wood. They taught a belletristic version of rhetoric that emphasized the appreciation and emulation of "beautiful" writing, while positioning themselves as models that drew out the "best" and most beautiful in their students. The conservative erotic of rhetorical emulation in Leache and Wood's opulent friendship thus animated their belletristic instruction for privileged white girls in the South.

While expanding intellectual opportunities for these young women, Wood and Leache's conservative form of the erotic as rhetorical power was grounded in and itself perpetuated the conditions of settler colonialism and slavery. While the same can be said for all the white women in this study, Wood and Leache most unabashedly approached difference with apparent "loathing," treating it in ways that were "divisive" rather than "creative."[17] The women rhetorically reproduced a normative, white femininity that emulated white, Western conceptions of beauty and embraced settler-colonial racism, cisheterosexism, and ableism. Advancing the ideology of eugenics, Wood explicitly articulated a role for this form of white femininity in defending racial and social hierarchies in order to preserve "the race" and "the nation" through pedagogical reproduction.[18] Ultimately, I argue, Wood and Leache's conservative erotic of emulating "beauty" functioned as a power fueling their rhetorical

---

16. Wood, *Story*, 311, NPL.
17. Lorde, "Age, Race, Class," 15; and Lorde, "Burst of Light," 209.
18. Wood, *Great Opportunity*, 10, JOCL.

practices and pedagogies on behalf of privileged girls in an effort to reproduce the white "race" and its settler-colonial nation.

## Conservative Erotic of Emulating Beauty

In order to set the stage for subsequent analysis of how the conservative erotic of Leache and Wood's opulent friendship fueled their rhetorical practices and instruction, this section characterizes the women's early pedagogical encounters and the development of their teacher-student relationship into a long-term romantic and professional partnership. Unfortunately, in the case of Leache and Wood, we do not have access to those primary sources most frequently consulted in histories of romantic friendship between women, romantic letters. Apparently Leache asked that a friend "destroy all of her correspondence."[19] Nor is most of Wood's correspondence extant.[20] Yet a good deal of information is available about the women's relationship, at least from Wood's perspective. My discussion draws especially from two memoirs that Wood published about the relationship following Leache's death, *The Story of a Friendship: A Memoir* (1901) and *Idyls and Impressions of Travel: From the Note-Books of Two Friends* (1904). Considered alongside the women's other writing, these books demonstrate how Wood's admiration of Leache developed into a shared passion for the emulation of white, Western beauty, in both a Platonic and a rhetorical sense. This erotic of emulating "beauty" energized the women's opulent friendship, which in turn shaped their work together as rhetors and teachers of belletristic rhetoric.

Leache and Wood were first brought together by their passionately shared desires for "intellectual production" within a homosocial educational setting for white girls and young women.[21] As previously introduced, Wood met Leache when she became a teacher at the Valley Female Seminary. Students and teachers referred to the seminary as Angerona, because it "was located in a building known as 'Angerona,' named after a heathen Roman goddess."[22]

---

19. Hofheimer, *Annie*, 2.
20. There are two exceptions of which I am aware. One is a letter from Wood to poet and essayist Virginia Taylor McCormick. In it, Wood praised one of McCormick's publications, writing in closing, "thank you dear Mrs. McCormick for the mental massage which you & your article have given me." Correspondence from Wood to McCormick, March 4, [1924?], CWM. A second exception includes a series of letters from Wood to Leache's coauthor, Louise Collier Willcox, in which Wood references progress on the Irene Leache Memorial Collection. Correspondence from Wood to Willcox, [undated], box 3, folder 3, UVA.
21. Lorde, "Uses of the Erotic," 56.
22. Engle, "Valley Seed," 1, WFHS.

Wood opened *The Story of a Friendship* (1901) with a description of the day in 1868 when her "eye first lighted on that rare woman whose influence was thenceforward to dominate my life."[23] That September day, Angerona's principal introduced Leache as "our new teacher" and "a marvel of . . . literary ability." Wood wrote that, "between fluttering lids . . . I set forth my gaze to meet that of the stranger, stranger no more after the first glance."[24] "Thus our acquaintance began," Wood continued, "she as a teacher, I as pupil: but such is the catholicity of true friendship that it masters all other ties, whether of blood or of marriage."

Whatever fluttering of lids may have occurred at first sight, it was another encounter in the school's garden where "spring flung beauties and bounties with a full hand."[25] Wood represented this same-sex garden encounter as erotic in ways consistent with Western rhetorical and literary traditions. In Plato's *Phaedrus*, Socrates's pedagogical seduction of Phaedrus occurred in "a charming resting place" with a "very beautiful" willow "in full bloom"; a "lovely and perfectly charming" scene; "the most delightful thing of all" being "the grass, as it grows on the gentle slope, thick enough to be just right when you lay your head on it."[26] Fragments of Sappho's lyric poetry suggest that she, too, delivered her seductive rhetoric, addressed to women, within the "lush beauty of natural spaces" like gardens.[27] Describing one such place, Sappho wrote, "here you will find a grove of / apple trees to charm you . . . here down from the leaves' bright flickering / entrancement settles."[28] According to Wood, she and Leache similarly met "in the garden . . . seated under a pear tree," where they spent hours reading, doing needlework, and talking.[29] Emphasizing the garden's opulence, Wood wrote that, "on account of a profusion of flowering shrubs and trees, the Virginia garden bloomed forth at its moment of rejuvenescence with a more unbridled fruitfulness."[30] "What a delight we found in wandering through this garden," she exclaimed, "giving to fancy all she craved of freedom, even spurring her forward to lift to the human plane all this flower-life."[31]

Wood's descriptions echo not only those Western garden scenes of same-sex pedagogical and rhetorical seduction familiar from Plato and Sappho but

---

23. Wood, *Story*, 3, NPL.
24. Wood, *Story*, 4, NPL.
25. Wood, *Story*, 19, NPL.
26. Plato, "Phaedrus," 140.
27. Jarratt, "Sappho's Memory," 16.
28. Jarratt, "Sappho's Memory," 18.
29. Wood, *Story*, 22, NPL.
30. Wood, *Story*, 19, NPL.
31. Wood, *Story*, 20, NPL.

also the imagery of flower gardens that characterized the "lesbian landscape tradition" made popular in eighteenth-century English poetry.[32] Materially speaking, such gardens were literal "grounds" of colonialism, settler colonialism, and slavery: most landscaped grounds and gardens of the period were built and maintained by the labor of recent immigrants and enslaved people.[33] Just as significantly, Wood's descriptions rhetorically framed the women's earliest meeting in ways that reproduced Western notions of rhetorical and aesthetic beauty. This cultural specificity is important to underscore, because, as I show later in this chapter, Leache and Wood did not merely embrace their own cultural traditions as white women. Rather, even as they gained privileged access to travel and opportunities to learn about other cultures around the world, the women retreated into the "sameness" of white femininity as a form of relational and cultural belonging.[34] In Lorde's words, Wood and Leache's responses to difference sought to "copy" what was culturally "dominant," whereas they "misnamed and misused" what they considered "subordinate."[35] In the former, it was white, Western culture that they emulated and even defined as superior.

Wood's account of her early relationship with Leache reflected Western notions of romantic love and marriage as well. After the "first glance" noted above, Wood narrated a move from initial passion to steadfast friendship.[36] "I was too much under the sway of passion," Wood wrote, "at the beginning our acquaintance."[37] Recalling the garden scene, she admitted, "there was a mutual past to be disclosed before our friendship could stand on a definite basis; and here I own to pangs of jealousy caused by the discovery that her experience was such a full one before touching mine."[38] While passion and jealousy are often associated with romantic love, Wood's jealousy was also that of a student looking up to her more experienced teacher. Wood's description of this pedagogical encounter brought together eroticized garden imagery and romantic love with metaphors of marriage. Following a remark that "young races . . . personify vegetation," Wood claimed that the spring garden scene with Leache "took on the aspect of a wedding, for which each plant in turn hurried to make ready."[39] After then describing the flowering landscape in detail, Wood

---

32. Cleves, *Charity*, 39. See also Moore, *Sister Arts*.
33. Greyser, *Sympathetic Grounds*.
34. Frankenberg, *White Women*, 72; and Carrillo Rowe, *Power Lines*, 131.
35. Lorde, "Age, Race, Class," 115.
36. Wood, *Story*, 4, NPL.
37. Wood, *Story*, 13, NPL.
38. Wood, *Story*, 22, NPL.
39. Wood, *Story*, 20, NPL.

asserted, "the centre of all this loveliness was the bride, a laurel, that leaned half of her snowy blossoms against a cedar, which, in his suit of perennial green, did us service for the groom. The maid of honor was a crab-apple."[40] "Fronting this bridal party," Wood went on, "stood a solitary yew, adding the semblance of a bishop in robes." As Censer suggests, this "description of the garden at Angerona that first spring suggests that a marriage, at least of their minds, had occurred there."[41] Like Censer, I, too, interpret Wood's garden scene as suggesting a progression from first glances to early passions and jealousies, from romantic love to a long-term marrying of minds.

Before turning to the rhetorical dimensions of this opulent friendship, I need to recognize alternative interpretations of the relationship. As with the other women in my study, it could be argued that Wood's description represents her friendship with Leache as romantic, but not erotic (or sexual). Indeed, accounts of the relationship between Wood and Leache, even more so than that between Putnam and Holley, reflect the complexities of debates about romantic friendships between women. Censer concludes that although "we can not determine the sexual orientation of these women," Wood's "narrative makes it clear that theirs was indeed a loving partnership."[42] The women are included in *Gay American History,* where Jonathan Ned Katz references their "intimate association lasting thirty-two years."[43] James Thomas Sears also mentions the women's "intimate relationship" within a list of "lesbian foremothers" from the South.[44] Yet in the most extensively researched account, former president of the Irene Leache Memorial Jo Ann Mervis Hofheimer refers to Leache and Wood as "celibate lovers."[45] Hofheimer recognizes that Wood "loved Irene Leache 'deeply, broadly, loftily,' and from that love came the growth of a community."[46] In concert with Marylynn Diggs's theorization of romantic friendship as a "cover" for potentially erotic and sexual relationships between privileged white women, Hofheimer also acknowledges that "the rare women who did live together as lovers were tolerated by society primarily because the attraction was so little understood."[47] Yet after recounting

---

40. Wood, *Story,* 21, NPL.
41. Censer, *Reconstruction,* 176.
42. Censer, *Reconstruction,* 176.
43. Katz, *Gay,* 656 n. 141. See also Rolle, *Celebrating.*
44. Sears, *Rebels,* 356 n. 12.
45. Hofheimer, *Annie,* 45.
46. Hofheimer, *Annie,* 162.
47. Diggs, "Romantic Friends," 319; and Hofheimer, *Annie,* 43–44. Hofheimer continued, however, "Whatever sexual feelings middle-class women might have felt for each other in the nineteenth century were thoroughly sublimated by Victorian mores and a total lack of knowledge of sexology."

an understanding of romantic friendship drawn from two books on women's history, Hofheimer claims that Wood and Leache "were thoroughly Victorian women" who "had neither the concept of, nor the terms for, a lesbian relationship. Therefore, when put into historical context, it is misleading and unsupportable to conclude any but the purist alliance."[48]

I share with Hofheimer an unwillingness to project twentieth-century notions of "lesbian" identity onto Leache and Wood's relationship. Nor is the presumption that nineteenth-century romantic friendships were necessarily celibate an uncommon view. Although the early scholarship arguing as such has since been complicated, that research is well-known and continues to be cited widely by scholars working outside of LGBTQ+ studies. My own work mainly sets aside questions about extratextual practices that present-day readers might understand as "sexual." Yet as already discussed, it is a specifically white femininity—idealized and desexualized—that lends itself to such assumptions of so-called sexual purity.[49] Moreover, if a "purist alliance" precludes any erotic relation other than complete celibacy, I am less confident than Hofheimer about how "misleading and insupportable" it would be to consider what concepts and terms for same-sex relationships were available to Leache and Wood within their "historical context."[50] I want to venture instead that if we reexamine the archives of Leache and Wood's romantic friendship, we find that Wood *was* well aware of figures associated with eroticized same-sex love from across historical periods in the West.[51] This awareness is significant because of how she seems to have emulated these historical figures as models for her own life and work with Leache.

Wood referenced a range of figures, both women and men, especially from ancient Greece and Rome. Writing in her unpublished commonplace albums about the Roman fresco of the Greek lyric poet from Lesbos, Wood asked of "this so-called Sappho," "is there in her expression a blending of the intellectual and the passionate?"[52] Another album includes a discussion of "sodomy," in which Wood mentioned "the classic Antonius" as an "ideal of manly beauty," noting his "certain feminine beauty of contour."[53] In one of Wood's published books, *The Psychology of Crime, Illustrated by Several Modern Poets*

---

48. Hofheimer, *Annie*, 45, emphasis added. The two books on women's history cited by Hofheimer are Duby, Perrot, and Fraisse, *History*; and Perkin, *Victorian Women*.

49. Bacon, *Humblest*, 43; and Franzen, *Spinsters*, 170–71.

50. Hofheimer, *Annie*, 45.

51. I further discuss questions about the archives of romantic friendship in VanHaitsma, "Stories."

52. Wood, [untitled album, n.d.], JOCL. All of Wood's unpublished albums are undated, and the pages are unnumbered.

53. Wood, [untitled album, n.d.], JOCL.

(n.d.), she wrote about one of the figures perhaps most associated with *eros* in Western rhetoric, Helen, offering a sketch in which Electra falls in "love" with Helen at first sight because of Aphrodite's curse.[54] In another, *Drama Sketches for Parlor Acting or Recitation* (1925), Wood wrote about Gilgamesh and Enkidu.[55] Both *The Story of a Friendship* (1901) and Wood's unpublished albums mention Pylades and Orestes as well as David and Jonathan.[56] All of these figures were same-sex friends whose relationships Wood variously treated as romantic or homoerotic in keeping with Western cultural history.

Closer to her own historical period, Wood's memoir about her friendship with Leache compares it to that between another white couple, Sarah Ponsonby and Eleanor Butler, or the "Ladies of Llangollen," who became "the model of Romantic Friendship" in late eighteenth-century colonial Europe.[57] Remarking on gender and same-sex friendships, Wood wrote, "here is another strange fact, that, in calling the roll of world-famous friendships, from David and Jonathan up to Tennyson and Arthur Hallam, we discover that these existed nearly altogether between men, if we except the attachment of the far-famed but little known Ladies of Llangollen."[58] Wood clearly knew about Ponsonby and Butler, whose romantic friendship was rumored to be more than platonic.[59] A comparison with the Ladies of Llangollen is also articulated in Edward Stevenson's early twentieth-century sexological study (1908), published after Leache's death. Leache and Wood, along with the Ladies of Llangollen, are *the* two examples provided to support the claim that "suggestive friendships of uraniad force and constancy are many among women of the intersexual type."[60] Stevenson's use of the term "intersexual" should not be confused with present-day uses by self-identified intersex advocates and

---

54. Wood, *Psychology*, 8, JOCL.

55. Wood, *Drama*, 4, JOCL.

56. Wood, *Story*, 111, NPL. References to Pylades and Orestes, as well as David and Jonathan, also appear in Wood's unpublished albums.

57. Vicinus, *Intimate Friends*, 6. For another perspective on the Ladies of Llangollen, see Castle, *Apparitional Lesbian*, 93–95.

58. Wood, *Story*, 5, NPL.

59. Diggs, "Romantic Friends," 319. Also see Moore, "'Something'"; and Whitbread, *I Know*, 210.

60. Stevenson, *Intersexes*, 404. This early use of the terms *intersexual* and *uraniad*, which designated "sexes" associated with homosexuality, should not be confused with the term *intersex* as used in the present. Stevenson described two "intersexes": "These Intersexes partake of the natures and temperaments and physiques of both the male and the female. . . . Departing from the first sex a man, we establish a second and 'intersexual' sex, known to European medico-psychologic literature as the Urning, or Uranian sex. . . . We next establish . . . a third sex, or intersex, called the Uraniad, which refers to the feminine, but the feminine sexually masculinized; of which sex many 'women-seeming' women are members" (19).

communities.⁶¹ Nor do I ascribe an "intersexual type" or present-day sexual identity to Leache and Wood. But I want to emphasize that, if we examine the primary materials carefully, rather than presuming what the women could have known, we find that Wood knew quite a bit about both contemporaneous models of white women's romantic friendships and examples of eroticized same-sex relationships from earlier periods. Again, her awareness is significant, because such models were central to the conservative erotic of emulating beauty that not only informed Wood and Leache's own opulent friendship but also shaped their rhetorical practices and pedagogy.

With respect to Leache's and Wood's rhetorical activities, two themes from the development of their opulent friendship are most noteworthy. First, their rhetorical labors were facilitated by a conservative erotic of emulation that emerged within their initial pedagogical encounters. As with the other women in this study, Leache and Wood first came together through their "sharing deeply" of intellectual and educational "pursuit."⁶² In the words of Elizabeth C. Engle, the women's "mutual love of books, art, music, poetry, history, and much else bound them together" as they formed a relationship that consisted of "reading and studying and conversations, stimulated by both ancient and contemporary authors."⁶³ The women's pedagogical encounters at Angerona inspired a passionate admiration that prompted Wood to see Leache as a rhetorical model of beauty. As previously introduced, emulation of an admired teacher is familiar from the history of rhetorical education between men in ancient Greece, where "intense homoerotic relationships often developed between mentor and pupil, which apparently were considered appropriate aids to emulation."⁶⁴ Predictably, as in the case of Putnam and Holley, there is no primary evidence suggesting that Wood and Leache engaged in the sexual power dynamic common to men's pedagogical admiration and seduction in ancient Greco-Roman contexts.⁶⁵ But "admiration" for Leache's "accomplishments" did motivate Wood, serving as an aid to rhetorical emulation.⁶⁶

Second, this emulation was grounded in a white, Western concept of "beauty" familiar from ancient rhetoric and philosophy. In Plato's *Phaedrus*, Socrates uses a seductive pedagogy with Phaedrus, yet dismisses rhetoric by likening it to mere seduction, sexual desire, and physical beauty—as opposed

---

61. For scholarship on *intersex* as a more recent historical and present-day category, see Malatino, *Queer Embodiment*. Within rhetorical studies, see Topp, "Against."
62. Lorde, "Uses of the Erotic," 56.
63. Engle, "Valley Seed," 3–4, WFHS.
64. Bizzell and Herzberg, *Rhetorical Tradition*, 26.
65. Bizzell and Herzberg, *Rhetorical Tradition*, 26.
66. Bizzell and Herzberg, *Rhetorical Tradition*, 26.

to the philosophical pursuit of truth, true love, and transcendent beauty. Like Plato's Socrates, Wood idealized beauty that purportedly transcended physical desire, in order to seek out what was truly "beautiful," what was the "best."[67] Declaring that Leache was the woman she "most loved and revered," with "Love" being that "which has changed the soul from passive to active, from bud to flower," Wood underscored how this love and reverence were activated by Leache's beauty.[68] Again, in the epigraph for this chapter, Wood wrote, "the subject of this memoir was a beautiful soul flooded with celestial light . . . but she was a beautiful personality because of her power to draw beauty out of the commonplace, and to make others do it too; because she shook, roused, and waked up those who slept, demanding of them their best."[69] It was not merely physical beauty that inspired Wood. She clarified, "have I given the impression that Miss Leache was a beautiful woman? If so, I have erred; for though full of beauties, she was not beautiful as judged by physical standards."[70] Instead, in more Platonic terms, Wood characterized Leache as a "beautiful soul" who could "draw . . . out" what was "best."

Even as Wood de-emphasized Leache's physical traits, both women's very conception of beauty was tied to specifically white, Western culture that the women saw as superior, as the "best." Even more than the other women in this archival study, Leache and Wood's erotic as rhetorical power was thus constrained by their ongoing investments in hierarchical distinctions, culturally as well as politically. I consider next how, in keeping with the women's early pedagogical encounters in the gardens at Angerona, Leache continued to function as an aid to emulating white femininity, with the erotic of the women's relationship inspiring them to draw out the beautiful within their own rhetorical practices and, in turn, teach their white students at Leache-Wood Seminary to do the same.

## Beauty in Commonplace Rhetorics

Leach and Wood's conservative erotic of emulating this culturally limited notion of "beauty" functioned "as a considered source of power" that fueled their own rhetorical practices as authors.[71] Throughout their lives, the women wrote letters, kept notebooks, and compiled commonplace books. Though the commonplace books were unpublished, there is evidence that Leache

---

67. Wood, *Story*, 310–11, NPL.
68. Wood, *Story*, 310, NPL.
69. Wood, *Story*, 310–11, NPL.
70. Wood, *Story*, 10, NPL.
71. Lorde, "Uses of the Erotic," 53.

and Wood did share them with each other and their broader pedagogical networks. With privileged access to the means to do so, Leache and Wood also published their writing in book form. After they had retired from formal teaching, Wood published several books in addition to the already discussed memoirs about her opulent friendship with Leache. Early in retirement, as the women embarked on their travels abroad, Wood's first books were two novels published under the pseudonym Algernon Ridgeway, *Diana Fontaine: A Novel* (1891) and *Westover's Ward* (1892).[72] The year the women returned to Virginia, Leache published a book with Louise Collier Willcox, who had been recruited to teach at the Leache-Wood Seminary. Published under Leache and Willcox's initials only, *Answers of the Ages* (1900) was "a book of inspirational quotations . . . 'gathered from the note-books of two friends.'"[73] Leache passed away that same year and, for the next two-plus decades, Wood focused on making arrangements in order to have Leache's life and cultural contributions memorialized. Then Wood returned to Italy, where she published three other books: *Drama Sketches for Parlor Acting or Recitation* (1925), *The Great Opportunity and Other Essays* (1926), and *The Psychology of Crime, Illustrated by Several Modern Poets* (n.d.).[74] According to one commentator, Wood "wrote . . . poor novels, but her . . . books on philosophy and art were considered highly creditable."[75] With Wood's and Leache's early publications appearing under pseudonyms and initials, the women obviously navigated constraints and opportunities that often faced privileged white women able to publish their writing.

Wood and Leache's opulent friendship practically supported the development of their unpublished and, later, published writing, because the relationship freed up the women's time from childbearing and childrearing responsibilities as well as other forms of domestic labor. In terms of what is documented within extant archives, however, evidence exists mainly for the ways their friendship influenced Wood's development of commonplace rhetorics (as opposed to its influence on Leache's rhetorical practices). In some respects, this direction of influence—by Leache on Wood—reflects the women's early teacher-student relationship. In other ways, the uneven evidence can be attributed to differences in longevity and, in turn, the shape of the available archive. Although the women were together for over thirty

---

72. Wood [as Algernon Ridgeway], *Diana*, JOCL; and Wood [as Algernon Ridgeway], *Westover's Ward*, JOCL.

73. Leache and Willcox [as I.K.L. and L.C.W.], *Answers*, JOCL, quoted in Hofheimer, *Annie*, 77.

74. Wood, *Drama*, JOCL; Wood, *Great Opportunity*, JOCL; and Wood, *Psychology*, JOCL. On the publication date of the latter, see Hofheimer, *Annie*, 191.

75. Engle, "Valley Seed," 3, WFHS.

years, Wood outlived Leache by forty years. In the simplest sense, Wood had more time after retiring from teaching in which to publish her work, and she published seven books to Leache's one. Moreover, while the available archives contain the published works of both women, most of the Chrysler's unpublished manuscript collection consists of Wood's rather than Leache's commonplace albums. Taken together, these materials make clear that Wood admired Leache and, with their opulent friendship fueled by a conservative erotic of emulating what they saw as the superiority of white, Western beauty, Wood developed what I am calling commonplace rhetorics. Through these commonplace rhetorics, Wood modeled both her commonplace books and published writing after Leache's white femininity and "power to draw beauty out of the commonplace."[76]

Wood admired, for instance, Leache's wartime rhetorical prowess and practices as a white woman who was invested in the Confederacy, its practices with respect to the institution of slavery, and anti-Black racism more broadly. Along these lines, *The Story of a Friendship* (1901) shares stories similar to those described in Harrison's study of Southern white women during the Civil War. While these women rarely had access to the traditional public podium as a site of overt persuasion, they developed more covert rhetorical strategies of hospitality and silence to deploy through conversation, including conversations with soldiers.[77] Wood wrote that, at a time when Northern soldiers occupied Leache's family's home, Leache's speech tricked an officer, making it possible for a Confederate soldier hidden in the attic to escape. Wood admired how Leache patiently waited for a kairotic moment after she "had woven" a "web of diplomacy" with "this wise end in view": to gain information to facilitate the soldier's escape while playing chess with a Northern general.[78] During the game of chess, Leache waited for the moment when, after the general dropped a piece of paper holding key information that would enable the soldier's escape, she was able to retrieve it. The general did not notice, because he was "too pleasantly engrossed" by Leache's conversation, "for it is not every day that a man finds himself" in the company of "young ladies . . . eager to take revenge upon him by every means in their power, from saucy challenge to polite rebuke."

Reflecting on Leache's rhetorical power, Wood pointed to Leache's "skill in finessing . . . this finest form of intrigue."[79] References to Leache's charming rhetoric of course show that Wood and Leache's version of the beautiful

---

76. Wood, *Story*, 311, NPL.

77. See Donawerth on the history of what she terms "conversational rhetorics" in her book by the same name.

78. Wood, *Story*, 51, NPL.

79. Wood, *Story*, 52, NPL.

necessarily departed from Plato's ideas about "true rhetoric."[80] Wood's characterization of Leache as a "lady," along with the assumption of sexual innocence even as Leache used sexualized "intrigue" to trick the soldier, are tied to the discourses of white femininity and sexual "purity" previously discussed. In addition, with the women's relationship animated by a conservative erotic of emulation, we see how admiring Leache's "beauty" included admiring her rhetorical accomplishments in service of the Confederacy. Insofar as these white women formed a rhetorical alliance with white men in support of the institution of slavery, Leache and Wood upheld, in the words of Lorde, "the dangerous fantasy" of white femininity.[81]

The written works that Leache and Wood found to be the "beautiful," the "best," and the most worthy of aesthetic appreciation were also marked by the whiteness of Western colonial and settler-colonial cultures. As referenced throughout this chapter, some of the authors and other cultural figures that Wood celebrated from Greco-Roman rhetorical and literary history include Sappho, Helen, Plato, Socrates, Aristotle, Cicero, and St. Augustine. That Wood and Leache admired the beauty of the culture and history into which they were born is by no means surprising. But their view of white, Western cultures as not simply beautiful but superior shaped their rhetorical practices (and teaching) in ways complicit with settler colonialism and slavery.

How Wood's admiration of Leache and white, Western culture played out is most apparent with respect to Wood's commonplace rhetorics. The term *commonplace* holds dual significance for invention in the history of Western rhetoric. First, there are commonplaces, as in common topics, often understood as places to which rhetors turn in order to invent their arguments.[82] Second, and more relevant to Leache's and Wood's rhetorical practices, there are commonplace books. These books are compiled collections, or spaces in which rhetors select, copy, and sometimes reflect on existing materials in service of their own invention.[83] Such invention through compilation may occur within the commonplace book itself and, simultaneously, serve future invention through more public-facing rhetorical practices. This complex

---

80. Bizzell and Herzberg, *Rhetorical Tradition*, 28, 82.
81. Lorde, "Age, Race, Class," 119.
82. The body of scholarship on commonplaces within the history of rhetoric is extensive. For a select sample of this work, see Aristotle, *Rhetoric*; Hesk, "'Despisers'"; Kimball, "Commonplace"; Marshall, "Warburgian"; McAdon, "'Special Topics'"; Quandahl, "Aristotle's Rhetoric'"; and Walzer, "Aristotle."
83. As with the commonplaces, commonplace books have been widely studied. A selection of this work within rhetoric, communication, and composition includes Almjeld, "Rhetorician's Guide"; Geraths and Kennerly, "Pinvention"; Lui, "Public Curation"; and Miller, *Assuming*. Across the humanities, also see Blair, "Humanist Methods"; V. E. Burke, "Recent Studies"; and Hobart and Schiffman, *Information*.

relationship with publicity made commonplace books particularly significant to women's invention, including into the nineteenth century. As Beth Ann Rothermel shows in her study of eighteenth- and nineteenth-century Quaker women, they did "more than just catalogue and copy rhetorically significant texts" into their commonplace books. Rather, the women used the books to "participate in and help shape their rhetorical culture by reenacting invention practices central to the creation of Quaker discourse."[84] Recognizing this importance of women's commonplace books to rhetorical history, I use the term *commonplace rhetorics* to refer to a cluster of invention practices, including selection, compilation, and reflection, which are associated with the commonplace book tradition but may be enacted in and through different textual forms.

Part of what distinguishes Wood's and Leache's development of commonplace rhetorics is how they used these practices of selection, compilation, and reflection in order to construct multiple types of texts. Among the texts were their unpublished albums, which are similar to commonplace books yet marked by an emphasis on the compilation of visual art pasted into the albums alongside writing. In one of the album entries already mentioned, Wood pasted a visual image of a Roman fresco of Sappho. Alongside the image, Wood reflected in writing, "is there in her expression a blending of the intellectual and the passionate?"[85] The visual distinctiveness of these commonplace albums is consistent with Leache and Wood's interest in the arts and their practice of collecting art during their travels abroad.

Moreover, in blurring generic lines between the commonplace book and other forms of the visual album, Leache and Wood were by no means alone. With commonplace books evolving over time, archives include a large body of materials from inventive rhetors who developed nineteenth-century iterations of what Ronald J. Zboray and Mary Saracino Zboray characterize as "'mixed material' items" or "'watchamacallits."[86] I have written elsewhere about genre-bending commonplace rhetorics that amounted to specifically genre-queer rhetorical practices.[87] More to my point here, as Zboray and Zboray document, "boundary-blurring items" like Leache's and Wood's commonplace albums reflect both a pattern of "common genre and format transformations" from the period and, at the same time, "occasional experimentation with

---

84. Rothermel, "Prophets," 72. On women's commonplace books, also see Edwards, "Legal World"; and Ophir, "Diary." On another closely related genre, see Ricker, "(De)Constructing."
85. Wood, [untitled album, n.d.], JOCL.
86. Zboray and Zboray, "Is It," 101.
87. VanHaitsma, *Queering*, 74–98.

genre."[88] The Chrysler's archival collection contains well over twenty of these genre-blurring commonplace albums, which unfortunately are undated. Most of the albums are attributed to Wood.[89]

Characteristic of Wood's commonplace rhetorics is an album that she explicitly titled on its first page "A Common-Place Book." Explaining the title, and noting the visual emphasis across her albums, Wood wrote that this album contained "a heterogeneous collection of pictures and Reflections." "The reflections have no connection with the pictures," Wood claimed, "but are an expression of everyday philosophy. The book is a species of diary recording observation." In actuality, most of Wood's "pictures" and "Reflections" do appear to "have . . . connection," as in the previously referenced Sappho example. The number of and emphasis on "pictures" marked her distinctive commonplace albums, whereas the traversal of generic lines between the commonplace book and "a species of diary" was typical for the period. Also typical was Wood's attempt to explain the album's contents and purposes. While her specific explanations varied by individual album, many included prefatory comments that introduced potential readers to the commonplace books.

That Wood compiled these books with an audience of readers in mind is apparent in another album that was seemingly composed while Leache was still alive. Here Wood's prefatory comments again acknowledged her inventive approach to visual compilation while denying the existence of a systematic relationship between her visual selections and written reflections. She asserted that "no system has been observed in the compilation of these prints and comments; chiefly because it was not possible to procure colored prints that could be used serially." Clarifying her compilation's purpose, Wood wrote, "there are plenty of books of information; so this little volume is only one of suggestion. As such we offer it to the dear home friends with whom we so often long to share even our random thoughts." "I might call these stray thoughts—Drift-Wood—(but not a pun on my name)," Wood concluded. Her references to "we" suggest that Leache was still alive and traveling with Wood when this album of "stray thoughts" was composed. Wood also referred to how the women sent their albums to friends back at "home" in Norfolk. In all probability, these friends were other white women whom Leache and Wood knew through their involvement in the Leache-Wood Seminary. "Ever the teacher," according to Hofheimer, Wood "used the albums to bring the great museums of Europe to her former students in Norfolk."[90] Through this sharing of the

---

88. Zboray and Zboray, "Is It," 101.
89. Hofheimer, *Annie*, 127.
90. Hofheimer, *Annie*, 126.

commonplace albums, they took on a pedagogical dimension among privileged women in the South.

Wood had learned to create the commonplace albums by modeling her rhetorical practices after what she found "beautiful" in Leache's white femininity and writing. While Leache clearly played some role in Wood's compilation of the above album, intentional emulation is evident in the ways that Wood composed her books about their friendship by following the model of Leache's invention strategies. Wood articulated Leache's influence in *The Story of a Friendship* (1901), published after Leache's passing. In a chapter dated much like a diary entry, "December 12, 1901," Wood wrote, "our beautiful life together is ended. To-day, therefore, I begin . . . to keep journals and notes, as she kept them . . . that I may retain her rounding influence." In *Idyls and Impressions of Travel* (1904), Wood further described how she invented her published books after the model of Leache's journals. Constructing the exigency for writing not one but two books about her life with Leache, Wood claimed, "I have acquired other writings of hers—notes upon travel, always sagacious."[91] From this writing, Wood selected what was beautiful. She "culled these notes from many sources, letters as well as journals . . . adding comments of my own."[92] Working with Leache's writing, Wood created a commonplace book of sorts. Wood's invention of this published book emulated what she considered to be Leache's "power to draw beauty out of the commonplace."[93] Again, this invention practice subscribed to white, Western notions of the beautiful and best. It also consisted, quite literally, of drawing from the texts of white femininity—of cultural sameness rather than difference—in order to rhetorically reproduce still more of the same. Inspired by the conservative erotic of emulation that marked the women's opulent friendship, Wood learned the invention strategies that constituted the rhetorical power of Leache's white femininity in order to write the story of their "beautiful life together."[94]

To be clear, my point is not merely that Wood selected, compiled, and reflected on Leache's letters and journals as a fellow white woman from the South. More significantly, in doing so, Wood was emulating the commonplace rhetorics that Leache herself used, including within her published work. Pointing to Leache's coauthored book *Answers of the Ages* (1900), Wood observed that the book "is made up of definitions of God, Soul, Religion. The quotations

---

91. Wood, *Idyls,* vii, HT.
92. Wood, *Idyls,* viii, HT.
93. Wood, *Story,* 311, NPL.
94. Wood, *Story,* 307, NPL.

are from spiritual teachers and thinkers of all countries and times."[95] Leache and her coauthor developed the book, in other words, by selecting and compiling from the writing of other teachers and thinkers. While Leache did not live to publish other books, Wood also emulated the commonplace rhetorics used by Leache within unpublished notebooks. Explaining Leache's journal writing, Wood wrote, "Miss Leache took her journals seriously, inasmuch as she had different ones for different uses, and she was faithful to this method of 'keeping a grasp on things' for over thirty-five years."[96] "The most interesting, perhaps, of these little volumes," Wood noted, "is one which she playfully called her 'Golden Book,' into which she entered whatever had been sifted down, or pronounced choice."[97] Wood characterized this "Golden Book" as consistent with the Western commonplace book tradition: Leache used it to select and compile what she "pronounced choice" from among those sources she encountered.

Wood modeled her commonplace rhetorics after Leache's not only within the already discussed memoirs of the women's friendship, which compiled selections from letters and journals, but also in publications that selected from the work of other authors for pedagogical and "psychological" purposes.[98] The title for *Drama Sketches for Parlor Acting or Recitation* (1925) suggests education through elocution training and parlor rhetorics, and Wood's forward also states that a portion of the book "was written for a study class."[99] The collection of sketches was compiled mainly from Western literature and history, including the "dramatic paraphrase" of the already mentioned "Romance of Gilgamish" [sic].[100] Another of Wood's books, *The Psychology of Crime, Illustrated by Several Modern Poets* (n.d.), consists of "a collection of poetical fragments, from a few celebrated authors, modified in several instances to suit the subject."[101] Wood stated in the forward to this book, and reaffirmed via didactic commentary inserted throughout, that "the purpose in these gathered fragments is not literary but psychological."[102] With this purpose in mind, she invented the book as follows: "the sentiment of their [the collected authors'] work has been in nowise altered, tho' condensation has been freely used

---

95. Wood, *Story*, 283, NPL; and Leache and Willcox, *Answers*, JOCL.
96. Wood, *Idyls*, vii–viii, HT.
97. Wood, *Idyls*, vii–viii, HT.
98. Wood, *Psychology*, 5, JOCL.
99. Wood, *Drama*, 3, JOCL. For discussion of women's elocution training and parlor rhetorics, see Buchanan, *Regendering*; Donawerth, *Conversational Rhetoric*; Gold and Hobbs, *Rhetoric*; and N. Johnson, *Gender*.
100. Wood, *Drama*, 7, JOCL.
101. Wood, *Psychology*, 1, JOCL.
102. Wood, *Psychology*, 5, JOCL.

where it has been deemed necessary to focus attention upon a given point." In developing both books, Wood deployed commonplace rhetorics for selecting and compiling from the work of other Western authors in service of her own invention and purposes.

The rhetorical practices involved in compiling commonplace books were alive and well among women in the long nineteenth century. Yet in the case of Leache and Wood, Wood developed her commonplace rhetorics by modeling them after Leache's practices in keeping with the specifically conservative erotic of emulation that characterized their opulent friendship as white women. Whether in Wood's actual commonplace books or her published works, she emulated Leache's rhetorical practice of selecting what is beautiful, best, or "choice" and then compiling those selections, "prefer[ing] to gather them just as they are and to present them to a sympathetic reader."[103] In Wood's commonplace albums, she selected visual images from art and culture encountered during her travels, compiling those images alongside her written reflections. In her published books, in turn, she "culled . . . notes from many sources, letters as well as journals, and to give continuity have woven them into a whole by adding comments of my own."[104]

Even where these selections were most varied, it was the "beauty" of white, Western culture, including white femininity, that the women treated as the "best." Admiring Leache as she had from their first pedagogical introductions—from the eroticized garden encounter at Angerona on the grounds of settler colonialism and slavery, to the rhetorical prowess of tricking soldiers in order to support the Confederacy—Wood followed the example of what she observed in Leache's rhetorical practices as a white woman. In doing so, Wood developed commonplace rhetorics through which both her commonplace albums and her published books were made possible by a conservative erotic of emulating white, Western notions of beauty, modeled as they were after Leache's own "power to draw beauty out of the commonplace."[105]

## Beautiful Writing and Belletristic Rhetorical Instruction

The same conservative erotic of emulating beauty that drove Wood's development of commonplace rhetorics also framed both women's teaching of rhetoric to white girls at the Leache-Wood Seminary. Extent records from the school are limited, as is common within histories of women's rhetoric and rhetorical

---

103. Wood, *Idyls*, viii, JOCL.
104. Wood, *Idyls*, viii, JOCL.
105. Wood, *Story*, 311, NPL.

education. In comparison with the relatively long-standing elite schools and colleges for young white men, nineteenth-century boarding schools for girls less often possessed the means to preserve their own archives. Fortunately, however, the special collections consulted for this chapter do contain a selection of Leache-Wood Seminary records, including school catalogs from 1880 and 1894. In order to understand how the erotic of Leache and Wood's opulent friendship enabled their teaching, I read the school catalogs alongside later efforts to memorialize the women and their pedagogical contributions. These memorializing efforts include the work of the Irene Leache Memorial, which Wood founded after Leache's passing in 1900, and the Leache-Wood Alumnae Association, through which former students continued to write and speak about the Leache-Wood Seminary even after Wood's own passing in 1940.[106] In addition to Wood's memoirs, the memorial writings from which I draw are "An Appreciation: Annie Cogswell Wood; Idealist, Steadfast in Friendship, Unswerving in Purpose, Obedient to Her Vision" (1940), Virginia Lyne Tunstall's "The Story of Two Remarkable Women and Their Living Memorial: A Short History of the Irene Leache Memorial" (1962), and Elizabeth C. Engle's "A Valley Seed Grows in Tidewater" (1991).

Taken together, these school records and memorial writings paint a clear picture of how Leache and Wood's opulent friendship was fueled by an erotic that enabled their teaching of rhetoric at the Leache-Wood Seminary. Energized by the conservative erotic of emulation within the women's initial pedagogical encounters and commonplace rhetorics, Leache and Wood taught their students to also draw out what was beautiful or best in keeping with the dominant values of white, Western culture. This teaching was carried out through belletristic rhetorical education as well as the example of Leache and Wood themselves as models of white femininity to emulate.

Typical to the period, rhetorical education at the Leache-Wood Seminary was what Nan Johnson terms "synthetic."[107] According to Johnson, nineteenth-century rhetoric was synthetic in that it combined the influences of competing rhetorical theories, including "classical assumptions" as well as "premises initially popularized in the late eighteenth-century English tradition."[108] In terms of a classical influence, primary materials document that Leache and Wood engaged with the thinking of many figures from the history of Western rhetoric: Sappho, Helen, Plato, Socrates, Aristotle, and Cicero (as well as St. Augustine). Against the backdrop of these classical influences, Leache's and Wood's synthetic instruction in rhetoric and writing was simultaneously

---

106. Hofheimer, *Annie*, 97. See also Hine, Oral history interview, May 14, 1982, AAA.
107. N. Johnson, *Nineteenth-Century Rhetoric*, 45.
108. N. Johnson, *Nineteenth-Century Rhetoric*, 19.

and distinctly belletristic. For example, the 1880 school catalog explained that "pupils of the Junior and Senior classes are thoroughly trained" in "Composition," "Ancient and Modern Languages," and "Belles-Lettres."[109] Similarly, the 1894 catalog characterized the "Classical and Academic Course" as covering "Modern Languages" and "Belles-lettres."[110] While these catalogs are straightforward in listing courses in belles-lettres, what I want to emphasize is how Leache and Wood enacted their rhetorical power through belletristic rhetorical education that encouraged the forms of emulating white femininity that also characterized their opulent friendship and commonplace rhetorics.

Belletristic rhetorical education emerged largely through the influence of eighteenth-century Scottish rhetorician Hugh Blair.[111] This form of instruction brought together rhetoric and poetics, emphasizing the study and emulation of literary models in order to develop "taste."[112] In the nineteenth-century US, according to Johnson, Blair's belletristic influence helped solidify the importance of imitation through "a recovery of the classical doctrine of *imitatio.*"[113] "Proper models," according to Blair's rhetorical theory, would "illustrate not only tasteful rhetorical effects but also the admirable ideas and elevated sentiments that the would-be writer or speaker should aspire to express."[114] Considering the various "pleasures of taste" in *Lectures on Rhetoric and Belles Lettres* (1783), Blair discussed "beauty" in his lecture by the same name. Blair emphasized that beauty applies not only to "every external object that pleases the eye" but "to a great number of the graces of writing," whether in the form of "an epic poem" or "an oration."[115] The influence of Blair's rhetorical theory is most evident at the Leache-Wood Seminary through instruction in rhetoric that involved the imitation of white, Western beauty that was modeled within literary works.

Similar to Blair's lectures, Leache's and Wood's instruction in belles lettres encouraged boarding school students to emulate beauty in writing. While school catalogs do not specify particular texts used in the courses on belles lettres, references to Western literary figures appear throughout materials

---

109. Leache-Wood Seminary, "Leache-Wood School," 1880, 7, NPL.
110. Leache-Wood Seminary. "Leache-Wood School," 1894, 8, NPL.
111. For other accounts of Blair and belletristic rhetorical education, including his influence on women's education in the US into the long nineteenth century, see Agnew, "Civic Function"; Bacon and McClish, "Reinventing"; Berlin, *Writing*; Golden and Corbett, *Rhetoric*; N. Johnson, *Gender*; Valdes, "Speaking"; Schaik, "How Belletristic"; Warnick, *Sixth Canon*; and Woods, *Debating*.
112. N. Johnson, *Nineteenth-Century Rhetoric*, 31–46.
113. N. Johnson, *Nineteenth-Century Rhetoric*, 82.
114. N. Johnson, *Nineteenth-Century Rhetoric*, 37.
115. Blair, *Lectures*, 57, 58, 64.

memorializing the school and its influence on alumnae. Referenced authors range from Virgil and Homer to Ralph Waldo Emerson and Robert Browning. Even in the memorial materials quoting Cicero at greatest length, the focus is on both oratory and poetry as would be the case within a belletristic approach. The inscription appearing on diplomas from the Leache-Wood Seminary was a translation of Cicero's *Pro Archia Poeta*, an oration in defense of the poet. As the memorial emphasized, "this inscription refers, of course, to the pursuit of knowledge and the love of literature."[116] At the Leache-Wood Seminary, cultivating rhetorical abilities involved sharing a passion for and emulating the beautiful writing of Western literature.

Leache's and Wood's pedagogical cultivation of beauty linked culturally specific notions of the beautiful to those of "the best," with a goal of modeling and then drawing out the most beautiful and best in students. Wood spells out this connection between the "beautiful" and the "best" at Leache-Wood Seminary in her two memoirs about the women's opulent friendship. As previously discussed, *The Story of a Friendship* (1901) characterizes Leache's beauty in terms of her "*power to draw beauty* out of the commonplace, and to make others do it . . . demanding of them *their best*."[117] Wood repeated this characterization of Leache's beauty in *Idyls and Impressions of Travel* (1904). Here Wood used commonplace rhetorics in order to select, compile, and reflect on "at least twenty letters" that documented Leache's influence on former students.[118] All of these letters, Wood claimed, contained statements to this effect. One student asserted that "the *best* that there is in my life today I trace back to Miss Leache."[119] Another student wrote, "I always felt when I was with Miss Leache as if she were quietly *drawing something from me* that I did not know was there, my *best self*, and when I left her it was with a feeling of encouragement to *do better* than I had ever done before."[120] "To dwell upon this feeling still more emphatically," the student continued, "I should say that *she drew mine, my very best*, from me, and for that *power to do this with almost everybody* I have never seen her equal."[121]

Recognizing the rhetorical dimensions of commonplace traditions, it is important to acknowledge that it was Wood who crafted this collection of quotations from student letters in order to serve her own purposes. Wood compiled the selections to help communicate to readers how she understood,

---

116. Tunstall, "Story," 12, JOCL.
117. Wood, *Story*, 311, emphasis added, NPL.
118. Wood, *Idyls*, ix, HT.
119. Wood, *Idyls*, ix, emphasis added, HT.
120. Wood, *Idyls*, ix, emphasis added, HT.
121. Wood, *Idyls*, ix, emphasis added, HT.

and wanted others to understand, Leache's pedagogical and cultural contributions. For Wood, Leache was beautiful because of her power to draw out the beautiful and to guide others, especially students who were also white women, to do the same. Particularly in Leache and Wood's own early pedagogical encounters, as the women developed their opulent friendship, Leache demanded of Wood her best. Then, when they became colleagues at the Leache-Wood Seminary, the conservative erotic of emulation in their opulent friendship functioned as a rhetorical power that inspired them to model white femininity and draw out what they considered to be the best in their students. Leache and Wood did so partly through rhetorical instruction that, in the tradition of Blair and other belletrists, emphasized the study of beautiful writing and treated Western literary works as the superior rhetorical models to emulate.

Alongside belletristic rhetorical education at the school, the Leache-Wood Seminary's impact on students was shaped by how Leache and Wood presented themselves as models of white womanhood. The intention to serve as models is clear in school catalogs. The 1894 catalog promised that the Leache-Wood Seminary would "offer every advantage for gentle culture and thorough training, under the direct personal influence of the Principals themselves."[122] The catalog followed this pedagogical promise about the "direct personal influence" of the school's principals as models for emulation with a signature line: "Misses Leache & Wood."[123] Leache and Wood's encouragement of modeling and emulation throughout the school is also apparent in the earlier 1880 catalog. "Under the supervision of the same teachers," the catalog explained, there was "an honorable spirit of emulation excited among the scholars."[124] Leache and Wood excited a spirit of emulation such that those white students who emulated their white teachers became scholars who emulated one another's white femininity.

Leache and Wood continued to be remembered as pedagogical models long after their retirement from the Leache-Wood Seminary in 1891. Another letter from a former student, according to Wood (1904), began with the words of Thomas á Kempis, author of *The Imitation of Christ*: "who can go unto the fountain of sweetness; or who, standing by a great fire does not feel some of the heat thereof?" "So it seems to me," the student reflected, "that nobody could live near Miss Leache and not feel some of her great warmth. She had the gift of helping people in an almost perfected state. How she encouraged

---

122. Leache-Wood Seminary. "Leache-Wood School," 1894, 15–16, NPL.
123. Leache-Wood Seminary. "Leache-Wood School," 1894, 16, NPL.
124. Leache-Wood Seminary. "Leache-Wood School," 1880, 8, NPL.

them in doing *their best!*"¹²⁵ The student continued, "I have been thinking so much about her lately and have taken out all the old composition books which she had corrected. . . . I have placed her as my ideal."¹²⁶ Wood's quotation and publication of this former student's letter reminds that Leache's influence was marked by an opulent "sweetness" and "warmth," a conservative erotic of emulating beauty. Just as this erotic fueled Wood's attraction to Leache, it did the women's pedagogical work. For students like the one above, Leache did not simply correct their composition books. She became an "ideal" of white femininity to emulate, "encourag[ing] them in doing their best!"¹²⁷

Other primary materials are consistent with the student letters that Wood compiled through her commonplace rhetorics. A 1910 yearbook recalled both women as models, describing Wood's "attractive personality" and Leache's "indescribable magnetism."¹²⁸ The yearbook declared that "their good opinion soon became the highest honor to which any pupil aspired, and their old girls like, to this day, to talk of their friendship and quote them as an authority."¹²⁹ Along similar lines, a 1962 memorial publication proclaimed, "it is the universal testimony of all who knew her, that Miss Leache was a wonderful teacher,—a wonderful teacher of so many different subjects that it might almost be said of her, as it was of [poet Oliver] Goldsmith, that 'she touched nothing that she did not adorn.'" As teachers and school administrators, Leache and Wood worked together to touch the lives of their white students. Just as Leache and Wood taught Western models of beautiful writing and belletristic rhetoric, they adorned even the commonplace through their own rhetorical practices and prompted Leache-Wood Seminary students to emulate their white femininity by doing the same.

Fully understanding the significance of these pedagogical contributions requires attention to the women's local context. Memorial materials characterized Leache and Wood as "the best" partly because of how they helped to open the Leache-Wood Seminary in response to the lack of education available to even the most privileged girls in Norfolk.¹³⁰ As Engle wrote (1991), "the excellent Norfolk Academy, long established for boys, had no counterpart for girls. In what was then a small, provincial, unsophisticated town whose main interests were ships, sailors, and seafood, the education of girls

---

125. Wood, *Idyls*, ix–x, emphasis added, HT.
126. Wood, *Idyls*, ix–x, HT.
127. Wood, *Idyls*, x, HT.
128. Leache-Wood Seminary, *Nods*, JOCL.
129. Leache-Wood Seminary, *Nods*, JOCL.
130. Tunstall, "Story," 1, JOCL.

had been neglected."[131] "Here was a challenge for the best," according to Tunstall's memorial (1962), "and here fate provided it—two people who were bold, energetic and imaginative enough to rise magnificently to this opportunity." While remembered as "the best," the two women who helped found the Leache-Wood Seminary had almost no pedagogical training. Their teaching was "more remarkable," Tunstall urged, "because [Leache] must have been literally self-educated."[132] Though Leache had taught previously at other schools, she was, according to Wood (1901), "without paraphernalia, without college or normal training, innocent of the science of pedagogy, with few friends, with no assistant but an inexperienced girl."[133] Leache and the "inexperienced girl," spurred on by the conservative erotic of their opulent friendship, sought out additional pedagogical training. "Some summers," according to Engle, Leache and Wood "studied in New England at the Concord Massachusetts School of Philosophy under such tutors as Ralph Waldo Emerson or the Alcott sisters."[134] Leache and Wood shared "deeply" their "pursuit" of desires for opulence, intellectual life, and white women's education.[135] The conservative erotic of emulating beauty in their opulent friendship made possible their teaching of belletristic rhetoric for Southern white girls who otherwise would not have had access to academic training.

As this analysis has detailed, Leache and Wood's friendship was a marrying of minds, overflowing with a passionate admiration and intellectual stimulation that functioned as a conservative erotic of rhetorical power animating all of their professional lives. Bringing together their family names, Leache and Wood's "marriage" produced the Leache-Wood Seminary. Here the women taught belletristic rhetoric and became models of white femininity themselves, encouraging their students to emulate what they considered to be the beautiful and the best in Western culture. Of course, this belletristic rhetorical education and its emphasis on appreciation and emulation was not uncommon in the long nineteenth century. Nor was the emulation of teachers by students, particularly within the same-sex educational environments of boarding schools (and women's colleges).[136] Yet Leache and Wood's pedagogy of belletristic emulation needs to be understood not only within the context of women's rhetorical education during the period but also in relation to Leache and Wood's opulent friendship. The women's teaching was both informed by

---

131. Engle, "Valley Seed," 4, WFHS.
132. Tunstall, "Story," 3, JOCL.
133. Wood, *Story*, 74, NPL.
134. Engle, "Valley Seed," 8, WFHS. See also Hofheimer, *Annie*, 66.
135. Lorde, "Uses of the Erotic," 56.
136. Gold and Hobbs, *Educating*, 43.

the conservative erotic of emulation within their same-sex opulent friendship and reinforced by their larger emphasis on drawing out the most beautiful—the best according to the values of Western culture—in their students. As such, Leache and Wood's legacy continued long after they had retired from their formal positions as teachers and school administrators. As claimed in a memorial booklet (1940) published after Wood's passing, the Leache-Wood Seminary "imbued a generation of Norfolk girls with a love of the fine arts that soon found an organized expression which, surviving to this day, has brought to flower a manifold garden of the arts in which was formerly, in this respect, a desert of unredeemed sterility."[137] While Leache and Wood lived out their lives together, rather than marrying and having biological children, their work as teachers and writers involved another sort of cultural reproduction through pedagogies of emulation across generations of white women in the South.

## Reproducing the Race and Nation through White Femininity

As the conservative erotic of Leache and Wood's opulent friendship animated their rhetorical instruction and practice on behalf of some girls in the South, it pedagogically reproduced a normative white femininity. The Leache-Wood Seminary was like most boarding schools for girls during the period in that it enrolled white girls and, among them, it "catered to the economically advantaged."[138] I do not mean simply that Leache and Wood were privileged women who labored only on behalf of young women like themselves (though they did). Rather, as already discussed, the conservative conception of beauty that Leache and Wood celebrated and emulated was grounded specifically in the whiteness of Western culture and settler colonialism. Nor was this a function of mere cultural proximity or a neutral familiarity. Instead, Wood's commonplace books and published writing show that she and Leache actively sought to "respond to human differences" in ways that maintained the status quo of social hierarchies and national distinctions.[139] Wood expressed opposition to reform movements and insisted that "civilization" depended on people staying in their place with respect to race, ethnicity, gender, class, and ability. Addressing settler white women in particular, the emphasis was on a

---

137. "Appreciation," 11, JOCL.
138. Hofheimer, *Annie*, 55.
139. Lorde, "Age, Race, Class," 115.

normative femininity that, in keeping with the ideology of eugenics, saw their role as preserving "the race" and "the nation."[140]

It is important to note, Leache and Wood admired white, Western notions of beauty not simply out of naive ignorance. These were not sheltered women, exposed only to white Southern culture. They traveled more than was typical for women—across not only Europe but also the Middle East and North Africa—with the purported intention of learning about people and art from non-Western cultures. Hofheimer details the women's travels, which began in the form of summer trips even before their nine-year retirement abroad.[141] "As late as 1890, it was noteworthy when a woman ventured to Europe" and "extraordinarily rare to go to . . . places, like Morocco and Turkey, as Leache and Wood did."[142] Leache and Wood's travels were connected to their pedagogical work, in that they saw travel as an opportunity to learn. Yet Leache and Wood's access to travel opportunities abroad was a function of colonialism and, more importantly, the women themselves upheld colonial notions of "learning" about and "knowing" other cultures.

Wood asserted in *The Story of a Friendship* (1901) that she and Leache "were deeply interested in the study of races."[143] "It is in comparing sections, peoples, races, one with another," Wood wrote, "that we come to understand our own section, our own people and ourselves."[144] Later in Wood's life, in one of her albums, she similarly claimed, "the best form of mental gymnastics . . . is the power to precipitate yourself from your own century into another; or, from the midst of your own people into the environment of an alien race." Of Leache, Wood declared (1901), "She revered the traditions of her native State, yet held through life an attitude of inquiry toward those subtler schools of thought which are the products of other lands and eras."[145] While perhaps notable for white women of their time, this "attitude of inquiry" was undermined by Leache and Wood's investments in a colonial logic of studying so-called "alien races." Such pursuits of "knowledge," as Anne McClintock explains, were less about "the expanded recognition of cultural difference" and more about "exploration . . . reassembled and deployed in the interests of . . . imperial power."[146] Within this logic, the women's so-called study, along with

---

140. Wood, *Great Opportunity*, 10, JOCL.
141. Hofheimer, *Annie*, 73.
142. Hofheimer, *Annie*, 73. Also see Engle, "Valley Seed," 9, WFHS.
143. Wood, *Story*, 80–81, NPL.
144. Wood, *Story*, 83, NPL.
145. Wood, *Story*, 84, NPL.
146. McClintock, *Imperial Leather*, 23.

their recording of it, ultimately functioned to uphold the existing status quo with respect to social hierarchies and national distinctions.¹⁴⁷

On the one hand, what Leache and Wood learned from their inquiries through travel made it into their published writing as well as the albums they sent back to former students and friends while traveling, thus modeling the practice of valuing at least some insights from cultures other than their own. As Hofheimer notes, Leache and Willcox's *Answers of the Ages* (1900) addressed its selection of spiritual and philosophical quotations to readers who were "'yearning to enlarge the boundaries of faith.'"¹⁴⁸ Crossing cultural boundaries, the "selections explore wide varieties of faith indeed, quoting most often from Swedenborg, Plato, Maeterlinck, the Kabbala, Porphyry, Récéjàc, the Upanishads, Schurré, the Bhagavad-Gita, Pythagorus [sic], Hermes Trismegistus, Pistis Sophia, and Kant."¹⁴⁹ "Yet the book could as easily have been compiled by Wood," Hofheimer explains, because in concert with Wood's already discussed emulation of Leache's commonplace rhetorics, "these same sources emerge again and again throughout her life in her own writing."¹⁵⁰ Still oriented primarily though not entirely to the whiteness of Western culture, Wood "was interested in and familiar with European theologians, neoplatonists, Hindu writings, Gnostic teachings, Belgian poets, and occult Hermetic writings from ancient Egypt."¹⁵¹ These sources reflect a well-read and well-traveled engagement with cultural and spiritual diversity, at least relative to what was typical for white women of the period.

On the other hand, even as Leache and Wood engaged with cultures other than their own, they believed that cultural distinctions and roles should be preserved for the sake of colonial and settler-colonial "civilization."¹⁵² In Wood's albums, she frequently criticized notions of social and intellectual equality, insisting that "every human being should be aware of his obligation to his sex, his race, his social standing." Asserting the necessity of class and race distinctions, Wood rehearsed ideas from the pseudoscience of phrenology, which was used to justify an ideology of European superiority.¹⁵³ "Some leisure class is necessary for the production of certain valuable, tho' invisible things," Wood asserted, "and leisure may often be as productive as labor." Echoing the rhetoric of phrenology, she claimed that "in proportion as a race

---

147. On this "imperial genre" of recording, see McClintock, *Imperial Leather*, 81.
148. Leache and Willcox, *Answers*, JOCL, quoted in Hofheimer, *Annie*, 77.
149. Hofheimer, *Annie*, 77.
150. Hofheimer, *Annie*, 77.
151. Hofheimer, *Annie*, 78.
152. Wood, [untitled album, n.d.], JOCL.
153. On imperialism and "scientific" racism, see McClintock, *Imperial Leather*.

becomes civilized, the skull tends to become more and more differentiated, hence civilization does not move towards intellectual equality but towards intellectual inequality. Anatomical and phrenological equality are only to be found in inferior races."[154] In passages like this one, Wood justified social inequality on grounds that were blatantly racist.

Not surprisingly, given this obvious desire to defend existing hierarchies, the women were opposed to most Progressive Era reform movements, educational and otherwise. Leache was remembered by one memorial publication as "an ardent Confederate" who "never permitted any discussion of the Civil War" at the school.[155] When founding the Irene Leache Memorial, Wood insisted that it "keep the intellectual and artistic activities . . . at the highest possible level, never popularizing them to suit the majority or an industrial element, the object of this Memorial being not reform but culture."[156] This goal for the group was consistent with an anti-reform rhetoric that appears throughout Wood's commonplace albums. These albums also criticized democratized mass education and democracy itself. Later in life, Wood even appeared to support Benito Mussolini and Italian fascism.[157]

On the surface, Wood and Leache's resistance to social reforms in the name of equality and democracy might seem at odds with their commitment to expanding educational opportunities for girls in the South. Yet, like many politically conservative white women, they sought to educate other white women as part of supporting, rather than undermining, hierarchies grounded in settler colonialism and slavery. Wood in particular decried the "fallacy" of "sex equality," feminism, the New Woman, and the "'progressive woman'" (which warranted scare quotes for Wood because "the so-called progressives are often regressives").[158] Wood's opposition to feminist reforms was inseparable from her racist thinking. In *The Great Opportunity and Other Essays* (1926), a book that made public many of the perspectives she explored in her commonplace albums, Wood's reflections about "the problem of sex" urged readers "to discharge one's obligation to oneself as well as to the race, for these two obligations are really *one*, either sex must discover its own directive purpose and then specialize in carrying it out."[159] "No less than sex," Wood urged, "races have each one its special directive purpose and this has formed

---

154. Wood, [untitled album, n.d.], JOCL.
155. Tunstall, "Story," 2, JOCL. Another source suggests that Leache more generally "did not allow it [the War] to be spoken of in her presence." See Engle, "Valley Seed," 3, WFHS.
156. Quoted in Hofheimer, *Annie*, 94.
157. Engle, "Valley Seed," 12, WFHS; and Hofheimer, *Annie*, 33.
158. Wood, *Great Opportunity,* 54, 57, JOCL.
159. Wood, *Great Opportunity,* 10, JOCL.

the contour of the racial soul. When this purpose is perverted by contact with too many alien people and surrender to them, the race soul is wrecked and the nation disintegrates."[160] Discussing next the "fall of the Roman Empire," Wood's thinking here and elsewhere drew on perspectives complicit with the eugenics movement of her time, which was on the rise in the settler-colonial nation of the US during the early twentieth century.

The eugenics movement drew on pseudoscience to advance the racist and ableist idea that the "human race" could be improved through a combination of exclusionary immigration and selective reproduction in order to eliminate those deemed "defective" or "deviant."[161] As Jay Timothy Dolmage asserts, "eugenics itself is always about sex."[162] Eugenics is about sex, most obviously, in that proponents of eugenics considered the biological reproduction of normative whiteness to be a crucial strategy for what eugenicist Charles Davenport (1911) characterized as "'the science of the improvement of the human race by better breeding.'"[163] Under the umbrella of this strategy, eugenicists are perhaps best known for advocating prohibitions against interracial relationships, (consensual) sex, and kinship, as well as discouraging reproduction and even supporting the forced sterilizations of women of color, low-income women, and disabled people.

Also under the umbrella, though, was an emphasis on reproducing norms for colonial sex, gender, and sexuality while excluding those whose sex, gender, or sexuality was deemed deviant. Eugenics discourse was enacted at Ellis Island, for instance, where people entering the settler-colonial US were inspected, both visually and discursively, to identify so-called defects and deviances.[164] These deviances included nonnormative sex and gender, as Dolmage discusses with respect to the examples of Frank Woodhull, from the occupied territories that are now Canada, and Donabet Mousekian, an Armenian Turk.[165] Moreover, the inspections included "questions about sexual preferences and histories," with the 1917 Immigration Act designating "'abnormal sex instincts' as a 'constitutional psychopathic inferiority.'"[166] In the words of Jennifer Terry, "eugenic doctrine of the first half of the 20th century placed

---

160. Wood, *Great Opportunity*, 10, JOCL.
161. Dolmage, *Disabled*, 12, 24. My characterization of the eugenics movement is informed by Dolmage's research. Here "human race," "defective," and "deviant" are in scare quotes, though this language can be found throughout eugenics discourse and scholarship about it.
162. Dolmage, *Disabled*, 99.
163. Dolmage, *Disabled*, 12.
164. Dolmage, *Disabled*, 101.
165. Dolmage, *Disabled*, 100–101. For further discussion of Woodhull and Mousekian, respectively, see Erica Rand, *Ellis Island*; and Nielson, *Disability*.
166. Dolmage, *Disabled*, 11 n. 3, 101. See also Luibhéid, *Entry*.

both racial and sexual purity at the top of its agenda.... White phobia about miscegenation ... paralleled a growing sex panic that inverts and perverts were everywhere."[167]

Echoing this emphasis on "both racial and sexual purity" within the eugenics movement, Wood saw an important role for normative femininity in the preservation of "civilization" and "the race."[168] She was disturbed by the relaxing of Victorian gender roles, writing in one of her commonplace books that she agreed with "a learned man" who claimed, "the man-woman always suggests to me Nature's great misfit and racial cripple, the Hermaphrodite." In *The Great Opportunity*, she lamented "an ever increasing number of individuals who belong to one sex physically but to an opposite sex psychically."[169] "These people are inverts," Wood wrote, "and while they may be both clever and efficient, yet, so far as the race is concerned, they are but sterile factors in its evolution." Because "if a man and a woman are fragments of two sexes instead of the completed whole of one," Wood claimed, "their gain to the race is also fractional and they end by jarring upon all the finer ideals of civilization."[170] Here Wood linked a normative femininity to rhetorics of race, disability, and sex that were propagated by the eugenics movement as well as sexology. By the early twentieth century, mainstream leaders perpetuated alarmist rhetorics about white women with class privilege who, in delaying marriage to become educated and then giving birth to fewer children, contributed to a "race suicide."[171]

Wood's criticism of "inverts" who were "sterile" with respect to "the race" may seem inconsistent with her own same-sex partnership with Leache, because of course they did not "marry the right men," in Lorde's words.[172] In McClintock's, they were "'nonproductive' women," meaning they did not preserve "the nation" or "the race" through the biological reproduction of settler white family.[173] They did so, however, by performing and teaching a normative white femininity. They developed a same-sex romantic partnership while simultaneously distancing themselves from many other people whose relationships were pathologized and subjected to violence in the name of eugenics and sexology. In other words, Leache and Wood used their privilege to

---

167. Terry, "Anxious," 138, quoted in Dolmage, *Disabled*, 11 n. 3, 101. For further discussion of linkages between normative race, sexuality, and purity, see Carter, *Heart*; McClintock, *Imperial Leather*; and Somerville, *Queering*.
168. Terry, "Anxious," 138; and Wood, *Great Opportunity*, 10, JOCL.
169. Wood, *Great Opportunity*, 57, JOCL.
170. Wood, *Great Opportunity*, 57, JOCL.
171. Franzen, *Spinsters*, 5.
172. Lorde, "Age, Race, Class," 119; and Wood, *Great Opportunity*, 10, JOCL.
173. McClintock, *Imperial Leather*, 47.

pedagogically reproduce the white "race" and its settler-colonial "civilization" in the South. Through their formal teaching of belletristic rhetoric and "beautiful" writing at the Leache-Wood Seminary, as well as their continued development of commonplace rhetorics that circulated their ideas through albums and published books, the women advanced a pedagogical reproduction of privilege through the emulation of white femininity.

## Conclusion

With the conservative erotic of their relationship made possible on the grounds of slavery and settler colonialism in the South, Leache and Wood rhetorically and pedagogically reproduced a normative version of femininity in support of the (white) "race" and (settler-colonial) "nation." Leache and Wood were not unique as privileged women whose rhetorical and pedagogical activities perpetuated social hierarchies, especially those of elitism, classism, racism, and ableism, in order to benefit similarly privileged girls while excluding most. That such a problematic is characteristic of available archives makes it no less noteworthy and, in fact, shows the importance of queer feminist erotohistoriography that desires to investigate not only the civic contributions but also the problematic implications of white women whose romantic friendships helped to enable their rhetorical practices and pedagogies. Moreover, and as Leache and Wood's case especially underscores, the erotic as rhetorical power within same-sex relationships between women needs to be recognized as a force with the potential to work toward divergent social and political ends. These ends include those that "entrench differences" according to systemic forms of oppression like white supremacist ideology.[174]

The erotic of emulating "beauty" that defined Leache and Wood's opulent friendship did serve as a "source of power," albeit a conservative one, in that it fueled their rhetorical practices and pedagogies.[175] From Leache and Wood's first eroticized pedagogical encounter in Angerona's garden, this friendship was marked by passionately shared desires for intellectual life and opulent "beauty" as understood with respect to white femininity and Western culture. As a student, Wood admired the beauty and power of Leache's intellectual and rhetorical prowess as a white woman. This erotic of emulation motivated Wood as she learned from and modeled herself after Leache in a version of the homoerotic recognized across Western rhetorical theory and history.

---

174. Gill, "In the Realm," 188.
175. Lorde, "Uses of the Erotic," 53.

Specifically, Wood emulated Leache's commonplace rhetorics for selecting what was the "best" and most "beautiful" in order to compile commonplace albums. Wood also used similar commonplace rhetorics to compose her published books. Whereas Leache was able to publish just one book before her death, Wood followed the model of Leache's rhetorical practices in publishing seven books—certainly a rhetorical achievement even for the most privileged women of her time. The conservative erotic of emulating white, Western beauty in Leache and Wood's opulent friendship also took shape through the development of their professional careers as teaching colleagues who lived and worked together at a boarding school for white girls in the South. At the Leache-Wood Seminary, they taught a form of belletristic rhetoric that encouraged students to model themselves and their rhetoric after what was traditionally "beautiful" in both literary writing and the example of Leache and Wood's own white femininity. Even after the women's retirement from teaching, they continued to address former students through commonplace albums compiled during their travels and sent back to Virginia. In these ways, Leache and Wood pedagogically reproduced through their work together at the Leache-Wood Seminary, shaping a future generation of privileged girls in Norfolk.

Leache and Wood shared their opulent friendship, which empowered their practices and teaching of rhetoric, for over three decades, until Leache's death in 1900. The conservative erotic of emulating "beauty" that fueled their lives and work together continued to shape Wood's writing and publications until her own passing four decades later. It was during this period that Wood emulated Leache's "power to draw beauty out of the commonplace" when composing and publishing multiple books.[176] Also during this period, Wood worked tirelessly to memorialize Leache's pedagogical and cultural contributions. As a testament to both women's rhetorical labors, former Leache-Wood Seminary students and teachers played a central role in this memorial work. As Engle describes (1991), Wood "organized the LeacheWood alumnae, asking them to spearhead a movement to establish the Irene Leache Memorial Library."[177] The movement was successful. Over time, they contributed to the founding of multiple educational and arts organizations, including the Norfolk Museum of Arts and Sciences—now the international Chrysler Museum, which holds the papers of the Irene Leache Memorial Collection.[178] As noted by Hofheimer, former president of the Memorial, Wood's primary "motivation was to per-

---

176. Wood, *Story*, 311, NPL.
177. Engle, "Valley Seed," 10, WFHS.
178. Engle, "Valley Seed," 11, 13, and WFHS; Hofheimer, *Annie*, 117. See also Norfolk Historical Society and Weinstein, "Norfolk."

petuate Irene Leache's name and memory."[179] When Wood passed away in 1940, she left an "estate estimated at about $70,000" to the Memorial.[180] At her funeral, Wood was celebrated for her "role as a teacher, writer, and civic leader."[181] With both women buried in Norfolk's Elmwood Cemetery, Wood's gravestone remembered her as "co-founder of the Leache-Wood Seminary and the founder of the Irene Leache Memorial."[182] The gravestone's inscription reads, "their words do follow them."[183] A memorial from that time reminisced (1940), "it is beautiful to reflect that the two friends, so closely united in life, will always be as one in the hearts of the old pupils."[184]

Memorials to Leache and Wood have persisted well into the late twentieth and early twenty-first centuries. Today the Chrysler Museum's website includes a short page that remembers Leache and Wood's role in the formation of the school and, later, museum.[185] But this site and others like it make no mention of the women's same-sex romantic friendship; nor are their complicities with white supremacist eugenics acknowledged. Along similar lines, an extensively researched Norfolk Historical Society presentation characterizes Leache and Wood's relationship in terms of an "older sister, mentor/mentee, teacher/student dynamic," noting that Leache was Wood's "travel companion, her best friend, her roommate, her business partner."[186] While these memorials all ring true, as in consistent with the available archives, the importance of Leache and Wood's specifically romantic friendship has been underappreciated, just as the problematic dimensions of their work together have been downplayed. But it was the distinctively conservative erotic of their opulent friendship—their passionately shared desires for intellectual life as well as emulation of the white, Western forms of beauty they considered superior—that functioned as a source of rhetorical power for their pedagogical and cultural activities at the Leache-Wood Seminary and through their own writing.

---

179. Hofheimer, *Annie*, 107.
180. Hofheimer, *Annie*, 158.
181. Hofheimer, *Annie*, 157.
182. Hofheimer, *Annie*, 157–58.
183. Hofheimer, *Annie*, 158.
184. "Appreciation," 6, JOCL.
185. Chrysler Museum of Art, "Two."
186. Norfolk Historical Society and Weinstein, "Norfolk."

# INTERLUDE 2

# My Husband

> What a pleasure it would be... to address you *My Husband* and if so do you think for one moment you would be where you are with out me? No, never....
>
> You are rec what you soul have been been thursting for you never could get it here that is to be in a society of intelligence & interlectural people. I know that you injoy it I only wish that I was their to see you.
>
> —Addie Brown, in a letter to Rebecca Primus, November 16, 1865

Addie Brown's extant letters to Rebecca Primus ceased in 1868, when Brown married Joseph Tines, which was the same year that Irene Leache and Annie Wood met at Angerona. Brown was working at another boarding school for white girls, Miss Porter's School, located on the occupied lands of Tunxis and Wappinger nations in Farmington, Connecticut.[1] Unlike Leache or Primus (and later Wood), Brown labored on behalf of the school not as a teacher but as a domestic who assisted the school's cook.[2] So even as her labor helped make other young women's education possible, she was excluded from that educational opportunity herself. Just three years before, Brown had written to Primus at the Primus Institute about a *soul thursting* for the *society of intelligence & interlectural people*.[3] Brown seemed happy for Primus to have found such intellectual company, although it was her teaching that took Primus away from Brown. But Brown imagined *what a pleasure it would be to address* Primus as *My Husband* and *wish* that she *was their to see her* and *injoy* the intellectual life of teaching in service of racial uplift and justice. I again join Brown in her *wish*, imagining how life might have played out differently if she were able to join Primus in their shared passions, not only teaching formerly

---

1. Native Land Digital.
2. Beeching, *Hopes*, 149; and Griffin, *Beloved Sisters*, 157, 237.
3. Correspondence from Brown to Primus, November 16, 1865, PF/CHS. Also quoted in Griffin, *Beloved Sisters*, 87.

enslaved students at the Primus Institute but living together as a married couple.

It is 1868. In the three years since Primus left Hartford, the women have written countless letters of longing. As each day's classes come to a close, Primus races to the mail, eager to read Brown's most recent letter. On this particular day, she receives a letter that, not for the first time, recalls the women's last night together before her departure for Royal Oak.

Browns is *seting on* Primus's *lap with* her *head on* Primus's *bosom.* She sinks into Primus's *loving arms,* leaning forward to *imprint sweet kisses* on Primus's *bosom.*[4] Primus leans back, gently guiding Brown's head. Brown looks up, trying to search what she can still see of Primus's face.

"Can I do the *other things connected with it?*"[5]

Primus answers affirmatively, pulling Brown's head down further, now with more urgency.

Both women, each in her own way, experience *a very thrilling sensation pass through* them.[6]

In Brown's letter about that night, she rehearses most of her fond memories, but teases Primus that she *will not tell* her those *other things* in writing, at least not *at present.*[7] Indeed, the letters themselves are a poor substitute for the physical intimacies of that night and so many others. Wracked with desire and longing for each other, the women find that each *Affec letter is like pieces of meat to hungre wolf.*[8]

Within their letters, the women's expressions of desire and pleasure intermix with flirtatious attempts to provoke jealousy. Brown writes to Primus about the *three rooms* where she visits other domestic workers at the boarding school *every night.*[9] *All of the occupants visit* Brown *also.*[10] *Two of* the women are *English—one of them* Brown calls her *female lover.* She *wants to sleep with* Brown, who speculates that *perhaps* she *will give* her *consent some of these*

---

4. Correspondence from Brown to Primus, September 29, 1861, PF/CHS. Also quoted in Griffin, *Beloved Sisters,* 49.

5. Correspondence from Brown to Primus, October 2, 1861, PF/CHS. Also quoted in Griffin, *Beloved Sisters,* 49.

6. Correspondence from Brown to Primus, January 8, 1864, PF/CHS. Also quoted in Griffin, *Beloved Sisters,* 75.

7. Correspondence from Brown to Primus, October 2, 1861, PF/CHS. Also quoted in Griffin, *Beloved Sisters,* 49.

8. Correspondence from Brown to Primus, May 24, 1861, PF/CHS. Also quoted in Griffin, *Beloved Sisters,* 35.

9. Correspondence from Brown to Primus, October 20, 1867; Oct. 27, 1867, PF/CHS. Also quoted in Griffin, *Beloved Sisters,* 225–26.

10. Correspondence from Brown to Primus, October 20, 1867, PF/CHS. Also quoted in Griffin, *Beloved Sisters,* 225.

*nights*, though she can *assure* that she is *not very fond of White*. Still, within the month, Brown explains that it is her *bosom that captivated the girl and made her want to sleep with me.*[11] She promises Primus to *try to keep you favorite one always for you*, but then teases, *should in my excitement forget you will pardon me I know.* Later Brown toys with Primus further, claiming, *I thought I told you about the girl sleeping with me. Whether I enjoyed it or not I can't say that I enjoyed it very much. I don't know what kind of excitement I refer to but I presume I know at the time.*[12] While Brown is more provocative in her teasing, Primus also writes about sleeping with others. After Primus reports on one such encounter, Brown exclaims, *Well dear Sister since you have been gone you have slept with a fellow! Who would of thought of that.*[13] Though the women remain playful about these affairs throughout their period of separation, both desire most strongly to be with each other.

The opportunity finally arises after three years of increasing enrollments at the Primus Institute. In response to Primus's fourth request for an assistant teacher, and following her successful fundraising campaign to build a new schoolhouse, the Baltimore Association for the Moral and Educational Advancement of Colored People agrees to her request.[14] They agree, as well, to Primus's suggestion that a former star pupil, Brown, would make an ideal fit for the assistant teacher position. Some hesitation follows after the Baltimore Association contacts the Hartford Freedmen's Aid Society, which relays local rumors about the women's relationship. Hartford community members report that Brown *thought as much of* Primus as if she *was a gentleman* and that *if either one of* them *was a gent*, Brown and Primus *would marry.*[15] Hartford locals allege that Brown in particular does *queer thing every now and then.*[16] Still, the need for an assistant teacher in Royal Oak is pressing, and Brown is well positioned to meet the need.

*I will be at your demand entirely,* Brown promises Primus after agreeing to the teaching position, *nothing to call me home.*[17] Soon Brown is *under* Primus's

---

11. Correspondence from Brown to Primus, November 17, 1867, PF/CHS. Also quoted in Griffin, *Beloved Sisters*, 228.

12. Correspondence from Brown to Primus, December 8, 1867, PF/CHS. Also quoted in Griffin, *Beloved Sisters*, 229.

13. Correspondence from Brown to Primus, June 17, 1866, PF/CHS. Also quoted in Griffin, *Beloved Sisters*, 131.

14. On the Baltimore Association, see Beeching, *Hopes*, 110.

15. Correspondence from Brown to Primus, January 21, 1866, PF/CHS.

16. Correspondence from Brown to Primus, February 24, 1867, PF/CHS. Also quoted in Griffin, *Beloved Sisters*, 173.

17. Correspondence from Brown to Primus July 28, 1867, PF/CHS. Also quoted in Griffin, *Beloved Sisters*, 215.

*charge* again, only now as her assistant teacher.[18] The women are able to be *with the object of their affections daily and hourly* and *nightly*, working alongside each other as freedmen's teachers while sharing their lives and home.

Primus and Brown live in a house on the land where the school is located, much like Putnam and Holley lived together at the Holley School site. The erotic that first brought Primus and Brown together continues to fuel their passionate sharing of intimacies.

It is their first night together in the house. Laying face to face on the new bed, Brown and Primus *hug and kiss*.[19] Brown unbuttons her *night dress*, directing Primus's *kisses* down to her *bosom*.

"*No kisses is like yours,*" Brown says.

Primus keeps moving down, taking Brown's *night dress* off and tossing it to the floor now that they can be completely alone. The door to their new home is locked.

The next morning at breakfast, Brown has a twinkle in her eyes, thinking about spending the whole night together in their shared bed. She feels emboldened to imagine another future.

"*You are the first Girl that I ever love,*" Brown says, "*you are the last one.*"[20]

Primus blushes and looks down at her biscuits, spreading the jam another time. She tucks a loose piece of hair behind her ear.

"*I mean just what I say,*" Brown goes on. "*If you was a man what would things come to?*"[21]

What *things come to*, over time, is *a marriage or something like it* between the two women.[22] Although Brown doesn't *address* Primus as *My Husband* outside of her letters, the women take *pleasure* in living together as a married couple.[23] At night in bed, Brown offers her *bosom* to Primus in their *favorite ways*.[24]

---

18. Correspondence from Brown to Primus, January 10, 1862, PF/CHS.
19. Correspondence from Brown to Primus, November 17, 1867; August 30, 1859, PF/CHS. Also quoted in Griffin, *Beloved Sisters*, 228, 21.
20. Correspondence from Brown to Primus, August 30, 1859, PF/CHS.
21. Correspondence from Brown to Primus, August 30, 1859, PF/CHS.
22. Cleves, *Charity*, x.
23. Correspondence from Brown to Primus, November 16, 1865, PF/CHS. Also quoted in Griffin, *Beloved Sisters*, 87. Brown's fantasies of addressing Primus as "husband," or of the women marrying if either of them were "a gent," raise questions about gender identity. Available letters show Brown imagining what would happen if either woman was a man only in the context of articulating desires to be together liked a married couple. That said, it is important to acknowledge nineteenth-century iterations of both same-sex and trans marriage. See Cleves, *Charity*; and Manion, *Female Husbands*.
24. Correspondence from Brown to Primus, November 17, 1867; August 30, 1859, PF/CHS. Also quoted in Griffin, *Beloved Sisters*, 228, 21.

The erotic of their marriage extends beyond its physical intimacies, with the erotic of the women's romantic friendship continuing to function as a rhetorical power enabling their self-education for racial uplift and justice. Their desires for each other, for intellectual life, and for racial justice interanimate and multiply as they live and work side by side. Primus and Brown find their *interlectual powers* are *like a deep well,* fueling the relationship and their teaching.[25] At the Primus Institute, the women teach a range of subjects to formerly enslaved African Americans. They act on their passionately shared desires, teaching rhetoric in service of racial uplift and their *hope* that *there will be justice, impartial justice, given to the colored people one of these days.*[26]

Their romantic letters stop, but only because they are with each other.

---

25. Correspondence from Brown to Primus, December 3, 1865, PF/CHS. Also quoted in Griffin, *Beloved Sisters,* 96.

26. Correspondence from Primus to family, April 7, 1866, PF/CHS. Also quoted in Griffin, *Beloved Sisters,* 118.

CHAPTER 3

# A Progressive Erotic of Sapphic Egalitarianism

*Communication and Leadership among Equals, 1897–1922*

> Miss Buck is here now and we are having a fine time. Needless to say she relieves me of many small cares which, though far from oppressive, eat much into my time. Of course no one knows so well as she just what things are to be done and just how to go about doing them. Every detail of the house as well as of the college work has grown up with her Knowledge, and all she needs to do is to press a button to make things move.
>
> —Laura Johnson Wylie, in a letter to Fanny Hart, 1916

Gertrude Buck (1871–1922) and Laura Johnson Wylie (1855–1932) were scholars of rhetoric and literature who met in 1897 when Wylie, head of the English department at Vassar College, hired Buck to direct their rhetoric and composition program.[1] Both were highly educated white women. Buck is widely known as the first person to earn a PhD in rhetoric, in 1898, having studied with Fred Newton Scott at the settler institution of the University of Michigan.[2] In 1894 Wylie was among the first women to earn a PhD at Yale, where she wrote her dissertation about literary criticism.[3] Although Wylie hired Buck, in time they were running Vassar's English department together as well as living with each other. Within the context of this personal and professional arrangement, the women were able to develop rhetorical practices beyond the classroom teaching that was mainly expected of even the most educated

---

1. Campbell, *Toward*, xxi. As previously introduced, Vassar is located on occupied Mohican, Munsee Lenape, and Schaghticoke territories. See Native Land Digital.

2. Also as introduced already, the University was founded and funded through the sale of land taken from the Ojibwe, Odawa, and Bodwéwadmi nations. See Tobin, "Wait."

3. Bordelon, *Feminist Legacy*, 16, 75; Campbell, *Toward*, xi, xix, xxii; and L'Eplattenier, "Investigating," 166.

women at the time.[4] As Wylie wrote in my epigraph, which is drawn from a letter to friend and Vassar colleague Fanny Hart, Buck "relieves me of many small cares which . . . eat much into my time."[5] Buck's "knowledge" could "make things move" with respect to "every detail of the house as well as of the college work." With this support from Buck, Wylie was able to take a leadership role in the white women's suffrage movement even while serving as head of the English department. Wylie similarly supported Buck, whose scholarly productivity was unique for the time in that she published not only rhetoric textbooks but also rhetorical theory. For nearly twenty-five years, until Buck's passing, the women shared their domestic and professional lives as a rhetorically active faculty couple.

Buck and Wylie's domestic and professional relationship can be understood as a romantic friendship. Barbara L'Eplattenier refers to the friendship as a Boston marriage, a form of relationship common among unmarried, educated women in the settler Northeast that "indicated a long-term financial and emotional commitment to each other" and may or may not have been "sexual in nature."[6] "After much consideration, and readings of other letters and papers," L'Eplattenier concludes, "I am compelled to argue that 'her great friend,'" the language used by Vassar's president, Henry Noble MacCracken, "was code for what we today would call a domestic partner—that is, recognition of the lesbian relationship, sexual or not, that existed between Wylie and Buck."[7] I understand Buck and Wylie's same-sex domestic partnership in similar terms. Both the romantic and the professional dimensions of this partnership were defined by an erotic of sapphic egalitarianism. I argue that this erotic of Buck and Wylie's romantic friendship amounted to a source of progressive rhetorical power. In this progressive iteration of the erotic, the women's intimate desires for each other interanimated with their passionately shared intellectual, pedagogical, and political desires for egalitarianism. Their egalitarianism idealized equality and cooperation but in "power-evasive" ways that actually ignored differences among women.[8] The political complexities of this sapphic erotic of egalitarianism not only shaped Buck and Wylie's own relationship but also informed their development of rhetorical theory, participation in suffrage activism, and administration of an English department that valued the study of Western rhetoric on par with literature.

---

4. L'Eplattenier, "Investigating."
5. Correspondence from Wylie to Hart, April 22, 1916, VCL.
6. L'Eplattenier, "Investigating," 60 n. 7.
7. L'Eplattenier, "Investigating," 86 n. 5.
8. Carrillo Rowe, *Power Lines*, 73. See also Frankenberg, *White Women*; and Lorde, "Age, Race, Class."

Working as teachers and administrators at the turn of the century, Buck and Wylie were among a generation of privileged women who gained access to advanced, doctoral-level training and faculty positions at white women's colleges like Vassar. The women's college during the late nineteenth and early twentieth centuries was a distinctive educational site in that its existence opened up considerable space for same-sex relationships like Buck and Wylie's. As Suzanne Bordelon explains in contextualizing their relationship, "the 'female twosome was an accepted institution on the faculties of women's colleges in America in the late-nineteenth and early-twentieth century.'"[9] "Their lives as faculty couples were openly played out on campus," according to Lillian Faderman, and "love between women in the early decades of the women's college was a noble tradition."[10] This "noble tradition" took on a tenuous position, however, as resistance to privileged white women's entrance into advanced scholarly and professional training increased. Those who opposed higher education for women argued that it would make students more "manly," less likely to marry and have children, and even "endanger their reproductive organs."[11] These arguments were tied up in the white supremacy and classism of eugenics discourse insofar as "alarms about the low birth-rate of middle-class white women" who became educated were tied to fears about a "resulting 'race suicide.'"[12] The woman's college was a complex site, then, creating space for relationships like Buck and Wylie's, but not without cultural concerns about highly educated white women having the option to forgo marriage and children.

In addition to their involvement in higher education, Buck and Wylie are also distinctive within this study because of a paradox marking the extant archives documenting their relationship and work. On the one hand, whereas Sallie Holley, Caroline Putnam, Irene Leache, and Annie Wood are largely unknown within rhetorical studies, Buck and Wylie have been widely studied by feminist historians of rhetoric, rhetorical education, and writing program administration.[13] Both women were published, and Buck in particular published more widely than the women in the other couples—as well as most rhetorical scholars of any gender during the period. On the other hand, though, few records exist of the specifically intimate dimensions of Buck and Wylie's

---

9. Faderman, foreword to *Wolf Girls*, xii–xiii, quoted in Bordelon, *Feminist Legacy*, 200 n. 13.

10. Faderman, foreword to *Wolf Girls*, xii, quoted in Bordelon, *Feminist Legacy*, 200 n. 13.

11. L'Eplattenier, "Investigating," 172, 166; and Horowitz, *Alma Mater*, 58–59.

12. Franzen, *Spinsters*, 5.

13. In addition to the already cited scholarship by Bordelon, Campbell, and L'Eplattenier, as well as other essays referenced in what follows, see Bordelon, "'Advance'"; and Lawrence, "Organisms," 32.

relationship. As JoAnn Campbell explains when introducing her edited collection of Buck's work, it "is based primarily on her published writings."[14] "Although I researched the archives of both institutions with which she was associated, the University of Michigan and Vassar College," Campbell continues, "I found little autographical material." Lisa S. Mastrangelo observes that, at Michigan, the papers of Buck's mentor Scott contain some professional letters from her. However, the papers of Wylie in the "Vassar archives have limited personal correspondence to [Buck], and it seems likely that her letters were destroyed at some point."[15]

More to the point given my study's focus, I have found no romantic letters between Buck and Wylie. Nor did either woman publish a posthumous memoir about their relationship in the way that Wood did about Leache. None of this is surprising. The history of same-sex romantic relationships is marked by the destruction of records—romantic letters especially.[16] Moreover, by the early twentieth century, sexological discourse had reached the mainstream, so published writing about the romantic and erotic dimensions of an ongoing relationship like Buck and Wylie's was more likely to arouse suspicion of so-called deviance. Still, because Buck and Wylie's personal and professional lives were so entwined, we can learn about the former through records of the latter. I thus examine the role of Buck and Wylie's intimate relationship in their more public work through research conducted in the settler-colonial archives at Vassar and the University of Michigan. This research builds on the prior feminist rhetorical studies of Buck and Wylie. Already these studies have acknowledged the women's relationship and its importance to their work together. Discussion of its erotic, however, is limited mainly to conjecture within a single paragraph or endnote.

My study underscores the erotic of Buck and Wylie's relationship, reclaiming its central role in their teaching and administration as well as their rhetorical theory and political participation. The chapter begins by characterizing the women's Boston marriage, showing how it was animated by passionately shared desires for egalitarianism. These desires reflected the ideals of the Progressive Era as well as theories of specifically "homogenic" and "sapphic" love. The ideals were undercut, however, by Buck and Wylie's "power-evasive

---

14. Campbell, *Toward*, xi.

15. Mastrangelo, "Building," 416–17. As Mastrangelo also points out, Buck's "papers are not collected together in one set of boxes or folders" at Michigan and Vassar. See Mastrangelo, "Lone Wolf," 258. On the limitations of available Buck archives, also see Yakel, "Searching," 108, 110.

16. Freedman, "'Burning.'" See also Bessette, *Retroactivism*, 82.

intimacy" with respect to differences among women.[17] Next I consider how this same progressive erotic of egalitarianism infused the women's rhetorical practices in terms of equality within their own relationship as white women, an equal valuing of both women's scholarly and activist roles, and the egalitarian view of cooperative communication that Buck theorized. Then, turning from rhetorical practices to rhetorical education, I show how passionately shared desires for egalitarianism also shaped the women's collaborative administration of a department in which Buck's leadership role and the teaching of Western rhetoric were valued in equal measure with, rather than subordinated to, Wylie's role and the teaching of English literature.

Through this progressive form of the erotic, the women enacted their ideals of egalitarianism primarily within their own relationship and shared leadership, marked as it was by an intimate "belonging" through "sameness" as two white women.[18] Although the women were motivated by ideals that were progressive relative to their own cultural and educational context, that shared context of Vassar was a racially and economically exclusive educational space during their tenure, one devoted to the teaching and learning of privileged young white women. In this way, the progressive erotic of Buck and Wyle's relationship and rhetoric, much like the conservative erotic of Leache and Wood's relationship, was grounded in settler colonialism and slavery.[19] Moreover, Buck's own theory of rhetoric as organic communication problematically reproduced the logics of difference that underwrote settler racism. Specifically, her theory of rhetoric and communication evaded questions about how "to respond to human differences" among women, while actively advancing Eurocentric views of race, education, and "civilization."[20] Ultimately, I argue that even as a progressive erotic of sapphic egalitarianism fueled Buck's and Wylie's rhetorical practices and pedagogies, the women nevertheless perpetuated Eurocentric arguments about education among white women.

## Progressive Erotic of Sapphic Egalitarianism

Before turning to my analysis of Buck's and Wylie's rhetorical practices and administration of the rhetoric program at Vassar, this section characterizes the women's relationship. Again, Buck and Wylie did not leave behind

---

17. Carpenter, *Homogenic Love*, 4; Wallace, "'Edith,'" 196, quoted in J. M. Allen, *Passionate Commitments*, 7; and Carrillo Rowe, *Power Lines*, 73.
18. Frankenberg, *White Women*, 72; and Carrillo Rowe, *Power Lines*, 131.
19. Greyser, *Sympathetic Grounds*.
20. Lorde, "Age, Race, Class," 115.

romantic letters of longing that were written during periods of physical separation like Putnam and Holley did. Nor did Wylie write a memoir of her romantic friendship with Buck like Leache did after Wood's passing. As such, what I examine are professional letters and letters of friendship, which were written by Buck to Scott and saved in his papers at Michigan as well as written to and from Wylie and preserved in her papers at Vassar. Also available are Buck's and Wylie's published writing about rhetoric, literature, and other topics, along with administrative documents related to the rhetorical training offered by Vassar's English department. These primary materials, examined in conjunction with prior feminist rhetorical scholarship about Buck and Wylie, show how the women's partnership was marked by a progressive erotic of egalitarianism in keeping with idealist theories of "homogenic" and "sapphic" love from the period.[21]

Although Buck and Wylie developed an egalitarian relationship, it is important to acknowledge how the conditions of their meeting in 1897 were marked by a power differential that could have developed differently. First, of all the couples in this study, their age difference was the greatest, with Wylie sixteen years older than Buck.[22] Second, and perhaps more importantly, Wylie hired Buck and, technically speaking, continued to serve as her professional superior throughout the women's lives together. After earning her PhD, Buck taught in other settings, including an Indianapolis high school and a Detroit normal school.[23] Buck's move to Vassar came after Wylie "read Buck's dissertation, was impressed, and hired her to run the composition and rhetoric program there."[24] While Buck administered that program in rhetoric and writing, Wylie would remain the head of the English department until Buck passed away in 1922. Yet, in spite of the difference in age and their placement in formal academic hierarchies, records suggest Buck and Wylie saw themselves as intellectual equals and professional colleagues.

In meeting through their work together at Vassar, Buck and Wylie participated in a relationship dynamic common among educated, professional women of the time—and particularly among those who formed faculty couples at women's colleges. From among women who earned a PhD between 1877 and 1924, 75 percent did not marry.[25] As Campbell recounts when describing

---

21. Carpenter, *Homogenic Love*, 4; and Wallace, "'Edith,'" 196, quoted in Allen, *Passionate Commitments*, 7.
22. Bordelon, *Feminist Legacy*, 95.
23. Campbell, *Toward*, xix. Also, according to Campbell, Buck "most likely attended John Dewey's course at the University of Chicago before going to Vassar College."
24. Campbell, *Toward*, xxi.
25. B. J. Harris, *Beyond*, 101, cited in Campbell, *Toward*, xxii.

Buck in these terms, "a life of service and sacrifice was expected of single women, whose devoted service to an institution at times literally took up all their personal space. While Buck and Wylie lived in a house in town, not all the teachers could afford to."[26] Although legally unmarried, not all of these women were "single"; nor was living with another faculty member necessarily a "sacrifice." Helen Lefkowitz Horowitz acknowledges that historians studying women's colleges and their faculty "have, sometimes unwittingly, uncovered their subjects' personal lives to find that these unmarried women were not selfless renunciating celibates, but passionate human beings who lived a rich and intense life within the emotional world of other women."[27] In addition to Wylie and Buck, for example, two other same-sex relationships between women faculty include those between Mount Holyoke president Mary Woolley and English department head Jeannette Marks, as well as Bryn Mawr president M. Carey Thomas and English professor Mamie Gwinn.[28] Same-sex romantic friendships between women faculty—like those between teachers at freedmen's schools and boarding schools for girls—were by no means unique, though Buck and Wylie are a particularly important case for the fields of rhetoric, communication, and composition.

While Buck and Wylie did not leave evidence (as far as we know) of the early passions common to romantic relationships or the erotic longings that marked physical separations when couples were unable to live together, existing records do document a comfortably established, long-term domestic partnership. In a typical letter from December of 1916, Wylie wrote to Hart about the faculty couple's winter break. Wylie was "delighted to be at the beginning of our vacation," relishing that "Miss Buck and I have spent the afternoon in the most flagrant idleness." "We are now feeling comfortably settled in the house for the evening," Wylie continued, "and I am especially enjoying the prospect of not having to start at the college at a set hour in the morning. It seems perfectly delightful to think that one may have five minutes more in bed of a morning!"[29] The nature of their relationship as a faculty couple is well captured by L'Eplattenier's designation of "Boston marriage."[30] Faderman explains that Boston marriages became possible for privileged women because of "the successes of the women's rights movement," such that "by the late nineteenth century . . . so-called romantic friendships of earlier eras could become 'Boston marriages': committed relationships between two women who, having

---

26. Campbell, *Toward,* xxii.
27. Horowitz, *Alma Mater,* 188.
28. Faderman, foreword to *Wolf Girls,* xiii, quoted in Bordelon, *Feminist Legacy,* 200 n. 13.
29. Correspondence from Wylie to Hart, December 22, 1916, VCL.
30. L'Eplattenier, "Investigating," 60 n. 7.

gone to college and then found decent-paying jobs, could set up a household together rather than marry men out of economic need."[31]

Along these lines, Campbell notes that Buck and Wylie "shared a household . . . and had a very stable relationship—at one time they even considered adopting a child."[32] The women did adopt a dog. Wylie mentioned "Miss Buck and our new little dog, a Boston terrier," in a letter from March of 1909.[33] Subsequent letters frequently mentioned the dog, Berlin, who the couple nicknamed Burly. Wylie signed a 1911 letter to Hart, for example, "with love from Miss Buck and me and a lick from Berlin."[34] It is impossible to know whether Buck and Wylie's long-term Boston marriage was "sexual in nature"—just as opposite-sex relationships rarely leave behind documentation confirming whether and to what extent sexual activity outside of reproduction was sustained over time.[35] But the women clearly shared a committed partnership, and a family, with their adoption of Burly, that was marked by love and affection.

Before shifting to my focus on the erotic as rhetorical power within this domestic partnership, I want to acknowledge existing representations of Buck and Wylie's relationship within the work of feminist rhetorical scholars. These scholars—like the interdisciplinary researchers studying Putnam, Holley, Wood, and Leache—have understood Buck and Wylie's relationship in concert with debates about romantic friendships between women. Bordelon introduces Wylie as Buck's "longtime professional associate, friend, and housemate," as her "colleague, friend, and housemate."[36] Bordelon contextualizes this relationship with reference to Faderman's already discussed account of faculty couples, emphasizing that "during this time female relationships were not 'yet widely stigmatized as "lesbian."'"[37] In an endnote, Bordelon discusses Faderman's work further, also citing Smith-Rosenberg's.[38] Campbell follows a similar arrangement. Where first introducing that Buck and Wylie "lived together for years," Campbell explains in a footnote how "the relatively low salaries of teachers at women's colleges made communal living

---

31. Faderman, *To Believe*, 6. For further discussion of the relational and professional possibilities enabled by Boston marriages—and by the "creative partnership" of Willa Cather and Edith Lewis specifically—see Homestead, *Only Wonderful Things*.
32. Campbell, *Toward*, xxii. On Buck and Wylie's consideration of adoption, also see Bordelon, *Feminist Legacy*, 100, 205 n. 8.
33. Correspondence from Wylie to Nina, March 13, 1909, VCL.
34. Correspondence from Wylie to Hart, April 20, 1911, VCL.
35. L'Eplattenier, "Investigating," 60 n. 7.
36. Bordelon, *Feminist Legacy*, 1–2, 15.
37. Bordelon, *Feminist Legacy*, 24.
38. Bordelon, *Feminist Legacy*, 200 n. 13.

a necessity."³⁹ Later mentioning how "stable" the women's "partnership" was, Campbell more fully recognizes its significance, but only in a footnote. She writes, "their relationship might have been what Carroll Smith-Rosenberg has called an 'intense female friendship,' and today we might call them lesbians, given their woman-centered lives and commitment to each other. Problems with using contemporary labels for the past should not erase the lives of woman-identified women."⁴⁰ L'Eplattenier goes the furthest in recognizing Buck and Wylie's romantic friendship, arguing, as already quoted, that Buck was Wylie's "domestic partner" and they had a "lesbian relationship, whether sexual or not."⁴¹ Here too, however, L'Eplattenier offers this interpretation in an endnote. What most stands out in the feminist rhetorical scholarship, then, is the recognition of the erotic and sexual possibilities of Buck and Wylie's romantic friendship and, simultaneously, the relegation of this recognition to side notes—quite literally, in the endnotes and footnotes.

In all of this work, I find it understandable that feminist scholars have focused first on establishing Buck's previously underexamined importance to the male-dominated history of Western rhetoric in the late nineteenth and early twentieth centuries. Moreover, Bordelon, Campbell, and L'Eplattenier, along with other feminist scholars writing about Buck and Wylie, have recognized the importance of the women's friendship to their work together. But as Bordelon asserts, "much more could be written about these women."⁴² More could be written, in my view, about the significance of the erotic to these women's rhetorical power.

Doing so requires that, while recognizing the complexities of romantic friendship in different periods, as well as the scholarly debates about it, we do not downplay the erotic and sexual possibilities of Buck and Wylie's romantic friendship. L'Eplattenier recognizes these possibilities in her endnote, where she quotes the work of Elaine Kendall on women's colleges. Kendall advances an understanding of romantic friendship that parallels Marylynn Diggs's take on its potential to function as a "cover."⁴³ "Passionate relationships between women, particularly those with advanced political ideas and great intellectual ambitions, were usual in that era and seemed to have been accepted as a matter of course," Kendall recognizes. "It was tolerance based upon naivete rather than on full understanding," though, "since women were generally viewed as

---

39. Campbell, *Toward*, xvi–xvii.
40. Campbell, *Toward*, xii.
41. L'Eplattenier, "Investigating," 86 n. 86.
42. Bordelon, *Feminist Legacy*, 189.
43. Diggs, "Romantic Friends," 319.

a sexually deficient species, virtually neuter until 'awakened' by a man, the most intense female associations could elude suspicion almost indefinitely."[44]

Again, assumptions about the nonsexual nature of romantic friendships could serve as a "cover" and "elude suspicion" specifically for middle-class white women because of sexist, racist, and classist stereotypes about their supposed sexual "purity."[45] As with the other couples in this study, I am not suggesting one way or another whether Buck and Wylie's relationship was sexual. Rather, I am interested in how the erotic dimensions of their romantic friendship enabled their public contributions, both as rhetors in their own right and as teachers responsible for administering the rhetoric program at Vassar. I ask, specifically, how their "sharing deeply"—of both "the passions of love" for each other and their desires for an idealized egalitarianism—functioned à la Audre Lorde as a progressive form of the erotic as power that fueled their rhetorical work.[46]

In shifting to analysis of Buck and Wylie's rhetorical activities, I want to underscore a set of themes from the development of their relationship. Buck and Wylie's rhetorical labors were facilitated by what I am calling a progressive erotic of egalitarianism, a shared desire for an idealized spirit of equality as well as cooperation. Excepting the specifically erotic dimensions of these ideals, a related point is made in both book-length studies of the women by Campbell and Bordelon, which connect Buck and Wylie's egalitarianism to protofeminist principles and Progressive Era ideals.[47] Campbell explains, "Buck's optimism about society's progress ... was, of course, a trait of the progressive era."[48] Writing for the University of Michigan's *Inlander* magazine, for example, Buck (1896) urged that "society shall come to recognize that which in the New Testament phrase is called love, in our practical modern vernacular co-operation, as essentially the law of life."[49] As Campbell interprets this passage, "by emphasizing love or cooperation as a law, Buck removed it from a romantic realm of emotion."[50] "Believing that love, or cooperation, was the primary law," Campbell continues, "Buck looked for it everywhere and objected to any teaching or theory that did not have a cooperative basis."[51] Bordelon emphasizes further "how Buck was not necessarily ahead of her

---

44. Kendall, *Peculiar Institutions*, 142, quoted in L'Eplattenier, "Investigating," 87 n. 5.
45. Franzen, *Spinsters*, 170.
46. Lorde, "Uses of the Erotic," 56.
47. For further discussion of Buck and Wylie's protofeminist principles, see Bordelon, *Feminist Legacy*, 2, 11; and Campbell, *Toward*, ix–x.
48. Campbell, *Toward*, xvii–xviii.
49. Buck, "Ethical Significance," 222, quoted in Campbell, *Toward*, xviii.
50. Campbell, *Toward*, xviii.
51. Campbell, *Toward*, xviii.

time but very much a product of her own period."⁵² Bordelon demonstrates this point especially in terms of the way Buck's theory of rhetoric reflected broader Progressive Era ideals: her "social" theory of rhetoric envisioned that "all would participate and that discourse had the potential to promote cooperation and equality."⁵³

While feminist scholars have located Wylie's and especially Buck's egalitarian ideals within the Progressive Era, and rightly so, the women's egalitarianism was also imbricated in the erotic of their same-sex romantic friendship. During the period, at least some practitioners of same-sex love advanced idealist theories of "homogenic" and "sapphic" friendship as particularly suited to egalitarian ethics and politics. As noted in my introductory chapter, Edward Carpenter—a British philosopher, poet, and socialist—theorized what he termed "homogenic love" across multiple pamphlets and publications, including *Homogenic Love, and Its Place in a Free Society* (1894). Carpenter understood *homogenic* according to the word's Greek roots, "*homos* 'same,' and *genos* 'sex,'" preferring it over the category *homosexual*.⁵⁴ Carpenter was interested in the role homogenic love could play in positive social transformation. In *The Intermediate Sex* (1908), he claimed that "eros is a great leveler," on which "perhaps the true Democracy rests."⁵⁵ Writing about the social role of same-sex *eros* in particular, Carpenter suggested, "I think myself that the best philanthropic work—just because it is the most personal, the most loving, and the least merely formal and self-righteous—has a strong fibre of the Uranian heart running through it."

In Robin Hackett's account, Carpenter's theory of homogenic love and larger body of work "argued for the existence of a sexual minority—a third sex—defined not only by same-sex erotic choice but also by a heightened commitment to social justice," in which "homoerotics and heightened ethical sensibilities are mutually constitutive."⁵⁶ Without delving into the complex relationship between Carpenter's writing and that ranging from Walt Whitman to the sexologists, I want to underscore that Carpenter acknowledged homogenic love among both men and women, and his ideas reached and were taken up by white women in the US.⁵⁷

---

52. Bordelon, *Feminist Legacy*, 5.
53. Bordelon, *Feminist Legacy*, 14.
54. Carpenter, *Homogenic Love*, 4.
55. Carpenter, *Intermediate Sex*, 107.
56. Hackett, foreword to *Passionate Commitments*, by Allen, xii.
57. Carpenter, *Homogenic Love*, 4.

Specifically, Carpenter developed "a system of 'homogenic and sapphic idealism' that influenced a generation of women."[58] Julia M. Allen characterizes this uptake of his ideas among women within her study of another white couple, Anna Rochester and Grace Hutchins, who worked for social and economic justice. "In the work of . . . Carpenter as well as in the lives of Hutchins and Rochester," Allen writes, "we find attempts to fuse a Platonic *eros*, or desiring love, with New Testament *agape*, or sacrificing love."[59] If we recognize more fully the homogenic love that Buck and Wylie shared, Buck's own statement about the New Testament and love can be reinterpreted in these terms, such that "love or cooperation" is not so much "removed . . . from a realm of emotion."[60] Rather, both forms of love may be "mutually constitutive" for same-sex couples whose shared desires fueled their intimate lives as well as their rhetorical labors.[61] This fusion of *eros* with *agape*, according to Allen, "meant both a recognition and a celebration of same-sex desire and a channeling of that desire away from personal gratification and into the work of creating a society based upon love and collectivity rather than individualism and greed."[62] Buck and Wylie did not evidence sustained commitments to socialism to the extent that Rochester and Hutchins did, though Buck was, at one point, a member of the Socialist Party of New York.[63] Nor should we make assumptions, one way or another, about how Buck and Wylie personally gratified their desires. In their lives and work together, though, there is ample evidence of the sapphic idealism that Allen has recognized in the lives of other women. In Allen's words, Rochester and Hutchins were "women, whose love for each other so clearly fueled their work to create a more egalitarian world."[64]

So, too, with Buck and Wylie. The progressive erotic of their shared desires for egalitarianism animated their relationship and their work together. This erotic enabled rhetorical practices and education that idealized equality and cooperation even as the couple enacted these ideals in ways that variously "ignore[d]" or "misnamed and misused" actual differences among women.[65]

---

58. Wallace, "'Edith,'" 196, quoted in Allen, *Passionate Commitments*, 7.
59. Allen, *Passionate Commitments*, 19.
60. Buck, "Ethical Significance," 222; and Campbell, *Toward*, xviii.
61. Hackett, foreword to *Passionate Commitments*, by Allen, xii.
62. Allen, *Passionate Commitments*, 19.
63. Bordelon, *Feminist Legacy*, 100.
64. Allen, *Passionate Commitments*, 1.
65. Lorde, "Age, Race, Class," 115.

## Egalitarian Theory and Activist Rhetoric

Buck and Wylie were rhetorically active as scholars and activists. "Wylie was the public figure," L'Eplattenier observes, "and Buck the private one."[66] Along these lines, Wylie was more active than Buck as an activist and leader in the white women's suffrage movement. Yet Buck was more rhetorically active in terms of published scholarly writing, which included textbooks as well as rhetorical theory. This section examines in turn each woman's primary participation, through rhetorical scholarship and then suffrage activism, with a focus on how the progressive erotic of egalitarianism that defined their "sapphic" love helped make possible these more public rhetorical practices. Reflecting the women's shared desires for equality and cooperation, each woman's rhetorical practices were equally supported and valued within the relationship, while the rhetorical practices themselves also were infused with the ideals of equality and cooperation. In both their relationship and rhetorical practices, however, the women idealized egalitarianism while ignoring—and thus contributing to the maintenance of—actual power differences between women.

For all of the white couples in this book, their rhetorical activities were made possible in practical terms because their relationships with each other, in contrast with most opposite-sex marriages, freed up the privileged women's time from some of the conventional responsibilities for childbearing, childrearing, and domestic labor. This reduction of reproductive labor (with no disrespect to Burly, or my readers who are LGBTQ+ pet parents), especially in combination with a more equitable sharing of what domestic labor remained, is an even more apparent factor in the relationship of Buck and Wylie. Whereas Putman played a behind-the-scenes role in relation to Holley's public speaking, and Wood became a published author mainly after Leache's passing, both Buck and Wylie were equally active as rhetors during the decades when they lived and worked together. In other words, the progressive erotic of egalitarianism that defined their entire relationship together played a part in their ability to cooperate so that each woman could contribute in her own right as published author and suffrage activist.

Buck's rhetorical practices took form primarily as scholarly publications. She authored and coauthored several textbooks, a number of which were used in Vassar rhetoric and writing courses: *A Course in Argumentative Writing* (1899); *A Course in Expository Writing* (1899) and *A Course in Narrative Writing* (1906), both written with a Vassar colleague, Elisabeth Woodbridge Morris; and *A Handbook of Argumentation and Debating*, written with another

---

66. L'Eplattenier, "Investigating," 91.

Vassar colleague, Kristine Mann (1906).[67] Other coauthored books oriented to teaching include *Organic Education: A Manual for Teachers in Primary and Grammar Grades* (1897), written with Harriett M. Scott, who was Buck's colleague at a normal school, and *A Brief English Grammar* (1905), written with Fred Newton Scott, Buck's mentor from Michigan.[68] Certainly Buck was prolific as a textbook author, guided by her scholarly expertise in rhetorical as well as pedagogical theory.

Perhaps more notable for a woman scholar of the period were her works of rhetorical theory. These publications include scholarly journal articles and still more books. Buck's article "The Present Status of Rhetorical Theory" (1900) is now recognized as an important work of nineteenth-century rhetorical theory.[69] In terms of scholarly books, and reflecting her early interest in the intersection of rhetorical theory with psychology, Buck published *Figures of Rhetoric: A Psychological Study* (1895) and then *The Metaphor: A Study in the Psychology of Rhetoric* (1899), which had been her master's thesis and dissertation. Buck also published *The Social Criticism of Literature* (1916), bringing rhetorical perspectives to bear on literary criticism in ways that reflected the cooperative relationship between Western rhetoric and literature in the English department under Buck and Wylie's shared leadership. Finally, *Poems and Plays* (1922) was a collection of her creative writing posthumously published under Wylie's editorship.[70]

Able to publish so widely with Wylie's support, Buck's rhetorical contributions were theoretically significant. This significance has been underscored across feminist scholarship, which counters sexist presumptions that women scholars were simply absent from the production of Western rhetorical theory during the period. This emphasis in feminist rhetorical scholarship is reflected in a relatively recent essay published about Buck. Writing about her theory of metaphor, Ashley Rose Mehlenbacher and Randy Allen Harris seek to "redress the erasure of her important contribution to theories of metaphor, especially to cognitive approaches to figure."[71] The problem, they explain, is that "despite Buck's dramatic re-framing of metaphor—a contribution that would remain unparalleled in rhetorical studies until I. A. Richard's work some 25 years later

---

67. Bordelon, *Feminist Legacy*, 18; Buck, *Course in Argumentative Writing*; Buck and Woodbridge, *Course in Expository Writing*; Buck and Morris, *Course in Narrative Writing*; Buck and Mann, *Handbook*; and Campbell, *Toward*, xxx.

68. Bordelon, *Feminist Legacy*, 18; and Buck and Scott, *Brief English Grammar*.

69. Buck, "Present Status"; and D. M. Gross, "Beginnings."

70. Buck, *Figures of Rhetoric*; Buck, *Metaphor*; Buck, *Social Criticism*; and Buck, *Poems*.

71. Mehlenbacher and Harris, "Figurative Mind," 80. Another study of Buck's work on metaphor is Vivian, "Gertrude." For further discussion of Buck's contributions specifically as a theorist of rhetoric, see Gross, "Beginnings."

. . . her work remains largely unknown to rhetoricians, unheard of by psychologists, philosophers, and linguists."[72] The importance of Buck's rhetorical theory is recognized already within feminist rhetorical studies. So instead of rehearsing other arguments in this vein, I am interested in the question of *how* she was able to be so productive as a rhetorical theorist.

"Perhaps what allowed Buck to write more than other women scholars of her time," Campbell ventures, "was her sense of herself not as an individual leader but as a member of an entire community interested in progressive education."[73] Perhaps, yes. Certainly her access to generational wealth, higher education, and the privileges of white femininity played a part. But perhaps the erotic of Buck's romantic friendship with Wylie also played a particular role. Within the context of their Boston marriage, marked as it was by a progressive erotic of sapphic egalitarianism, Buck's life and work included time free from domestic responsibilities, in which she could read, think, and write. Even if these activities were less obviously or immediately public than Wylie's suffrage activism, Buck's rhetorical practices were equally valued within the relationship—given both the time they took and the respect they deserved.

With the equality and cooperation in Buck and Wylie's relationship helping to make possible Buck's writing, in a practical sense, a progressive ideal of egalitarianism also infused Buck's ideas within the theory of rhetoric that she advanced. In an article for *Educational Review* (1901), Buck defined rhetoric "as the science or theory of the process of communication by language."[74] Most relevant here is Buck's "communication theory of discourse," which emphasized an equality of and cooperation between speakers (or writers) and listeners (or readers). Buck emphasized this theory in her early work on metaphor (1899), explaining, "this theory is that known as the communication theory of discourse, which has, in the later rhetorical systems, largely superseded the one-sided theories of discourse as persuasion and as self-expression."[75] Turning to her emphasis on equality, Buck continued, "the theory that discourse is self-expression has reference only to the speaker; the hypothesis that it is persuasion makes the hearer all-important. When discourse is regarded as communication, the two factors in the process are equally emphasized."[76] Buck developed this ideal of equality in communication further in "The Present Status of Rhetorical Theory" (1900), where she aligned her views with

---

72. Mehlenbacher and Harris, "Figurative Mind," 80.
73. Campbell, *Toward*, xlii.
74. Buck, "What"; also quoted in Campbell, *Toward*, 53.
75. Buck, *Metaphor*, 30. This passage is also quoted in Vivian, "Gertrude," 100, as well as reprinted in Campbell, *Toward*, 38.
76. Buck, *Metaphor*, 30.

those of Plato and against Sophistic theory.⁷⁷ In her interpretation of Plato, "both the Platonic and the modern theory of discourse make it not an individualistic and isolated process for the advantage of the speaker alone, but a real communication between the speaker and hearer to the equal advantage of both, and thus a real function of the social organism."⁷⁸ Buck's theory of rhetoric thus highlighted social equality between rhetors and audiences even though it failed to account for actually existing hierarchies of difference.

Equality as well as cooperation have been recognized within feminist rhetorical scholarship as central to Buck's egalitarian view of communication. As Campbell observes, Buck saw "persuasion as violence" but approached "argument as cooperation."⁷⁹ "Buck shared [Fred Newton Scott's] distrust of persuasion," Campbell explains, "and interpreted rhetoric as a truer form of communication, taking an epistemic approach whereby both speaker and hearer learn something."⁸⁰ Writing about the same passage I quote above, Bordelon locates these ideals of equality and cooperation within Buck's Progressive Era context. Bordelon offers, "Buck's modern theory of discourse responds to Progressive Era insistence on furthering democracy by fostering communication that benefits all individuals in the community."⁸¹ In *The Social Criticism of Literature* (1916), Buck similarly theorized literature as "a social activity," a "process" of communication rather than a product, in which both "the writer's action" and "the reader's reaction" were of equal importance to the cooperative endeavor.⁸²

Buck's view of rhetoric (and literature) as communication between equals likely seems overly idealized, and this is exactly the point. On the one hand, she and Wylie were motivated by an erotic of egalitarianism that was characterized by equality and cooperation as ideals. This egalitarianism was a product, certainly, of the Progressive Era. But just as much, it was part of "a system of 'homogenic and sapphic idealism' that influenced a generation of women."⁸³ For Buck and Wylie, this sapphic idealism took shape through a shared desire for an idealized cooperation between equals. On the other hand, and precisely because Buck's writing about equality within communication was so idealized, her theory of rhetoric was not matched by an acknowledgment of—much less

---

77. Certainly Plato is not associated primarily with ideals of equality in present-day rhetorical theory. For another feminist interpretation of Sophistic rhetorical theory, see Jarratt, *Rereading*.

78. Buck, "Present Status," 174. For discussion of Buck's rhetorical theory with respect to composition instruction, see Mulderig, "Gertrude."

79. Campbell, *Toward*, 45.

80. Campbell, *Toward*, xxxviii.

81. Bordelon, *Feminist Legacy*, 69.

82. Buck, *Social Criticism*, quoted in Campbell, *Toward*, 67.

83. Wallace, "Edith," quoted in Allen, *Passionate Commitments*, 7.

any accounting for—the hierarchies of difference that interfered with such cooperation within the late nineteenth- and early twentieth-century context of the settler-colonial US.

Consider more fully, for example, Buck's "The Present Status of Rhetorical Theory." In it, she idealized communication in which "speaker and hearer stand on a footing of at least approximate equality"; then, through discourse, any "original inequality" based on a "truth" perceived by a speaker or writer rather than the audience "is removed," so that "equilibrium is at this point restored to the social organism."[84] Buck contrasted this cooperative communication with discourse that restores and maintains "the dominance of the strong" speaker or writer.[85] She likened the latter discourse, quite tellingly, to "a primitive aggression" in which "the stronger of two tribal organizations subdues and eventually enslaves the weaker."[86] Thus, in the "modern" communication that Buck advocated, equality was not sought or achieved across the hierarchical differences of race, nation, and class, or even of gender and sexuality, that actually constituted her historical context. Rather, equality was "restored" between people who were already "approximate[ly] equal" apart from differential access to some specific knowledge, subject, or "truth." When Buck idealized communication that was not "cut off from all relations to the world," then, she was imagining a world of sameness, a world in which socially meaningful differences in power did not exist. This was a world in which the "primitive," the "weak," and the "enslave[d]" were absent. A world, perhaps, like the elite, settler-colonial institution of Vassar—a world that actively excluded anyone who was unable to belong through sameness such as privileged white femininity. It was a world, finally, that only existed through the active denial and exclusion of difference.

In these respects, Buck's theory of rhetoric resembled the practices of many white women both before and after her. This refusal to address differences between women, as opposed to being concerned only with similarly privileged white women, has marked white feminism from the women's suffrage movement of Buck and Wylie's period, to the critiques of women of color feminists during Lorde's time, and into the present.[87] Indeed, this problematic refusal is part of what her Black lesbian feminist theories of the erotic and difference persistently countered throughout the 1970s and 1980s. Buck's refusal or "silence" is that of all white women who claim to value or even idealize egalitarianism, equality, and cooperation but who simultaneously remain silent about difference. Across her body of work, Lorde labored "to break that

---

84. Buck, "Present Status," 171.
85. Buck, "Present Status," 169.
86. Buck, "Present Status," 169–70.
87. Zakaria, *Against White Feminism*.

silence and bridge some of those differences . . . for it is not difference which immobilizes us, but silence."[88] As Aimee Carrillo Rowe explains, this silence marks the "power-evasive communication styles" that are common among white women but flourish especially within the sort of "power-evasive intimacy" and "segregated belongings" that defined both a romantic relationship like Buck and Wylie's and an institutional setting like Vassar.[89] A problematically idealized erotic of egalitarianism thus fueled not only Buck and Wylie's romantic friendship but also the rhetorical theory Buck was able to produce with the support and cooperation of that relationship of sameness between equals.

While Buck and Wylie's relationship as women in a Boston marriage obviously provided the space in which to devote time and energy to rhetorical scholarship rather than the forms of reproductive labor expected of most privileged women in opposite-sex marriages, there are also direct textual traces in the archives of Wylie's support and respect for Buck's writing. In Bordelon's words, "Buck's life at Vassar with Laura Johnson Wylie profoundly influenced her view of rhetoric."[90] This supportive influence is apparent in the expected places, such as the acknowledgments paragraph included at the end of some of Buck's book prefaces.[91] In her and Morris's *A Course in Narrative Writing* (1906), for example, the acknowledgments paragraph concludes the preface as follows: "to Professor Laura Johnson Wylie of Vassar College and to Miss Katherine Warren, formerly instructor in English in Vassar College, especial gratitude is due for invaluable counsel and criticism during the preparation of this book."[92] Acknowledgments like this one, which usually begin with thanks to Buck's mentor Scott, also evidence Wylie's support as a colleague.

However, in Wylie's own editorial introduction to Buck's final, posthumous publication, Wylie insisted that she held more of an "insider" perspective on Buck's life as a theorist and writer—one that went beyond being mere colleagues and relied clearly on their having shared a household and vacationed together within the context of their Boston marriage. Wylie's support for Buck's writing is apparent in Wylie's effort to edit and publish the collection *Poems and Plays* (1922), which was a departure from Buck's more typical publications of rhetorical textbooks and theory. Introducing the book, Wylie acknowledged that to most people, and "even to her friends," Buck was "primarily the teacher, the thinker, the administrator." "But, however apparently

---

88. Lorde, "Transformation," 43.
89. Carrillo Rowe, *Power Lines*, 73. See also Frankenberg, *White Women*.
90. Bordelon, *Feminist Legacy*, 72.
91. On acknowledgments as a genre, see Micciche, *Acknowledging*.
92. Buck and Morris, *Course in Narrative Writing*, ix. For another example of Buck acknowledging Wylie, see Buck, *Social Criticism*, vi.

absorbed in such tasks," Wylie continued, "there was never a time when Miss Buck was not directly occupied with some piece of imaginative writing."[93] Explaining further, based on the women's experiences sharing an intimate life beyond work, Wylie wrote, "the strength of her imaginative bent showed itself throughout her life in the use she made of such scanty leisure as came to her. A few days of vacation were prized less that she might hear or see some new thing than because in them her imagination, released from daily service, could work out some one of the many themes always revolving in her mind." Wylie concluded the preface by reiterating that "the editor stresses these points [about Buck] in view of their relation to the more obvious aspect of her life and work" and underscoring how the book reveals "a key to much that, though implicit in everything she did, was not always evident to those who knew her chiefly as teacher or critic." Wylie knew Buck as much more than a teacher and a critic. Their Boston marriage was characterized by an erotic of sapphic egalitarianism that functioned as a source of rhetorical power such that Wylie supported, inspired, and helped make possible Buck's rhetorical practices as a writer and theorist.

Through this same erotic of sapphic egalitarianism, Buck supported Wylie's rhetorical practices in equal measure. While Wylie was more active in the suffrage movement, it is important to acknowledge that she, too, was a scholar who published her literary criticism. Notably, Wylie was the first woman to publish her dissertation, which was titled *Studies in the Evolution of English Criticism* (1894), after earning a PhD from Yale.[94] Wylie's other publications include a book, *Social Studies in English Literature* (1916), and "edited school editions" of other literary texts.[95] Buck respected Wylie's scholarship, citing it in her own work. In *The Social Criticism of Literature* (1916), for example, Buck referenced Wylie's *Studies in the Evolution of English Criticism* (1894) when making a point about "more penetrating thinkers, of the type of Coleridge."[96] Still, the extent of Wylie's scholarly publications does not begin to compare to that of Buck. Rather, Wylie's public rhetorical practices were oriented mainly to suffrage activism among white women.

Not surprisingly, given the progressive erotic of egalitarianism that defined Buck and Wylie's romantic friendship, both women supported the movement for equality in voting rights between white women and white men. But Wylie was not merely a supporter; she was a local leader. In the words of Wylie's obituary, published in the *New York Times* (1932), "she was a leader in the

---

93. Wylie, preface to *Poems*, by Buck. There is no pagination in Wylie's preface to the edited collection.
94. Bordelon, *Feminist Legacy*, 75; and Wylie, *Studies*.
95. Bordelon, *Feminist Legacy*, 75; and Wylie, *Social Studies*.
96. Buck, *Social Criticism*, quoted in Campbell, *Toward*, 74.

suffrage movement from 1910 to 1918."[97] As early as 1909, Wylie cooperated with Vassar colleagues and other local women to help found Poughkeepsie's Equal Suffrage League.[98] In 1910, Wylie was elected as president of the organization. "Under her leadership," the group "hosted many events in which women and men congregated over issues that were plaguing the enfranchisement of women."[99] "Wylie brought in dynamic speakers," and she "led the League in canvassing neighborhoods leading up to the 1917 referendum," which amended New York's state constitution in favor of women's suffrage.[100] With the League's goal achieved, Wylie then helped found the Women's City Club in 1918, which was later renamed the Women's City and Country Club.[101] Along with leading these local organizations, Wylie spoke publicly on the suffrage question. In 1913, she outlined "three reasons why we should be interested in Woman Suffrage," delivering her address "to an interested gathering of the Mothers and Teachers Association . . . of the Suffrage League, at the Cannon Street School."[102] Wylie's address linked her suffrage activism to the values of equality and cooperation, claiming, "the whole suffrage movement in America . . . grew up as part of the great movement for wider rights for men and women" and "democracy" itself.[103]

Wylie's rhetorical practices and local leadership on behalf of white women's suffrage take on particular significance within the context of her role as a faculty member and department leader alongside Buck at Vassar. For both faculty and students, campus involvement in the suffrage movement was actively discouraged. James Monroe Taylor, the president of the College from 1886 to 1914, "believed that students should be able to pursue their studies without interference from various political or social reform movements."[104] "So, although Vassar students were allowed to argue about suffrage in their debate clubs and to discuss it among themselves," according to Bordelon, "they were not allowed to form a suffrage club on campus."[105] Taylor's policy was met with resistance.[106] In 1908, students and supporters circumvented the policy by electing to hold a suffrage meeting in a cemetery right next to campus.

---

97. "Miss Laura Wylie." For discussion of her obituary in the *Poughkeepsie Courier,* see Boice, "Woman," 42.
98. Hesler, "Lost Legacy," 68; and Boice, "Woman," 40.
99. Hesler, "Lost Legacy," 69.
100. Hesler, "Lost Legacy," 69.
101. Hesler, "Lost Legacy," 69; and Boice, "Woman," 40–43.
102. Wylie, "Address."
103. Wylie, "Address."
104. Bordelon, *Feminist Legacy,* 94.
105. Bordelon, *Feminist Legacy,* 94.
106. Similar policies existed at the other Seven Sisters colleges of the period. Boice, "Woman," 37. See also Conway, "Woman."

According to news reporting (1908) about the meeting, it "consisted of about forty undergraduates, ten alumnae, two male visitors, and Mrs. Hariot Stanton Blatch, Mrs. Charlotte Perkins Gilman, Miss Helen Hoy, corporation counsel for the Equality League of Self-Supporting Women, and Miss Rose Schneiderman of the Cap Makers Union and Cooper Union fame."[107] The meeting would have been larger except that, in the words of "an alumna," Taylor was "terribly opposed to woman suffrage, and even to the discussion of it in the college." The report concludes by noting that faculty who were "avowed suffragists, conceded to Dr. Taylor's wishes so far as to stay from the cemetery meeting." Neither Wylie nor Buck are named in this report. The conflict makes clear, however, that Wylie's choice to hold leadership positions within the suffrage movement, and to speak publicly on the issue, was a move in keeping not with dictates from Vassar's academic hierarchy but with her and Buck's egalitarianism and especially their valuing of equality between white men and women with respect to voting rights.[108]

Wylie's suffrage leadership was both consistent with and enabled by the complexities of the progressive erotic of sapphic egalitarianism that characterized her relationship with Buck. In a way that is more often celebrated within feminist rhetorical scholarship, as Bordelon emphasizes, the same "progressive ideals of cooperation . . . and equality" that "were at the heart of Buck's . . . theory of discourse . . . were also central to the suffrage movement" in which Wylie cooperated with other women and took a leadership role.[109] Buck's support for Wylie's rhetorical practices on behalf of suffrage was rooted in this shared passion for egalitarian values. Most simply, Buck, too, supported the movement, even if her own rhetorical practices were more orientated to her scholarly writing. An exception to Buck's focus on writing textbooks and rhetorical theory while she was alive, for example, was the publication of poetry she wrote about suffrage.[110] Buck's poetry suggests that, whatever criticism or "anti-suffrage sentiments" Wylie might have encountered at Vassar or in public, her partner at home saw through them and provided a domestic space

---

107. "Vassar Meets in Graveyard."

108. For more detailed discussions of the conflicts surrounding suffrage at Vassar, see Bordelon, *Feminist Legacy*, 94–102; Campbell, *Toward*, xxiii–xxviii; and L'Eplattenier, "Investigating," 151–53.

109. Bordelon, *Feminist Legacy*, 112.

110. One piece, "Anti-Suffrage Sentiments" (1913), poked fun at the counterarguments leveled by those who opposed the movement in which Wylie was so actively involved. In the first verse, "a delicate Angora cat" insists that she does not "want to vote" because her "place is at home on the mat." In the second, a rooster says to a hen that holding an umbrella, "'Tiss man's privilege, love," and then he "held it above / His own head, so it dripped in her ear." Buck, "Anti-Suffrage Sentiments," 9.

in which Wylie's rhetorical power found support.[111] Nor was this an enclosed domestic space with Buck and apart from public life, as Buck ventured out to join Wylie at "suffrage parades."[112] Moreover, the women's home itself became a site for suffrage activism. In the words of MacCracken, who followed Taylor as president, "Buck and Wylie's home 'in the center of old Poughkeepsie became a rallying place for suffrage and for many other movements.'"[113]

Again, however, the progressive erotic of egalitarianism that animated the women's romantic relationship and rhetorical practices was marked by not only an idealization of equality in the abstract but also an apparent indifference to racial or ethnic equity in reality. Situating Wylie's suffrage activism within its broader context, the racism of the white women's suffrage movement has been widely documented.[114] Analyses of this racism, as V. Jo Hsu and Jen McDaneld both note, often center white suffragist opposition to the Fifteenth Amendment as well as blatantly racist statements by well-known leaders in the movement. Earlier in the century, for example, Elizabeth Cady Stanton infamously prompted readers, "think of Patrick and Sambo and Hans Yung Tung, who do not know the difference between a monarchy and a republic, who can not read the Declaration of Independence or Webster's spelling-book, making laws for Lucretia Mott, Ernestine L. Rose, and Anna E. Dickinson."[115]

The lesser-known Wylie, unlike Stanton, does not appear to have left behind elaborate statements about suffrage, especially with respect to the Fifteenth Amendment or the voting rights of men (and women) of color. Records are also limited for the local Equal Suffrage League turned Poughkeepsie Woman Suffrage Party, of which Wylie was a leader.[116] But what documentation does exist suggests still more "power-evasive communication" with respect to race and "segregated belongings" among Wylie, other white women activists, and their white male allies in these suffrage groups.[117] Speakers known to have been hosted by the organizations during Wylie's tenure include, for example, author Charlotte Perkins Gilman; labor union organizer Rose Schneiderman; British journalist Ethel Arnold; socialist editor and

---

111. Buck, "Anti-Suffrage Sentiments," 9.

112. Bordelon, *Feminist Legacy*, 24. "Buck's involvement in women's issues was supported," Bordelon continued, "through her relationship with Wylie."

113. Bordelon, *Feminist Legacy*, 24. On this same point, also see Hesler, "Lost Legacy," 71.

114. Ginzberg, *Elizabeth*; Goodier, "Doublespeak"; Hsu, "Voting"; M. S. Jones, *Vanguard*; McDaneld, "White Suffragist"; Palczewski, "1919"; Sneider, "Impact"; and Tetrault, *Myth*.

115. Stanton, "Manhood," qtd. in Hsu, "Voting," 272; and McDaneld, "White Suffragist," 246. See also Flexner, *Century*, 138; Ginzberg, *Elizabeth*, 130; Newman, *White*, 5; and Tetrault, *Myth*, 28.

116. Boice, "Woman," 41.

117. Carrillo Rowe, *Power Lines*, 73. See also Frankenberg, *White Women*; and Lorde, "Age, Race, Class."

cofounder of the Men's League for Woman Suffrage, Max Eastman; socialist child labor activist Florence Kelley; labor educator Hilda Smith; first president of the National League of Women Voters, Maud Wood Park; peace activist Ruth Morgan of the League of Women Voters; and Eleanor Roosevelt. This is, to put it simply, an exclusively white group. Notably absent are Black women suffragettes.[118] Notably present is Gilman, whose racism and xenophobia have been analyzed already.[119] There is no reason to presume, then, that Wylie's rhetorical practices on behalf of white women's suffrage addressed questions of difference among women any more than did Buck's rhetorical theory. Instead, the progressive erotic of sapphic egalitarianism that fueled their rhetorical labors was one of "power-evasive intimacy."[120]

Recognizing these complicities, it remains remarkable that Wylie was able to be so politically and rhetorically active in the white women's suffrage movement even as she held considerable administrative responsibilities as a department head at Vassar. Though Buck and Wylie exercised their rhetorical power most fully in different arenas, through published scholarly writing and suffrage activism respectively, they cooperated so that their romantic friendship could function as an equal source of rhetorical power for both women. Their rhetorical practices were animated, at the same time, by the values of equality and cooperation that defined their sapphic ideals and erotic of egalitarianism. Buck's published writing theorized an idealized rhetoric as cooperative communication between equals, while Wylie worked with fellow suffrage activists to advocate for equal voting rights for white women and men. In both forms of rhetorical practice, these women idealized equality in the abstract, but they evaded actual power differences and advocated for equality only on behalf of other similarly privileged white women. This same erotic of sapphic egalitarianism that infused the women's rhetorical practices, in its ideals as well as shortcomings, also made possible their rhetorical power as enacted through shared administration of Vassar's English department and its rhetoric program.

## Egalitarian Administration of Rhetorical Education

Turning from Buck's and Wiley's rhetorical practices to their pedagogical work as a faculty couple, this section considers how a progressive erotic of

---

118. On Black women's suffrage activism, see August, "Strained Sisterhood"; Bailey, "Between"; "Black Women's Suffrage Collection"; Gold, "Creating"; Jones, *Vanguard*; Samek, "(White) Women"; and White, *Too Heavy*.
119. Knight, "Charlotte."
120. Carrillo Rowe, *Power Lines*, 73.

egalitarianism also infused their administration of rhetorical education at Vassar. Even with romantic letters between the women unavailable, there are a range of primary sources that document their administrative and pedagogical labors. These records include letters exchanged with other friends and colleagues, Buck's published textbooks that were used in Vassar courses on rhetoric and writing, administrative records from the English department, and memorial accounts written by former students. In existing archival research with these materials, feminist rhetorical scholars have noted the importance of Buck and Wylie's working relationship to the rhetorical education and writing program administration within the department. "At the heart of the English department," in L'Eplattenier's words, "was the great friendship between Gertrude Buck and Laura Wylie . . . as well as the intellectual connection between these two women."[121] My own analysis extends feminist arguments about Buck and Wylie's administration of rhetorical education at Vassar by showing how the progressive erotic of sapphic egalitarianism that animated their same-sex romantic friendship also shaped their cooperative academic leadership as two equals. This shared leadership in turn informed the rhetoric curriculum at Vassar in ways that were productive for young women—but only for those privileged by whiteness.

Before I detail how the erotic of Buck and Wylie's relationship animated their administrative work, it is important to emphasize the extent to which this rhetorical labor reinforced existing hierarchies of difference among women. Buck and Wylie carried out their rhetorical labors at a settler institution, Vassar, that produced "segregated belongings" for the benefit of already privileged young white women.[122] While the racism and classism at Vassar was not unique among private women's colleges of the period, it remains necessary to recognize (including in contrast with Putnam's and Holley's experiences at Oberlin and their later rhetorical and pedagogical labors in collaboration with African Americans). As pointed out by Linda M. Perkins, in her work on racial integration across the Seven Sisters, Vassar was the last of these institutions to change their formal policy in order to allow the admission of students of color, which they did not do until 1940.[123] Moreover, when it was discovered during the late nineteenth century that Vassar had admitted a light-skinned African American student, Anita Florence Hemmings, this discovery led to "scandal." Hemmings still managed to successfully complete her studies, becoming the first (known) African American graduate of Vassar in 1897. But Vassar administrators "clearly felt that the presence of African-

---

121. L'Eplattenier, "Investigating," 71.
122. Carrillo Rowe, *Power Lines*, 73.
123. Perkins, "Racial Integration," 106, cited in Bordelon, *Feminist Legacy,* 9–10.

American women, even those with a slight tinge of black blood, would detract from the image it sought to project as an institution for the aristocratic and genteel women."[124]

The interconnectedness of settler-colonial racism and classism at Vassar is further evident in MacCracken's emphasis on the need for Wylie to hire English teachers "who had the 'appropriate' social and economic background and who could help students 'enter into possession of their racial and national inheritance in the humanities.'"[125] This "racial and national" intellectual inheritance at Vassar—in E Cram's terms, this "violent inheritance"—was clearly that of the dominant white settler culture.[126] At Vassar, the inheritance of Western rhetoric and English was now handed down to not only young men but also young women, though only those who were privileged by nation, race, and class.

To be sure, this increased access to education, even and particularly for white women, was under debate and not at all taken for granted during the period. As previously discussed, opposition to privileged women's higher education was often articulated through assertions that it would make them less likely to marry and have children. While women graduates did indeed marry and have children at lower rates, such assertions were bound up with not only gendered expectations but also the white supremacy and classism of eugenics discourse.[127] Again, "alarms about the low birth-rate of middle-class white women" who became educated were tied to fears about a "resulting 'race suicide.'"[128] As Campbell writes with respect to Vassar students, these "young women . . . entered universities amidst public debate over . . . the future of white civilization."[129] This debate was discussed at the infamous graveyard suffrage meeting held by students and supporters just outside of Vassar. When Gilman addressed the group (1908), "she contemptuously dismissed President Roosevelt's race suicide scare" (though, again, many of Gilman's own ideas were racist and xenophobic).[130] Operating within this same context, Buck and Wylie themselves did not work to preserve "the nation" or "the race" through the biological reproduction of white family. However, insofar as their actions

---

124. Perkins, "Racial Integration," 107, quoted in Bordelon, *Feminist Legacy,* 9–10. Also see Perkins, "African American."

125. L'Eplattenier, "Investigating," 168. Wylie's response to MacCracken is reprinted in Campbell, *Toward,* 271.

126. Cram, *Violent Inheritance.*

127. On the lower marriage and birth rates among college educated women, see Campbell, *Toward,* 167.

128. Franzen, *Spinsters,* 5.

129. Campbell, *Toward,* xliii.

130. "Vassar Meets in Graveyard"; and Knight, "Charlotte."

as academic leaders and educators focused on making higher education—and the range of kinship and professional options it afforded—available to young women at Vassar, this rhetorical labor perpetuated hierarchies of difference by serving only those women already privileged by white femininity and its "racial and national inheritance."[131]

Where Wylie and Buck's administrative labor did challenge existing power differentials was in the institutional realm of the academy. Although Wylie served as department head, had hired Buck, and was her supervisor, the women shared leadership for the department in ways that reflected the egalitarianism of their romantic friendship more so than the hierarchies of the academy (and most other workplaces too, to be sure). Wylie put her ideals of equality and cooperation into practice, as Bordelon notes, in that she and Buck "revised the traditional power of the chair by developing a collaborative model."[132] This model involved a sharing of power by Wylie and Buck, as well as greater involvement of the faculty writ large. Wylie described their approach in a departmental report addressed to MacCracken (1921), claiming that "from 1886 at least, we have worked co-operatively whenever co-operation was possible" in a "democratically organized department."[133] This spirit of democratic cooperation animated departmental leadership and faculty governance just as it did Buck and Wylie's intimate relationship. According to Campbell, writing about Buck and Wylie's professional relationship, it was "at the center of the democratic harmony within the department."

Buck and Wylie's progressive erotic of egalitarianism was matched by concrete actions with respect to not only the cooperation among faculty but also the equalization of faculty salaries. Administrative records show that Wylie repeatedly advocated for promotions and raises for Buck. In a 1909 department report, Wylie even offered the following recommendation: "that Professor Buck's salary be made equal to that of the head of the department."[134] Explaining her rationale, Wylie continued, "this has for some time seemed just to me, because of the size, and consequent administrative work of the department of English. Of this administrative work, Miss Buck does her full share, relieving me entirely of a great deal of it. Indeed, if we did not work together in entire harmony, it would probably be necessary either for me to do considerably less teaching, or to divide the department."[135] According to Campbell,

---

131. L'Eplattenier, "Investigating," 168.
132. Bordelon, *Feminist Legacy*, 79.
133. Quoted in Campbell, *Toward*, 273. The report itself is reprinted in Campbell's collection, and this same passage is also discussed in L'Eplattenier, "Investigating," 71.
134. Quoted in L'Eplattenier, "Investigating," 81. Also see Bordelon, *Feminist Legacy*, 85–86.
135. Quoted in L'Eplattenier, "Investigating," 81; and Bordelon, *Feminist Legacy*, 86.

also writing about Wylie's advocacy for Buck's equal pay, Wylie saw Buck as "an equal and was grateful for the administrative duties she performed."[136] It is important to keep in mind that in advocating for equal pay for Buck, Wylie was seeking, in effect, an increase to her own household income. I point this out not to undermine the significance of Wylie's egalitarianism. Rather, it was because of both women's egalitarianism that they sought to cultivate equal respect—and compensation—for each woman's labor at both home and work. Nor did they act on this value only within the context of their relationship as a couple. In another departmental report (1919), Buck similarly argued for broader salary equity across the department's faculty, asserting that "justice demands the equalization and the increase of salaries in each rank."[137]

The egalitarian sense of justice that informed the women's leadership involved a sharing of not only power but also labor. As Wylie exclaimed in a 1916 letter to Hart, "it is a very great relief to have Miss Buck back in her place, as she carries a lot of work that last year went, all too largely, without being done."[138] Letters like this one echo, albeit in more familiar language, the same claims that Wylie made in administrative reports, about the work Buck "carries." Returning to the epigraph that opened this chapter, Wylie (1916) similarly wrote that Buck "relieves me of many small cares which, though far from oppressive, eat much into my time." Buck did not simply carry out tasks, however, but took a leadership role, using her expertise to guide administrative action within the department. "Of course no one knows so well as she just what things are to be done," Wylie continued, "and just how to go about doing them. Every detail of the house as well as of the college work has grown up with her Knowledge, and all she needs to do is to press a button to make things move." The "many small cares" that Wylie mentioned included the work of hiring, training, and mentoring instructors in the department. The women's cooperative approach to this labor is apparent in a memorial recollection by a Vassar alumna, Elizabeth Kemper Adams, who was hired to teach in the department. After explaining that she had been hired by Wylie to return as an instructor in 1899, Adams wrote (1934), "But from the first, both she and Miss Buck were most helpful and friendly, and for the first time I began to think about the teaching process and found a new and engrossing intellectual stimulation." Adams discussed how, with Buck and Wylie's mentoring, she went on to pursue graduate training at the University of Chicago with Professor

---

136. Campbell, *Toward,* xxii.
137. Quoted in Campbell, *Toward,* 254.
138. Correspondence from Wylie to Hart, October 21, 1916, VCL. This typewritten letter is dated "October 21, 1916." In the archives, however, it is included between two other letters dated 1919 in box 3, folder 5.

John Dewey, whom Buck knew from her studies at Michigan. Whether in departmental reports, Wylie's letters, or the recollections of former students and instructors, "it seems apparent," L'Eplattenier concludes, "that Wylie and Buck shared in the administrative work of the department."[139]

Buck and Wylie's manner of working together, in their public-facing professions as well as their intimate relationship, is evident in the daily writing that carried out the quotidian details of both arenas of life. Each woman in her writing, whether in the form of department reports or letters to friends and colleagues, frequently spoke on behalf of the other. In a letter from Buck to her mentor Scott, she wrote (1909), "Miss Wylie joins me in regards to you. If you are in the east at any time during the year we should be most happy to have you stop over and see the college and us."[140] In another letter to Scott, Buck spoke on behalf of Wylie when recommending a Vassar student for Michigan's graduate program and an assistantship.[141] After describing the student's strengths, Buck continued (1913), "Miss Wylie has often spoken of her as a future member of our own department so you may know we think as highly as possible of her."[142] This writing on behalf of each other extended to more formal documents. In 1900, when Wylie was unwell, Buck wrote the department's report, noting in the report that she had done so and indicating Wylie had "authorized me to sign this for her."[143] L'Eplattenier suggests further and provides compelling evidence "that—whether orally or through drafting or copying—Buck and Wylie co-authored the majority of official documents that emerged from the English department's offices."[144]

The women also wrote cooperatively, with and on behalf of each other, within the more personal documents of their relationship. I quoted previously the 1911 letter to Hart that Wylie signed, "with love from Miss Buck and me and a lick from Berlin."[145] Other letters to Hart use the first person plural, "we," seemingly in reference to Wylie and Buck, though there was apparently no need to specify the pronoun reference.[146] Wylie's papers even include notes and letters to Hart from Burly the dog, from Burly and "Miss Buck," and from

---

139. L'Eplattenier, "Investigating," 84.
140. Correspondence from Buck to Scott, October 28, 1909, BHL.
141. Mastrangelo, "Building," 415.
142. Correspondence from Buck to Scott, April 3, 1913, quoted in Mastrangelo, "Building," 416.
143. Campbell, *Toward*, 253, 262.
144. L'Eplattenier, "Investigating," 78. See also 79, 96, 100.
145. Correspondence from Wylie to Hart, April 20, 1911, VCL.
146. See, for example, the description of travel plans in Correspondence from Wylie to Hart, March 23, 1909, VCL.

"Berlin C. Wylie"![147] Setting aside the cuteness of writing from the perspective of their dog, I mean to emphasize that Buck and Wylie wrote as a unit, the voice of each white woman able to speak for the other, as they worked in close cooperation. In this way, their letters and departmental records make clear how enjoined the women's lives were, in both intimate and professional terms, as companions and colleagues.

This cooperation and equality that defined Buck and Wylie's erotic as rhetorical power also carried forward within the curriculum for privileged young women in at least two important ways.[148] First, the department valued the whiteness of Western rhetoric on par with the whiteness of English literature. In the department report from 1900, referenced above, Buck and Wylie wrote that "the rhetorical side of English . . . maintains in all our courses a relation with the literature [sic] at once coequal and complementary."[149] The women saw rhetoric and literature as equally important areas of teaching and learning. This curricular perspective was consistent with both women's scholarly writing. Again, in Buck's communication theory of discourse, she idealized rhetoric as well as literature as forms of cooperative communication between equals—while ignoring the actual power differentials at play across the "human differences" of age, race, class, and so on that Lorde underscores.[150] Wylie, for her part, brought such limited yet rhetorically inflected social perspectives to bear in her literary criticism. In Bordelon's words, "rhetoric for Buck is a broad, interdisciplinary study of communication; it is also interconnected with literary criticism."[151]

Perhaps more remarkable than Buck seeing literature as equal to rhetoric was that Wylie, as a literary scholar and head of an English department, shared this view. Wylie offered her perspective in the report where she argued for Buck's salary to be made equal to her own. After noting that, without Buck's administrative involvement, Wylie may need "to do considerably less teaching," she continued, "or to divide the department, as has been unfortunately done in many places, into the departments of English or Rhetoric, and of Literature."[152] As Campbell writes, it was Buck and Wylie's "partnership"—a partnership, I want to emphasize again, that was both professional and romantic—which "served as a reference point for the close connection between

---

147. Correspondence to Hart, August 2, 1912, August 29, 1912, April 18, 1914, VCL.
148. Administration of the program is also examined in L'Eplattenier and Mastrangelo, *Historical Studies*.
149. Quoted in Campbell, *Toward*, 260. Also quoted in Bordelon, *Feminist Legacy*, 38.
150. Lorde, "Age, Race, Class," 115.
151. Bordelon, *Feminist Legacy*, 40.
152. Quoted in L'Eplattenier, "Investigating," 81; and Bordelon, *Feminist Legacy*, 86.

rhetoric and literature within the curriculum."[153] In L'Eplattenier's words, "the great friendship" between the women "allowed for the creation of an English department that functioned cooperatively and attempted to decrease as much as possible the privileging of Literature over Writing."[154]

While Wylie and Buck valued the whiteness of Western rhetoric and English literature equally, with their leadership modeling cooperation between two areas of the department, the women's erotic of egalitarianism also informed the curriculum in a second way, at the level of pedagogy within its courses in rhetoric, writing and, to a lesser extent, speech. Existing feminist scholarship has examined this rhetorical education at length, albeit without a focus on the romantic dimensions of Buck and Wylie's relationship.[155] Most notably, Bordelon offers an extended analysis of Buck's textbooks and how they informed instruction in rhetoric for white women at Vassar. Especially in *A Course in Argumentative Writing* (1899) and *A Handbook for Argumentation and Debate* (1906), Buck's pedagogy prompted these socially privileged and educationally segregated students to debate and develop arguments about topics such as suffrage, slavery, unions, and coeducation.[156] As Bordelon's analysis shows, Buck "encouraged young women to question received opinion, to evaluate critically their own thought processes, and to act in a way that promoted equality and cooperation."[157] Buck's approach to debate and argumentation obviously reflected the political potential and limitations of her theory of rhetoric, already discussed, and this approach was in many ways unique for the period.[158] Importantly, she enacted this approach at Vassar with Wylie's approval as department head. Part of what is significant about the rhetorical education that Buck and Wylie made possible at Vassar is how the progressive erotic of the women's relationship enabled their shared leadership of the department and its program in rhetoric, just as the program itself emphasized learning and developing rhetoric in service of egalitarian values of equality and cooperation—but only through the "power-evasive communication styles" generally

---

153. Carrillo Rowe, *Power Lines*, 73; and Campbell, *Toward*, xxii.

154. L'Eplattenier, "Investigating," 71.

155. For analysis of the students' commencement speeches as evidence of rhetorical education, see Bordelon, "Composing."

156. Campbell, *Toward*, xxxii–xxxiii.

157. Bordelon, *Feminist Legacy*, 103.

158. Additional analyses of rhetorical education via Buck's textbooks are available in Bordelon, "Gertrude Buck's Approach"; and Bordelon, "Gertrude Buck: Revisioning." For discussion of what made rhetorical education at Vassar unique for the period, see L'Eplattenier, "Investigating," 75.

"contingent upon segregated belongings" among exclusively privileged white women.[159]

These are the values, both promising and problematic, that drove virtually all of Buck and Wylie's lives and work together as white women. Their romantic friendship, which took the form of a late nineteenth- and early twentieth-century Boston marriage, was fueled by an erotic of egalitarianism that reflected not only Progressive Era ideals but also the homogenic and sapphic idealism of the same period. Within this idealized view of same-sex relationships, the erotic characterizing them was understood as oriented to social transformation in service of democracy and social justice. Along these lines, the egalitarian erotic shared by Buck and Wylie was a source of rhetorical power that enabled their romantic friendship as well as their rhetorical labors. In terms of rhetorical education at Vassar, a segregated institution for other privileged white women, Buck and Wylie's egalitarian ideals fueled their cooperation as equals in a faculty couple as well as shared leadership of the English department and its program in rhetoric. These ideals also informed the curriculum in the department, such that Western rhetoric was valued on par with English literature as in Buck's communication theory of discourse. Students were taught to participate in discourse with attention to questions of democratic social reform and through practices that relied on a valuing of equality and cooperation within communication—but that relied on segregation and exclusion in order to ignore the realities of hierarchal differences among people. In these ways, the erotic of Buck and Wylie's same-sex relationship functioned as a source of rhetorical power that helped to make possible their shared administration of rhetorical education for women at Vassar.

Sapphic idealism was just that, however. As referenced throughout, Buck and Wylie's intimate and professional "alliance," in Carrillo Rowe's terms, was the sort of rhetorical collaboration through which white women "get things done," yet only insofar as "they are propelled by affective investments . . . forged through the reproduction of sameness grounded in institutional power."[160] The erotic of Buck and Wylie's relationship did indeed function as a source of rhetorical power, in other words, but such power was forged through both intimate and institutional alliances of segregation and sameness among white women. In this way and others, Buck and Wylie were like the other couples in this study—and so many white women reformers throughout the long nineteenth century and into the present—who have fallen short in enacting their idealism.

---

159. Carrillo Rowe, *Power Lines*, 73. See also Carrillo Rowe, *Power Lines*, 80, 145; and Frankenberg, *White Women*, 43–55, 142–57.

160. Carrillo Rowe, *Power Lines*, 140.

## Reproducing Eurocentrism among White Women

So far this chapter has shown how Buck and Wylie's romantic friendship, fueled by a progressive erotic of sapphic egalitarianism, enabled their development of rhetorical theory and suffrage activism as well as their administration of rhetorical education at Vassar. Although Buck and Wylie's erotic of egalitarianism was explicitly progressive, with the women idealizing equality and cooperation, their joint efforts to write, teach, and administer according to those ideals occurred mainly within segregated settings like the settler institution of Vassar and the white women's suffrage movement. Nor did Buck and Wylie leave behind a record of addressing inequalities among women even within these educational and activist settings. In Campbell's words, writing about Buck in particular, her "conception of community could be criticized for ignoring lines of power and differences within the community."[161] However, the problem is not only that Buck and Wylie reproduced the segregation and sameness of white institutions and activism by working on behalf of white women while leaving unaddressed the power differentials between women. Rather, Buck and Wylie also directly advanced the logics of colonialism and slavery through Eurocentric arguments about education, race, and civilization.

These Eurocentric views are present from Buck's earliest publications. During her days as a student at Vassar herself, she wrote an account of her spiritual and religious transformation from Methodism to Unitarianism. In the essay, she echoed Carpenter's theory of homogenic love and, at the same time, what Carrillo Rowe characterizes as the "loveless encounter" of "the civilizing and Christianizing processes through which the colonial subject . . . encounters . . . the colonizer."[162] For example, Buck described becoming less "selfish" through her "association with a real humanity-lover, interested in people, as such—especially in the so-called 'lower classes.'"[163] "I burned at first to preach to them," Buck wrote of her own "civilizing and Christianizing" desires, and "later just to live among and love them. My heart seemed bursting with love for all the loveless." Without questioning her own colonizing presumptions about who was "loveless," Buck continued, "I could scarcely restrain myself, passing on the street a gross and discontented-looking negro girl, or bent, forlorn old day-laborer, from throwing my arms about them, holding my face to theirs and saying—'I love you! I love you with all my heart. And your Father loves you.'" One can only hope that Buck did restrain her racist, classist, and colonizing desires, leaving alone her fellow passersby.

---

161. Campbell, *Toward*, xliii.
162. Carpenter, *Homogenic Love*, 4; and Carrillo Rowe, *Power Lines*, 186.
163. Buck, "Religious Experience," reprinted in Campbell, *Toward*, 23.

At least in part, Buck's words should be understood as she presented them: as those of a young person coming to a broader spiritual awareness and a relatively expanded sense of "love." However, these words were later reprinted in the *Vassar Miscellany Monthly* as late at 1923, just after Buck had passed away but still during Wylie's tenure.[164] Buck's language is obviously patronizing to African Americans, poor people, and physical laborers. This patronizing language is consistent with the white saviorism and Eurocentrism common among white women teachers who look down on those they believe they are "helping." The language is also rooted in a much longer history of British imperialism and Christianizing colonialism. While at least some of Buck's views may have changed over time, her perspective as a young white woman was reproduced among the similarly privileged students at Vassar through posthumous publication in the school's paper. Especially when read alongside Buck and Wylie's broader pattern of "power-evasive communication styles," such patronizing language and Eurocentric views must be understood as reproducing the logics of slavery and settler colonialism.[165]

Eurocentric colonialist views of education are most evident in what Buck called her "organic" theory of education. This theory of education relied on racist ideas from social Darwinism that informed a "culture-epoch" theory of education among children.[166] Bordelon makes this point in her analysis of Buck's *Organic Education: A Manual for Teachers in Primary and Grammar Grades* (1897), which was coauthored with normal school teacher Harriet Scott before Wylie hired Buck to return to Vassar to teach.[167] The book's "approach resembled the 'culture-epoch' theory of education," Bordelon explains, "which viewed child development as a 'repetition in little of the history of civilization,'" with student progress through "different grade levels . . . supposedly matching the 'progress' of civilization, or 'certain period[s] of race development.'"[168] Civilization was "an explicitly racial concept" at the time, according to Gail Bederman: "human races were assumed to evolve from simple savagery, through violent barbarism, to advanced and valuable civilization. But only the white races had, as yet, evolved to the civilized stage."[169] As Bordelon points out, "this racialized view of civilization is evident in Scott and Buck's curriculum, which includes no mention of African Americans and

---

164. Campbell, *Toward*, 19.
165. Carrillo Rowe, *Power Lines*, 73.
166. Bordelon, *Feminist Legacy*, 50–51; and McClintock, *Imperial Leather*, 37.
167. A selection of the book is reprinted in Campbell, *Toward*, 3–18.
168. Buck and Scott, *Organic Education*, 4, 13, quoted in Bordelon, *Feminist Legacy*, 50.
169. Bederman, *Manliness*, 25, quoted in Bordelon, *Feminist Legacy*, 51.

places white Anglo-Saxons at the top of the civilization ladder."[170] The women's deployment of culture-epoch theory within their organic theory of education "is obviously racist."[171]

Along with being racist, Buck and Wylie's advance of organic and culture-epoch theories of education was colonialist, tied to the larger project of British imperialism. Specifically, these theories of education echo a related but broader set of ideas exemplified by the "figure" of "the evolutionary family Tree of Man."[172] As Anne McClintock explains, such ideas similarly drew on social Darwinism, which was "first applied to nature" and "now applied to cultural history," in order to construct "a global allegory of 'natural' social difference" and thus naturalize imperialism. Consider, for example, Paolo Mantegazza's visual rhetoric in "Morphological Tree of the Human Races." As McClintock outlines, this tree image represents all of global history through "a single, European Ur-narrative" in which history is "an organic process of upward growth, with the European as the apogee of progress." The tree's branches are labeled according to a hierarchy of racial and ethnic categories: "Aryans" are listed at the top, "Negritos" at the bottom, and "Semites," "Japanese," "Americans," and "Australians" in between, to name just a few from among many more categories.[173] In this figure, hierarchies of difference get naturalized as historical "progress" in keeping with scientific racism, much as they were naturalized as pedagogical progress or "learning" in culture-epoch theories of education like Buck's.

Lest it be assumed that Buck's ideas in *Organic Education* were an exception to her and Wylie's overall approach to education, it is important to consider how Buck advanced similarly racist and colonialist arguments in other publications. In another article already in print (1896) when Wylie decided to hire Buck, she wrote about how the Detroit Normal Training School was based on the "idea . . . of the 'culture-epochs' in education.'"[174] "In brief," she explained, the idea "may be stated as follows: Every child repeats in his own development the history of the race; therefore his education should follow, as closely as may be, the lines of progress drawn by the civilization of the race." Illustrating this "development" in Eurocentric terms, Buck explained that the first grade in the school began with stories, lessons, and other activities about "*Hiawatha*, the little Indian boy" from "a type of the nomadic period in

---

170. Bordelon, *Feminist Legacy*, 51.
171. Bordelon, *Feminist Legacy*, 51.
172. McClintock, *Imperial Leather*, 37.
173. McClintock, *Imperial Leather*, 38.
174. Buck, "Another Phase," 376.

civilization."[175] Next, in this Eurocentric view of civilization's "development," are classrooms focused on "*Kablu,* a little early Aryan boy," Greece and Rome, and then the Renaissance.[176] By the start of the fourth grade, classroom lessons were, in Buck's slightly US Americanized version of racial and ethnic hierarchies, "devoted to the Puritans in England, in Holland, and in America."[177] All of the lessons were oriented, she concluded, to the need for "cooperation" within a civilization.[178] Buck's emphasis on cooperation reflected the egalitarian values present throughout her work. That she reached this conclusion about cooperation within a discussion of such a Eurocentric and colonizing pedagogical approach may seem strange on the surface but is indicative of the problematic complexities of her and Wylie's life and work together. They idealized cooperation and equality among white people while rhetorically reproducing Eurocentric hierarchies of difference and education.

Nor was this problematic side of Buck and Wylie's rhetorical labors limited to just a couple of Buck's earliest writings on a single topic. Similar to the racism and colonialism in her views on education, Buck compared "the modern" with "the primitive consciousness," and "the child in a civilized nation" with "the savage," when developing her theory of metaphor in *The Metaphor: A Study in the Psychology of Rhetoric* (1899).[179] She also perpetuated racist stereotypes in her coauthored textbook *A Handbook of Argumentation and Debating* (1906). On the one hand, as Bordelon acknowledges in her analysis of the textbook, Buck and Mann offered students "examples . . . drawn from social issues concerning various disadvantaged and oppressed groups" as well as pointed students to texts written by Booker T. Washington and W. E. B. Du Bois.[180] On the other hand, the book includes "negative" examples that "could be seen as reinscribing racial stereotypes."[181] "Students are asked," Bordelon recounts, "to group a list of assertions into a few main headings 'for the exclusion of Chinese laborers from the United States.'"[182] The assertations on the list include as follows: "because they gamble," "because they carry on a secret system of slavery," and "because they are barbarous."[183] Although "these and the other examples could also be viewed as encouraging students to focus on broader social issues and patterns of oppression within society," any such

---

175. Buck, "Another Phase," 377.
176. Buck, "Another Phase," 378.
177. Buck, "Another Phase," 382.
178. Buck, "Another Phase," 384.
179. Buck, *Metaphor,* reprinted in Campbell, *Toward,* 42.
180. Bordelon, *Feminist Legacy,* 115.
181. Bordelon, *Feminist Legacy,* 115.
182. Buck and Mann, *Handbook,* 14, quoted in Bordelon, *Feminist Legacy,* 115.
183. Buck and Mann, *Handbook,* 14, quoted in Bordelon, *Feminist Legacy,* 115.

encouragement is undermined by the framing of social issues in ways so thoroughly bound up in logics of colonialism and slavery.[184]

That Buck and Wylie advanced the Eurocentric arguments about education, race, and civilization considered throughout this section only reinforces my earlier point about their progressive erotic of sapphic egalitarianism: that, even as it idealized equality and cooperation, their rhetorical practices and pedagogies were power-evasive in ways that reinforced hierarchical differences within and beyond the segregated institutional and activist settings of the women's rhetorical labors. Buck's and Wylie's evasion of difference was not passively neutral or indifferent, in other words, but actively exclusionary. The narrow equality they worked for was only among relatively privileged white women and with their white male counterparts. Within this conception of equality, "the primitive" was not equal or even included; nor was the "gross and discontented-looking negro girl" (or the "bent, forlorn old daylaborer").[185] In this sense, as Carrillo Rowe discusses, the segregated relations of institutions like Vassar allowed these "white women to experience power and marginality as an exclusively gender-based phenomenon."[186] At the same time, in those exceptional instances where Buck and Wylie actually did address rather than evade social differences, they reinforced the damaging colonial and racist thinking that was used to justify not only educational segregation but also systemic imperialism, colonialism, and slavery both in and beyond what is now the US.

This is not to say that Buck and Wylie's simultaneous embrace of egalitarian ideals and reproduction of racist logics was the same as Leache and Wood's direct denouncements of equality, support for the Confederacy in the South, and embrace of sexual and racial "purity" as defined within eugenics discourse. Yet, even in Buck and Wylie's progressive erotic of sapphic egalitarianism, they, too, reinscribed difference through investments in the "dangerous fantasy" of white femininity.[187] Buck and Wylie advanced rhetorical theories and pedagogies fueled by an erotic of sapphic egalitarianism and, simultaneously, theorized education and taught white women in ways that reproduced the Eurocentrism of settler colonialism and slavery. Considering the example of Buck and Wylie alongside Leache and Wood—as well as Holley and Putnam—illustrates what I emphasize as the political variability of the erotic as rhetorical power. The erotic can fuel public speaking, published writing, and the teaching of rhetoric to multiple political ends—radical, conservative, and

---

184. Bordelon, *Feminist Legacy*, 115.
185. Buck, "Religious Experience"; reprinted in Campbell, *Toward*, 42, 23.
186. Carrillo Rowe, *Power Lines*, 131.
187. Lorde, "Age, Race, Class," 119.

progressive. Moreover, even at its most radical or progressive, the potential for the erotic as rhetorical power to productively engage with questions of difference is merely a *potential*—one in which, as Lorde herself theorizes, difference may be responded to in various ways that both challenge and entrench existing structures of power.[188]

## Conclusion

The erotic of rhetorical power that characterized Buck and Wylie's relationship was both productive and problematic—much like that of the other white couples in this study and along with many other reformers and educators across the long nineteenth century. With the erotic of Buck and Wylie's relationship made possible through slavery and settler colonialism, the women rhetorically reproduced Eurocentric views of education among white women at Vassar. There is little archival evidence to suggest they challenged institutional racism and classism at Vassar. Still more, Buck's published writing advanced a theory of education grounded in racist, settler-colonial logics of "race development" and "civilization."

At the same time, and reflecting the complexities of the erotic as a source of rhetorical power, the progressive erotic of sapphic egalitarianism animating Buck and Wylie's relationship empowered their labors as rhetors, educators, and administrators who worked toward at least some egalitarian values. This egalitarian erotic of their relationship reflected not only the Progressive Era values common among reformers but also the homogenic and sapphic idealism embraced within same-sex romantic friendships, which were understood as holding particular potential for the pursuit of those values. In keeping with this erotic of sapphic egalitarianism, Buck and Wylie's own relationship was a cooperative partnership between equals in which both women respected and supported the other's rhetorical practices in different realms. Buck was active primarily as a published writer of rhetorical theory and textbooks. Her writing theorized rhetoric as a cooperative form of communication between speakers and listeners, between readers and writers, as equals. At the same time, she advanced a narrow understanding of equality that evaded actual differences. This idealized view of rhetoric spanned what was, for Buck, an incredibly productive record of multiple publications—a record more substantive than that of most rhetorical scholars, from all genders, during the period.

---

188. Lorde, "Age, Race, Class," 115.

Whereas Wylie encouraged Buck's intellectual devotion to writing, Buck supported Wylie's rhetorical activity in connection to the white women's suffrage movement. Wylie was a local movement leader in Poughkeepsie, where she collaborated with other women to advocate for equal voting rights on behalf of privileged white women. She maintained this visible leadership and local activity in spite of opposition to suffrage activism from the president's office at Vassar. With the erotic of Buck and Wylie's relationship animating their rhetorical practices, these practices were enabled further, practically speaking, because as privileged women involved in a faculty couple rather than married to men, their time for writing and activism was freed up from some of the reproductive labor usually expected of married women. The women's Boston marriage also made it possible for them to be active as administrators in the racially segregated setting of Vassar's English department and program of rhetorical education. The women administered the department as equals, modeling cooperation among the faculty as a whole. Buck and Wylie fostered a curriculum in which Western rhetoric was valued on par with English literature, and students were taught to use rhetoric as a form of communication in service of cooperation and equality—though only within segregated relations among white people.[189]

Buck and Wylie shared their same-sex romantic friendship and their rhetorical labors for almost twenty-five years, until Buck's passing in 1922. Wylie stepped down from her role as department chair that year.[190] She retired from Vassar shortly after, in 1924, at which point she went on to teach at "the Bryn Mawr School for Women Workers, a pioneer effort in extending higher education opportunities to working-class women."[191] Wylie herself passed away in 1932. According to the *Poughkeepsie Courier* (1932), Wylie was "cremated and the ashes buried in the grave of her friend, Gertrude Buck, in Woodlands Cemetery, Philadelphia."[192] Wylie's will directed that "sufficient money be given the cometary to care for the permanent upkeep of the grave."[193] In addition, according to the *Packer Alumna* (1932), Wylie's "will set[ ] up a fund of $10,000 called the Gertrude Buck Fund."[194] The memorial fund named after Buck honored her founding, with Wylie's support, of the Community Theatre

---

189. Bordelon also considers the rhetorical influence of Buck and Wylie with respect to the teaching that their former students went on to do. In addition to the concluding chapter of Bordelon's book, *Feminist Legacy* (153–91), see Bordelon, "Contradicting"; Bordelon, "Muted Rhetors"; and Bordelon, "Restructuring."

190. Bordelon, *Feminist Legacy*, 11.

191. Bordelon, *Feminist Legacy*, 10.

192. Quoted in Campbell, *Toward*, xxii.

193. Quoted in Campbell, *Toward*, xxii.

194. "Laura Johnson Wylie," *Packer Alumna*, VCL.

of Poughkeepsie. The Buck Fund was designated for "use in this work" of "bring[ing] about a closer relation between the city and the college."

Former colleagues, students, and friends also worked to preserve the memory of Wylie. None other than Eleanor Roosevelt spoke at Wylie's funeral, noting her "gift for friendship."[195] Wylie, in addition to establishing the Buck Fund, had "bequeathed" the women's shared "home to the Women's City and Country Club to use rent-free for six months."[196] Club members set up "the Wylie Memorial Fund, with members donating money to help the organization purchase and maintain the house and Wylie's memory."[197] While at least some sources speak of Wylie's home and memory, it is more accurate to memorialize what was the home of Wylie *and* Buck—the center of a domestic and professional relationship animated by an erotic that made possible rhetorical labors by and for privileged white women at and beyond Vassar.

---

195. Roosevelt, "Tribute," VCL. See also Boice, "Woman," 48.
196. Hesler, "Lost Legacy," 71.
197. Hesler, "Lost Legacy," 71.

CONCLUSION TO INTERLUDES

## Future Archives

By 1897, when Gertrude Buck and Laura Wylie first met, there are no extant letters of Addie Brown or even Rebecca Primus. The last available letter mailed from Primus to her family, while she was still teaching at the Primus Institute, is from 1869. Brown passed away in 1870, not long after marrying Joseph Tines. The last letter to Primus is from her mother in 1872, the year before she married Charles Thomas. Yet, even as the archives of Brown and Primus's correspondence become quiet, Primus actually outlived Buck by a decade, passing away in 1932, the same year Wylie did. Crucially, as previously discussed, archival research about Brown and Primus's romantic friendship is possible only because Primus saved the letters from Brown for over sixty years, until her own death in 1932. "The collection of family letters and documents she had kept for so many years found its way to the Hobby Shop in Hartford," Farah Jasmine Griffin explains, "and in 1934 this collection was acquired by the Connecticut Historical Society."[1] Sadly, Primus's letters to Brown are not available—meaning, they have not been preserved (that we know of) and made available to the public for research.

But what if Brown was able to save Primus's letters and, at some point in the future, those letters are acquired by an archive?

---

1. Griffin, *Beloved Sisters*, 284.

This question imagines an alternative past that could make possible an alternative future, a future archive, one that aspires to align with Alexis Pauline Gumbs's speculative *M Archive*.[2] Within the context of settler colonialism, systemic racism, and capitalism, multiple factors worked against Brown's ability to preserve Primus's letters. Brown does not appear to have had access to a family home or other physical place where she could store intimate papers over the course of time.[3] In needing to work mainly as a domestic servant, Brown moved from one occupied territory to the next, across Connecticut and New York, usually living with whichever family or institution employed her.[4] At times, she moved from one white employer to the next because they refused to pay her agreed-upon wages. As Barbara Beeching notes, during the years from 1859 to 1867 alone, Brown "worked for fourteen different employers that we know of."[5] In a letter to Primus, Brown (1861) characterized her working and living situation as "roving around this unfriendly world."[6] This "roving" existence created far from ideal conditions under which to store Primus's letters. Brown probably was not in a position to save the letters, much less to garner the interest of nineteenth-century settler-colonial archives, which did not acquire, appraise, and provide access to the papers of African American women working as domestics.

However, it is not completely out of the question to imagine other letters or records that may exist, even if they have not been acquired by an archive thus far. With respect to Primus, a second collection has become available in recent years. Whereas the Primus family papers were acquired by the Connecticut Historical Society in 1934, the Rebecca Primus papers were acquired by the Arthur and Elizabeth Schlesinger Library as recently as 2017.[7] What I imagine, then, is a third archival collection, the Addie Brown papers, which contain the romantic letters from Primus and saved by Brown. Even if it is another eighty-three years before this collection is located and sold or donated, I imagine these letters offering new information and perspectives about Primus's desires in the women's romantic friendship. Did she, too, write about fantasies of marrying Brown? Of being Brown's teacher or teaching colleague? Of inviting her to live and work at the Primus Institute?

2. Gumbs, *M Archive*.
3. VanHaitsma, "Archival Framework," 32–33.
4. These were mainly white families and white-owned institutions. However, Brown did work as a domestic in at least one Black family, and it is likely that she boarded with the Primus family for a short time. Griffin, *Beloved Sisters*, 27, 18.
5. Beeching, *Hopes*, 145.
6. Correspondence from Brown to Primus, PF/CHS.
7. See PF/CHS; and SLRI.

In one sense, I ask these questions in recognition of how we limit our imaginations when we assume that the settler archives currently available are the only materials in existence. In another sense, though, imagining this possibility of an alternative past and future archive—and imagining *all* of the other possibilities that I have within these interludes—has risked imposing still more limitations on Brown and Primus as African American women.

First, my erotohistoriography risked and indeed encountered the limits of my own imagination. The archives of Brown and Primus's relationship are rich, and they include references to both women's other relationships (and affairs) with "people of more than one gender."[8] On the question of romantic relationships alone, "critical imagination" and "critical fabulation" grounded in these archives could generate many other alternate pasts for Brown and Primus.[9] Yet, in working within the scope of this project, I have limited my imagination to a romantic friendship between Brown and Primus as presumably cisgender women teachers who were able to live and work together as a couple, sustain that relationship over time, and have documentation of it preserved within archives. Importantly, this limited scope was envisioned by myself, a cis white scholar, and led to a project focused mainly on apparently cis white women. While I have imagined these alternative pasts for Brown and Primus as part of my effort to show how the erotic functioned as a source of rhetorical power in different ways for different women, Saidiya Hartman's reflections on "inevitable failure" echo in my mind (although my own failures are distinctly white, to be sure).[10]

Second, in developing imaginative interludes as a white woman, I risked the limitations and even the violence of my desires. Here, too, I return to Hartman's words. Reflecting on her critical fabulation about two Black girls who were enslaved, she writes, "initially I thought I wanted to represent the affiliations severed and remade in the hollow of the slave ship by imagining the two girls as friends, by giving them each one another."[11] "But in the end," Hartman continues, "I was forced to admit that I wanted to console myself." In my own ways, I am "forced to admit" that the alternate pasts I have imagined for Brown and Primus—whatever else they may or may not accomplish where intervening in the settler whiteness of feminist and LGBTQ+ histories of rhetoric—were born of my own desires to "console myself." I desired, wanted, and ached for a version of what was possible for the other women in the study to have been possible for Brown and Primus. Of course it cannot and could

---

8. Ochs, "Bisexual"; and VanHaitsma, "Archival Framework," 31.
9. Royster, *Traces*, 83; and Hartman, "Venus," 11.
10. Hartman, "Venus," 12.
11. Hartman, "Venus," 9.

not be. And in consoling myself, in seeking to satisfy my own desires, my erotohistoriography "replicates the very order of violence that it writes against by placing yet another demand upon [Brown and Primus], by requiring that [their] li[ves] be made useful or instructive, by finding in [them] a lesson for our future or a hope for history."[12]

Still, I imagine it: that future archives will make possible a different historiography of the erotic as a source of rhetorical power for more diverse women, that this book itself will have a different story to tell.

---

12. Hartman, "Venus," 14.

CONCLUSION

# Erotics of Rhetorical Power

This book has advanced a theory of the erotic as a source of rhetorical power. I conceive of the erotic as an interanimation of desires simultaneously intimate, intellectual, pedagogical, and political.[1] In being passionately shared, these desires gather the creative power to forge connections and foment change. This creative power takes on rhetorical valence as intimate connections blur the boundaries between so-called private and public life, fueling rhetorical practices that include public speaking, published writing, and the teaching of rhetoric oriented to social and political change.

I build this argument primarily through erotohistoriographic engagements with settler-colonial archives documenting white women's intimate relationships, rhetorical practices, and teaching careers over the course of the long nineteenth century. From the abolitionist movement to the backlash during Reconstruction and then resistance to white women's suffrage, the erotic of these women's romantic friendships animated their writing and speaking on questions of abolition, educational access, and voting rights as well as their teaching of rhetoric at freedmen's schools, boarding schools, and women's colleges. The archival studies across my chapters thus build not only over time, across different historical periods and social movements, but also through consideration of couples that were varied with respect to where they taught

---

1. Lorde, "Uses of the Erotic."

and, more importantly, to what ends. Reflecting the couples' divergent educational, social, and political desires, their intimate friendships and rhetorical activities were shaped by diverse erotics of antislavery affection, emulating beauty, and sapphic egalitarianism.

## From Ideals to Complexities

Attending to such diverse erotics underscores the need to theorize the erotic as rhetorical power in ways that recognize this form of power as politically complex rather than ideal. Central to this book's concept of the erotic as rhetorical power is my argument that although the same-sex erotic between cisgender women is often idealized for transcending differences in service of social transformation, that change may be oriented in radical, progressive, and/or conservative directions, thus challenging some harmful power dynamics while reproducing others. Moreover, even where the erotic as rhetorical power is directed to radical and progressive change, relatively privileged women still develop rhetorical practices and pedagogies that are materially grounded in—and rhetorically reproduce—settler colonialism and slavery. The erotic as rhetorical power is best understood not as an orientation to social justice, then, but as a seed of a multifaceted potentiality that can move in multiple and frequently competing directions. This more complex understanding of the erotic complicates surface-level treatments of Audre Lorde's broad body of thinking and writing about that erotic and difference. Simultaneously, this conception points to the significance of the erotic for investigating rhetorical power across positionalities and political orientations while remaining persistently attentive to questions of difference.

Rather than romanticize how the erotic as rhetorical power enabled the privileged women in this study to sustain their romantic friendships, public rhetorical activities, and teaching careers, it is necessary to emphasize how this same erotic was made possible by settler colonialism and slavery. On these material "grounds," privileges of nation, race, and class played a crucial role in the ability of Sallie Holley, Caroline Putnam, Irene Leache, Annie Wood, Gertrude Buck, and Laura Wylie to sustain their lifelong relationships and careers. Similar possibilities can be critically imagined for, but were not available to, African American and other BIPOC women like Addie Brown and Rebecca Primus.[2] As such, my research has focused mainly on the erotic as rhetorical power under specific conditions: for presumably cisgender women

---

2. Greyser, *Sympathetic Grounds*.

in same-sex relationships whose privileges of nation, race, and class made possible their educational access and professional opportunities.

Yet this politically complex erotic was not merely an "inheritance" for the white women in my study.[3] Rather, the women themselves rhetorically reproduced the problematic dynamics of settler colonialism and slavery. Whether through a radical erotic of antislavery affection, a conservative erotic of emulating "beauty," or a progressive erotic of sapphic egalitarianism, each couple passionately shared intellectual, pedagogical, and political desires that enlivened their intimate relationships and energized their public work together. Yet, even as the rhetorical labors of Holley, Putnam, Leache, Wood, Buck, and Wylie advanced at least some forms of positive social change, these women all perpetuated rhetorics of settler colonialism and slavery. The erotic as rhetorical power animating those practices and pedagogies was variously complicit with white saviorism, anti-Black racism against Southern worship practices, eugenics discourse, and Eurocentric culture-epoch theories.

By showing the importance of the erotic, both productive and problematic, to the broader history of rhetoric, my research not only advances rhetorical scholarship by uncovering the rhetorical activities of the women in my study. It also reinvigorates the study of romantic friendship while bringing together and building on feminist and LGBTQ+ historiography. I illustrate how romantic friendships were far from simplistic instances of social constraint, sexual repression, or equality across difference within intimate relations. Rather, these multidimensional relationships were marked by an erotic of rhetorical power that fueled rhetorical pedagogies and practices to socially and politically varied ends that were promising as well as troubling. The erotic of these romantic friendships held significance in the women's own time, for reform movements and rhetorical education on behalf of white girls and women and African Americans, and also holds significance now, for the theory and erotohistoriography of feminist and LGBTQ+ rhetorics. Indeed, I see potential for this theory that extends much wider than the focus of my archival research on the long nineteenth century. With an eye toward future studies of women's and LGBTQ+ rhetoric across historical periods, I urge that the erotic is a politically complex source of rhetorical power that is not marginal but central to the theory, practice, and teaching of rhetoric as well as to LGBTQ+ historiography.

---

3. Cram, *Violent Inheritance*.

## From Queer to Erotic

My archivally grounded theory of the erotic as rhetorical power stretches the study of LGBTQ+ rhetorics past a preoccupation with that which is queer, as in nonnormative. Queer rhetorics scholarship, including most of my own prior work, has tended to focus on the nonnormative, as in instances of "critical engagement with normative discourses of sexuality."[4] Certainly this queer engagement may take multiple forms, as Jonathan Alexander and Jacqueline Rhodes emphasize: it "torques [normative discourses] to create different or counter-discourses, giving voice and agency to multiple and complex sexual experiences." Moreover, this attention to an embrace of queerness "works against" the normative "cordoning off of the erotic" that Lorde pointed to and which persists in both rhetorical studies and much public discourse.[5] However, an overemphasis on nonnormative iterations of sexual experience or LGBTQ+ rhetoric tends to obscure the rhetorical power of the erotic for at least some people, forms of relationship, and periods of history.

Setting aside queerness in order to grapple with the richness of the erotic has been necessary for examining the rhetorical activities made possible by same-sex romantic friendships between the presumably cisgender women in this study. They strayed from the heteronormative path of opposite-sex marriage and biological reproduction. But their rhetoric, like that of most nineteenth-century women, has gone underexamined within queer rhetorics scholarship partly because their lives were not understood, then or now, as nonnormative with respect to sexuality. Nor did they publicly critique normative discourses of sexuality. Instead, romantic friendship was largely accepted, at least insofar as it was practiced by white women whose passions were presumed to be nonsexual and "pure." Within the teaching profession in particular, privileged women in romantic friendships were even seen as contributing to the pedagogical (if not biological) reproduction of the "white race" and settler "nation."

Holley and Putnam faced social ostracization among white people not because of their romantic friendship but because of their work on behalf of racial justice for African Americans in the South. Leache and Wood were conservative women whose teaching and writing defended normative gender and sexuality as well as social and racial hierarchies. Buck and Wylie's relationship, even at the turn of the century when discourses of sexuality and sexology had started to shift into greater public view, was also seen as a positive

---

4. Alexander and Rhodes, "Queer Rhetoric."
5. Alexander and Rhodes, "Queer Rhetoric."

contribution to the education of white women. Though they idealized egalitarianism, they advanced culture-epoch theories of education that reinforced Eurocentric views of "civilization." In all of these women's relationships and careers, they reproduced as much as they undermined normativity. There may be little purchase, then, in insisting on the queerness per se of these women's romantic friendships.

But the rhetorical implications of their same-sex relationships are certainly important to the history of LGBTQ+ rhetoric, and investigating the erotic more so than normativity provides an inroad to studying the rhetorical possibilities and limitations of these couples. In a similar vein, yet thinking outside of the specificity of romantic friendship between cisgender women, shifting our attention from queer rhetorics to the erotics of rhetorical power may serve the development of histories of LGBTQ+ rhetoric from historical periods and cultural contexts in which people did not understand themselves or organize into movements based on categories of sexual identity. A shift to investigating erotics of rhetorical power also opens up attention, just as importantly, to the rhetorical practices of LGBTQ+ people from any period who did not (or could not) embrace the public rhetorical performance of nonnormativity as an ideal (or option).

Finally, whereas I am invested primarily in the development of LGBTQ+ rhetorical study and historiography, I see potential for greater attention to the erotics of rhetorical power in a range of romantic relationships and domestic arrangements, including those understood as cisheterosexual. Here I think of work by Lindal Buchanan on the importance of collaborative relationships to women's rhetoric, as well as that by J. P. Hanly on the romantic and rhetorical alliance of Lucy Stone with Henry B. Blackwell.[6] In many ways, attention to multiple erotics of rhetorical power may uncover the intimate relationships inextricably connected with public practices of rhetoric.

## From Individual Couples to Multiple Connections

Even in turning from queerness to the erotic, my theory of the erotic as rhetorical power works to methodologically queer the field of feminist rhetorical studies. My archival research on the couple relationships between Holley and Putnam, Leache and Wood, and Buck and Wylie recognizes more fully the contributions and limitations of women whose lives were not circumscribed

---

6. Buchanan, *Regendering*, 134, 147; and Hanly, "'Then Alone.'" See also Buchanan, "Forging."

by the heteronormative imperatives of opposite-sex marriage, biological childbirth, and associated domestic responsibilities. Specifically, I build on existing scholarship in feminist rhetorics and women's history that variously acknowledges the women's close relationships in passing but without showing how central the erotic was to their activities as teachers of rhetoric, public speakers, and published writers. Focusing on long-term couples who sustained their relationships for decades also helps make possible an erotohistoriography that is based on robust archives. Quite simply, it was the long-term couple form that produced and accumulated rich repositories of letters between the women, memoirs and memorial publications created by one woman in honor of the other's legacy, and commentary about their relationships by others in their professional and activist networks. There is much to be gained, in other words, through a focus on romantic friendships that took the form of long-term couples.

Ideally, though, future work will find ways to examine the erotics of rhetorical power that fueled other relational forms, beyond the couple, which may be more difficult to recognize and trace within existing settler-colonial archives. Lorde urges that the sharing of passions that constitutes the erotic may take many forms, that it "does not have to be called *marriage*" or take shape through "certain proscribed erotic comings-together."[7] Ela Przybylo's theory of asexual erotics also recognizes the need to set aside "the couple formation" in order to consider "other forms of relating—including friendship networks, polyamory, and . . . the single life."[8] So, too, in the work of Aimee Carrillo Rowe, who urges that we avoid conceptions of the erotic as "contained within the popular register of love—safely shuttled to the depoliticized space of normative coupling."[9]

In pointing to relations not taking the form of the couple, the example of Brown and Primus is instructive. While they did not live together as a couple for the remainder of their lives, like the white women in this study were able to, it is Brown and Primus's relationship as a pair that has been studied most closely within scholarship on same-sex romantic friendship, even though there is at least some evidence of other romantic and erotic relations in their lives.[10] This emphasis on the couple form is partly a function of its centrality within Western conceptions of romantic love. Yet it is also the case that longer-lasting couple relationships are more available for study

---

7. Lorde, "Uses of the Erotic," 57, 59.
8. Przybylo, *Asexual Erotics*, 69.
9. Carrillo Rowe, "Erotic Pedagogies," 1041.
10. Griffin, *Beloved Sisters*, 224–29; VanHaitsma, "Archival Framework," 34–38; and VanHaitsma, *Queering Romantic Engagement*, 60–61.

because of the written records they produce and accrue. Whereas Brown and Primus amassed substantial correspondence over the course of nine years, the other women (and men) who populated their romantic and erotic encounters receive only fleeting mentions in those letters. I have no easy answers to offer in terms of how to examine the erotics of rhetorical power where even less documentation exists. But a broadened view of the erotics of rhetorical power would consider not only Brown and Primus's epistolary exchange with each other but also their epistolary networks consisting of multiple people, encounters, and affairs, however difficult to trace.

Relatively recent historical periods, including into the present, may offer more in the way of archives available for studying uncoupled erotics of rhetorical power. Working with a conception of "the archive" common in the humanities, Przybylo's book collects and analyzes an archive of asexual erotics not delimited by coupled relationships.[11] I think especially of how erotics often animate LGBTQ+ communities, movements, and activism. As Claire Potter notes in a discussion with John D'Emilio about Eleanor Roosevelt's same-sex relationship and romantic correspondence with Lorena Hickok, effective political networks are "sometimes glued together through an erotic charge."[12] Shifting from the long-term primary-couple relationship to other kinds of relations and networks would allow for study of how such an erotic charge functions as rhetorical power for individuals and communities. Closer to Lorde's historical context, for example, are the erotics of rhetorical power as enacted within lesbian feminist communities.[13] I offer these examples, while brief and outside of the historical scope of my study, as glimpses intended to be suggestive of other erotics of rhetorical power that are available for archival study if we decenter the couple as the locus of the erotic.

## From Settler to Erotic Archives

My theory of the erotic as rhetorical power is grounded in settler-colonial archives and, at the same time, persistently attentive to that which is absent in those archives. Partly because of the focus already delineated, on women for whom settler colonialism and slavery grounded their ability to sustain their relationships and amass records over time, my study has benefited from research in over twenty archival collections. This extensive documentation

---

11. Przybylo, *Asexual Erotics*, 15, 29.
12. Potter and D'Emilio, "Letters." On the Roosevelt-Hickok correspondence, see Cloud, "First Lady's Privates."
13. Przybylo, *Asexual Erotics*, 33; and Rhodes, *Once a Fury*.

has allowed me to flesh out a textured, in-depth account of how the passionately shared desires of the same-sex romantic friendships of Holley, Putnam, Leache, Wood, Buck, and Wylie enabled their rhetorical practices and pedagogies even as the women reproduced problematic dynamics of power, privilege, and difference. At the same time, my imaginative engagements with the archives of Brown and Primus's relationship have interrupted the dominant historiographic narrative in order to underscore the limitations of available archives. Inspired by the imaginative interludes, and especially by Jacqueline Jones Royster's and Saidiya Hartman's methodologies for "critical imagination" and "critical fabulation," I want to urge that we avoid limiting our imaginations, as well as feminist and LGBTQ+ erotohistoriographies of rhetoric, to archival records of what actually occurred.[14]

What I begin to imagine, in closing, is a theory of the erotics of rhetorical power that goes even further in releasing the hold of settler archives. What I imagine is not a disengagement *from* but a different engagement *with* archives as typically understood and approached within histories of rhetoric. The different engagement that I am gesturing toward, in concert with Elizabeth Freeman's theorization of erotohistoriography, is a distinctly and thoroughly erotic relationship to archives. By that I mean, it is not a relation of *drawing from* or *drawing away from* archives but a relation of passionate *sharing between* ourselves, our work, and the archives. This is a passionate sharing that is open to imagination as "creative power" and "creative energy," in Lorde's words, a sharing that embraces "erotic knowledge."[15] It is a passionate sharing that attends to "the erotic relay" in archival work itself—"the historian's erotic desire for her archived object . . . All of this lust becoming the archive itself"—but while recognizing that, as Julietta Singh's book by the same name so does, *No Archive Will Restore You*.[16] "The loss of stories sharpens the hunger for them," realizes Hartman, "so it is tempting to fill in the gaps and to provide closure where there is none."[17] In place of closure, I imagine this erotics of archival engagement as its own rhetorical power for fueling future feminist and LGBTQ+ historiographies.

---

14. Royster, *Traces*, 83; and Hartman, "Venus," 11.
15. Lorde, "Uses of the Erotic," 55–56.
16. Singh, *No Archive*, 111. See also Olivares, "Thoughts."
17. Hartman, "Venus," 8.

# BIBLIOGRAPHY

"Acknowledgement of Land—Office of the Vice Provost for Educational Equity." Pennsylvania State University. Accessed February 22, 2023. http://equity.psu.edu/acknowledgement-of-land.

Adams-Campbell, Melissa, Ashley Glassburn Falzetti, and Courtney Rivard. "Introduction: Indigeneity and the Work of Settler Archives." *Settler Colonial Studies* 5, no. 2 (2015): 109–16.

Agnew, Lois. "The Civic Function of Taste: A Re-Assessment of Hugh Blair's Rhetorical Theory." *Rhetoric Society Quarterly* 28, no. 2 (1998): 25–36.

Ahmed, Sara. "Orientations: Toward a Queer Phenomenology." *GLQ: A Journal of Lesbian and Gay Studies* 12, no. 4 (2006): 543–74.

Aiken, Zora. "Holley Graded School: Preserving an Icon of Education on the Northern Neck." *The House and Home Magazine*, January 6, 2020. http://thehouseandhomemagazine.com/api/content/7540db42-30c9-11ea-adfc-1244d5f7c7c6/.

Alexander, Jonathan, and Jacqueline Rhodes. "Queer Rhetoric and the Pleasures of the Archive." *Enculturation: A Journal of Rhetoric, Writing, and Culture* 13 (2012). http://enculturation.net/files/QueerRhetoric/queerarchive/Home.html.

Allaire, Christian. "How Pride Organizers Will Uplift the Black LGBTQ+ Community This Month." *Vogue*, June 4, 2020. https://www.vogue.com/article/gay-pride-events-june-black-lives-matter.

Allen, Jafari S. *Venceremos? The Erotics of Black Self-Making in Cuba*. Durham: Duke University Press, 2011.

Allen, Julia M. *Passionate Commitments: The Lives of Anna Rochester and Grace Hutchins*. Albany: State University of New York, 2013.

Almjeld, Jen. "A Rhetorician's Guide to Love: Online Dating Profiles as Remediated Commonplace Books." *Computers and Composition*, no. 32 (2014): 71–83.

Altintas, Evrim, and Oriel Sullivan. "Fifty Years of Change Updated: Cross-National Gender Convergence in Housework." *Demographic Research* 35, no. 16 (2016): 455–70.

"Anti-Slavery Lecture." *Liberator,* no. 18 (May 6, 1853): 72. NCN.

"An Appreciation: Annie Cogswell Wood; Idealist, Steadfast in Friendship, Unswerving in Purpose, Obedient to Her Vision." [Norfolk, 1940]. JOCL.

Aristotle. *Rhetoric.* Edited by Edward P. J. Corbett. Translated by W. Rhys Roberts. New York: McGraw Hill, 1984.

Arondekar, Anjali. *Abundance: Sexuality's Historiography.* Durham: Duke University Press, 2023.

———. "In the Absence of Reliable Ghosts: Sexuality, Historiography, South Asia." *Differences* 25, no. 3 (2014): 98–122.

Asante, Godfried. "Decolonizing the Erotic: Building Alliances of (Queer) African Eros." *Women's Studies in Communication* 43, no. 2 (2020): 113–18.

Audre Lorde Project. "About ALP." Accessed February 23, 2023. https://alp.org/about.

August, Anita. "Strained Sisterhood in the WCTU: The Lynching and Suffrage Rivalry between Ida B. Wells and Frances E. Willard." *Rhetoric Review* 40, no. 1 (2021): 1–15.

B., C. "Sallie Holley in Montague." *Liberator,* no. 52 (December 24, 1858): 206. AHN.

Bacon, Jacqueline. "'Do You Understand Your Own Language?': Revolutionary *Topoi* in the Rhetoric of African-American Abolitionists." *Rhetoric Society Quarterly* 28, no. 2 (1998): 55–75.

———. *The Humblest May Stand Forth: Rhetoric, Empowerment, and Abolition.* Columbia: University of South Carolina Press, 2002.

Bacon, Jacqueline, and Glen McClish. "Reinventing the Master's Tools: Nineteenth-Century African-American Literary Societies of Philadelphia and Rhetorical Education." *Rhetoric Society Quarterly* 30, no. 4 (2000): 19–47.

Bailey, Megan. "Between Two Worlds: Black Women and the Fight for Voting Rights." National Park Service, October 9, 2020. https://www.nps.gov/articles/black-women-and-the-fight-for-voting-rights.htm.

Baker, Christina N. "Revisiting Audre Lorde's Uses of the Erotic through Contemporary Film." *Women's Studies in Communication* 44, no. 4 (2021): 470–76.

Ballif, Michelle. *Seduction, Sophistry, and the Woman with the Rhetorical Figure.* Carbondale: Southern Illinois University Press, 2001.

Banks, William P. "Written through the Body: Disruptions and 'Personal' Writing." *College English* 66, no. 1 (2003): 21–40.

Bauer, Gerrit. "Gender Roles, Comparative Advantages and the Life Course: The Division of Domestic Labor in Same-Sex and Different-Sex Couples." *European Journal of Population* 32 (2016): 99–128.

Baylor, Cherry Revona. "Emancipation, Land, and Education: Emily Howland Discovers Northumberland County during Reconstruction." *Bulletin of the Northumberland County Historical Society,* no. 48 (2011): 79–92.

———. "The Holley School and Zion Church: A Hotbed of Issues of Race, Gender, and Religion." *Bulletin of the Northumberland County Historical Society,* no. 52 (2015): 10–20.

———. "The Holley School at Lottsburg: The Cost of Freedom and Conscience." *Bulletin of the Northumberland County Historical Society,* no. 51 (2014): 58–74.

———. "The Holley School for Freedmen in Lottsburg: The First Decade of Challenges and Successes." *Bulletin of the Northumberland County Historical Society,* no. 49 (2012): 53–64.

———. "The Second Decade at the Holley School: A Series of Celebrations of Openings to Freedom." *Bulletin of the Northumberland County Historical Society*, no. 50 (2013): 13–18.

Beckley, R. D. "Letter from R. D. Beckley." *New National Era and Citizen*. November 20, 1873. LOC.

Bederman, Gail. *Manliness and Civilization: A Cultural History of Gender and Race in the United States, 1880–1917*. Chicago: University of Chicago Press, 1995.

Beeching, Barbara. *Hopes and Expectations: The Origins of the Black Middle Class in Hartford*. Albany: State University of New York Press, 2017.

———. "The Primus Papers: An Introduction to Hartford's Nineteenth Century Black Community." Master's thesis, Trinity College, 1995.

Bereano, Nancy K. Introduction to Lorde, *Sister Outsider*, 7–11.

Bergin, Celia. "Remembering Stonewall: How Are Pride and BLM Linked?" *The Boar*, June 28, 2020. https://theboar.org/2020/06/remembering-stonewall-how-are-pride-and-blm-linked/.

Berlin, James. *Writing Instruction in Nineteenth-Century American Colleges*. Carbondale: Southern Illinois University Press, 1984.

Bessette, Jean. "Queer Rhetoric in Situ." *Rhetoric Review* 35, no. 2 (2016): 148–64.

———. *Retroactivism in the Lesbian Archives: Composing Pasts and Futures*. Carbondale: Southern Illinois University Press, 2017.

Bianchi, Suzanne M., Liana C. Sayer, Melissa A. Milkie, and John P. Robinson. "Housework: Who Did, Does or Will Do It, and How Much Does It Matter?" *Social Forces* 91, no. 1 (2012): 55–63.

Biesecker, Barbara A. "Of Historicity, Rhetoric: The Archive as Scene of Invention." *Rhetoric and Public Affairs* 9, no. 1 (2006): 124–31.

Bizzell, Patricia. "Chastity Warrants for Women Public Speakers in Nineteenth-Century American Fiction." *Rhetoric Society Quarterly* 40, no. 4 (2010): 385–401.

Bizzell, Patricia, and Bruce Herzberg, eds. *The Rhetorical Tradition: Readings from Classical Times to the Present*. 2nd ed. New York: Bedford, 2001.

Black Lives Matter. "Herstory." Accessed October 21, 2021. https://blacklivesmatter.com/herstory/.

"Black Women's Suffrage Collection." *Digital Public Library of America*. Accessed October 27, 2021. https://blackwomenssuffrage.dp.la/about.

Blair, Ann. "Humanist Methods in Natural Philosophy: The Commonplace Book." *Journal of the History of Ideas* 53, no. 4 (1992): 541–51.

Blair, Hugh. *Lectures on Rhetoric and Belles Lettres*. London: Strahan, 1783.

Boice, Eva C. "Woman Suffrage, Vassar College, and Laura Johnson Wylie." *Hudson River Valley Review* 20, no. 2 (2004): 37–49.

Booth, Jean Norris. "A Study of the Holley School for Negroes, Lottsburg, Virginia: 'Our Three Acres.'" Master's thesis, University of Richmond, 1956.

Bordelon, Suzanne. "The 'Advance' toward Democratic Administration: Laura Johnson Wylie and Gertrude Buck of Vassar College." In *Historical Studies of Writing Program Administration: Individuals, Communities, and the Formation of a Discipline*, edited by Barbara E. L'Eplattenier and Lisa S. Mastrangelo, 91–116. West Lafayette: Parlor Press, 2004.

———. "Composing Women's Civic Identities during the Progressive Era: College Commencement Addresses as Overlooked Rhetorical Sites." *College Composition and Communication* 61, no. 3 (2010): 510–33.

———. "Contradicting and Complicating Feminization of Rhetoric Narratives: Mary Yost and Argument from a Sociological Perspective." *Rhetoric Society Quarterly* 35, no. 3 (2005): 101–24.

———. *A Feminist Legacy: The Rhetoric and Writing of Gertrude Buck*. Carbondale: Southern Illinois University Press, 2007.

———. "Gertrude Buck: Revisioning Argumentation and the Role of Women in a Participatory Democracy." *Nineteenth-Century Prose* 27, no. 2 (2000): 138–58.

———. "Gertrude Buck's Approach to Argumentation: Preparing Women for a More Active and Vocal Role in Democracy." *Journal of Teaching Writing* 16, no. 2 (1998): 233–62.

———. "Muted Rhetors and the Mundane: The Case of Ruth Mary Weeks, Rewey Belle Inglis, and W. Wilbur Hatfield." *College Composition and Communication* 64, no. 2 (2012): 332–56.

———. "Restructuring English and Society through an Integrated Curriculum: Ruth Mary Weeks's *A Correlated Curriculum*." *Rhetoric Review* 29, no. 3 (2010): 257–74.

Borge, Jonathan. "The Queer Black History of Rioting." *Refinery 29*, June 15, 2020. https://www.refinery29.com/en-us/2020/06/9861317/first-pride-riots-history-black-lgbtq-blm.

Bradway, Tyler. "How to Do History with Pleasure." *Postmodern Culture* 22, no. 1 (2011): 1–7.

Breitborde, Mary-Lou. "Learning about Each Other: Two Teachers Negotiate Race, Class, and Gender in the Civil War South." *American Educational History Journal* 40, no. 1/2 (2013): 37–57.

Brewster, Melanie E. "Lesbian Women and Household Labor Division: A Systematic Review of Scholarly Research from 2000 to 2015." *Journal of Lesbian Studies*, no. 21 (2017): 47–69.

Britannica. S.v. "William Bradford: Plymouth Colony Governor." Accessed November 2, 2022. https://www.britannica.com/biography/William-Bradford-Plymouth-colony-governor.

Brooks, Lonny J. Avi. "Cruelty and Afrofuturism." *Communication and Critical/Cultural Studies* 15, no. 1 (2018): 101–7.

brown, adrienne maree. *Emergent Strategy: Shaping Change, Changing Worlds*. Chico: AK Press, 2017.

Brown, Ira Vernon. *Mary Grew, Abolitionist and Feminist, 1813–1896*. Selinsgrove: Susquehanna University Press, 1991.

Browne, Stephen H. *Angelina Grimké: Rhetoric, Identity, and the Radical Imagination*. East Lansing: Michigan State University Press, 1999.

Buchanan, Lindal. "Forging and Firing Thunderbolts: Collaboration and Women's Rhetoric." *Rhetoric Society Quarterly* 33, no. 4 (2003): 43–63.

———. *Regendering Delivery: The Fifth Canon and Antebellum Women Rhetors*. Carbondale: Southern Illinois University Press, 2005.

Buck, Gertrude. "Another Phase of the New Education." *Forum*, November 1896, 376–84.

———. "Anti-Suffrage Sentiments." *The Masses* 4, no. 9 (June 1913): 9.

———. *A Course in Argumentative Writing*. New York: Henry Holt and Company, 1899.

———. "The Ethical Significance of 'Coriolanus.'" *The Inlander: A Monthly Magazine by the Students of Michigan University* 6, no. 6 (March 1896): 217–22.

———. *Figures of Rhetoric: A Psychological Study*. Edited by Fred Newton Scott. Ann Arbor: Inland Press, 1895.

———. *The Metaphor: A Study in the Psychology of Rhetoric*. Edited by Fred Newton Scott. Ann Arbor: Inland Press, 1899.

———. *Poems and Plays*. Edited by Laura Johnson Wylie. New York: Duffield and Company, 1922.

———. "The Present Status of Rhetorical Theory." *Modern Language Notes* 15, no. 3 (March 1900): 167–74.

———. "The Religious Experience of a Skeptic." *The Vassar Miscellany Monthly,* February 9, 1923, 21–29.

———. *The Social Criticism of Literature.* New Haven: Yale University Press, 1916.

———. "What Does 'Rhetoric' Mean?" *Educational Review,* no. 22 (September 1901): 197–200.

———. "What Does 'Rhetoric' Mean?" In *Toward a Feminist Rhetoric: The Writing of Gertrude Buck,* edited by JoAnn Campbell, 52–55. Pittsburgh: University of Pittsburgh Press, 1996.

Buck, Gertrude, and Kristine Mann. *A Handbook of Argumentation and Debating.* Orange: Orange Chronicle, 1906.

Buck, Gertrude, and Fred Newton Scott. *A Brief English Grammar.* Chicago: Scott, Foresman and Company, 1905.

Buck, Gertrude, and Harriet M. Scott. *Organic Education: A Manual for Teachers in Primary and Grammar Grades.* Boston: D. C. Heath and Co., 1897.

Buck, Gertrude, and Elisabeth Woodbridge [Morris]. *A Course in Expository Writing.* New York: Henry Holt and Company, 1899.

Buck, Gertrude, and Elisabeth Woodbridge Morris. *A Course in Narrative Writing.* New York: Henry Holt and Company, 1906.

Burke, Kenneth. *A Rhetoric of Motives.* Berkeley: University of California Press, 1950.

Burke, Victoria E. "Recent Studies in Commonplace Books." *English Literary Renaissance* 43, no. 1 (2013): 153–77.

Butchart, Ronald E. *Schooling the Freed People: Teaching, Learning, and the Struggle for Black Freedom, 1861–1876.* Chapel Hill: University of North Carolina Press, 2010.

Byrd, Rudolph P. "Introduction: Create Your Own Fire, Audre Lorde and the Tradition of Black Radical Thought." In Lorde, *I Am Your Sister,* 3–36.

Campbell, JoAnn, ed. *Toward a Feminist Rhetoric: The Writing of Gertrude Buck.* Pittsburgh: University of Pittsburgh Press, 1996.

Carbine, Rosemary P. "Erotic Education: Elaborating a Feminist and Faith-Based Pedagogy for Experiential Learning in Religious Studies." *Teaching Theology and Religion* 13, no. 4 (2010): 320–38.

Carlacio, Jami. "'Ye Knew Your Duty, But Ye Did It Not': The Epistolary Rhetoric of Sarah Grimké." *Rhetoric Review* 21, no. 3 (2002): 247–63.

Carpenter, Edward. *Homogenic Love, and Its Place in a Free Society.* Manchester, United Kingdom: Labour Press Society Limited, 1894.

———. *The Intermediate Sex: A Study of Some Transitional Types of Men and Women.* New York: Mitchell Kennerley, 1908.

Carrillo Rowe, Aimee. "Erotic Pedagogies." *Journal of Homosexuality* 59, no. 7 (2012): 1031–56.

———. *Power Lines: On the Subject of Feminist Alliances.* Durham: Duke University Press, 2008.

Carter, Julian. *The Heart of Whiteness: Normal Sexuality and Race in America, 1880–1940.* Durham: Duke University Press, 2007.

Castle, Terry. *The Apparitional Lesbian: Female Homosexuality and Modern Culture.* New York: Columbia University Press, 1993.

Caswell, Michelle. "'The Archive' Is Not an Archives: On Acknowledging the Intellectual Contributions of Archival Studies." *Reconstruction: Studies in Contemporary Culture* 16, no. 1 (2016). https://escholarship.org/uc/item/7bn4v1fk.

Cavanagh, Sheila L. *Sexing the Teacher: School Sex Scandals and Queer Pedagogies.* Vancouver: University of British Columbia Press, 2007.

Censer, Jane Turner. *The Reconstruction of White Southern Womanhood, 1865–1895.* Baton Rouge: Louisiana State University Press, 2003.

Chadwick, John White, ed. *A Life for Liberty: Anti-Slavery and Other Letters of Sallie Holley.* New York: G. P. Putnam's Sons, 1899.

Chambers-Schiller, Lee Virginia. *Liberty, a Better Husband: Single Women in America; The Generations of 1798–1840.* New Haven: Yale University Press, 1984.

Chávez, Karma R. "Beyond Inclusion: Rethinking Rhetoric's Historical Narrative." *Quarterly Journal of Speech* 101, no. 1 (2015): 162–72.

———. *The Borders of AIDS: Race, Quarantine, and Resistance.* Seattle: University of Washington Press, 2021.

Chrysler Museum of Art. "Two Women, One Remarkable Gift." Accessed January 14, 2021. https://chrysler.org/about/two-women-one-remarkable-gift/.

Chude-Sokei, Louis, Ariane Cruz, Amber Jamilla Musser, Jennifer C. Nash, L. H. Stallings, and Kirin Wachter-Grene. "Race, Pornography, and Desire: A TBS Roundtable." *Black Scholar* 46, no. 4 (2016): 49–64.

Cima, Gay Gibson. *Performing Anti-Slavery: Activist Women on Antebellum Stages.* Cambridge: Cambridge University Press, 2014.

Cimbala, Paula. *Under the Guardianship of the Nation: The Freedmen's Bureau and the Reconstruction of Georgia, 1862–1875.* Athens: University of Georgia Press, 1997.

Claflin, Jehiel. "Miss Holley in Vermont." *Liberator*, no. 28 (July 9, 1858): 111. APS.

Cleves, Rachel Hope. "Beyond the Binaries in Early America: Special Issue Introduction." *Early American Studies* 12, no. 3 (2014): 459–68.

———. *Charity and Sylvia: A Same-Sex Marriage in Early America.* New York: Oxford University Press, 2014.

Clifford, Geraldine J. *Those Good Gertrudes: A Social History of Women Teachers in America.* Baltimore: Johns Hopkins University Press, 2014.

Cloud, Dana. "The First Lady's Privates: Queering Eleanor Roosevelt for Public Address Studies." In Morris, *Queering Public Address*, 23–44.

Cobb, Amanda J. *Listening to Our Grandmothers' Stories: The Bloomfield Academy for Chickasaw Females, 1852–1949.* Lincoln: University of Nebraska Press, 2000.

Collins, Patricia Hill. *Black Feminist Thought: Knowledge, Consciousness, and the Politics of Empowerment.* New York: Routledge, 1991.

———. *Black Sexual Politics: African Americans, Gender, and the New Racism.* New York: Routledge, 2005.

Conway, Kathryn M. "Woman Suffrage and the History of Rhetoric at the Seven Sisters Colleges, 1865–1919." In *Reclaiming Rhetorica: Women in the Rhetorical Tradition*, edited by Andrea A. Lunsford, 203–26. Pittsburgh: University of Pittsburgh Press, 1995.

Cornelius, Janet Duitsman. *"When I Can Read My Title Clear": Literacy, Slavery, and Religion in the Antebellum South.* Columbia: University of South Carolina Press, 1991.

Corrigan, Lisa M. "Queering the Panthers: Rhetorical Adjacency and Black/Queer Liberation Politics." *QED: A Journal in GLBTQ Worldmaking* 6, no. 2 (2019): 1–25.

Costa, Jade Crimson Rose da. "Pride Parades in Queer Time: Disrupting Time, Norms, and Nationhood in Canada." *Journal of Canadian Studies* 54, no. 2/3 (2020): 434–58.

Coviello, Peter. *Tomorrow's Parties: Sex and the Untimely in Nineteenth-Century America*. New York: New York University Press, 2013.

Cox, Matthew B., and Michael J. Faris. "An Annotated Bibliography of LGBTQ Rhetorics." *Present Tense: A Journal of Rhetoric in Society* 4, no. 2 (2015). http://www.presenttensejournal.org/volume-4/an-annotated-bibliography-of-lgbtq-rhetorics/.

Cram, E. *Violent Inheritance: Sexuality, Land, and Energy in Making the North American West*. Oakland: University of California Press, 2022.

Cruz, Ariane. *The Color of Kink: Black Women, BDSM, and Pornography*. New York: New York University Press, 2016.

Cushman, Ellen, Rachel Jackson, Annie Laurie Nichols, Courtney Rivard, Amanda Moulder, Chelsea Murdock, David M. Grant, and Heather Brook Adams. "Decolonizing Projects: Creating Pluriversal Possibilities in Rhetoric." *Rhetoric Review* 38, no. 1 (2019): 1–22.

D., F. "Lotsburgh [sic], Virginia." *New National Era* 43, no. 2 (October 24, 1872). LOC.

Davis, Angela Y., and Dylan Rodriguez. "The Challenge of Prison Abolition: A Conversation." *Social Justice* 27, no. 3 (2000): 212–18.

Davis, Khyree D. "Transnational Blackness at Toronto Pride: Queer Disruption as Theory and Method." *Gender, Place and Culture* 28, no. 11 (2021): 1541–60.

Dennehy, Kevin, and Susan Gonzalez. "Yale Publicly Confronts Historical Involvement in Slavery." *YaleNews*, November 1, 2021. https://news.yale.edu/2021/11/01/yale-publicly-confronts-historical-involvement-slavery.

De Veaux, Alexis. *Warrior Poet: A Biography of Audre Lorde*. New York: W. W. Norton, 2004.

Dickerson, Dianna Watkins. "'Don't Get Weary': Using a Womanist Rhetorical Imaginary to Curate the Beloved Community in Times of Rhetorical Emergency." *Journal of Communication and Religion* 43, no. 3 (2020): 62–74.

Diggs, Marylynne. "Romantic Friends or a 'Different Race of Creatures'? The Representation of Lesbian Pathology in Nineteenth-Century America." *Feminist Studies* 21, no. 2 (1995): 317–40.

Dixon, Chris. "Grew, Mary (01 September 1813–10 October 1896), Abolitionist and Women's Rights Advocate." American National Biography. Accessed September 17, 2020. http://www.anb.org/view/10.1093/anb/9780198606697.001.0001/anb-9780198606697-e-1500893.

Dolmage, Jay Timothy. *Disabled Upon Arrival: Eugenics, Immigration, and the Construction of Race and Disability*. Columbus: The Ohio State University Press, 2018.

Donawerth, Jane. *Conversational Rhetoric: The Rise and Fall of a Women's Tradition, 1600–1900*. Carbondale: Southern Illinois University Press, 2012.

Donner, Francesca. "The Household Work Men and Women Do, and Why." *New York Times*, February 12, 2020. https://www.nytimes.com/2020/02/12/us/the-household-work-men-and-women-do-and-why.html.

Driskill, Qwo-Li. *Asegi Stories: Cherokee Queer and Two-Spirit Memory*. Tucson: University of Arizona Press, 2016.

———. "Call Me Brother: Two-Spiritedness, the Erotic, and Mixedblood Identity as Sites of Sovereignty and Resistance in Gregory Scofield's Poetry." In *Speak to Me Words: Essays on Contemporary American Indian Poetry*, edited by Dean Rader and Janice Gould, 223–34. Tucson: University of Arizona Press, 2003.

———. "Stolen from Our Bodies: First Nations Two-Spirits/Queers and the Journey to a Sovereign Erotic." *Studies in American Indian Literatures* 16, no. 2 (2004): 50–64.

Duberman, Martin B., Martha Vicinus, and George Chauncey, eds. *Hidden from History: Reclaiming the Gay and Lesbian Past.* New York: Meridian, 1990.

Duby, Georges, Michelle Perrot, and Geneviève Fraisse, eds. *A History of Women in the West.* Cambridge: Belknap Press of Harvard University Press, 1993.

Duggan, Lisa. *Sapphic Slashers: Sex, Violence, and American Modernity.* Durham: Duke University Press, 2000.

Dunbar, Anthony W. "Introducing Critical Race Theory to Archival Discourse: Getting the Conversation Started." *Archival Science* 6, no. 1 (2006): 109–29.

Dunn, Thomas R. *Queerly Remembered: Rhetorics for Representing the GLBTQ Past.* Columbia: University of South Carolina Press, 2016.

Edwards, Laura F. "The Legal World of Elizabeth Bagby's Commonplace Book: Federalism, Women, and Governance." *The Journal of the Civil War Era* 9, no. 4 (2019): 504–23.

Emens, Elizabeth F. "Compulsory Sexuality." *Stanford Law Review* 66, no. 2 (2014): 303–86.

Engle, Elizabeth C. "A Valley Seed Grows in Tidewater." Paper presented to the Century Club of Winchester, VA, February 26, 1991. WFHS.

Enoch, Jessica. *Refiguring Rhetorical Education: Women Teaching African American, Native American, and Chicano/a Students, 1865–1911.* Carbondale: Southern Illinois University Press, 2008.

———. "A Woman's Place Is in the School: Rhetorics of Gendered Space in Nineteenth-Century America." *College English* 70, no. 3 (2008): 275–95.

Ensor, Sarah. "Spinster Ecology: Rachel Carson, Sarah Orne Jewett, and Nonreproductive Futurity." *American Literature* 84, no. 2 (2012): 409–35.

Epps-Robertson, Candace. *Resisting Brown: Race, Literacy, and Citizenship in the Heart of Virginia.* Pittsburgh: University of Pittsburgh Press, 2018.

Erickson, Keith V., and Stephanie Thomson. "Seduction Theory and the Recovery of Feminine Aesthetics: Implications for Rhetorical Criticism." *Communication Quarterly* 52, no. 3 (2004): 300–319.

Espinal, Isabel, Tonia Sutherland, and Charlotte Roh. "A Holistic Approach for Inclusive Librarianship: Decentering Whiteness in Our Profession." *Library Trends* 67, no. 1 (2018): 147–62.

Faderman, Lillian. Foreword to *Wolf Girls of Vassar: Lesbian and Gay Experiences 1930–1990*, edited by Anne MacKay, xi–xv. New York: St. Martin's, 1992.

———. *Surpassing the Love of Men: Romantic Friendship and Love between Women from the Renaissance to the Present.* New York: Harper Paperbacks, 1998.

———. *To Believe in Women: What Lesbians Have Done for America—A History.* Boston: Houghton Mifflin Harcourt, 2000.

Farnham, Christie. *The Education of the Southern Belle: Higher Education and Student Socialization in the Antebellum South.* New York: New York University Press, 1994.

Faulkner, Carol. *Women's Radical Reconstruction: The Freedmen's Aid Movement.* Philadelphia: University of Pennsylvania Press, 2011.

Feintzeig, Rachel. "Women Still Do More of the Housework. Here's How to Share the Load." *Wall Street Journal,* September 23, 2021. https://www.wsj.com/articles/women-more-house-work-11632330725.

Ferguson, Roderick A. *Aberrations in Black: Toward a Queer of Color Critique.* Minneapolis: University of Minnesota Press, 2004.

———. "Of Sensual Matters: On Audre Lorde's 'Poetry Is Not a Luxury' and 'Uses of the Erotic.'" *WSQ: Women's Studies Quarterly* 40, no. 3/4 (2013): 295–300.

Fiesta, Melissa. "Homeplaces in Lydia Maria Child's Abolitionist Rhetoric, 1833–1879." *Rhetoric Review* 25, no. 3 (2006): 260–74.

Fitzsimons, Tim. "Pride Started with 'Revolutionary Riots': Advocates Point to the Movement's Radical Roots." *NBC News,* June 1, 2020. https://www.nbcnews.com/feature/nbc-out/pride-started-revolutionary-riots-advocates-point-movement-s-radical-roots-n1221416.

Flexner, Eleanor. *Century of Struggle: The Woman's Rights Movement in the United States.* Cambridge: Belknap, 1959.

Foucault, Michel. *The History of Sexuality.* Vol. 1. Translated by Robert Hurley. New York: Pantheon, 1978.

Frankenberg, Ruth. *White Women, Race Matters: The Social Construction of Whiteness.* Minneapolis: University of Minnesota Press, 1993.

Franzen, Trisha. *Spinsters and Lesbians: Independent Womanhood in the United States.* New York: New York University Press, 1996.

Freedman, Estelle B. "'The Burning of Letters Continues': Elusive Identities and the Historical Construction of Sexuality." *Journal of Women's History* 9, no. 4 (1998): 181–200.

Freeman, Elizabeth. *Time Binds: Queer Temporalities, Queer Histories.* Durham: Duke University Press, 2010.

Freeman, Mary Tibbetts. "The Politics of Correspondence: Letter Writing in the Campaign against Slavery in the United States." PhD diss., Columbia University, 2018.

Garber, Marjorie. *Vice Versa: Bisexuality and the Eroticism of Everyday Life.* New York: Simon and Schuster, 1995.

Garza, Alicia. "A Herstory of the #BlackLivesMatter Movement." *Feminist Wire,* October 7, 2014. https://thefeministwire.com/2014/10/blacklivesmatter-2/.

Geraths, Cory, and Michele Kennerly. "Pinvention: Updating Commonplace Books for the Digital Age." *Communication Teacher* 29, no. 3 (2015): 166–72.

Ghisyawan, Krystal. "Social Erotics: The Fluidity of Love, Desire and Friendship for Same-Sex Loving Women in Trinidad." *Journal of International Women's Studies* 17, no. 3 (2016): 17–31.

Gill, Lyndon K. "In the Realm of Our Lorde: Eros and the Poet Philosopher." *Feminist Studies* 40, no. 1 (2014): 169–89.

Gilliland, Anne J., and Michelle Caswell. "Records and Their Imaginaries: Imagining the Impossible, Making Possible the Imagined." *Archival Science,* no. 16 (2016): 53–75.

Ginzberg, Lori D. *Elizabeth Cady Stanton: An American Life.* New York: Hill and Wang, 2009.

Giuliani-Hoffman, Francesca. "LGBTQ Communities Are Elevating Black Voices during Pride Month in Solidarity." *CNN,* June 9, 2020. https://www.cnn.com/2020/06/07/us/lgbtq-pride-month-events-in-solidarity-with-black-lives-matter-trnd/index.html.

Gold, David. "Creating Space for Black Women's Citizenship: African American Suffrage Arguments in the Crisis." *Rhetoric Society Quarterly* 50, no. 5 (2020): 335–51.

———. *Rhetoric at the Margins: Revising the History of Writing Instruction in American Colleges, 1873–1947.* Carbondale: Southern Illinois University Press, 2008.

Gold, David, and Catherine Hobbs. *Educating the New Southern Woman: Speech, Writing, and Race at the Public Women's Colleges, 1884–1945.* Carbondale: Southern Illinois University Press, 2014.

———, eds. *Rhetoric, History, and Women's Oratorical Education: American Women Learn to Speak.* New York: Routledge, 2013.

Golden, James L., and Edward P. J. Corbett. *The Rhetoric of Blair, Campbell, and Whately.* Carbondale: Southern Illinois University Press, 1990.

Gomez, Jewelle L., and Sally R. Munt. "Femme Erotic Independence." In *Butch/Femme: Inside Lesbian Gender*, 101–8. London: Caswell, 1998.

Goodier, Susan. "Doublespeak: Louisa Jacobs, the American Equal Rights Association, and Complicating Racism in the Early US Women's Suffrage Movement." *New York History* 101, no. 2 (2020–21): 195–211.

Glenn, Cheryl, and Jessica Enoch. "Drama in the Archives: Rereading Methods, Rewriting History." *College Composition and Communication* 61, no. 2 (2009): 321–42.

Grasso, Linda M. "Edited Letter Collections as Epistolary Fictions: Imagining African American Women's History in Beloved Sisters and Loving Friends." In *Letters and Cultural Transformation in the United States, 1760–1860*, edited by Theresa Strouth Gaul and Sharon M. Harris, 249–67. Burlington: Ashgate Publishing Company, 2009.

Greey, Ali. "Queer Inclusion Precludes (Black) Queer Disruption: Media Analysis of the Black Lives Matter Toronto Sit-In during Toronto Pride 2016." *Leisure Studies* 37, no. 6 (2018): 662–76.

Greyser, Naomi. *On Sympathetic Grounds: Race, Gender, and Affective Geographies in Nineteenth-Century North America*. New York: Oxford University Press, 2017.

Griffin, Farah. *Beloved Sisters and Loving Friends: Letters from Rebecca Primus of Royal Oak, Maryland, and Addie Brown of Hartford, Connecticut, 1854–1868*. New York: Ballantine Publishing Group, 1999.

Gross, Daniel M. "Beginnings and Ends of Rhetorical Theory: Ann Arbor 1900." *Philosophy and Rhetoric* 53, no. 1 (2020): 34–50.

Gross, Terry. "Pandemic Makes Evident 'Grotesque' Gender Inequality in Household Work." *National Public Radio*, May 21, 2020. https://www.npr.org/2020/05/21/860091230/pandemic-makes-evident-grotesque-gender-inequality-in-household-work.

Gumbs, Alexis Pauline. *M Archive: After the End of the World*. Durham: Duke University Press, 2018.

———. *Survival Is a Promise: The Eternal Life of Audre Lorde*. New York: Farrar, Straus and Giroux, 2024.

Gunderson, Erik. *Declamation, Paternity, and Roman Identity: Authority and the Rhetorical Self*. Cambridge: Cambridge University Press, 2003.

Gupta, Kristina. "Compulsory Sexuality: Evaluating an Emerging Concept." *Signs: Journal of Women in Culture and Society* 41, no. 1 (2015): 131–54.

Hackett, Robin. Foreword to *Passionate Commitments: The Lives of Anna Rochester and Grace Hutchins*, by Julia M. Allen, xi–xii. Albany: State University of New York, 2013.

Halberstam, Jack. *Female Masculinity*. Durham: Duke University Press, 1998.

Hall, Ashley R. "Slippin' In and Out of Frame: An Afrafuturist Feminist Orientation to Black Women and American Citizenship." *Quarterly Journal of Speech* 106, no. 3 (2020): 341–51.

Hanly, J. P. "'Then Alone Could the Morning Stars Sing Together for Joy': Engendering Rhetorical Alliance in the Stone-Blackwell Courtship Correspondence." *Rhetoric Review* 38, no. 3 (2019): 285–96.

Hansen, Karen. "'No Kisses Is Like Youres': An Erotic Friendship between Two African-American Women during the Mid-Nineteenth Century." In *Lesbian Subjects*, edited by Martha Vicinus, 178–207. Bloomington: Indiana University Press, 1996.

Harris, Barbara J. *Beyond Her Sphere: Women and the Professions in American History*. Westport: Greenwood Press, 1978.

Harris, Leslie J. "Motherhood, Race, and Gender: The Rhetoric of Women's Antislavery Activism in the *Liberty Bell* Giftbooks." *Women's Studies in Communication* 32, no. 3 (2009): 293–319.

———. *State of the Marital Union: Rhetoric, Identity, and Nineteenth-Century Marriage Controversies*. Waco: Baylor University Press, 2014.

Harrison, Kimberly. *Civil War Diaries and Confederate Persuasion: The Rhetoric of Rebel Women*. Carbondale: Southern Illinois University Press, 2013.

Hartman, Saidiya. "Venus in Two Acts." *Small Axe: A Caribbean Journal of Criticism* 12, no. 2 (2008): 1–14.

———. *Wayward Lives, Beautiful Experiments: Intimate Histories of Social Upheaval*. New York: W. W. Norton and Company, 2019.

Hartocollis, Anemona. "The Major Findings of Harvard's Report on Its Ties to Slavery." *New York Times*, April 26, 2022, sec. US. https://www.nytimes.com/2022/04/26/us/harvard-slavery-report.html.

Hawhee, Debra. *Bodily Arts: Rhetoric and Athletics in Ancient Greece*. Austin: University of Texas Press, 2004.

Hawkins, Ames. *These Are Love(d) Letters*. Detroit, MI: Wayne State University Press, 2019.

Heath, Shirley Brice. "Finding in History the Right to Estimate." *College Composition and Communication* 45, no. 1 (1994): 97–102.

Henry, Katherine. "Angelina Grimké's Rhetoric of Exposure." *American Quarterly* 49, no. 2 (1997): 328–55.

Herbig, Katherine Lydigsen. "Friends for Freedom: The Lives and Careers of Sallie Holley and Caroline Putnam." PhD diss., University of Michigan, 1977.

Hertz, Larry. "Hidden History—Slavery in the Hudson Valley?" *Vassar Stories*, February 10, 2021. https://stories.vassar.edu/2021/hidden-history-slavery-in-the-hudson-valley.html.

Hesk, Jon. "'Despisers of the Commonplace': Meta-Topoi and Para-Topoi in Attic Oratory." *Rhetorica* 25, no. 4 (2007): 361–84.

Hesler, Samantha M. "The Lost Legacy of Laura Johnson Wylie: An Exploration of Her Achievements in Local Women's History." *Hudson River Valley Review: A Journal of Regional Studies* 35, no. 2 (2019): 64–72.

Hine, Lela Marshall. Oral history interview, May 14, 1982. AAA.

Hobart, Michael E., and Zachary S. Schiffman. *Information Ages: Literacy, Numeracy, and the Computer Revolution*. Baltimore: Johns Hopkins University Press, 2000.

Hobsbawm, Eric J. *The Age of Capital, 1848–1875*. New York: Vintage Books, 1996.

———. *The Age of Empire, 1875–1914*. New York: Pantheon Books, 1987.

———. *The Age of Revolution: Europe 1789–1848*. New York: Praeger Publishers, 1969.

Hochschild, Arlie Russell, and Anne Machung. *The Second Shift*. New York: Avon Books, 1999.

Hoffert, Sylvia D. "Earnest Efforts to Be Friends: Teacher-Student Relationships in the Nineteenth-Century South." *Journal of Southern History* 84, no. 4 (2018): 813–44.

Hoffman, Nancy. "'Inquiring After the Schoolmarm': Problems of Historical Research on Female Teachers." *Women's Studies Quarterly* 22 (1994): 104–18.

———. "Teaching about Slavery, the Abolitionist Movement, and Women's Suffrage." *Women's Studies Quarterly* 14, no. 1/2 (1986): 2–6.

Hofheimer, Jo Ann Mervis. *Annie Wood, a Portrait: The Life and Times of the Founder of the Irene Leache Memorial*. Norfolk: Irene Leache Memorial; Norfolk: Chrysler Museum of Art, 1996.

Hoganson, Kristin. "Garrisonian Abolitionists and the Rhetoric of Gender, 1850–1860." *American Quarterly* 45, no. 4 (1993): 558–95.

Holland, Sharon Patricia. *The Erotic Life of Racism*. Durham: Duke University Press, 2012.

Holley, I. B., Jr. "Schooling Freedmen's Children." *New England Quarterly* 74, no. 3 (2001): 478–94.

Holley, Sallie. "Address to the Legislative Committee on Caste Schools in Rhode Island." *Liberator* 29, no. 23 (June 10, 1859): 91. NCN.

———. Commonplace book, [1847]–52. RH/CHS.

———. "Letter from Sallie Holley." *Liberator*, no. 28 (October 29, 1858). AHN.

———. Letter to Abigail Kelley Foster, [1851?]. AAS.

———. Letter to Caroline Putnam, November 9, 1867. FHSC.

———. Letter to Theodore Dwight Weld, November 12, 1879. WG/CLMT.

———. Letter to Wendell Phillips, March 14, 1874. WF/HL.

Holley Graded School. "Home." Holley Graded School Historic Site. Accessed July 7, 2021. http://holleyschool.weebly.com.

"Holley School Histories." *Holley School Histories*. Accessed July 8, 2021. http://holleyschoolhistories.weebly.com/.

Holmes, Kwame. "What's the Tea: Gossip and the Production of Black Gay Social History." *Radical History Review*, no. 122 (2015): 55–69.

Homestead, Melissa J. *The Only Wonderful Things: The Creative Partnership of Willa Cather and Edith Lewis*. New York: Oxford, 2021.

hooks, bell. "Eros, Eroticism and the Pedagogical Process." *Cultural Studies* 7, no. 1 (1993): 58–63.

Horowitz, Helen Lefkowitz. *Alma Mater: Design and Experience in the Women's Colleges from Their Nineteenth-Century Beginnings to the 1930s*. Amherst: University of Massachusetts Press, 1993.

Howland, Emily. Letter to Hannah [Letchworth Howland], November 13, 1873. FHSC.

Hsu, V. Jo. *Constellating Home: Trans and Queer Asian American Rhetorics*. Columbus: The Ohio State University Press, 2022.

———. "(Trans)Forming #MeToo: Toward a Networked Response to Gender Violence." *Women's Studies in Communication* 42, no. 3 (2019): 269–86.

———. "Voting Rights, Anti-Intersectionality, and Citizenship as Containment." *Quarterly Journal of Speech* 106, no. 3 (2020): 269–76.

Huxman, Susan Schultz. "Mary Wollstonecraft, Margaret Fuller, and Angelina Grimké: Symbolic Convergence and a Nascent Rhetorical Vision." *Communication Quarterly* 44, no. 1 (1996): 16–28.

Hylton, Antonia. "Black Lives Matter Forces LGBTQ Organization to Face Its History of Racial Exclusion." *NBC News*, June 22, 2020. https://www.nbcnews.com/feature/nbc-out/black-lives-matter-forces-lgbtq-organization-face-its-history-racial-n1231816.

Inness, Sherrie A. "Mashes, Smashes, Crushes, and Raves: Woman-to-Woman Relationships in Popular Women's College Fiction, 1895–1915." *NWSA Journal* 6, no. 1 (1994): 48–68.

Jabour, Anya. *Scarlett's Sisters: Young Women in the Old South*. Chapel Hill: University of North Carolina Press, 2009.

Japp, Phyllis M. "Esther or Isaiah? The Abolitionist-Feminist Rhetoric of Angelina Grimké." *Quarterly Journal of Speech* 71, no. 3 (1985): 335–48.

Jarratt, Susan C. "Classics and Counterpublics in Nineteenth-Century Historically Black Colleges." *College English* 72, no. 2 (2009): 134–59.

———. *Rereading the Sophists: Classical Rhetoric Refigured*. Carbondale: Southern Illinois University Press, 1991.

———. "Sappho's Memory." *Rhetoric Society Quarterly* 32, no. 1 (2002): 11–43.

Jeffrey, Julie Roy. *The Great Silent Army of Abolitionism: Ordinary Women in the Antislavery Movement*. Chapel Hill: University of North Carolina Press, 1998.

Johnson, E. Patrick. *Black. Queer. Southern. Women: An Oral History*. Chapel Hill: University of North Carolina Press, 2018.

———. "A Revelatory Distillation of Experience." *Women's Studies Quarterly* 40, no. 3/4 (2012): 311–14.

———. *Sweet Tea: Black Gay Men of the South*. Chapel Hill: University of North Carolina Press, 2008.

Johnson, J. R. "Sallie Holley in Connecticut." *Liberator*, no. 6 (February 8, 1856): 22. NCN.

Johnson, Nan. *Gender and Rhetorical Space in American Life, 1866–1910*. Carbondale: Southern Illinois University Press, 2002.

———. *Nineteenth-Century Rhetoric in North America*. Carbondale: Southern Illinois University Press, 1991.

Jones, Jacqueline. *Soldiers of Light and Love: Northern Teachers and Georgia Blacks, 1865–1873*. Athens: University of Georgia Press, 1980.

Jones, Martha S. *Vanguard: How Black Women Broke Barriers, Won the Vote, and Insisted on Equality for All*. New York: Basic Books, 2020.

Kahan, Benjamin. *Celibacies: American Modernism and Sexual Life*. Durham: Duke University Press, 2013.

Kaschak, Ellyn, ed. *Intimate Betrayal: Domestic Violence in Lesbian Relationships*. Binghamton: Haworth Press, 2001.

Katz, Jonathan Ned. *Gay American History: Lesbians and Gay Men in the USA*. New York: Thomas Y. Crowell, 1992.

Kelley, William. "Rhetoric as Seduction." *Philosophy and Rhetoric* 6, no. 2 (1973): 69–80.

Kelly, Maura, and Elizabeth Hauck. "Doing Housework, Redoing Gender: Queer Couples Negotiate the Household Division of Labor." *Journal of GLBT Family Studies* 11, no. 5 (2015): 1–27.

Kemp, Yakini B. "Writing Power: Identity Complexities and the Exotic Erotic in Audre Lorde's Writing." *Studies in the Literary Imagination* 37, no. 2 (2004): 21–36.

Kendall, Elaine. *Peculiar Institutions: An Informal History of Seven Sister Colleges*. New York: G. P. Putnam's Sons, 1976.

Kennerly, Michele. *Editorial Bodies: Perfection and Rejection in Ancient Rhetoric and Poetics*. Columbia: University of South Carolina Press, 2018.

Kent, Kathryn R. *Making Girls into Women: American Women's Writing and the Rise of Lesbian Identity*. Durham: Duke University Press, 2003.

Kim, Eunjung. "Asexuality in Disability Narratives." *Sexualities* 14, no. 4 (2011): 479–93.

Kimball, Elizabeth. "Commonplace, Quakers, and the Founding of Haverford School." *Rhetoric Review* 30, no. 4 (2011): 372–88.

Knight, Denise D. "Charlotte Perkins Gilman and the Shadow of Racism." *American Literary Realism* 32, no. 2 (2000): 159–69.

Kraft-Ebing, Richard von. *Psychopathia Sexualis*. Translated by F. J. Rebman. 12th ed. 1886. Reprint, Chicago: Login Brothers, 1929.

Kranidis, Rita S. *The Victorian Spinster and Colonial Emigration: Contested Subjects.* New York: St. Martin's Press, 1999.

Kumbier, Alana. *Ephemeral Material: Queering the Archive.* Sacramento: Litwin Books, 2014.

Kurdek, Lawrence A. "The Allocation of Household Labor by Partners in Gay and Lesbian Couples." *Journal of Family Issues,* no. 28 (2007): 132–48.

"Laura Johnson Wylie." *Packer Alumna.* June 1932. VCL.

Lawrence, LeeAnn. "Organisms vs. Machines: Gertrude Buck and the Direction of Early Twentieth-Century Rhetorical Theory." *Women and Language* 15, no. 2 (1992): 32.

Leache, Irene Kirke, and Louise Collier Willcox [as I.K.L. and L.C.W.]. *Answers of the Ages.* Chicago: Herbert S. Stone, 1900. JOCL.

Leache-Wood Seminary. "Leache-Wood School for Young Ladies, No. 138 Granby Street, Norfolk, VA" [school catalog]. 1880. NPL.

———. "Leache-Wood School for Young Ladies, No. 138 Granby Street, Norfolk, VA" [school catalog]. 1894. NPL.

———. *Nods and Becks* [yearbook]. Norfolk: Burke and Gregory, 1910. JOCL.

"Lectures of Miss Holley." *Liberator,* no. 27 (December 25, 1857): 206. APS.

Lee, Jamie A. "Be/Longing in the Archival Body: Eros and the 'Endearing' Value of Material Lives." *Archival Science,* no. 16 (2016): 33–51.

———. *Producing the Archival Body.* New York: Routledge, 2021.

Lee, Robert, and Tristan Ahtone. "Land-Grab Universities." *High Country News,* March 30, 2020. https://www.hcn.org/issues/52.4/indigenous-affairs-education-land-grab-universities.

LeMaster, Lore/tta (Benny). "Felt Sex: Erotic Affects and a Case for Critical Erotic/a." *Departures in Critical Qualitative Research* 9, no. 3 (2020): 105–39.

L'Eplattenier, Barbara E. "Investigating Institutional Power: Women Administrators during the Progressive Era, 1890–1920." PhD diss., Purdue University, 1999.

L'Eplattenier, Barbara E., and Lisa S. Mastrangelo, eds. *Historical Studies of Writing Program Administration: Individuals, Communities, and the Formation of a Discipline.* Anderson: Parlor Press, 2004.

"Letter from Miss Sallie Holley, March 7, 1868." *National Anti-Slavery Standard* 28, no. 44 (March 7, 1868).

Libby, Peter. "Sallie Holley in Maine." *Liberator,* no. 35 (September 2, 1859): 138. NCN.

Lobel, Kerry, ed. *Naming the Violence: Speaking Out about Lesbian Battering.* Seattle: Seal Press, 1986.

Logan, Shirley Wilson. *Liberating Language: Sites of Rhetorical Education in Nineteenth-Century Black America.* Carbondale: Southern Illinois University Press, 2008.

———. "Literacy as a Tool for Social Action among Nineteenth-Century African American Women." In *Nineteenth-Century Women Learn to Write,* edited by Catherine Hobbs, 179–96. Charlottesville: University Press of Virginia, 1995.

———. "'To Get an Education and Teach My People': Rhetoric for Social Change." In *Rhetorical Education in America,* edited by Cheryl Glenn, Margaret M. Lyday, and Wendy B. Sharer, 36–52. Tuscaloosa: University of Alabama Press, 2004.

———. *We Are Coming: The Persuasive Discourse of Nineteenth-Century Black Women.* Carbondale: Southern Illinois University Press, 1999.

———, ed. *With Pen and Voice: A Critical Anthology of Nineteenth-Century African American Women.* Carbondale: Southern Illinois University Press, 1995.

Lorde, Audre. "An Address Delivered as Part of the 'Litany of Commitment' at the March on Washington, August 27, 1983." In *I Am Your Sister: Collected and Unpublished Writings of Audre Lorde,* by Audre Lorde, Rudolph P. Byrd, Johnnetta B. Cole, and Beverly Guy-Sheftall, 212. New York: Oxford University Press, 2009.

———. "Age, Race, Class, and Sex: Women Redefining Difference." In Lorde, *Sister Outsider,* 114–23.

———. "A Burst of Light: Living with Cancer." In Lorde, *I Am Your Sister,* 81–149.

———. "Commencement Address: Oberlin College, May 29, 1989." In Lorde, *I Am Your Sister,* 213–18.

———. "Difference and Survival: An Address at Hunter College." In Lorde, *I Am Your Sister,* 201–4.

———. "Foreword to the English Edition of *Farbe Bekennen: Afro-Deutsche Frauen auf den Spuren Ihrer Geschichte.*" In Lorde, *I Am Your Sister,* 169–76.

———. *I Am Your Sister: Collected and Unpublished Writings of Audre Lorde.* Edited by Rudolph P. Byrd, Johnnetta B. Cole, and Beverly Guy-Sheftall. New York: Oxford University Press, 2009.

———. "Learning from the 60s." In Lorde, *Sister Outsider,* 134–44.

———. "The Master's Tools Will Never Dismantle the Master's House." In Lorde, *Sister Outsider,* 110–13.

———. "My Words Will Be There." In Lorde, *I Am Your Sister,* 160–68.

———. "Poetry Is Not a Luxury." In Lorde, *Sister Outsider,* 36–39.

———. "Poetry Makes Something Happen." In Lorde, *I Am Your Sister,* 184–87.

———. *Sister Outsider: Essays and Speeches by Audre Lorde.* Berkeley: Crossing Press, 1984.

———. "There Is No Hierarchy of Oppression." In Lorde, *I Am Your Sister,* 219–20.

———. "The Transformation of Silence into Language and Action." In Lorde, *I Am Your Sister,* 39–43.

———. "Turning the Beat Around: Lesbian Parenting, 1986." In Lorde, *I Am Your Sister,* 73–80.

———. "Uses of the Erotic: The Erotic as Power." In Lorde, *Sister Outsider,* 53–59.

———. "What Is at Stake in Lesbian and Gay Publishing Today: The Bill Whitehead Award Ceremony, 1990." In Lorde, *I Am Your Sister,* 221–23.

———. "When Will the Ignorance End? Keynote Speech at the National Third World Gay and Lesbian Conference, October 13, 1979." In Lorde, *I Am Your Sister,* 207–11.

———. *Zami: A New Spelling of My Name.* Berkeley: Crossing Press, 1982.

Lorde, Audre, and Pat Parker. *Sister Love: The Letters of Audre Lorde and Pat Parker, 1974–1989.* Edited by Julie R. Enszer. Introduced by Mecca Jamilah Sullivan. Dover: Sinister Wisdom, 2018.

Lorde, Audre, and Susan Leigh Star. "Sadomasochism: Not about Condemnation; an Interview with Audre Lorde." In Lorde, *I Am Your Sister,* 50–56.

Love, Heather. *Feeling Backward: Loss and the Politics of Queer History.* Cambridge: Harvard University Press, 2007.

———. "Gyn/Apology: Sarah Orne Jewett's Spinster Aesthetics." *ESQ: A Journal of the American Renaissance* 55, no. 3 (2009): 305–34.

Lui, Debora. "Public Curation and Private Collection: The Production of Knowledge on Pinterest.com." *Critical Studies in Media Communication,* no. 32 (2015): 128–42.

Luibhéid, Eithne. *Entry Denied: Controlling Sexuality at the Border.* Minneapolis: University of Minnesota Press, 2002.

Lundy, Sandra E., and Beth Leventhal, eds. *Same-Sex Domestic Violence: Strategies for Change.* Thousand Oaks, CA: Sage Publications, 1999.

Machado, Carmen Maria. *In the Dream House: A Memoir.* Minneapolis: Graywolf Press, 2019.

Malatino, Hil. *Queer Embodiment: Monstrosity, Medical Violence, and Intersex Experience.* Lincoln: University of Nebraska Press, 2019.

———. *Trans Care.* Minneapolis: University of Minnesota Press, 2020.

Mandziuk, Roseann M., and Suzanne Pullon Fitch. "The Rhetorical Construction of Sojourner Truth." *Southern Communication Journal* 66, no. 2 (2001): 120–38.

Manion, Jen. *Female Husbands: A Trans History.* New York: Cambridge University Press, 2020.

Marcus, Sharon. "The State's Oversight: From Sexual Bodies to Erotic Selves." *Social Research* 78, no. 2 (2011): 509–32.

Marshall, David L. "Warburgian Maxims for Visual Rhetoric." *Rhetoric Society Quarterly* 48, no. 4 (2018): 352–79.

Mastrangelo, Lisa S. "Building a Dinosaur from the Bones: Fred Newton Scott and Women's Progressive Era Graduate Work at the University of Michigan." *Rhetoric Review* 24, no. 4 (2005): 403–20.

———. "Lone Wolf or Leader of the Pack? Rethinking the Grand Narrative of Fred Newton Scott." *College English* 72, no. 2 (2010): 248–68.

McAdon, Brad. "The 'Special Topics' in the Rhetoric: A Reconsideration." *Rhetoric Society Quarterly* 36, no. 4 (2006): 399–424.

McClintock, Anne. *Imperial Leather: Race, Gender, and Sexuality in the Colonial Contest.* New York: Routledge, 1995.

McClish, Glen. "'To Furnish Specimens of Negro Eloquence': William J. Simmons's *Men of Mark* as a Site of Late-Nineteenth-Century African American Rhetorical Education." *Rhetoric Society Quarterly* 44, no. 1 (2014): 46–67.

McDaneld, Jen. "White Suffragist Dis/Entitlement: The Revolution and the Rhetoric of Racism." *Legacy* 30, no. 2 (2013): 243–64.

McHenry, Elizabeth. "'Dreaded Eloquence': The Origins and Rise of African American Literary Societies and Libraries." *Harvard Library Bulletin* 6, no. 2 (1995): 32–56.

McKinney, Cait. *Information Activism: A Queer History of Lesbian Media Technologies.* Durham: Duke University Press, 2020.

McNinch, James. "Queering Seduction: Eros and the Erotic in the Construction of Gay Teacher Identity." *Journal of Men's Studies* 15, no. 2 (2007): 197–215.

Mehlenbacher, Ashley Rose, and Randy Allen Harris. "A Figurative Mind: Gertrude Buck's *The Metaphor* as a Nexus in Cognitive Metaphor Theory." *Rhetorica* 35, no. 1 (2017): 75–109.

Mesch, Rachel. *Before Trans: Three Gender Stories from Nineteenth-Century France.* Stanford: Stanford University Press, 2020.

Meyer, Moe. "The Signifying Invert: Camp and the Performance of Nineteenth-Century Sexology." *Text and Performance Quarterly* 15, no. 4 (1995): 265–81.

Micciche, Laura. *Acknowledging Writing Partners.* Fort Collins: Colorado State University Open Press, 2017.

Mihesuah, Devon A. *Cultivating the Rosebuds: The Education of Women at the Cherokee Female Seminary, 1851–1909.* Urbana: University of Illinois Press, 1993.

Miller, Susan. *Assuming the Positions: Cultural Pedagogy and the Politics of Commonplace Writing.* Pittsburgh: University of Pittsburgh Press, 1998.

Miller-Young, Mireille. *A Taste for Brown Sugar: Black Women in Pornography.* Durham: Duke University Press, 2014.

"Miss Laura Wylie, Educator, Is Dead: Professor of English at Vassar for 27 Years Passes Away at Age of 75." *New York Times*, April 3, 1932.

Montgomery, Nick, and Carla Bergman. *Joyful Militancy: Building Resistance in Toxic Times.* Chico: AK Press, 2017.

Moore, Lisa L. *Sister Arts: The Erotics of Lesbian Landscapes.* Minneapolis: University of Minnesota Press, 2011.

———. "'Something More Tender Still than Friendship': Romantic Friendship in Early-Nineteenth-Century England." *Feminist Studies*, no. 18 (1992): 499–520.

Morgan, Joan. "Why We Get Off: Moving Towards a Black Feminist Politics of Pleasure." *Black Scholar* 45, no. 4 (2015): 36–46.

Morris, Charles E, III. "Archival Queer." *Rhetoric and Public Affairs* 9, no. 1 (2006): 145–51.

———. "Hard Evidence: The Vexations of Lincoln's Queer Corpus." In *Rhetoric, Materiality, and Politics*, edited by Barbara Biesecker and John Lucaites, 185–214. New York: Peter Lang Publishers, 2009.

———. "My Old Kentucky Homo: Abraham Lincoln, Larry Kramer, and the Politics of Queer Memory." In Morris, *Queering Public Address*, 93–120.

———, ed. *Queering Public Address: Sexualities in American Historical Discourse.* Columbia: University of South Carolina Press, 2007.

———. "Sexuality and Public Address: Rhetorical Pasts, Queer Theory, and Abraham Lincoln." In *The Handbook of Rhetoric and Public Address*, edited by Shawn J. Parry-Giles and J. Michael Hogan, 398–421. Hoboken: John Wiley and Sons, 2010.

———. "Sunder the Children: Abraham Lincoln's Queer Rhetorical Pedagogy." *Quarterly Journal of Speech* 99, no. 4 (2013): 395–422.

Morris, Robert C. *Reading, 'Riting, and Reconstruction: The Education of Freedmen in the South, 1861–1870.* Chicago: University of Chicago Press, 1981.

Moss, Beverly J. "'Phenomenal Women,' Collaborative Literacies, and Community Texts in Alternative 'Sista' Spaces." *Community Literacy Journal* 5, no. 1 (2010): 1–24.

Moulder, M. Amanda. "Cherokee Practice, Missionary Intentions: Literacy Learning among Early Nineteenth-Century Cherokee Women." *College Composition and Communication* 63, no. 1 (2011): 75–97.

Mulderig, Gerald P. "Gertrude Buck's Rhetorical Theory and Modern Composition Teaching." *Rhetoric Society Quarterly* 14, no. 3/4 (1984): 95–104.

Muñoz, José Esteban. "Ephemera as Evidence: Introductory Notes to Queer Acts." *Women and Performance: A Journal of Feminist Theory* 8, no. 2 (1996): 5–16.

Murphy, Mollie K., and Tina M. Harris. "White Innocence and Black Subservience: The Rhetoric of White Heroism in *The Help*." *Howard Journal of Communications* 29, no. 1 (2018): 49–62.

Musser, Amber Jamilla. "On the Erotic." In *Gender: Sources, Perspectives, and Methodologies*, edited by Renée C. Hoogland, 69–82. Farmington Hills: Macmillan Reference, 2016.

———. "Queering the Pinup: History, Femmes, and Brooklyn." *GLQ: A Journal of Lesbian and Gay Studies* 22, no. 1 (2016): 55–80.

———. "Re-Membering Audre: Adding Lesbian Feminist Mother Poet to Black." In *No Tea, No Shade: New Writings in Black Queer Studies*, edited by E. Patrick Johnson, 346–61. Durham: Duke University Press, 2016.

Nash, Jennifer C. *The Black Body in Ecstasy: Reading Race, Reading Pornography*. Durham: Duke University Press, 2014.

National Domestic Violence Hotline. "Power and Control: Break Free from Abuse." *National Domestic Violence Hotline*. Accessed July 2, 2021. https://www.thehotline.org/identify-abuse/power-and-control/.

Native Land Digital. Accessed October 28, 2022. https://native-land.ca/.

Newman, Louise Michele. *White Women's Rights: The Racial Origins of Feminism in the United States*. New York: Oxford University Press, 1999.

Nielson, Kim E. *A Disability History of the United States*. New York: Penguin Books, 2012.

Norfolk Historical Society and Josh Weinstein. "Norfolk Museum of Arts and Sciences." YouTube, February 8, 2017. https://www.youtube.com/watch?v=Oc_OkVXl17k.

Oberlin College and Conservatory. "Oberlin History." February 23, 2017. https://www.oberlin.edu/about-oberlin/oberlin-history.

Ochs, Robyn. "Bisexual." *Robyn Ochs*. Accessed February 15, 2019. https://robynochs.com/bisexual/.

O'Connor, Lillian. *Pioneer Women Orators: Rhetoric in the Ante-Bellum Reform Movement*. New York: Columbia University Press, 1954.

O'Dell, Jeff. "Holley Graded School." National Register of Historic Places Registration Form. Lottsburgh, VA. US Department of the Interior, National Park Service, 1990.

Olivares, Christina. "Thoughts on the Erotic in Audre Lorde's Archive." *Makhzin*, no. 3 (November 2018). https://www.makhzin.org/issues/dictatorship/thoughts-on-the-erotic-in-audre-lorde-s-archive.

Olson, Lester C. "Anger among Allies: Audre Lorde's 1981 Keynote Admonishing the National Women's Studies Association." *Quarterly Journal of Speech* 97, no. 3 (2011): 283–308.

———. "Intersecting Audiences: Public Commentary Concerning Audre Lorde's Speech, 'Uses of the Erotic: The Erotic as Power.'" In *Standing in the Intersection: Feminist Voices, Feminist Practices in Communication Studies*, edited by Karma R. Chávez and Cindy L. Griffin, 125–46. Albany: State University of New York Press, 2012.

———. "Liabilities of Language: Audre Lorde Reclaiming Difference." *Quarterly Journal of Speech* 84, no. 4 (1998). 448–70.

———. "On the Margins of Rhetoric: Audre Lorde Transforming Silence into Language and Action." *Quarterly Journal of Speech* 83, no. 1 (1997): 49–70.

———. "The Personal, the Political, and Others: Audre Lorde Denouncing 'The Second Sex Conference.'" *Philosophy and Rhetoric* 33, no. 3 (2000): 259–85.

———. "Traumatic Styles in Public Address: Audre Lorde's Discourse as Exemplar." In Morris, *Queering Public Address*, 249–82.

Ophir, Ella. "The Diary and the Commonplace Book: Self-Inscription in the Note Books of a Woman Alone." *Biography* 38, no. 1 (2015): 41–55.

"Oral Histories." *Holley School Histories*. Accessed July 8, 2021. http://holleyschoolhistories.weebly.com/oral-histories.html.

Oram, Allison. *Women Teachers and Feminist Politics, 1900–1939*. Manchester, United Kingdom: Manchester University Press, 1996.

Orbuch, Terri L., and Sandra L. Eyster. "Division of Household Labor among Black Couples and White Couples." *Social Forces* 76, no. 1 (1997): 301–32.

Owen, Ianna Hawkins. "On the Racialization of Asexuality." In *Asexualities: Feminist and Queer Perspectives*, edited by Karli June Cerankowski and Megan Milks, 119–35. New York: Routledge, 2014.

———. "Still, Nothing: Mammy and Black Asexual Possibility." *Feminist Review* 120, no. 1 (2018): 70–84.

Palczewski, Catherine H. "The 1919 Prison Special: Constituting White Women's Citizenship." *Quarterly Journal of Speech* 102, no. 2 (2016): 107–32.

Partner, Nancy F. "Making Up Lost Time: Writing on the Writing of History." *Speculum* 61, no. 1 (1986): 90–117.

Pease, William, and Jane Pease. "Sallie Holley." In *Notable American Women, 1607–1950*, edited by Edward T. James, Janet Wilson James, and Paul S. Boyer, 205–6. Cambridge: Belknap, 1971.

Perkin, Joan. *Victorian Women*. New York: New York University Press, 1995.

Perkins, Linda. "The African American Female Elite: The Early History of African American Women in the Seven Sister Colleges, 1880–1960." *Harvard Educational Review* 67, no. 4 (1997): 718–57.

———. "The Racial Integration of the Seven Sister Colleges." *Journal of Blacks in Higher Education*, no. 19 (1998): 104–8.

Petermon, Jade D., and Leland G. Spencer. "Black Queer Womanhood Matters: Searching for the Queer Herstory of Black Lives Matter in Television Dramas." *Critical Studies in Media Communication* 36, no. 4 (2019): 339–56.

Pfeffer, Carla A. "'Women's Work'? Women Partners of Transgender Men Doing Housework and Emotion Work." *Journal of Marriage and Family*, no. 72 (2010): 165–83.

Pirker, Eva Ulrike, and Judith Rahn. "Afrofuturist Trajectories across Time, Space and Media." *Critical Studies in Media Communication* 37, no. 4 (2020): 283–97.

Plato. "Phaedrus." In *The Rhetorical Tradition: Readings from Classical Times to the Present*, edited by Patricia Bizzell and Bruce Herzberg, translated by H. N. Fowler, 138–68. 2nd ed. New York: Bedford, 2001.

Potter, Claire, and John D'Emilio. "Letters from Eleanor: When Do Private Acts Have Public Consequences?" *Queer America*, episode 8. Accessed July 26, 2021. https://www.learningforjustice.org/podcasts/queer-america/letters-from-eleanor-when-do-private-acts-have-public-consequences.

Powell, Malea. "Dreaming Charles Eastman: Cultural Memory, Autobiography, and Geography in Indigenous Rhetorical Histories." In *Beyond the Archives: Research as Lived Process*, edited by Gesa E. Kirsch and Liz Rohan, 115–27. Carbondale: Southern Illinois University Press, 2008.

Pritchard, Eric Darnell. "'As Proud of Our Gayness, as We Are of Our Blackness': Race-ing Sexual Rhetorics in the National Coalition of Black Lesbians and Gays." In *Sexual Rhetorics: Methods, Identities, Publics*, edited by Jonathan Alexander and Jacqueline Rhodes, 159–71. New York: Routledge, 2015.

———. *Fashioning Lives: Black Queers and the Politics of Literacy*. Carbondale: Southern Illinois University Press, 2017.

———. "'Like Signposts on the Road': The Function of Literacy in Constructing Black Queer Ancestors." *Literacy and Composition Studies* 2, no. 1 (2014): 29–56.

Przybylo, Ela. *Asexual Erotics: Intimate Readings of Compulsory Sexuality*. Columbus: The Ohio State University Press, 2019.

Przybylo, Ela, and Danielle Cooper. "Asexual Resonances: Tracing a Queerly Asexual Archive." *GLQ: A Journal of Lesbian and Gay Studies* 20, no. 3 (2014): 297–318.

Putnam, Caroline. Letter to Frederick Douglass, April 19, 1888. FD/LOC.

———. Letters to Sallie Holley, 1868–71. CP/CLMT.

———. Letters to Sallie Holley and Emily Howland, 1852–58. CRNL.

———. Letters to Samuel May, 1887–93. MHS.

———. Letter to Wendell Phillips, June 28, 1874. WF/HL.

Quandahl, Ellen. "Aristotle's Rhetoric: Reinterpreting Invention." *Rhetoric Review* 4, no. 2 (1986): 128–37.

Ramirez, Mario H. "Being Assumed Not to Be: A Critique of Whiteness as an Archival Imperative." *The American Archivist* 78, no. 2 (2015): 339–56.

Rand, Erica. *The Ellis Island Snow Globe*. Durham: Duke University Press, 2005.

Rand, Erin J. *Reclaiming Queer: Activist and Academic Rhetorics of Resistance*. Tuscaloosa: University of Alabama Press, 2014.

Rao, Aliya Hamid. "Even Breadwinning Wives Don't Get Equality at Home." *The Atlantic*, May 12, 2019. https://www.theatlantic.com/family/archive/2019/05/breadwinning-wives-gender-inequality/589237/.

Rasheed, Shaireen. "Sexualized Spaces in Public Places: Irigaray, Levinas, and an Ethics of the Erotic." *Educational Theory* 57, no. 3 (2007): 339–50.

Rawson, K. J. "The Rhetorical Power of Archival Description: Classifying Images of Gender Transgression." *Rhetoric Society Quarterly* 48, no. 4 (2017): 1–25.

Rhodes, Jacqueline. *Once a Fury*. Documentary feature. Morrigan House, 2020. https://onceafury.com/.

Rhodes, Jacqueline, and Jonathan Alexander. *The Routledge Handbook of Queer Rhetoric*. New York: Routledge, 2022.

Reed, Alison Rose. *Love and Abolition: The Social Life of Black Queer Performance*. Columbus: The Ohio State University Press, 2022.

Rich, Adrienne. "Compulsory Heterosexuality and Lesbian Existence." *Signs: Journal of Women in Culture and Society* 5, no. 4 (1980): 631–60.

Richardson, Elaine. "'To Protect and Serve': African American Female Literacies." *College Composition and Communication* 53, no. 4 (2002): 675–704.

Ricker, Lisa Reid. "(De)Constructing the Praxis of Memory-Keeping: Late Nineteenth-Century Autograph Albums as Sites of Rhetorical Invention." *Rhetoric Review* 29, no. 3 (2010): 239–56.

Rifkin, Mark. *The Erotics of Sovereignty: Queer Native Writing in the Era of Self-Determination*. Minneapolis: University of Minnesota Press, 2012.

Ristock, Janice L. *No More Secrets: Violence in Lesbian Relationships*. New York: Routledge, 2002.

Robertson, Stacey M. "Remembering Antislavery: Women Abolitionists in the Old Northwest." *Proteus* 19, no. 2 (2002): 65–71.

Rodsky, Eve. *Fair Play: A Game-Changing Solution for When You Have Too Much to Do (and More Life to Live)*. New York: G. P. Putnam's Sons, 2019.

Rolle, Elisa. *Celebrating LGBT History One Story at a Time.* CreateSpace Independent Publishing Platform, 2014.

Roosevelt, Eleanor. "Tribute to Miss Wiley by Eleanor Roosevelt." In *Miss Wylie of Vassar,* edited by Elisabeth Woodbridge Morris. New Haven: Yale University Press, 1934. VCL.

Rothblum, Esther D., and Kathleen A. Brehony, eds. *Boston Marriages: Romantic but Asexual Relationships among Contemporary Lesbians.* Amherst: University of Massachusetts Press, 1993.

Rothermel, Beth Ann. "Prophets, Friends, Conversationalists: Quaker Rhetorical Culture, Women's Commonplace Books, and the Art of Invention, 1775–1840." *Rhetoric Society Quarterly* 43, no. 1 (2013): 71–94.

Royster, Jacqueline Jones. *Traces of a Stream: Literacy and Social Change among African American Women.* Pittsburgh: University of Pittsburgh Press, 2000.

Royster, Jacqueline Jones, and Gesa E. Kirsch. *Feminist Rhetorical Practices: New Horizons for Rhetoric, Composition, and Literacy Studies.* Carbondale: Southern Illinois University Press, 2012.

Royster, Jacqueline Jones, and Jean C. Williams. "History in the Spaces Left: African American Presence and Narratives of Composition Studies." *College Composition and Communication* 50, no. 4 (1999): 563–84.

Rycenga, Jennifer. "A Greater Awakening: Women's Intellect as a Factor in Early Abolitionist Movements, 1824–1834." *Journal of Feminist Studies in Religion* 21, no. 2 (2005): 31–59.

Sahli, Nancy. "Smashing: Women's Relationships Before the Fall." *Chrysalis,* no. 8 (1979): 17–27.

"Sallie Holley." *Frederick Douglass' Paper,* no. 9 (February 19, 1852). NCN.

Samek, Alyssa A. "(White) Women on the Move: Suffrage Memory and the 1977 International Women's Year Conference." *Quarterly Journal of Speech* 106, no. 3 (2020): 277–84.

Savage, Maddy. "How COVID-19 Is Changing Women's Lives." *BBC News,* June 30, 2020. https://www.bbc.com/worklife/article/20200630-how-covid-19-is-changing-womens-lives.

Schaik, Marjan A. van. "How Belletristic Rhetorical Theory in the Liberal Arts Tradition Led to Civic Engagement: Turn-of-the-Century Rhetoric Instruction at Bryn Mawr College." *Rhetoric Review* 33, no. 2 (2014): 113–31.

Sears, James T. *Rebels, Rubyfruit, and Rhinestones: Queering Space in the Stonewall South.* New Brunswick: Rutgers University Press, 2001.

Sedgwick, Eve Kosofsky. *Epistemology of the Closet.* Berkeley: University of California Press, 1990.

Shelden, Mary Lamb. "'A Broad, Generous Stream of Love and Bounty': The Concord Sewing Circle and the Holley School for Freedmen." *Documentary Editing,* no. 32 (2011): 22–35.

———. "'Deep in Barrels': Friendship and Support from the Alcott Family of Concord, Massachusetts, for the Holley School for Freedmen." *Bulletin of the Northumberland County Historical Society,* no. 47 (2010): 96–98.

———. "'Such a Great Light': Letters to Louisa and Abba Alcott from the Holley School for Freed People and the Story of Winnie Beale's Emancipation." *Resources for American Literary Study,* no. 37 (2014): 67–151.

Siejk, Cate. "Awakening the Erotic in Religious Education." *Religious Education* 96, no. 4 (2001): 546–62.

Simpson, David. "Symposium on Native Land Acknowledgement to Feature Indigenous Stakeholders." Old Dominion University, October 30, 2022. https://www.odu.edu/article/symposium-native-land-acknowledgement-to-feature-indigenous-stakeholders.

Singh, Julietta. *No Archive Will Restore You.* Santa Barbara: Punctum Books, 2018.

Sloop, John M. "Lucy Lobdell's Queer Circumstances." In Morris, *Queering Public Address,* 149–73.

Smilges, J. Logan. *Queer Silence: On Disability and Rhetorical Absence.* Minneapolis: University of Minnesota Press, 2022.

Smith, Barbara. "Toward a Black Feminist Criticism." *Women's Studies International Quarterly* 2, no. 2 (1979): 183–94.

Smith-Rosenberg, Carroll. "Discourses of Sexuality and Subjectivity: The New Woman, 1870–1936." In *Hidden from History: Reclaiming the Gay and Lesbian Past,* edited by Martin Duberman, Martha Vicinus, and George Chauncey Jr., 264–80. London: Penguin, 1991.

———. "The Female World of Love and Ritual." In *Disorderly Conduct: Visions of Gender in Victorian America,* 53–76. New York: Oxford University Press, 1985.

Sneider, Allison L. "The Impact of Empire on the North American Woman Suffrage Movement: Suffrage Racism in an Imperial Context." *UCLA Historical Journal,* no. 14 (1994): 14–32.

Snorton, C. Riley. *Black on Both Sides: A Racial History of Trans Identity.* Minneapolis: University of Minnesota Press, 2017.

Somerville, Siobhan B. *Queering the Color Line: Race and the Invention of Homosexuality in American Culture.* Durham: Duke University Press, 2000.

Spade, Dean. *Normal Life: Administrative Violence, Critical Trans Politics and the Limits of Law.* Boston: South End Press, 2011.

Speicher, Anna M. *The Religious World of Antislavery Women: Spirituality in the Lives of Five Abolitionist Lecturers.* Syracuse: Syracuse University Press, 2000.

Stallings, L. H. *Funk the Erotic: Transaesthetics and Black Sexual Cultures.* Chicago: University of Illinois Press, 2015.

Stanley, Eric A., Nat Smith, and CeCe McDonald, eds. *Captive Genders: Trans Embodiment and the Prison Industrial Complex.* Stirling, United Kingdom: AK Press, 2015.

Stanton, Elizabeth Cady. "Manhood Suffrage." *Revolution,* no. 24 (December 24, 1868): 392–93.

Stevens, H. "Sallie Holley in Montague." *Liberator,* no. 52 (December 24, 1858): 206. NCN.

Stevenson, Edward Irenaeus Prime [as Xavier Mayne]. *The Intersexes: A History of Similisexualism as a Problem in Social Life.* 1908. Reprint, New York: Arno Press, 1975.

Stewart, Maria W., and Marilyn Richardson. *Maria W. Stewart, America's First Black Woman Political Writer: Essays and Speeches.* Bloomington: Indiana University Press, 1987.

Stoler, Ann Laura. "Colonial Archives and the Arts of Governance." *Archival Science,* no. 2 (2002): 87–109.

Sullivan, Oriel. "The Gendered Division of Household Labor." In *Handbook of Sociology of Gender,* edited by Barbara J. Risman, Carissa M. Froyum, and William J. Scarborough, 377–92. Cham, Switzerland: Springer International, 2018.

Sutphin, Suzanne. "The Division of Child Care Tasks in Same-Sex Couples." *Journal of GLBT Family Studies,* no. 9 (2013): 474–91.

Taylor, Diana. *The Archive and the Repertoire: Performing Cultural Memory in the Americas.* Durham: Duke University Press, 2003.

Taylor, Judith. "Enduring Friendship: Women's Intimacies and the Erotics of Survival." *Frontiers: A Journal of Women Studies* 34, no. 1 (2013): 93–113.

Terry, Jennifer. "Anxious Slippages between 'Us' and 'Them': A Brief History of the Scientific Search for Homosexual Bodies." In *Deviant Bodies: Critical Perspectives on Difference in Sci-*

*ence and Culture,* edited by Jennifer Terry and Jacqueline L. Urla, 129–69. Bloomington: Indiana University Press, 1995.

Tetrault, Lisa. *The Myth of Seneca Falls: Memory and the Women's Suffrage Movement, 1848–1898.* Chapel Hill: University of North Carolina Press, 2017.

Thomas, M. Carey. *The Making of a Feminist: Early Journals and Letters of M. Carey Thomas.* Edited by Marjorie Houspian Dobkin. Kent: Kent State University Press, 1979.

Tinsley, Omise'eke Natasha. *Thiefing Sugar: Eroticism between Women in Caribbean Literature.* Durham: Duke University Press, 2010.

Tobin, James. "Wait . . . When Did the University Start?" *Michigan Today,* November 16, 2013. https://michigantoday.umich.edu/2013/11/16/wait-when-did-the-university-start/.

Topp, Sarah S. "Against the Quiet Revolution: The Rhetorical Construction of Intersex Individuals as Disordered." *Sexualities* 16, no. 1/2 (2013): 180–94.

Tornello, Samantha L. "Division of Labor among Transgender and Gender Non-Binary Parents: Association with Individual, Couple, and Children's Behavioral Outcomes." *Frontiers in Psychology* 11, no. 15 (2020). https://www.frontiersin.org/articles/10.3389/fpsyg.2020.00015/full.

Towne, Laura Matilda, and Rupert Sargent Holland. *Letters and Diary of Laura M. Towne: Written from the Sea Islands of South Carolina, 1862–1884.* New York: Negro Universities Press, 1969.

Tunstall, Virginia Lyne. "The Story of Two Remarkable Women and Their Living Memorial: A Short History of the Irene Leache Memorial." Norfolk, 1962. JOCL.

Valdes, Annmarie. "Speaking and Writing in Conversation: Constructing the Voice of Eleanor Parke Custis Lewis." In *Rhetoric, History, and Women's Oratorical Education: American Women Learn to Speak,* edited by David Gold and Catherine Hobbs, 60–77. New York: Routledge, 2013.

VanHaitsma, Pamela. "African-American Rhetorical Education and Epistolary Relations at the Holley School (1868–1917)." *Advances in the History of Rhetoric* 21, no. 3 (2018): 293–313.

———. "An Archival Framework for Affirming Black Women's Bisexual Rhetorics in the Primus Collections." *Rhetoric Society Quarterly* 51, no. 1 (2021): 27–41.

———. "Between Archival Absence and Information Abundance: Reconstructing Sallie Holley's Abolitionist Rhetoric through Digital Surrogates and Metadata." *Quarterly Journal of Speech* 106, no. 1 (2020): 25–47.

———. "Gossip as Rhetorical Methodology for Queer and Feminist Historiography." *Rhetoric Review* 35, no. 2 (2016): 135–47.

———. "'Opulent Friendships,' Rhetorical Emulation, and Belletristic Instruction at Leache-Wood Seminary." In *Women at Work: Rhetorics of Gender and Labor in the US,* edited by David Gold and Jessica Enoch, 56–68. Pittsburgh: University of Pittsburgh Press, 2019.

———. *Queering Romantic Engagement in the Postal Age: A Rhetorical Education.* Columbia: University of South Carolina Press, 2019.

———. "Queering 'the Language of the Heart': Romantic Letters, Genre Instruction, and Rhetorical Practice." *Rhetoric Society Quarterly* 44, no. 1 (2014): 6–24.

———. "Romantic Correspondence as Queer Extracurriculum: The Self-Education for Racial Uplift of Addie Brown and Rebecca Primus." *College Composition and Communication* 69, no. 2 (2017): 182–207.

———. "Stories of Straightening Up: Reading Femmes in the Archives of Romantic Friendship." *QED: A Journal in GLBTQ Worldmaking* 6, no. 3 (2019): 1–24.

"Vassar Meets in Graveyard: College Girls Hold Suffrage Powwow." *New York Sun,* June 9, 1908.

Veracini, Lorenzo. "Introducing: Settler Colonial Studies." *Settler Colonial Studies* 1, no. 1 (2011): 1–12.

Vicinus, Martha. "Distance and Desire: English Boarding-School Friendships." *Signs: Journal of Women in Culture and Society* 9, no. 4 (1984): 600–622.

———. *Intimate Friends: Women Who Loved Women, 1778–1928*. Chicago: University of Chicago Press, 2004.

Virginia Department of Historic Resources. "066-0112 Holley Graded School." Accessed July 7, 2021. https://www.dhr.virginia.gov/historic-registers/066-0112/.

Vivian, Barbara G. "Gertrude Buck on Metaphor: Twentieth-Century Concepts in a Late Nineteenth-Century Dissertation." *Rhetoric Society Quarterly* 24, no. 3/4 (1994): 96–104.

Vleuten, Maaike van der, Eva Jaspers, and Tanja van der Lippe. "Same-Sex Couples' Division of Labor from a Cross-National Perspective." *Journal of GLBT Family Studies* 17, no. 2 (2021): 150–67.

Wallace, Jo-Ann. "Edith Ellis, Sapphic Idealism, and *The Lover's Calendar* (1912)." In *Sapphic Modernities: Sexuality, Women and National Culture*, edited by Lauren Doan and Jane Garrity, 183–99. New York: Palgrave MacMillan, 2006.

Wallace-Sanders, Kimberly. *Mammy: A Century of Race, Gender, and Southern Memory*. Ann Arbor: University of Michigan Press, 2008.

Walzer, Arthur E. "Aristotle on Speaking 'Outside the Subject': The Special Topics and Rhetorical Forums." In *Rereading Aristotle's Rhetoric*, edited by Alan G. Gross and Arthur E. Walzer, 38–54. Carbondale: Southern Illinois University Press, 2000.

Warnick, Barbara. *The Sixth Canon: Belletristic Rhetorical Theory and Its French Antecedents*. Columbia: University of South Carolina Press, 1993.

Werner, Maggie M. "Seductive Rhetoric and the Communicative Art of Neo-Burlesque." *Present Tense: A Journal of Rhetoric in Society* 5, no. 1 (2015): 1–11.

Whitbread, Helena. *I Know My Own Heart: The Diaries of Anne Lister, 1791–1840*. New York: New York University Press, 1992.

White, Deborah Gray. *Too Heavy a Load: Black Women in Defense of Themselves, 1894–1994*. New York: W. W. Norton and Company, 1999.

Wiegman, Robyn, and Elizabeth A. Wilson. "Introduction: Antinormativity's Queer Conventions." *Differences* 26, no. 1 (2015): 1–25.

Willey, Angela. *Undoing Monogamy: The Politics of Science and the Possibilities of Biology*. Durham: Duke University Press, 2016.

Williams, Heather Andrea. *Self-Taught: African American Education in Slavery and Freedom*. Durham: University of North Carolina Press, 2005.

Williams, Stacie M., and Jarrett M. Drake. "Power to the People: Documenting Police Violence in Cleveland." *Journal of Critical Library and Information Studies* 1, no. 2 (2017). https://journals.litwinbooks.com/index.php/jclis/article/view/33.

Wilson, Kirt H. "The Racial Politics of Imitation in the Nineteenth Century." *Quarterly Journal of Speech* 89, no. 2 (2003): 89–108.

———. *The Reconstruction Desegregation Debate: The Politics of Equality and the Rhetoric of Place, 1870–1875*. East Lansing: Michigan State University Press, 2002.

Wood, Anna Cogswell. *Drama Sketches for Parlor Acting or Recitation*. Florence, Italy: Succ. B. Seeber [Editori Librai], 1925. JOCL.

———. *The Great Opportunity and Other Essays*. Florence, Italy: Succ. B. Seeber, 1926. JOCL.

———. *Idyls and Impressions of Travel from the Note-Books of Two Friends.* New York: Neale Publishing, 1904. HT.

———. *The Psychology of Crime, Illustrated by Several Modern Poets.* Florence, Italy: TIP Giuntina, n.d. JOCL.

———. *The Story of a Friendship: A Memoir.* New York: Knickerbocker Press, 1901. NPL.

———. [Untitled albums, n.d.]. JOCL.

Wood, Anna Cogswell [as Algernon Ridgeway]. *Diana Fontaine: A Novel.* Philadelphia: J. B. Lippincott, 1891. JOCL.

———. *Westover's Ward.* London: Richard Bentley and Son, 1892. JOCL.

Woods, Carly S. *Debating Women: Gender, Education, and Spaces for Argument, 1835–1945.* East Lansing: Michigan State University Press, 2018.

Wylie, Laura Johnson. "An Address on Woman Suffrage: Before Mothers and Teachers' Association by Prof. Laura J. Wylie Tuesday Afternoon. At Cannon St. School." *Poughkeepsie Daily Eagle*, February 5, 1913.

———. Preface to *Poems and Plays,* by Gertrude Buck. New York: Duffield and Company, 1922.

———. *Social Studies in English Literature.* New York: Houghton Mifflin, 1916.

———. *Studies in the Evolution of English Criticism.* Boston: Ginn and Company, 1894.

Yakel, Elizabeth. "Searching and Seeking in the Deep Web: Primary Sources on the Internet." In *Working in the Archives: Practical Research Methods for Rhetoric and Composition,* edited by Alexis E. Ramsey, Wendy B. Sharer, Barbara E. L'Eplattenier, and Lisa S. Mastrangelo, 102–18. Carbondale: Southern Illinois University Press, 2012.

Yee, Shirley J. *Black Women Abolitionists: A Study in Activism, 1828–1860.* Knoxville: University of Tennessee Press, 1992.

Young, Nikki. "'Uses of the Erotic' for Teaching Queer Studies." *Women's Studies Quarterly* 40, no. 3/4 (2012): 303–7.

Zaeske, Susan. "The 'Promiscuous Audience' Controversy and the Emergence of the Early Woman's Rights Movement." *Quarterly Journal of Speech* 81, no. 2 (May 1995): 191–207.

———. "Signatures of Citizenship: The Rhetoric of Women's Antislavery Petitions." *Quarterly Journal of Speech* 88, no. 2 (2002): 147–68.

Zakaria, Rafia. *Against White Feminism: Notes on Disruption.* New York: W. W. Norton and Company, 2021.

Zboray, Ronald J., and Mary Saracino Zboray. "Is It a Diary, Commonplace Book, Scrapbook, or Whatchamacallit? Six Years of Exploration in New England's Manuscript Archives." *Libraries and the Cultural Record* 44, no. 1 (2009): 101–23, 154–55.

# INDEX

## A

ableism, 96, 119, 123, 124, 125

abolitionism, 27, 48, 176; activism, 2, 9; lecture circuit, 9, 45–46; modern iterations of, 57n65; women's romantic friendships connected with, 24n110. *See also* erotic of antislavery affection; Holley/Putnam romantic friendship

abolitionist rhetoric: erotic of antislavery affection and, 46, 86; Holley School curriculum and, 67–68, 69; Holley/Putnam romantic friendship and, 50–51, 60, 65, 74, 84

Adams, Elizabeth Kemper, 159–60

Adams-Campbell, Melissa, 33

African American women: as abolitionists, 65; author's research on, xix; imagined pasts of, xvii, 2, 41–42; papers of, 173; racist assumptions about sexuality of, 30, 61, 65; romantic friendships of, 31–32, 177 (*see also* Brown/Primus romantic friendship); Southern, religious practices of, 49–50, 56, 178; as suffragists, 155; as teachers, 22, 47n8, 67n112, 84–85; white women and, 13; women's colleges and, 156–57

African Americans: culture-epoch theory and, 165–66; educational opportunities for, 26, 46–47; literacy education of, 68, 68n118, 77n158; Lottsburgh (VA) community, 69, 74, 77, 77n160, 81, 85; Northern white teachers and, 77n158; rhetorical education of, 47, 68n119; Southern, religious practices of, 75–76; voting rights activism, 56

African diaspora, 27, 29

Afrofuturism, 40n10

*agape*, 144

Aguilar, Grace, 88

Ahmed, Sara, 18n78

Alcott family, 48, 73n145, 118

Alexander, Jonathan, 16–17, 179

Allen, Jafari S., 4n17

Allen, Julia M., 7, 144

American Anti-Slavery Society, 45, 55–56, 57, 69, 83

American Missionary Association, 47, 65

Angerona. *See* Valley Female Seminary (Winchester, VA)

*Answers of the Ages* (Leache and Willcox), 105, 110–11, 121

## 212 · INDEX

Anthony, Susan B., 81n184
"Anti-Suffrage Sentiments" (poem; Buck), 153n110
Antonius, 101–2
Arbery, Ahmaud, xviii
archival imaginaries, 40n10
archives: birth of concept of, 33; "conditions of possibility" for, 3, 32, 33–36, 173; couple form and, 180–82; erotic relationship to, 183; future, 172–75; of Leache/Wood romantic friendship, 95–96; limitations of, 183; narratives exceeding bounds of, 38–39, 41n16 (*see also* imagined pasts); repertoires vs., 34; settler-colonial, 176, 182–83; women's abusive relationships and, 81n184
Aristotle, 107, 113
Arnold, Ethel, 154
Arthur and Elizabeth Schlesinger Library on the History of Women in America, 40, 173
Asante, Godfried, 4
asexuality, 19–20, 19n81, 181, 182
Augustine, Saint, 107

## B

Bacon, Jacqueline, 64
Baltimore Association for the Moral and Educational Advancement of the Colored People, 39, 130
Banks, William P., 8
Baylor, Cherry Revona, 83
Beale, Winnie, 68n122
Beckley, R. D., 78
Bederman, Gail, 165
Beecher, Henry Ward, 88
Beeching, Barbara, 173
Bessette, Jean, 16–17
"Between Archival Absence" (VanHaitsma), 57n66
BIPOC activism, xviii
BIPOC archives, 32, 33
BIPOC women, 31–32, 43, 177
Bishop, Elizabeth, 81n184
Bizzell, Patricia, 8, 61
Black feminism, 35

Black lesbian feminist theory, 3, 3n6, 149–50
Black Lives Matter movement, xviii
Black women, 40, 40n10. *See also* African American women
Blackwell, Glasgow, 68, 68n122, 69–70
Blackwell, Harold, 85n211
Blackwell, Henry B., 180
Blackwell, Ruth, 85
Blackwell, Susie, 67n112, 85
Blair, Hugh, 114
Blake, Jacob, xviii
Blatch, Hariot Stanton, 153
boarding schools. *See* Leache-Wood Seminary (Norfolk, VA); women's boarding schools
Bodwéwadmi territory, 28, 29
Bordelon, Suzanne, 135, 140, 141, 142–43, 148, 152, 158, 161, 162, 165–66, 167–68
Bradford, William, 29
Bradway, Tyler, 36
*Brief English Grammar, A* (Buck and Scott), 146
British imperialism, 165, 166
Brown, Addie: biographical sketch, xiii, 39; correspondence of, 172; death of, 172; as domestic laborer, xvii, 24, 39, 128, 173; education of, xvi; imagined past of, 173; imagined past of, xvii, 2, 41, 87–91, 128–32; marriage of, 31, 39, 128, 172; self-education of, 88. *See also* Brown/Primus romantic friendship
Brown, Emma V., 47n8
Brown, Hallie Quinn, 47n8
Brown, John, 69
Browning, Robert, 115
Brown/Primus correspondence, 87; archives of, 32–33, 39–40, 43, 182, 183; author's research on, xv–xvi, 36; end of, 31, 128, 132, 172; erotic/sexual nature of, 39, 128, 129–32, 131n23; imagined archive of, 172–75
Brown/Primus romantic friendship: author's research on, xv–xvii; as cross-class relationship, 24, 31; documentation of, 32–33, 174; end of, 31; erotic as rhetorical power and, 9, 38, 42, 132; imagined past of, 38–39, 41, 42, 43–44, 87–91, 128–32, 174–75

Bryn Mawr College (Bryn Mawr, PA), 25n117, 139
Bryn Mawr School for Women Workers, 170
Buchanan, Lindal, 51, 58, 60, 74, 180
Buck, Gertrude: biographical sketch, xiv; correspondence of, 136, 160; death of, 26, 134, 138, 165, 170; dissertation of, 138; education of, 28–29, 133, 138, 138n23; educational theory of, 165–68; erotic as rhetorical power and, 43, 169; feminist rhetorical scholarship on, 146–47; memorialization of, 170–71; papers of, 136; privilege and, 28–29; progressive politics of, 142–43; published writings of, 145–46, 162, 169; religious views of, 164; rhetorical practices of, 133–34, 145–51, 155, 169–70; rhetorical theory of, 137, 143, 146–50, 155, 161–62, 163, 167–68; as women's college teacher, 26. *See also* Buck/Wylie romantic friendship
Buck Fund, 170–71
Buck/Wylie romantic friendship: archival studies of, 2, 38, 135–36; beginnings of, 29, 133, 138, 172; as Boston marriage, 134, 136, 139–40, 147, 150, 151, 163, 170; correspondence in, 136, 137–38, 156; educational setting for, 9, 26; erotic as rhetorical power in, 9, 10, 134–35, 136–37, 142–44, 155, 168–71, 177 (*see also* erotic of sapphic egalitarianism); Eurocentrism reproduced through, 164–69; feminist rhetorical scholarship on, 140–42; memorialization in, 170–71; normativity and, 179–80; pedagogical efforts in, 137, 144, 155–63; power dynamics of, 30–31, 138–39, 145, 153–54, 155, 158–59; "power-evasive intimacy" of, 134, 136–37, 150, 154–55, 168; privilege and, 29, 177–78; research on, 16; rhetorical practices in, 133–34, 137, 145–55, 169–70, 178; settler colonialism/slavery and, 137, 163
Burleigh, Cyrus, 24n110
Burleigh, Margaret Jones, 24n110, 45
Burly (dog), 140, 160–61
Butchart, Ronald E., 47n8, 77n158
Butler, Eleanor, 102

C

Campbell, JoAnn, 136, 138–39, 140–41, 142, 147, 148, 158–59, 161–62, 164
Canandaigua (NY), 27

Cap Makers Union, 153
capitalism, 10, 12, 32, 41, 173
Carpenter, Edward, 6–7, 8, 143–44, 164
Carrillo Rowe, Aimee, 6, 8, 12, 72, 150, 163, 164, 168, 181
Caswell, Michelle, 40n10
Censer, Jane Turner, 93, 100
Chadwick, John White, 45, 46, 50, 84
Chambers-Schiller, Lee Virginia, 53, 79–80
Chávez, Karma R., 16–17
Chesapeake territory, 95
Child, Lydia Maria, 69n123
Christianity, 61–62, 75–76, 165
Chrysler Museum of Art (Norfolk, VA), 95, 106, 109
Cicero, 107, 113, 115
cisgender women, 21, 177–78
cisheterosexism, 18, 32, 96
Civil Rights Movement, 11n50
Civil War (1861–1865), 91, 94–95, 106, 122, 122n155
classism: of eugenics discourse, 135, 157; at Vassar, 156–57, 169; white femininity and, 19–20, 30, 61, 142; women's romantic friendships and reproduction of, 75, 76n155, 125, 169, 177
Clifford, Geraldine J., 21–23, 54
colonialism, 33n155, 67, 165, 166–68. *See also* settler colonialism
commonplace books, 52n34, 92, 95, 96, 104–5, 107–10
commonplace rhetorics, 96
Community Theatre of Poughkeepsie, 170–71
Concord Massachusetts School of Philosophy, 118
Confederate ideology, 94–95, 106, 122, 168
Connecticut Historical Society, 39, 87n2, 172, 173
Conner, Eliza, 67n112, 85
Cooper Union, 153
*Course in Argumentative Writing, A* (Buck and Morris), 145, 162
*Course in Expository Writing, A* (Buck and Morris), 145
*Course in Narrative Writing, A* (Buck and Morris), 145, 150

Cram, E, 16–17, 27, 157
critical fabulation, 35, 40–41, 40n10, 174, 183
critical imagination, 35, 40, 40n10, 174, 183
"crushes," 51
Cruz, Ariane, 5n19
Cullors, Patrice, xviii
culture-epoch theory, 165–67, 169, 178, 180

## D

Davenport, Charles, 123
Day, Alexander, 69
De Veaux, Alexis, 3
DeLarveric, Stormé, xviii
D'Emilio, John, 182
desexualization, 19–20
Deveaux, Jane, 47n8
Dewey, John, 138n23, 159–60
*Diana Fontaine* (Wood), 105
Dickinson, Anna E., 64, 154
difference: Buck's rhetorical theory and, 148–50, 168; as diversity, 11n50; erotic as rhetorical power and, 10–13, 125, 168–69, 177; hierarchies of, 1, 12, 13, 148, 149, 156; logics of, 137; privilege and, 11, 12; white femininity and, 99; white supremacist ideology and, 125; in women's romantic friendships, 30–31, 119
Diggs, Marylynne, 18, 18nn75–76, 29, 54–55, 100, 141
Dolmage, Jay Timothy, 123, 123n161
domestic responsibilities, xvi, xvii–xviii, 21, 21n93, 58, 59–60, 106, 145, 159, 181
domestic skills, 93–94
Donawerth, Jane, 63
Douglass, Frederick, 48, 66, 69, 77, 77n160, 78, 88, 90
*Drama Sketches for Parlor Acting or Recitation* (Wood), 102, 105
Driskill, Qwo-Li, 5, 16–17, 18
Du Bois, W. E. B., 167
Dunn, Thomas R., 16–17

## E

Eastman, Max, 154–55
education, 38, 165–69

*Educational Review*, 147
egalitarianism, 137, 142, 180. *See also* erotic of sapphic egalitarianism
elitism, 125
Emerson, Ralph Waldo, 115, 118
employment discrimination, 32
Engle, Elizabeth C., 103, 113, 117–18, 126
Enoch, Jessica, 22, 47, 66
epistolary networks, 72, 74, 182
epistolary practices, queer, xv–xvi
Equality League for Self-Supporting Women, 153
Erie territory, 28, 45n1
*eros*, 102, 143, 144
erotic, the: classroom and public articulation of, 8; defined, 1; etymology of, 8; sex vs., 4–5, 4nn16–17; in women's romantic friendships, 3
erotic as rhetorical power: alliance/coalition-building and, 4n9; author's archival research on, 32, 176–77, 182–83; author's conception of, 13–14, 176–83; cisgender women and, 177–78; "conditions of possibility" for, 3, 27–32, 49–50, 177–78 (*see also* classism; racism; settler colonialism; slavery); couple form and, 180–82; defined, 44, 176; difference and, 10–13, 125, 168–69, 177; erotohistoriography and, 32–37; in homosocial educational settings, 7–8; imagined pasts and, 42; influences on, 2–3; during long nineteenth century, 2–3; Lorde's theory of, 177; normativity and, 179–80; political variability of, 13, 168–69, 177–78; potentials for, 178, 182, 183; privilege and, 43–44; queer rhetorics and, 179, 180; significance of, 3; theorization of, xv, 1; white women teachers and, 9–10, 21–26, 87–88; women's romantic friendships and, 14–20, 38, 125, 176–77. *See also* erotic of antislavery affection; erotic of "beauty" emulation; erotic of sapphic egalitarianism
erotic of antislavery affection: Holley/Putnam romantic friendship and, 9, 28, 79–83, 177, 178; pedagogical efforts in, 65–74; as power source, 46, 49, 58–60, 65, 70, 83–84, 86; racism reproduced through, 75–79, 76n155; rhetorical practices in, 57–65, 178; settler colonialism/slavery and, 28, 49

erotic of "beauty" emulation: influences on, 103–5; Leache/Wood romantic friendship and, 9, 28, 93, 95–97, 105–6, 177, 178; models and, 103; pedagogical practices and, 112–19; as power source, 105, 125–27; rhetorical practices and, 105–12, 178; settler colonialism/slavery and, 28; white superiority and, 93, 119–25

erotic of sapphic egalitarianism: activist rhetoric and, 145–55; Buck/Wylie romantic friendship and, 9, 28–29, 134–35, 136–37, 142–44, 147, 155, 169–71, 177, 178; defining qualities of, 155; Eurocentrism and, 137, 164–69; as power source, 30–31, 169–71; rhetorical education and, 155–63, 178; settler colonialism/racism and, 28–29, 156–57, 164–69

erotohistoriography: Brown/Primus imagined past and, 174–75; couple form and, 181; erotic as rhetorical power and, 42; of feminist/LGBTQ+ rhetorics, 178, 183; Freeman's conception of, 35–36, 183; imagined pasts and, 43–44; queer feminist, 125; in settler-colonial archives, 32–37, 176

eugenics: classism and, 135, 157; defined, 123; erotic as rhetorical power and, 178; Leache/Wood romantic friendship and, 30, 96–97, 123–25, 127, 168; movement promoting, 123–24, 123n161; white femininity and, 120; white superiority and, 30, 96–97, 120, 135, 157; women's education and, 157

Eurocentrism, 30, 137, 164–69, 178, 180

## F

Faderman, Lillian, 16, 21, 46, 54, 59, 135, 139–40

Falzetti, Ashley Glassburn, 33

Farmington (CT), 128

fascism, 122

feminism, 122, 149

feminist historiography, 3, 19, 33n154, 125, 135, 178, 183

feminist rhetorical studies, 16, 135, 136, 140–42, 146–47, 153, 180

feminist scholarship, xix, 162

Ferguson, Roderick A., 5

*Figures of Rhetoric* (Buck), 146

Floyd, George, xviii

Foster, Abigail Kelley, 45, 48, 50–51, 57n66, 79

Franzen, Trisha, 21, 23, 26

*Frederick Douglass' Paper*, 59

freedmen's aid movement, 56

Freedmen's Bureau, 47, 65, 68, 72, 77

freedmen's schools: historical accounts of, 47n8; rhetorical education at, 46–47, 66–67, 176; as segregated public schools, 80; women teachers at, 23–24, 24n110, 48n12; women's romantic friendships at, 26. *See also* Holley School (Lottsburgh, VA); Primus Institute (Royal Oak, MD)

Freeman, Elizabeth, 35–36, 183

friendship networks, 181

## G

Garnet, Henry Highland, 88, 90

Garrisonian Anti-Slavery platform, 45, 51

Garza, Alicia, xviii

*Gay American History* (Katz), 100

gender: division of labor and, 50, 57, 63, 66, 72, 83–84; domestic responsibilities and, xvi, 21; intersections of, 21; LGBTQ+ rhetorical studies and, 16–17; "power-evasive intimacy" and, 12; teaching and, 21–22; white femininity and, 19–20, 60, 63; women orators and, 65; women teachers and, 93–94; women's education and, 157

gender identity, 131n23

genocide, 32

genre-queer rhetorical strategies, 108–9

gentrification, 32

Gill, Lyndon K., 11

Gilliland, Anne J., 40n10

Gilman, Charlotte Perkins, 153, 154, 155, 157

Gold, David, 94

*Great Opportunity and Other Essays, The* (Wood), 105, 122–23, 124

Greece, ancient, 8, 51, 101–2, 107

Greek mythology, 102, 107

Grew, Mary, 24n110, 45

Greyser, Naomi, 27

Griffin, Farah Jasmine, 172

Griffin-Gracy, Miss Major, xviii

Grimké, Charlotte Forten, 47n8

Gumbs, Alexis Pauline, 173
Gwinn, Mamie, 25n117, 139

# H

Hackett, Robin, 143
*Handbook of Argumentation and Debating, A* (Buck and Mann), 145–46, 162, 167
Handley Regional Library (Winchester, VA), 95
Hanly, J. P., 180
Harper, Frances Ellen Watkins, 88
Harris, Blanche V., 47n8
Harris, Randy Allen, 146
Harrison, Kimberly, 94, 106
Hart, Fanny, 133, 139, 159
Hartford (CT), 39, 87, 88, 91
Hartford Freedmen's Aid Society, 39, 91, 130
Hartman, Saidiya, 35, 40–41, 40n10, 42–43, 174, 183
Harvard College, 28, 29
Haudenosaunee territory, 27
Hawkins, Ames, 17
Hemmings, Anita Florence, 156
Herbig, Katherine Lydigsen, 46, 50, 51, 52, 54, 57, 62–63, 64, 80
Herzberg, Bruce, 8
heteronormativity, 41
heterosexism, 12, 18, 18n78, 29–30, 61, 78
heterosexuality, compulsory, 18, 19n81
Hickok, Lorena, 182
Higginson, Thomas Wentworth, 69n123
Highgate, Edmonia, 47n8
historiography, politics of, 68n122
history, 34–35
Hobbs, Catherine, 94
Hobsbawm, Eric J., 2n5
Hofheimer, Jo Ann Mervis, 100–101, 100n47, 109, 120, 121, 126–27
Holland, Sharon Patricia, 6, 10, 11, 36
Holley, I. B., Jr., 59, 59n74
Holley, Myron, 27, 50, 59n74
Holley, Sarah ("Sallie"): as antislavery lecturer, 45–46, 51–52, 53, 55n55, 57–61, 57n66, 83–84; biographical sketch, xiii; correspondence of, 57n66, 72–73, 73n145, 76n155, 77n160; death of, 24, 46, 74, 81, 84; education of, 27, 45, 63; epistolary networks of, 72, 74; erotic as rhetorical power and, 43; as freedmen's teacher, 24, 46–47, 48n12, 54, 56, 69n123; "promiscuous audiences" of, 27, 56, 57–58, 83–84; racist/classist views of, 76n155; scrapbooks of, 48, 52n34; settler colonialism and, 27–28. *See also* Holley/Putnam correspondence; Holley/Putnam romantic friendship
Holley Graded School (Lottsburgh, VA), 85–86
*Holley Graded School Historic Site* (website), 86
Holley School (Lottsburgh, VA): Douglass visit to, 77, 77n160; faculty of, 67n112; founding of, 48, 48n12, 54, 70, 86; fundraising for, 72–74, 73n145, 78; histories of, 68n122; Holley/Putnam as teachers at, 9, 24, 54, 84, 130; memorialization of, 85–86, 85n211; political discussions discouraged at, 77–78, 77n160; press coverage of, 81–82, 81n185; as private school, 47, 65, 73, 80; renaming of, 46; rhetorical education at, 66–69, 72, 84; as segregated public school, 85; as settler-colonial institution, 65, 78–79, 84; students at, 71
*Holley School Histories* (website), 86
Holley/Putnam correspondence: archives of, 47–48; author's research using, 50; on Holley School, 65–66, 67; Holley/Putnam romantic friendship and, 52–55, 58, 69–72, 79–80
Holley/Putnam romantic friendship: as abusive, 79–83, 80n176; anti-Black racism of, 49 50, 75–79; archival studies of, 2, 38, 47–48, 58; beginnings of, 7, 24, 28, 45, 49, 50–51, 73, 130; erotic as rhetorical power in, 9, 46–47, 48–50, 54–55, 83–84, 87–88, 168–69, 177 (*see also* erotic of antislavery affection); as nonsexual, 51, 60–61; normativity and, 179–80; pedagogical efforts in, 65–74, 69n123; power dynamics of, 30–31, 45–46, 48–49, 51–52, 56–57, 58, 62–64, 66, 72, 74–75, 79, 83–84; privilege and, 24, 177–78; racism reproduced through, 75–79, 76n155; research on, 15–16; rhetorical practices in, 57–65, 57n66, 83–84, 178; as virtual marriage, 46, 53
Holmes, Oliver Wendell, 69n123

Homer, 115
homoerotic pedagogies, 51
homoeroticism, 8
homogenic idealism, 144, 148
homogenic love, 6–7, 143–44, 163, 164, 169
*Homogenic Love, and Its Place in a Free Society* (Carpenter), 143
homosocial educational settings, 24–26, 94, 97–100
hooks, bell, 4, 8
Horowitz, Helen Lefkowitz, 139
housing crises, 32
Howland, Emily, 48, 48n12, 53, 70, 79, 81
Hoy, Helen, 153
Hsu, V. Jo, 17, 154
Hutchins, Grace, 144

## I

identity categories, 15
*Idyls and Impressions of Travel* (Wood), 97, 115
imagined pasts: critical imagination/fabulation and, 35, 40–42, 40n10, 41n16; erotohistoriography and, 35–36, 174–75; goal of, 42; privilege and, 38, 43–44; risks of, 36–37, 41n16, 42–43, 174–75. *See also* Brown/Primus romantic friendship: imagined past of
imagined records, 40n10
Immigration Act (1917), 123
Indigenous peoples: culture-epoch theory and, 166–67; erasure of, 33–34; settler colonialism and occupied lands of, 27–29, 33–34, 45n1, 65, 87, 95, 128
Indigenous women, 13, 30, 61
*Inlander* magazine, 142
*Intermediate Sex, The* (Carpenter), 143
intersexuality, 102–3, 102n60
intimacy, shared, 4, 6
invention, 96, 107–8, 110
Irene Leache Memorial, 113, 122, 126

## J

Jackson, Ellen Garrison, 47n8
Jacobs, Louisa, 47n8
Johnson, E. Patrick, 17

Johnson, Marsha P., xviii
Johnson, Nan, 113, 114

## K

Kalamazoo (MI), 28
Kaskaskia territory, 28, 45n1
Katz, Jonathan Ned, 100
Kelley, Abigail, 62. *See also* Foster, Abigail Kelley
Kelley, Florence, 155
Kendall, Elaine, 141–42
Kim, Eunjung, 19
King, Susie, 47n8

## L

Ladies of Llangollen, 18n75, 102
Lady of Cofitachequi, 18
Leache, Irene Kirke: as author, 92–93, 97, 105–6, 110–11, 121; biographical sketch, xiii; as boarding school cofounder, 25; conservative politics of, 94–95, 106, 122, 122n155; correspondence of, 97, 97n20; death of, 92, 95, 97, 105, 106, 113, 126; education of, 28, 92, 118; erotic as rhetorical power and, 43; memorialization of, 113, 115–16, 122, 126–27; papers of, 95; privilege and, 28; retirement of, 105, 116; rhetorical practices of, 96, 105, 106–12, 121; settler colonialism and, 28; slavery and, 28. *See also* Leache/Wood romantic friendship
Leache Memorial Collection, 95, 126
Leache-Wood Alumnae Association, 113, 126
Leache/Wood romantic friendship, 99; alternative interpretations of, 100–103; archival studies of, 2, 38, 95–96, 101, 106–7; beginnings of, 28, 92, 96, 97–100, 103, 128; erotic as rhetorical power in, 9, 93, 95–97, 105–6, 125–27, 168–69, 177 (*see also* erotic of "beauty" emulation); legacy of, 119; as marriage alternative, 93, 118; memorialization in, 113, 115–16, 122, 126–27, 138; normativity and, 179–80; pedagogical efforts in, 103, 112–19, 126–27; power dynamics of, 30–31, 94, 103, 105; privilege and, 28, 93, 105, 124–25, 177–78; research on, 16; rhetorical practices in, 103, 104–12, 125–26, 178; settler colonialism/slavery reproduced through,

96–97, 119–25, 137, 168; travels, 92, 105, 108, 109, 120–21

Leache-Wood Seminary (Norfolk, VA), 25; catalog of, 116; conservative politics at, 94–95; faculty of, 105, 109; founding of, 92, 117–18; Leache/Wood as teachers/administrators at, 9, 92, 116–19, 126; privilege and, 119; records from, 95, 112–13; rhetorical education at, 9, 92, 93, 112–19, 126; significance of, 119

LeMaster, Lore/tta, 9

L'Eplattenier, Barbara, 134, 139, 141, 156, 160, 162

lesbian feminist theory, 19n81

lesbian landscape tradition, 99

lesbianism: pathologization of, 17; spinster figure and, 23; women's romantic friendships and, 100–101, 140–41

LGBTQ+ archives, 32, 33

LGBTQ+ communities, xviii, 182

LGBTQ+ historiography: archival shortcomings and, 33n154, 34, 44; development of, 180; erotic as rhetorical power and, 3, 14, 180; future, 183; identity categories, 15; romantic friendships and, 15, 16–17, 19, 178

LGBTQ+ identities, 19

LGBTQ+ rhetorical studies, 16–17, 180

LGBTQ+ rhetorics, 14, 179, 180

*Liberator, The*, 59, 62, 63, 64

*Life for Liberty, A* (Chadwick), 45, 84

Lincoln, Abraham, 17n71, 69n123

Lister, Anne, 18n75

literacy bans, 32

literacy education, 47, 68, 68n118

literary criticism, 151

literature, 148, 161–62, 163

Logan, Shirley Wilson, 47

Lorde, Audre, 55; Black lesbian feminist theory of, 3, 3n6, 6; on difference, 10–11, 11n50, 31, 75, 99, 149–50, 169, 177; erotic theory of, 3, 3n6, 4–5, 4n9, 7, 9, 12, 13, 44, 57, 177, 179, 181; on marriage, 124; on pornography, 5n19; on white femininity, 107

Lottsburgh (VA), 48n12, 65, 66, 70, 78, 85. *See also* Holley School (Lottsburgh, VA)

Lumbee territory, 95

## M

*M Archive* (Gumbs), 173

MacCracken, Henry Noble, 134, 154, 157, 158

Macedo Soares, Lota de, 81n184

Machado, Carmen Maria, 81n184

Manahoac territory, 28

Manion, Jen, 20n91

Mann, Kristine, 145–46, 167

Mantegazza, Paolo, 166

Marks, Jeannette, 25n117, 139

marriage: Boston, 134, 139–40, 150, 151, 163, 170; metaphors of, 99–100; opposite-sex, 180–81; same-sex, 131n123; trans, 131n123; women's education and, 135, 157; women's romantic friendships as alternative to, 45, 46

marriage bar laws, 22–23, 26

Mary Grew's School for Young Women (Philadelphia, PA), 24n110

Maryland, 87n3, 91

Massachusetts, 27

Massawomeck territory, 28

Mastrangelo, Lisa S., 136

May, Samuel, 48, 69n123, 81–83

May, Samuel, Jr., 64

McClintock, Anne, 120, 124, 166

McCormick, Virginia Taylor, 97n20

McDaneld, Jen, 154

McKim, James Miller, 64

McKinney, Cait, 7

Mehlenbacher, Ashley Rose, 146

memoirs, 181

memorial publications, 181

Men's League for Woman Suffrage, 154–55

men's romantic friendships, 8, 17n71

*Metaphor, The* (Buck), 146, 167

Michigan Anti-Slavery Society, 48

migrations, forced, 32

Milton (PA), 29

miscegenation, 12, 124

Miss Porter's School (Farmington, CT), 128

models, 103, 114–15

Mohican territory, 29

Morgan, Joan, 4–5, 5n18
Morgan, Ruth, 155
Morris, Charles E., III, 17, 17n71
Morris, Elisabeth Woodbridge, 145, 150
Mott, Lucretia, 154
Mount Holyoke College (South Hadley, MA), 25n117, 139
Mousekian, Donabet, 123
Munsee Lenape territory, 29
Murray, Ellen, 24n110
Musser, Amber Jamilla, 10, 36
Mussolini, Benito, 122

## N

*Narrative of the Life of Frederick Douglass* (Douglass), 88
Nash, Ephraim, 69
*National Anti-Slavery Standard,* 56, 68n122, 69
National Coalition of Black Lesbians and Gays, 11n50
National League of Women Voters, 155
National Register of Historic Places (NRHP), 85, 86
*New National Era,* 77
*New National Era and Citizen,* 78
New Woman, 122
*New York Times,* 151–52
nineteenth century, long: erotic as rhetorical power during, 2–3; Indigenous women as teachers during, 22n99; same-sex/trans marriage during, 131n23; sexuality during, 15n63; use of term, 2n5; white femininity as viewed during, 12, 63; women's diaries during, 18, 18n75; women's romantic friendships during, 14, 22n99
Norfolk (VA), 95
Norfolk Museum of Arts and Sciences, 126
Norfolk Public Library (Norfolk, VA), 95
normativity, 179–80

## O

Oberlin College (Oberlin, OH): as first coeducational college, 7; founding of, 45n1; Holley as student at, 52n34, 63; Holley/Putnam meet at, 7, 24, 49, 50–51, 73; Putnam as student at, 27–28, 63; as settler-colonial institution, 27, 27n1, 45n1
O'Connor, Lillian, 58
Odawa territory, 29
Ojibwe territory, 29
Olson, Lester C., 8, 17
*Organic Education* (Buck and Scott), 146, 165–66

## P

*Packer Alumna,* 170
Park, Maud Wood, 155
Parker, Garfield, 85, 85n211
Partner, Nancy, 34–35
patriarchy, 10, 12, 16, 55, 57, 60–61
Peake, Mary S., 47n8
Penn School (St. Helena Island, SC), 24n110
Peoria territory, 28
Phaedrus, 8, 98, 103–4
*Phaedrus* (Plato), 98, 103–4
Philadelphia Female Anti-Slavery Society, 24n110
Phillips, Wendell, 48, 69, 77n160
phrenology, 121–22
Pillsbury, Parker, 45
*Pioneer Women Orators* (O'Connor), 58
Plato, 8, 98, 103–4, 107, 113, 148, 148n77
*Poems and Plays* (Buck), 146, 150–51
poetics, 114
poetry, 3n6
police brutality, xviii
polyamory, 181
Ponsonby, Sarah, 102
Poquonock territory, 39
pornography, 5, 5n19
positionality, xix
potentiality, 13
Potter, Claire, 182
Poughkeepsie (NY), 29, 154
*Poughkeepsie Courier,* 170
Poughkeepsie Equal Suffrage League, 152, 154

Poughkeepsie Woman Suffrage Party, 154
poverty, 32
"power-evasive" communication, 12, 150, 154–55, 162–63, 165, 168
"Present Status of Rhetorical Theory, The" (Buck), 146, 147–48, 149
Pride, xviii
Primus, Holdridge, 88–89
Primus, Mehitable Esther (Jacobs), 88–89
Primus, Rebecca: biographical sketch, xiii, 39; correspondence of, 172; death of, 39, 172; family papers of, 39–40, 87n2; as freedmen's teacher, xvi, 23–24, 31, 39, 47n8, 87, 128–29; imagined past of, xvii, 2, 41; marriage of, 39, 172; papers of, 173; relocation to Maryland, 87n3, 91; self-education of, 88. *See also* Brown/Primus romantic friendship
Primus family papers, 173
Primus Institute (Royal Oak, MD): Brown's imagined past at, 128–29, 130, 132; founding of, 39, 91; Primus as teacher at, 24, 91, 172
Pritchard, Eric Darnell, 5, 9, 11n50, 17
*Pro Archia Poeta* (Cicero), 115
Progressive Era, 2, 122, 142–43, 148, 163, 169
protofeminism, 142
Przybylo, Ela, 4, 19, 181, 182
pseudonyms, 105
*Psychology of Crime, The* (Wood), 101–2, 105, 111–12
public/private distinction, xix, 49, 145
Pugh, Sarah, 45
Putnam, Caroline F.: antislavery activism of, 51–52, 56–57, 83–84; biographical sketch, xiii; correspondence of, 81–83, 81n185; death of, 24, 46, 74, 85; education of, 27–28, 45, 63; erotic as rhetorical power and, 43; as freedmen's teacher, 24, 46–47, 48n12, 53–54, 69n123; papers of, 48; as postmistress, 73n142; retirement of, 84; rhetorical practices of, 56, 58, 71–72. *See also* Holley/Putnam correspondence; Holley/Putnam romantic friendship

## Q

Quaker discourse, 108
queer, 17

queer feminist erotohistoriography, 125
queer relationships, xvi–xvii
queer rhetorics, 108–9, 179, 180

## R

race: "alien," study of, 120–21; intersections of, 21; white femininity and, 19–20, 60
racial justice: Brown/Primus romantic friendship and, 90, 132; freedmen's curriculum and, 76; Holley/Putnam romantic friendship and, 9, 46–47, 50, 53, 55–56, 83–84, 86, 179; Leache/Wood romantic friendship and, 94–95; rhetorical education for, 24, 49, 65–71, 74–75, 84; undermining of, 30, 94–95. *See also* erotic of antislavery affection
racial uplift, 75, 88, 128, 132, 179
racism: archives and, 173; of culture-epoch theory, 165–67; difference and, 12, 75; Holley/Putnam and, 49–50; Holley/Putnam romantic friendship and reproduction of, 83; imagined pasts beyond limitations of, 41; Leache/Wood romantic friendship and reproduction of, 106, 119–25, 168; power dynamics of, 50; reinforcement of, 13–14, 75–79, 178; sexuality and, 64–65; at women's colleges, 156–57; women's romantic friendships and, 32; in women's suffrage movement, 154, 155
Rand, Erin J., 17
Rawson, K. J., 17
reform movements, 119, 122
regionalism, 75
repertoires, 34
rhetoric: activist, 145–55; belletristic, 9, 25, 92, 93; commonplace, 93, 96, 105–12, 115–16; conversational, 45–46, 56, 62–63; feminist histories of, 94; seductive, 71–72, 98; social, 143, 147–50, 161–62, 163; Western, whiteness of, 161
rhetorical education: African American, 24; belletristic, 25, 94, 96, 112–19, 126; at freedmen's schools, 46–47, 66–67, 176; for racial justice, 24, 49, 65–71, 74–75, 84; women teachers and, 25, 26, 94; at women's boarding schools, 176; at women's colleges, 176; women's romantic friendships and, 176. *See also under specific schools*
rhetorical studies, 135

rhetorical theory, 3
Rhodes, Jacqueline, 17, 179
Richards, I. A., 146–47
Rivard, Courtney, 33
Rivera, Sylvia, xviii
Robertson, Stacey M., 75
Rochester, Anna, 144
Rochester Ladies' Anti-Slavery Society, 48
romantic letter genre, 52–53
Roosevelt, Eleanor, 155, 171, 182
Roosevelt, Theodore, 157
Rose, Ernestine L., 154
Royal Oak (MD), 39
Royster, Jacqueline Jones, 22, 35, 40, 40n10, 41, 41n16, 47, 68, 68n119, 183

## S

sameness, 99
same-sex relationships, xvi–xvii, 81n184, 131n23, 180–81. *See also* women's romantic friendships
sapphic idealism, 144, 148–49, 155, 163, 169. *See also* erotic of sapphic egalitarianism
Sappho, 98, 101, 107, 108, 109, 113
Sargent Memorial Collection, 95
"savage" stereotype, 76, 83, 165, 167
Schaghticoke territory, 29
Schneiderman, Rose, 153, 154
school records, 33
school segregation, 55n55
Scott, Fred Newton, 133, 136, 146, 148, 150, 160
Scott, Harriet M., 146, 165–66
scrapbooks, 33, 48, 52n34
Sears, James Thomas, 100
seductive rhetoric, 98
Sekakawon territory, 65
self-education, 88
Seneca territory, 27
settler colonialism: archives and, 32, 33–36, 173; difference and, 12; erotic as rhetorical power and, 27, 177; gardens as "grounds" of, 99; Holley/Putnam romantic friendship and reproduction of, 83; imagined pasts beyond limitations of, 41; Indigenous territories occupied through, 27–29, 33–34, 45n1; Leache/Wood romantic friendship and reproduction of, 96–97, 119–25, 137; Leache/Wood support of, 95; logic of, 27; power dynamics of, 30, 50; reinforcement of, 13–14, 164–69, 178; "savage" stereotype and, 76; spinster figure and, 23; westward expansion as goal of, 45n1; white saviorism and, 67, 84–85; whiteness and, 107, 119; women abolitionist lecturers and, 61–62; women teachers and, 26, 49–50; women's romantic friendships and, 1–2, 30–31, 32

Seven Sisters, 25–26, 156
sex: ephemeral nature of, 20n91; the erotic vs., 4–5, 4nn16–17; eugenics movement and, 123–24
sex equality, 122
sexism, 29, 59, 146
sexology, 17, 54, 60, 100n47, 102, 124, 179
sexuality: histories of, 33n155; intersections of, 21; LGBTQ+ studies and, 16–17; nineteenth-century, 15n63; normativity discourse and, 179–80; racist assumptions about, 29–30, 64–65; women's romantic friendships and, 15–20, 18n78, 45, 60, 141–42
Shaw, Robert Gould, 69n123
Shawandasse Tula territory, 28
Shelden, Mary Lamb, 50, 68n122, 85n211, 86
Sicaog (Saukiog) territory, 39
Singh, Julietta, 36, 183
singlehood, 181
slavery: archives and, 32; Buck/Wylie romantic friendship and reproduction of, 164–69; erotic as rhetorical power and, 27, 177; Holley/Putnam romantic friendship and reproduction of, 83; imagined pasts beyond limitations of, 41; Leache/Wood romantic friendship and reproduction of, 96–97, 137; logic of, 27; power dynamics of, 30; reinforcement of, 178; women teachers and, 26, 49–50; women's romantic friendships and, 1–2
"smashes," 51
Smilges, J. Logan, 17
Smith, Cora, 67n112, 84–85
Smith, Gerrit, 69n123
Smith, Hilda, 155

Smith-Rosenberg, Carol, 15–16, 140–41
*Social Criticism of Literature, The* (Buck), 146, 148, 151
social Darwinism, 165, 166
*Social Studies in English Literature* (Wylie), 151
socialism, 144
Socrates, 8, 103–4, 107, 113
Sophism, 148
South, the: African American religious practices in, 49–50, 56, 75–76, 178; Northern white teachers in, 75; stereotypes about, 94
speeches, 33
Speicher, Anna M., 62, 75–76
spinster figure, 23
Stanley, Sara G., 47n8
Stanton, Elizabeth Cady, 154
sterilizations, forced, 123
Stevens, Thaddeus, 69n123
Stevenson, Edward, 102, 102n60
Stewart, Maria W., 58
Stone, Lucy, 180
*Story of a Friendship, The* (Wood), 92, 97–98, 102, 104, 106, 110, 115, 120
"Story of Two Remarkable Women and Their Living Memorial, The" (Tunstall), 113
Stowe, Harriet Beecher, 88
*Studies in the Evolution of English Criticism* (Wylie), 151
suffrage movement, 9–10. See also women's suffrage movement
Sumerian mythology, 102
Sumner, Charles, 69
Susquehannock territory, 29

## T

Taylor, Breonna, xviii
Taylor, Diana, 34
Taylor, James Monroe, 152, 153, 154
Terry, Jennifer, 123–24
Thomas, Charles, 39, 40, 172
Thomas, M. Carey, 25n117, 139
Tines, Joseph, 39, 128, 172

Tinsley, Omise'eke Natasha, 5
Tometi, Ayọ, xviii
Towne, Laura, 24n110
trans marriage, 131n23
transphobia, 12
Tree of Man, 166
Truth, Sojourner, 45
Tunstall, Virginia Lyne, 113, 118
Tunxis territory, 39, 128

## U

*Uncle Tom's Cabin* (Stowe), 88
University of Chicago, 138n23, 159–60
University of Michigan: author's research at, 136; Buck as student at, 26, 29, 133, 142; faculty of, 146; graduate program at, 160; Putnam papers at, 48; as settler-colonial institution, 29, 133, 133n2
University of Virginia, 95
Uraniad, 6, 6n31, 102, 102n60
"Uses of the Erotic" (Lorde), 3, 10–11

## V

Valley Female Seminary (Winchester, VA), 28, 92, 97–100, 103, 105, 128
"Valley Seed Grows in Tidewater, A" (Engle), 113
VanHaitsma, Pamela, 57n66
Vassar College (Poughkeepsie, NY): archives of, 136; author's research at, 136; Buck/Wylie as teachers/administrators at, 9, 25–26, 29, 133–34, 138–39, 142, 155; faculty of, 134, 157; privilege and, 137, 165; racism at, 156–57; rhetorical education at, 9, 142, 145–46, 155–63, 164; salaries at, 158–59; as settler-colonial institution, 29, 149, 150, 156–57, 163, 168; suffrage activism discouraged at, 152–53, 157, 170
*Vassar Miscellany Monthly*, 165
Vicinus, Martha, 5
Virgil, 115
Virginia, 28
Virginia Department of Historic Resources, 85
voting rights, 9, 56, 70, 176. *See also* women's suffrage movement

## W

Wanguk territory, 39

Wappinger territory, 128

Warren, Katherine, 150

Washington, Booker T., 167

Waxhaw women, 18–19

Weld, Theodore Dwight, 48, 73

Weld-Grimké Papers, 48

Western culture: beauty as conceived in, 104, 106, 110, 119; Leache/Wood romantic friendship and, 104, 107; literary models in, 114–15; rhetoric in, 161; romantic love as conceived in, 181; whiteness of, 119

*Westover's Ward* (Wood), 105

white femininity: desexualized notions of, 61, 62, 63, 64–65, 101, 107; difference reinscribed through, 12, 168; erotic of, 72; Leache/Wood as models of, 96, 106–7, 110, 114, 116, 119; nineteenth-century fantasies of, 12, 60, 63; normative, reproduction of, 49–50, 119–20, 124–25; privileges of, 30, 31, 147, 149; sameness and, 99, 110

white feminism, 67

white saviorism: Buck/Wylie romantic friendship and reproduction of, 165; of current white feminism, 67; erotic as rhetorical power and, 178; Holley/Putnam romantic friendship and reproduction of, 30, 49, 66, 67, 69–70, 71–72, 74, 76, 83, 84–85; white freedmen's teachers and, 77n158, 77n160

white superiority, 93, 106, 119–25

white supremacy, xviii, 125, 135, 157

white women: as authors, 105; educational opportunities for, 26, 97–100, 119–20, 122, 135, 157, 176; erotic as rhetorical power and, 9–10; Eurocentrism and, 164–69; "power-evasive" communication styles among, 12, 150, 162–63; privilege and, 93, 156; racist assumptions about sexuality of, 29–30; as suffragists, 56, 134, 176; as teachers, 22, 25–26, 83. *See also* white femininity

Whittier, John Greenleaf, 69n123

Willcox, Louise Collier, 97n20, 105, 110–11, 121

Williams, Fannie Barrier, 47n8

women: desexualized, 19–20; diaries of, 18, 18n75; differences among, 10–11, 11n50, 137, 145, 149–50, 156; domestic responsibilities of, xvii–xviii; educational opportunities for, 135; invention strategies of, 108; as "ladies," 63; as public speakers, 59, 60–62, 64–65; published writings of, 105; rhetorics acceptable for, 45–46; as scholars, 146; sexist stereotypes about, 146

women of color, 123, 149

women teachers: educational sites available to, 23–26, 24n110, 93; erotic as rhetorical power and, 7, 43; historical accounts of, 47n8; Indigenous, 22n99; marriage bar laws and, 22–23; as models for students, 93–94; same-sex relationships and, 21–26, 22n99, 138–39; settler colonialism and, 26; slavery and, 26; subjects taught by, 25; white, 9–10, 42, 43, 67n112, 165

women's boarding schools: as homosocial educational setting, 7, 24; privilege and, 119; relationship dynamics at, 93–94; rhetorical education at, 176; women's romantic friendships at, 24–25, 26. *See also* Leache-Wood Seminary (Norfolk, VA); Valley Female Seminary (Winchester, VA)

Women's City and Country Club (Poughkeepsie, NY), 152, 171

women's colleges: as homosocial educational setting, 7–8, 24; racism/classism at, 156; relationship dynamics at, 51, 138–39; rhetorical education at, 176; salaries at, 140–41; white women teachers at, 25–26; women's romantic friendships at, 24–25, 25n117, 26, 135, 140–41. *See also* Vassar College (Poughkeepsie, NY)

*Women's Friendship* (Aguilar), 88

women's movement, 95, 123, 139

women's rights movement, 139, 149

women's romantic friendships: abusive, 81n184; archives of, 1, 15, 32–33, 33n154, 181–82; as "cover," 18, 20, 29, 60–61, 100, 141–42; debates about, 100; erotic as rhetorical power and, 14–20, 38, 125, 176–77; erotic in, 3; historically specific notions of, 14–15; as nonsexual, 15–20, 18n78, 45, 60, 141–42; opposite-sex relationships vs., 7n33, 180–81; power dynamics of, 30–31; "power-evasive intimacy" of, 12; privilege and, 1–2, 29–30, 31–32, 38, 43–44; rhetorical implications of, 179–80; scholarship on, 15–17, 17n71; settler colonialism and, 30–31; shared intimacy in, 183; slavery and, 30–31; sustained, 31–32,

38, 44; teaching and, 21–26, 22n99; use of term, 20; at women's colleges, 25n117, 135, 138–39. *See also specific romantic friendships*

women's suffrage movement, 10, 134, 149, 151–55, 170, 176

Wood, Anna Cogswell ("Annie"): as author, 92–93, 99–100, 101–2, 105, 105–6, 111–12, 119; biographical sketch, xiv; as boarding school cofounder, 25; commonplace books of, 101, 104–5, 109–10, 119, 122; commonplace rhetorics of, 105–12, 121; conservative politics of, 94–95, 119, 121–25, 168; death of, 113, 119, 127; education of, 28, 92, 118; erotic as rhetorical power and, 43; invention practices of, 96; Leache memorialized by, 113, 126–27; memoirs of, 113; memorialization of, 127; papers of, 95; privilege and, 28; pseudonym of, 105; retirement of, 105, 116; settler colonialism and, 28. *See also* Leache/Wood romantic friendship

Woodhull, Frank, 123

Wooley, Mary, 25n117, 139

Wylie, Laura Johnson: biographical sketch, xiv; correspondence of, 133, 134, 136, 139, 159, 160–61; death of, 170, 172; dissertation of, 151; education of, 29, 133; erotic as rhetorical power and, 43; memorialization of, 171; obituary of, 151–52; papers of, 136; privilege and, 29; published writings of, 151; retirement of, 170; rhetorical practices of, 133–34, 147, 151–55, 170; as suffrage activist, 147, 151–55, 170; as women's college teacher, 26, 138. *See also* Buck/Wylie romantic friendship

Wylie Memorial Fund, 171

# X

xenophobia, 154, 155, 157, 167

# Y

Yale University, 29, 133, 151

# Z

Zaeske, Susan, 60

Zakarja, Rafia, 67

Zboray, Mary Saracino, 108–9

Zboray, Ronald J., 108–9

# INTERSECTIONAL RHETORICS
KARMA R. CHÁVEZ, SERIES EDITOR

This series takes as its starting point the position that intersectionality offers important insights to the field of rhetoric—including that to enhance what we understand as rhetorical practice, we must diversify the types of rhetors, arguments, frameworks, and forms under analysis. Intersection works on two levels for the series: (1) reflecting the series' privileging of intersectional perspectives and analytical frames while also (2) emphasizing rhetoric's intersection with related fields, disciplines, and research areas.

*The Erotic as Rhetorical Power: Archives of Romantic Friendship between Women Teachers*
PAMELA VanHAITSMA

*A Nation's Undesirables: Mixed-Race Children and Whiteness in the Post-Nazi Era*
TRACEY OWENS PATTON

*Inscrutable Eating: Asian Appetites and the Rhetorics of Racial Consumption*
JENNIFER LIN LEMESURIER

*Constellating Home: Trans and Queer Asian American Rhetorics*
V. JO HSU

*Inconvenient Strangers: Transnational Subjects and the Politics of Citizenship*
SHUI-YIN SHARON YAM

*Culturally Speaking: The Rhetoric of Voice and Identity in a Mediated Culture*
AMANDA NELL EDGAR

www.ingramcontent.com/pod-product-compliance
Lightning Source LLC
Chambersburg PA
CBHW030135240426
43672CB00005B/136